AFTER ISIS

**America, Iran and the Struggle
for the Middle East**

Fascinating, terrifying, and highly insightful, a superb account of the rise and fall of ISIS by a writer who is both a roving war reporter who has visited and observed all over the region and an acute and shrewd analyst of war and power in the Middle East. Excellent. Essential reading.

– *Simon Sebag Montefiore, author of* Jerusalem: The Biography

This book is a must-read for policy-makers and everyone interested in the rise and defeat of ISIS and what happens next. A seasoned Middle East war reporter, Seth Frantzman has travelled to many of the places he writes about and met the protagonists. His unique insights help us understand the global jihadist phenomenon, its wider consequences and how to deal with it.

– *Colonel Richard Kemp* CBE, *Former Head of International Terrorism Intelligence,* UK *Cabinet Office*

Insightful and gripping reporting from the nightmare ISIS made. A tour de force of today's, and probably tomorrow's, bloody frontlines in the Middle East.

– *Ambassador Alberto Fernandez, President, Middle East Broadcasting Networks*

A panoramic, fascinating account of how the ISIS "Caliphate" emerged, rose up and was destroyed. *After ISIS* combines a cogent analysis of the Islamic State phenomenon, with a compassionate empathy for those caught up in the terrible suffering wrought by this organization.

– *Jonathan Spyer, journalist and Middle East analyst; author of* Days of the Fall: A Reporter's Journey in the Syria and Iraq Wars

A man of conviction whose work is so important and his reports on Mosul will always be considered when we review the history of what happened.

– *Mohammed Omar, founder, Mosul Eye*

Often lost in the coverage of ISIS's barbarity were the victims. Seth Frantzman provides a chilling on-the-ground account of the people who suffered at the hands of the militant group and paints a terrifying picture of just how close the modern Middle East came to being wiped off the map.

– *Conor M. Powell, veteran foreign correspondent*

In *After ISIS*, Seth Frantzman has masterfully combined field reporting with high-quality analysis. This book is a unique contribution from one of the most authoritative voices in the field.

– *Sirwan Kajjo, Kurdish affairs analyst*

AFTER ISIS

America, Iran and the Struggle for the Middle East

SETH J. FRANTZMAN

gefen
publishing house
JERUSALEM ◆ NEW YORK   Est. 1981

Cover Photos: Seth Frantzman
Cover Design: Benjie Herskowitz
Typeset in Arno Pro by Raphaël Freeman, Renana Typesetting

ISBN: 978-965-7023-09-9

1 3 5 7 9 8 6 4 2

Gefen Publishing House Ltd.
6 Hatzvi Street
Jerusalem 94386, Israel
+972-2-538-0247

Gefen Books
140 Fieldcrest Ave.
Edison NJ, 07081
516-593-1234

orders@gefenpublishing.com
www.gefenpublishing.com

Printed in Israel

* * *

Library of Congress Control Number: 2019909191

For Kasaey

Contents

Preface

The war on ISIS is now largely behind us. But its effects will be felt throughout this century. In many ways the conflict formed a bookend to the optimism that emerged from the end of the Cold War. The brutal horrors of the selling of people into slavery and of mass murder that ISIS perpetrated in Iraq and Syria were made even more real by being carried out through social media, using the latest technology. If news of Auschwitz had to be smuggled out and could be dismissed as terrible rumor, ISIS boasted on Twitter, Facebook and elsewhere of its crimes.

The war on ISIS ends without a clear victory. This presents the question of whether winning the war will mean winning the peace. The US appears to be at a crossroads in its foreign policy, seeking to withdraw from Syria and wrap up the conflict while still leading a seventy-nine-member Global Coalition to Defeat ISIS. With the Syrian civil war largely over, the major winners are Iran, Russia and Turkey.

The ISIS war took place against the backdrop of the Syrian conflict and a changeover in US administrations. This means that it occurred during the rise and fall of the Iran nuclear deal. That places it at a key point in history, not only for the Middle East but also for the US and Iran. Emerging from the rubble of the war is a more robust and powerful Iran. The defeat of some of the last ISIS remnants near Baghuz, Syria, in February 2019 coincided with the fortieth anniversary of the Islamic

Revolution in Iran. As President Hassan Rouhani boasted in Tehran of success, Iran's foreign minister Javad Zarif traveled to Lebanon.

For US allies, such as Israel, the post-ISIS period presents new uncertainty. From the chaos and instability of years of conflict come new question marks about US commitment to the Middle East and whether the end of one war will lead to another, much as the end of the Second World War led to the Cold War.

There is creeping pessimism in world affairs after the ISIS conflict. Authoritarianism is on the rise. Some of that authoritarianism is a response to the extremism and terrorism that gave rise to ISIS. Some of it is a response to the period of international instability that flowed from the end of the Cold War, when US hegemony quickly gave way to a variety of states seeking to challenge the US. It is no surprise that Britain's move to leave the European Union began during the ISIS war as the waves of refugees fleeing Syria and elsewhere, some of them caused by this fight, fueled Brexit. These conflicts are all connected.

The lesson of five years of global war against ISIS is that local conflicts cannot be ignored and that they will have unexpected repercussions. The after-ISIS period calls on us to be more vigilant and to confront groups like ISIS early on, before they commit genocide and alter the course of history.

Jerusalem, 2019

Prologue

Iraq, Sinjar, December 2015. Major Adel Sleman poured more sweet tea into a small glass. It was cold outside the half-built shed we were sitting in, and we inched closer to the jet-black stove. Kurdish men stood next to small mattresses they had arranged on top of cinder blocks around the stove. Each man seemed to have a different style of camouflage. The pot-bellied major with his loose-fitting fatigues looked dressed ready to blend into a jungle. His colleague Major Hussein Yusuf wore forest green. Even though it was cold, the two men didn't put on coats.

"I've spent nineteen years working in demining," said Sleman. Born in 1963 in northern Iraq's Kurdish region, he had been a Peshmerga, or Kurdish soldier, since the 1990s. The younger men under his command, making their beds in a nearby house, were new to soldiering. "Sometimes we are here for a month, or up to six months. It depends on necessity."

Here, for now, was an abandoned house at the foot of Mount Sinjar in northern Iraq. I'd arrived at night, so the mountain looming behind us only appeared in my imagination. A long hump rising out of the tan desert was what it was supposed to look like, according to photos I'd seen online. The drive over the mountain that night had been done in pitch black. There was no electricity in this part of Iraq. The infrastructure, such as power lines, had been destroyed during the battles to liberate the area from Islamic State.

At night your surroundings become increasingly intimate in a place without electricity. A car feels like a lonely spacecraft. At the abandoned house, there was a generator the Peshmerga were using, but it was only enough for a few lights. In the distance another generator hummed. There was another unit of soldiers somewhere out there. One of the younger soldiers shined a large flashlight on the houses and hills around us. Poking into the distance, the light found a ridgeline. The extremists of Islamic State had been cleared from this area a month before I arrived, in November 2015. But the men were cautious. Their AK-47s were slung over their backs or perched nearby.

Sleman had been one of the first Peshmerga to enter a US-led coalition demining training course. His team of engineers was then given an MRAP or Mine-Resistant Ambush Protected armored vehicle, and sent into the field. But it had not been easy. "We lost six men from the same family, and they died because we don't have the right equipment to destroy the mines."

This was a suicide mission, Sleman thought. On his Samsung phone he showed photos of the last weeks his men had spent in Sinjar city, just south of the mountain, combing through tunnels and houses for what ISIS had left behind. They had come as liberators, but they found a city of ghosts. This was the city ISIS had overrun in August 2014. It was where thousands of Yazidi women and children had been taken before being sold into slavery. More than thirty mass graves, filled with the decaying bodies of men and elderly women, pockmarked the fields around the city. These killing fields had been found in the last few days between the city of Sinjar and the former Yazidi villages beyond. Many of them were within shouting distance of the front line. "Daesh [ISIS] must be punished and revenge taken for what they did," Sleman said. "It's not my job to decide whether they go to heaven or hell, but rather to send them to Allah to decide."

How cold can it get in northern Iraq, I'd joked when packing to come to Sinjar. It's a desert. It's Iraq. It's warm. But in December it's cold, and the cold creeps up on you. Major Sleman offered me lodgings with his officers. "Do you snore?" he wondered. I did, and anyway the mattress next to the outdoor stove looked more comfortable than sleeping on the floor of what had once been a modest two-room house. Outside, under the stars. So I waddled back to the stove; its rusted exterior held the bits of warmth of a dying fire. The young man with the flashlight, tall and handsome with large eyebrows, came over to sit. He was supposed to be doing guard duty. So with his AK-47 propped against my makeshift bed, I pulled up my jacket, put down an old shirt for a pillow, and curled up next to the fire. Several hours later I awoke to the cold and a sense of shuffling. The major was there with a giant blanket that he tucked over me. I went back to sleep.

In the morning the sound of animals, some kind of sheep-like noises and a man shouting woke me. The sun wasn't up yet, and it was that beautiful, special time of dawn. No one was awake in the compound, save the Peshmerga on guard duty. He was slumped by the still slightly warm fire.

Last night the pitch black had obscured the settings. Now the small house at the back of the walled compound was visible. Kurdish graffiti in Arabic script was spray-painted on it. There were two adjacent doors to the rooms occupied by officers and men of the demining team. Behind the house the foothills of Mount Sinjar, drab and khaki-colored, stretched into the distance. Little trees dotted them. Walking up toward the little trees was the source of the bleating and clanging, a herd of sheep and a young man out for a morning graze.

The rectangular compound, besides the two-room house and the stove with a shed built over it, included a concrete outhouse and another small enclosure against one wall. The outhouse, which the men used, was freezing cold, far colder than the outside air. It was as if it had absorbed all the cold of the night and kept it inside. At least this masked the wretched smells from below. In northern Iraq, many toilets are of the squat variety, just a hole in the ground. There was no toilet paper, just a small watering can, like one might use for flowers, to wash after.

Near to the entrance of the compound was a blue tarp propped over a bunch of gray buckets, tin cans, an oil drum and bottles. Wires and chunks of concrete and bits of tape were fastened to the buckets and cans. These were the leftovers of the demining. Over the years ISIS had become experts in making improvised explosive devices or IEDs. They'd learned this skill from years of insurgency and terror against the Iraqi government and the US Army before 2014. Now ISIS handiwork had ended up here, in this compound. It was a bit disconcerting that I'd been sleeping so close to all these explosives. They had been neutralized, their wires cut like in some movie, but they still contained dangerous explosives.

"Breakfast?" Vager Saadullah asked. Saadullah was a local journalist turned fixer. We had driven out together to Sinjar. While I'd been checking out the outhouse and IEDs, the compound had begun to wake up. Major Yusuf, the skinny commander, was up and doing calisthenics. He did chin-ups above a door of the house. One of the young Peshmerga put a pan on the stove and threw on some eggs. These were the eggs we'd bought from Shariah, a Yazidi refugee camp, the day before. When they were fried, Saadullah brought a plastic plate with a wedge of soft cheese. The eggs were an explosion of flavor, more complex and tastier than eggs I'd remembered. Perhaps I was just hungry, but it seemed odd to find such a wonderful egg in the cold in the compound of soldiers in the midst of a vicious war.

Introduction

"I was wounded in the first days of the war," Captain Rizgar Jabar recalled. He was part of a group of Peshmerga soldiers manning a sandbagged position in northern Iraq in August 2014.[1] For two months they had been facing "new neighbors," as some Kurds referred to the black-flag-carrying extremists who had suddenly appeared in Iraq. ISIS had swept all before it, taking over Mosul and other Sunni Arab areas in June of that year. Like a black tide rising, they inched closer to the Kurdish mountains.

Jabar and his men looked out at these neighbors. They'd seen jihadists before. They'd seen insurgents. Their parents had fought Saddam Hussein's army. For them it was all the same. More enemies in the plains below. They hoped that ISIS would move south, toward Baghdad. It would rid them of the burden of the Iranian-backed federal government in Baghdad that had been bullying the Kurdish region. Let ISIS and the Iranians fight each other. They knew Grand Ayatollah Ali Sistani, the spiritual leader of Iraq's Shi'ites, had issued a fatwa urging Shi'ite men to flock to the banners of Popular Mobilization Units in southern Iraq. Now the Shi'ite militias were on the march. They would meet the black flags of the Sunni jihadists somewhere in the middle of Iraq, and they would fight to the death. And Kurdistan would be free.

"My commander thought he would do a test to see if the ISIS fighters are good snipers," Jabar recalled about that hot August day. So the young captain held up a helmet over the sandbags. "After a minute a bullet went through it." The bullet ricocheted off the inside of the cheap helmet and went into Jabar's leg. He was evacuated and sent home to his village in the mountains near the historic town of Amedi, not far from the Turkish border. For Jabar, the war was over. For hundreds of thousands of others, it had just begun.

I caught up with Jabar and four friends at a smoke-filled shisha bar near Dereluk, in the Kurdish region, in December 2015. I was coming back from seeing the aftermath of ISIS genocide of Yazidis that took place in August 2014. Jabar and his friends sat and joked. The war was stretching into its second year. It would continue into the fall of 2017, when most of the ISIS presence in Iraq would be eradicated.

The aftershocks of ISIS will be felt for generations in Iraq and the rest of the Middle East. The region has seen many wars, but what ISIS wrought was different. It grew out of the hope of the Arab Spring. Where youth protesting in Deraa in southern Syria or in Cairo hoped for peace, there were others who hoped only for war and killing. ISIS was an anomaly in some ways. It built upon the existing extremist infrastructure that had come before. It used the smuggling routes that insurgents had used to get from Syria into Iraq after 2003. Its leaders had been members of other groups going back to al Qaeda in Iraq. Some of them had been officers in Saddam's army.

But ISIS sought to do more than al Qaeda or other insurgents had done. It sought to replace them all with a "caliphate" or new superstate. It also wanted to erase the borders of Iraq and Syria, uniting the region for the first time since the Ottoman Empire had fallen one hundred years before. Although ISIS leader Abu Bakr al-Baghdadi was from Iraq, he used Raqqa in Syria as a base. His forces in Iraq moved into Fallujah in January and into Tikrit on June 11, 2014. Using captured American-made Humvees, they took Mosul the same day, and several days later they took Tal Afar. The extremists were still on a winning streak when they rolled into Ramadi in May 2015, just kilometers from Baghdad. In July 2015, the UN estimated that eight million people were living under ISIS control; it controlled at least ten million at its height, and 100,000 square kilometers.[2] That's about the size of the Republic of Ireland and Northern Ireland combined.[3]

At its most brutal, ISIS was a genocidal organization seeking to cleanse the areas under its rule of minorities. At Camp Speicher in June 2014, it murdered fifteen hundred mostly Shi'ite Iraqi army cadets. At Badush prison, it killed 670 Shi'ite prisoners on June 10. It systematically expelled Christians from Mosul in July. In August, when it attacked Sinjar and the Kurdish region, it put in motion a campaign of enslavement and genocide against Yazidis, members of an ancient minority. The full scale of its crimes may never be known. Hundreds of mass graves have been found and continue to be uncovered in Iraq and Syria. In mid-February 2018, a mass grave was found near Raqqa. Forensic teams were flown in to see if the bodies might be Westerners murdered by Jihadi John, one of ISIS's brutal executioners.[4] In the same month, the bodies of ninety people were found near the village of Al-Haj in Iraq near Qayarrah.

After ISIS was done killing people and expelling others, it systematically destroyed the heritage of the region. It bulldozed shrines and blew up archaeological sites. It destroyed churches and temples. Some of these sites will never recover. Others could be reconstructed if funding is found. Most likely the destruction at places such as Nimrud, an ancient Assyrian city in Iraq, will be everlasting. ISIS sought to rip out the cultural heart of the region. After ISIS, the region has a clean slate to begin a new chapter.

The battle against ISIS became a major cultural struggle in the Middle East. The percolating Islamist extremist views that had underpinned groups such as al Qaeda and led to the assassination of Anwar Sadat in 1981 and the Algerian Civil War of 1991–2002 posed a challenge to local regimes. However, the emergence of ISIS was something else altogether. It threatened to overturn the entire region. This was tantamount to the effect Nazism or Communism had in the twentieth century. The battles against ISIS in the region became a larger Kulturkampf against a pernicious ideology. It led to reform of religious institutions in Saudi Arabia and at Egypt's iconic Al-Azhar. The flirtations with Salafism and Wahhabism that had taken place in the twentieth century were now seen as more deadly serious than in the past.

Much of this struggle against extremism and terror and the chaos it produced was conducted by local governments. The US-led coalition of seventy-nine countries and partners fighting ISIS provided the firepower of the greatest and largest alliance of countries in world history. This was symbolic of the threat ISIS posed in Europe, Asia and Africa. It picked up where al Qaeda and local groups such as the Taliban or Abu Sayyef had left off. But it had much larger dreams. It wasn't al Qaeda 2.0, it was sui generis. With its decline, many would ask whether there will be an ISIS 2.0, but the likelihood is that ISIS was a unique threat and had entered a unique vacuum. It preyed upon a certain kind of chaos, just as Nazism had preyed on chaos in the 1920s.

ISIS also was far more successful at attracting foreign jihadists than previous groups had been. The US coalition estimated it had killed fifty thousand ISIS members by 2016.[5] These fighters came by the thousands from Russia and various European countries, as well as from China and even as far away as the Caribbean. Even in defeat in Iraq and Syria, the tentacles of ISIS still threaten the world.

In the areas ISIS destroyed, the thousands of improvised explosive devices the group sewed into the landscape will take more than a decade to remove. I traveled to dozens of villages and towns that are still in ruins and will remain in ruins. The people are afraid to come back. This is especially true of the hundreds of thousands of Yazidis living in camps in the Kurdish region of northern Iraq, or still in tents and shacks on Mount Sinjar. In 2018, years after ISIS arrived and more than two years after being liberated from ISIS, the people had not returned.

Ruin. Depopulation. Demographic and religious change. Destruction of heritage. Those are some of the main, obvious effects of ISIS. But there are much larger political outcomes. ISIS led the US to return to Iraq in 2014. US president Barack Obama had sought to leave Iraq in 2011. In August 2014, Obama declared that he would authorize targeted air strikes to slow the ISIS advance toward the Kurdistan Regional Government's capital of Erbil and to provide humanitarian aid to Yazidis trapped on Mount Sinjar.[6] It was a momentous decision that sent Americans surging into Iraq for the fourth time in a quarter century.

For the US, the war on ISIS become a massive form of "mission creep." It began with a few air strikes and ended with a seventy-nine-member coalition and the US deeply involved in training yet another Iraqi army. In eastern Syria, the US built airstrips and put down roots to support the mostly Kurdish Syrian Democratic Forces. This has brought the US into brief conflict with Russian contractors and the Syrian air force and led to a major crisis with Turkey.[7] Now the US appears prepared to stay in eastern Syria. The Iraq and Syria model of "by, with and through" partner forces has become a new paradigm for how to fight terror throughout the world, most notably in Africa. The war on ISIS has transcended one administration, as Donald Trump picked up where Obama left the ball for him. Brett McGurk, Obama's anti-ISIS czar, stayed on as well.

Whereas ISIS created the cause and the vacuum that brought the US back into Iraq and then into Syria in an unprecedented intervention, it has also empowered Iran in the region. The Shi'ite militias in Iraq control the interior ministry, and since the fall of 2016 they are official forces. Now they will craft Iraqi politics for the foreseeable future. ISIS left behind a shattered Syria, part of the much larger civil war. It also gave Turkey and Russia an excuse to intervene in Syria, as both claimed to be fighting ISIS. Even the Syrian regime sought to label its legitimate opposition as "ISIS" terrorists in order to tar them as extremists. And ISIS has spread beyond these countries, threatening Israel, Egypt, Jordan, Lebanon and other states. It has led to the greatest changes in the region in a century, since the fall of the Ottoman Empire.

In December 2018, Trump decided to withdraw from Syria. The US withdrawal and the rise of Turkey and Iranian influence in the region have created a new set of alliances and power struggles. Israel and Iran are on a collision course in Syria. The region is at a crossroads. Totalitarian regimes have returned in one country after another. Elections have been postponed. The hopes of the Arab Spring are gone, as are the hopes for democratization foreseen by the George W. Bush administration. But the Islamists have no hope for the future, either. They too have been mostly defeated. Arab nationalism is a thing of the past. What remains is a shattered region trying to recover. When Jordan hosted Saudi Arabia, Bahrain, the United Arab Emirates, Egypt and Kuwait at the Dead Sea in January 2019, it discussed regional stability and the need for peace. With the Syrian civil war largely over, the last independent groups to emerge from the civil war are on the verge of being rapidly, totally sidelined. This may bring a form of peace after years of brutal war.

This book is not about ISIS. Others, such as Michael Weiss and Hassan Hassan's ISIS: Inside the Army of Terror, have covered its rise and doctrine. This book is about the effects of ISIS. It is about the men and women whose lives were transformed by ISIS. It is about the US Army that was transformed, the Kurdish fighters, Turkish society, refugees in Jordan, the glittering towers of Dubai, Iraq's Shi'ite militias and Cairo's Islamic theologians. It is the story of the volunteers who came from abroad to aid locals, and the foreign jihadi fighters, as well as the former ISIS members. It is about the year zero in the Middle East, which 2018 became. A new curtain is rising on a region that has been changed by the events that began in 2011 and built to a tragic crescendo in 2014. The defeat of ISIS is a kind of bookend to one great chapter. It is a chapter that has many beginnings.

Based on four years of trips throughout the region, what follows does not seek to tell the full tale of every country and every group involved. It aims to illuminate the challenges and solutions that came about as a result of the rise and fall of ISIS. From the tents of Peshmerga commanders in northern Iraq to the refugee camps of Turkey and the superannuated diplomats of Egypt's old elite in Cairo, it looks at the old Middle East and the new. It is based on six trips to Iraq, two to Jordan and Turkey, and one each to Egypt, the UAE and Senegal, as well as a decade of experience reporting on the region from Jerusalem. It is also based on two trips to Europe, one in 2015 during the height of the refugee crisis, and another in the following year to see the effects of ISIS, the growing security crackdown and presence of soldiers at train stations and iconic sites such as Florence's Doumo.

Part I
Holding the Line, 2014–2015

"The problem we face here is that ISIS fighters want to die, and we want to live."

– Peshmerga commander, June 2015

Chapter 1
A Band-Aid for Sykes-Picot

The Shadow of a Century

The BBC's Tarek Osman argued in December 2014 that "border lines drawn with a ruler in WWI still rock the Middle East," implying that European colonialism is the primary source of the current trouble.[8] Modern-day Iraq and Syria are the clearest examples of the impact of the colonial legacy. The border between them, at least in part, was drawn with ruler-like sharpness. It was the product of a May 19, 1916, meeting between Sir Mark Sykes of Great Britain and François Georges-Picot of France.

It's easy to reductively boil down all the problems of the Middle East to that. In some ways the chaos and conflict that erupted in 2011 with the Arab Spring and later with the rise of ISIS were a hundred-year bookend to the events of 1914–1918. The unresolved problems – ethnic groups such as the Kurds who wanted independence, states that lacked natural borders, unresolved demands – percolated. The tragedy that emerged in 2014 with ISIS and its defeat several years later by a global coalition echoes the First World War. It is also not the only lens through which to see the region.

Much greater movements were taking place. The Ottoman Empire collapsed at the end of the First World War, and the colonial powers did divide it partly based on the 1916 lines. However, in northern Iraq, it was Turkey that once sought to annex Mosul. Instead, the British kept the Kurdish region and Mosul as part of Iraq so that their chosen man, King Faisal, would have a Sunni majority in the country. Otherwise he would have been a Sunni king plucked from Hijaz of a largely Shi'ite rump state. One result of the decline of the Ottoman Empire and the rise of the colonial powers denied the Kurds a state.

Much of what happened in the region in the war on ISIS was not merely about ISIS, it was also about Kurdish aspirations. That the war against ISIS in Iraq ended in 2017 with a Kurdish independence referendum illustrates how much Kurdish demands and the chaos spread by ISIS dovetailed with one another. The same is true in Syria. The destruction of ISIS came mostly at the hands of valiant Kurdish fighters. Turkey eventually intervened in the Syrian civil war, moving into parts of northern Syria to counter what Ankara called "terrorist" groups, including the Kurdish People's Protection Units (YPG) and ISIS. The Turkish aspirations in Afrin and northern Syria are connected to century-old grievances involved in the border changes of Hatay Province in the 1930s. The Ottoman Empire had returned.

Ankara's agenda of "neo-Ottomanism" was a result of the vacuum created by ISIS. It not only angered Syrian nationalists connected to the Assad regime but also ruffled feathers in the Gulf. In December 2017, the UAE's foreign minister Sheikh Abdullah bin Zayed al-Nahyan retweeted a tweet by an Iraqi dentist. "Did you know that in 1916, Turkish [Governor] Fahreddin Pasha committed a crime against the people of Medina, stole their properties, and put them on a train en route to Damascus and Istanbul? Also the Turks stole the handwritten books in Mahmoudia Library and took them to Istanbul. This is the history of [Turkish president] Erdogan's ancestors and what they did to Muslim Arabs."[9] In response, the municipality of Ankara renamed the street in front of the UAE embassy "Fakhreddin Pasha Street."

The argument between Abu Dhabi and Ankara is not an isolated incident. In the last days of December 2017, Erdogan called Syria's Bashar al-Assad a "terrorist."[10] Syria's foreign ministry replied that the accusation was due to Turkey's "illusions of the past," which has made Erdogan "forget that his old empire has vanished and that the free people of the world have the choice to make their national decisions."

The Sykes-Picot agreement haunts the Middle East a hundred years later in other ways as well. The agreement is interesting because it gave rise to the colonial-era mandates in Syria and Iraq, which in turn eventually gave way to the rise of Arab socialism or Ba'athism in Iraq and Syria. The rise of Sunni jihadists in both countries is directly linked to that, as are Kurdish grievances and Iran's influence. In Syria, the Ba'ath regime came to be dominated by an Alawite minority government of the family of Hafez al-Assad and then his son Bashar. In Iraq, it led to Saddam Hussein and his Arab nationalist policies. It led to almost a decade of war with Iran and then the war with the US-led coalition in 1991. Finally, it led to Saddam's death by hanging after the US invasion in 2003. It is tempting to see that invasion as leading to the chaos that produced ISIS. Mosul, which played a key role in the ISIS rise in Iraq, was also a city that provided the highest per capita number of officers for Saddam's army. Later it played a central role in the insurgency against the Americans.

The bulwark in Iraq that helped stem the flow of ISIS also had its roots in an earlier era. The origins of the modern-day Kurdistan Regional Government in Iraq are found not in 2003 but in the 1990s, when the US entered northern Iraq in Operation Provide Comfort and created a no-fly zone. Many of the leaders in Iraq who led Shi'ite militias against ISIS had served with Iran in the 1980s against Saddam Hussein. They were closely linked to Iran's Islamic Revolutionary Guard Corps. The US invasion of 2003 empowered the Kurds and the Shi'ites. Sunni Arabs, who formerly ran the country, found themselves marginalized.

Many of the long-term problems in the region that led to ISIS and extremism were already there before the US invasion. In Syria, religiously inspired rebels had poked their heads up in 1982 with the Muslim Brotherhood rebellion against the Syrian regime, resulting in Hafez al-Assad's razing of Hama.

The Arab nationalist regimes in the region were weakened by the Arab Spring protests. Their ossification made them more susceptible to protests. In Tunisia and Egypt, long-serving dictators were overthrown. Protests, however, were stamped out in Bahrain. In Syria, the protests led to a brutal crackdown by the regime, and soon a civil war broke out. The Arab monarchies in the Gulf and Jordan held the line against the brewing chaos. Iran, which was already allied with Damascus and had gained influence in Baghdad because of the reelection of Nouri al-Maliki as prime minister in 2010, saw the chaos as an opportunity. Emma Sky, who served in Iraq as an adviser to the US Army, said the seeds of "Iraq's unraveling" were sown after 2010. Iran's goal in Iraq was to work through the ruling Islamic Dawa Party.[11]

In 2014, when ISIS threatened Baghdad, it was Iranian-backed Shi'ite militias that helped turn the tide. Grand Ayatollah Ali al-Sistani issued a fatwa in June 2014 calling on citizens to defend Iraq. Eventually, a hundred thousand mostly Shi'ite men from southern Iraq flocked to the colors of various armed groups. Abu Mahdi al-Muhandis, once wanted by the Americans for a bombing in Kuwait, became a leader of these Popular Mobilization Units (PMU). Hadi al-Amiri's Badr Organization, which had once served alongside the Iranians in the 1980–1988 Iran-Iraq War, became a central bulwark against ISIS. Badr also took up the reins of the Ministry of Interior in Iraq, rebuilding the Federal Police into an effective fighting unit to combat the extremists.

As the Iraqi army melted away in the summer of 2014, the vacuum was filled by these new sectarian militias. Qais al-Khazali, who had once served time in a US military prison at Camp Cropper in Iraq, gathered men under the banner of Asaib Ahl al-Haq or "The League of the Righteous."[12]

The growth of Iranian influence is a direct result of ISIS. Where ISIS sought to erase the borders of Iraq and Syria, Iran only wants to blur the borders. Hezbollah fighters from Lebanon served in Syria and Iraq. Shi'ite militias in Iraq were modeled on Hezbollah, and the National Defence Forces in Syria was based on this prototype as well. As the war against ISIS wound down in 2017 and 2018, a coterie of pro-Iranian leaders from Iraq made the pilgrimage to southern Lebanon, usually to threaten Israel while standing by Hezbollah. Their threats represent how Tehran had exploited the war on ISIS to paste over Sykes-Picot with a Band-Aid of Shi'ite militia influence.

Problems with Turkey's Neighbors

The First World War still haunts the Middle East, and nowhere more so than in Istanbul. No longer the capital of Turkey, it is still a center of politics and trade.[13] A sprawling, massive city on both sides of the Bosphorus, it has seventeen million residents. From here the Ottoman fleets once controlled the Mediterranean. Here the Crusaders once marched on their way to the Holy Land. This was the target of the ill-fated Allied 1915 armada that came to nought at the battle of the Dardenelles and Galilipoli. It was through that battle that Ataturk gained fame and therefore came to rule Turkey after the war. It was through Istanbul that thousands of foreign volunteers for ISIS passed on their way to Syria, using the two local airports to transit closer to the border. So it is from Istanbul that we must begin to understand the post-ISIS Middle East.

Directly across from Istanbul's Taksim Gezi Park is the grandiose Marmara Hotel. In 2013, a wave of popular protests swept through Gezi Park. They were sparked by a small environmentalist protest against development plans. The protests grew into a major gathering of a cross-section of society angered by what they saw as an erosion of the country's secular values at the hands of the ruling Justice and Development Party (AKP). The AKP and its leader Recep Tayyip Erdogan had been in power since 2002.

The protests in Gezi Park were also connected to other government policies, such as Ankara's support for the rebellion in Syria and the increasing religious conservativism of government policy in Turkey. This had resulted in a ban on public advertising of alcohol in May 2013. Eventually this morality legislation would include the ban on hundreds of "immoral" songs and increasing incitement against the secular public.

In December 2014, I went to Turkey to see how the country was coping with a variety of crises. As one flies into Sabiha Gokcen International Airport, the hills of Asiatic Turkey spill out into the horizon. A country of eighty million stretching over almost 800,000 square kilometers, Turkey is an economic, military and cultural linchpin between the Middle East and Europe. The drive from Sabiha Gokcen, one of two airports that service Istanbul, takes more than an hour into the center, in massive traffic jams.

At the Marmara Hotel, things were quiet. Outside it was cold. Inside I took the elevator to the twentieth-floor Raika Restaurant and its panoramic views over the city. There, in an immaculate suit, stood Yasar Yakis, a founding member of the AKP. Yakis, who was born in a small town on the Black Sea, was foreign minister of Turkey from 2002 to

2003. "Thirteen hundred ships pass here a day," he said, surveying the Bosphorus seaway that links the Black Sea to the Mediterannean.[14]

Turkey's agenda in 2014, according to Yakis, faced a series of challenges. Turkey wanted better economic relations with Russia, but it was opposed to Moscow's policy in Syria. "Turkey gives the highest priority to overthrowing the Assad regime, whereas Russia thinks that [the choice of] who is going to govern Syria must be left to the Syrian people, and foreign countries should not create the ground for the overthrow of Assad." Yakis argued that Russia and Turkey had successfully compartmentalized Syria from their relationship on other issues. "I think Turkey did the right thing at the beginning in Syria, when the dictator and the people faced each other, and Turkey acted with the international community to do it."

However, then Turkey's policy began to diverge from the West's. "When the international community discovered the weapons given to the opposition were ending up in the wrong hands, and the Western countries put the brakes on, Turkey was left in a kind of 'off-sides' position and could not adjust itself to the new reality," Yakis said in 2014. From the point of view of Turkey's leaders, Turkey was a frontline state in the Syrian conflict, but after initially working in concert with Washington and the West, it was increasingly alone after 2014 as the Syrian rebellion became more radicalized and Islamist. By 2014, the West had lost its adoration for the rebels as more and more Westerners were kidnapped after crossing the border from Turkey to travel toward Aleppo.

British war correspondent John Cantlie was kidnapped near the Bab al-Hawa border crossing in July 2012, rescued a week later, and then kidnapped again in November. In June 2013, French correspondent Didier François and photographer Edouard Elias were kidnapped traveling the fifty kilometers from Turkey to Aleppo, Syria's second largest city. On August 4, 2013, American-Israeli journalist Steven Sotloff was captured as well. Reporters Theo Padnos, James Foley and others were kidnapped. Many ended up in the hands of ISIS. Foley and Sotloff were murdered in 2014.

"There are indications it has roots here in Turkey," Yakis said of ISIS in 2014. "In June during Ramadan, the Daesh supporters organized a sermon on the outskirts of Istanbul," he recalled. There would be ramifications, and it put Turkey in a critical situation. "Turkey cannot take as daring decisions as other countries would do, because it could have negative effects. You only need one suicide bombing... If it happens in a place like Antalya, then we will be deprived of tourism and have negative effects on the economy." In short, Turkey had to tread carefully because of the potential blowback from Syria. The blowback had already begun. In May 2013, two bombs rocked the border town of Reyhanli, killing fifty-one people.

In 2014, Erdogan was still putting his weight behind a cease-fire with the Kurdistan Workers' Party (PKK) and attempts to reconcile with Kurds in eastern Turkey. Ankara could solve its problems by working closely with the Kurdistan Regional Government in northern Iraq and through discussions with the PYD, the leading Kurdish party in Syria. The AKP also relied on Kurdish votes in Turkey and was hopeful that in 2015 elections, it would prevail in Kurdish districts in the east.

Yakis's optimism in 2014 showed the degree to which Turkey was treading a thin line on its next move. The architect of Turkey's policy in the region, including Syria, was Ahmet Davutoglu, foreign minister from 2009 to 2014 and then prime minister from 2014 to 2016. Davutoglu claimed that his policy was one of "zero problems with our neighbors," but under his leadership Turkey ran into more problems than it had since 1918.[15] Davutoglu's agenda was laid out in his 2001 book *Strategic Depth*, in which he argued for greater Turkish involvement in the region. He wanted to alter Turkey's focus from integration with Europe to integration with the Middle East. This policy was dubbed "neo-Ottomanism" by critics. Neo-Ottomanism has stepped on many toes in the region and put Turkey at odds with its neighbors, rather than leading to "zero problems."

Ankara recalled its ambassador from Israel after a controversial flotilla of pro-Palestinian activists tried to reach Gaza in 2010. It withdrew its ambassador to Washington over a US Congress vote on the Armenian genocide. In 2013, the Turkish ambassador in Egypt was recalled in protest at the overthrow of the Muslim Brotherhood.

But the biggest problem was Syria. In 2014, a truck loaded with humanitarian aid, guns and ammunition was stopped by Turkish gendarmerie near the Syrian border. The truck was understood to belong to the

Turkish intelligence service, Can Dundar later wrote. "The gendarmerie and the intelligence officials in control of the convoy pulled guns on each other. This was the moment the two blocks vying to rule the state came face to face."[16] After a search and intervention from the government, the truck continued on its way.

In May 2015, the *Cumhuriyet* daily published the details of the truck fiasco, after acquiring footage of the incident. "It was clearly visible that the truck was loaded with arms. It was thus documented that the intelligence service was illegally carrying arms into the civil war raging in a neighboring country." Dundar was charged with revealing state secrets in his report. Clandestine support for the rebels would continue in Turkey.

For supporters of the AKP, the real struggle in Ankara in 2014 was between the "deep state" and the reforms that Erdogan has tried to put in place. Depending on whom one speaks to, the "deep state" includes old elites, journalists, people in media, the court system, and a nefarious network of coup-supporting members of the military and security establishment. A series of trials between 2010 and 2013 alleged that a coup plot called Ergenekon had been in the works to overthrow the AKP. A total of 275 suspects were arrested. Nineteen received life sentences, while two dozen were acquitted. A subsequent 2016 ruling overturned many of the convictions. A related coup plot nicknamed "Sledgehammer" saw three hundred suspects sentenced to prison terms. By 2014 the government was convinced that Fethullah Gulen, a cleric living in exile in the US, was behind plots against the government. When I was in Turkey in 2014, officials claimed that Gulen was behind the Gezi Park protests.

Before traveling to staid Ankara, I took in some nightlife in Istanbul. Down in the Ortakoy neighborhood, dozens enjoyed the view of the iconic mosque and the Bosphorus Bridge, one of three that span the Bosphorus. Built in 1973, it was once the fourth-largest suspension bridge in the world. In July 2016 it would be one of the centers of the attempted coup and be renamed the "15 July Martyrs Bridge." After a stop by the bridge, I went up the street for dinner at the Mavi Balik fish restaurant. Laid out at the entrance were all manner of fish resting on ice. Inside, the windows overlooked the water, and customers enjoyed tables full of *mezze*. Less than a kilometer away, the "see and be seen" of

Istanbul were lined up at Reina nightclub. At a New Year's party in 2017, a gunman loyal to ISIS would walk into the club and murder thirty-nine people with an AK-47. In 2014, though, everything seemed detached from the tragedy that would unfold. There were Syrian beggars in the streets, some of the 3.5 million who entered Turkey as refugees, but for the most part the city was gyrating to its own rhythms.

Ankara was fundamentally different. I flew in at the same time that a high-level delegation from Qatar was arriving. Qatari emir Sheikh Tamim al-Thani was greeted on arrival by Finance Minister Mehmet Simsek and Turkish National Intelligence (MIT) head Hakan Fidan. A who's who of Erdogan's inner circle took part in the meetings on December 19 at Erdogan's newly constructed, massive presidential palace, including National Defense Minister Ismet Yilmaz, then-Izmir parliamentarian Binali Yildirim and Ibrahim Kalin, a close adviser and spokesman for the president. Yildirim would become prime minister in 2016. Sheikh Tamim was trying to cement his relationship with Turkey in the meetings. He rose to power in 2013 after his father abdicated. In December 2014, Erdogan and Tamim discussed the need for "solidarity" in the region, including in Syria and in dealing with threats posed by ISIS.[17]

In Ankara, I drove to the AKP's party headquarters, located in a large, modern building. Ankara was declared the capital in 1923 and still feels like a provincial city. It is spread out and lacks the congestion of Istanbul. At the AKP headquarters, the party magazines featured Erdogan and Davutoglu. Down corridors and more corridors, we came to the office of the foreign policy wing of the party. Yakis's portrait hung on the wall among many others, but his views on display in Istanbul – favoring the West and constructive peace efforts – were in stark contrast to the thinking in Ankara.

"The war on ISIS is creating Islamophobia," said Yasin Aktay, then a deputy chairman of the AKP holding a foreign affairs portfolio. "ISIS is not Islamic; there is nothing Islamic in it. Many people think ISIS is a conspiracy against Muslims and against Islamists," he claimed. "Muslim countries support war against it. It is marginal; actually, we are not worried about the impact of ISIS on Muslims." In his view it had nothing to do with Islamic culture or civilization.

Aktay argued that Turkey was stuck in a kind of paradox. "The world is benefiting from the wealth of the region, such as oil, but does not make any contribution to solve its problems." In that sense Turkey again saw itself as abandoned on the front line. Oil from Iraq's Kurdistan region flowed through Turkey at the rate of up to 600,000 barrels a day from 2014 to 2017.[18] Turkey benefited economically from this link, but the feeling in 2014 was one of long-term resentment against Western powers, including NATO, using Turkey for a base without Turkey receiving enough in return except for chaos on its southern flank.

"After the war in Iraq we heard the US will bring democracy to the region," Aktay said in 2014. "But when they brought democracy by force [to Iraq], they left a country in a sort of civil war. When we are asked about relationships with ISIS, I say it emerged in a country governed by the US for eleven years." The AKP politician pointed out that ISIS used US weapons raided from Iraqi army arms caches, "not weapons made in Turkey." He also noted that ISIS members had emerged from US prisons in Iraq. "ISIS is a sort of unintended consequence of the war in Iraq. But that is the disappointing thing, given the size of intelligence, weapons and possibilities the US brought to this region."

Aktay stressed that Davutoglu rejected the term *neo-Ottomanism* for Turkish policy. "We are trying to build a new world, not a new Ottomanism." When the Ottoman Empire fell, it left many problems in the region. "We are in a new world and following the necessities of the new world," he claimed. "We have good relations with the US, EU, and are trying to be a bridge between Europe and the Middle East and Central Asia and mediate between Russia and Europe." For Aktay and the leadership, neo-Ottomanism was a "narrowing" lens, while Turkey's aspirations were actually broader. "Turkey is still going on in its process of joining the EU," he said. But there was negative discourse in Europe against Turkey. "Some parties in the EU think the EU is a Christian club."

The optimism of late 2014 would become darker in 2015. In June and November of 2015, Turkey held elections. In June, the AKP had only taken 40 percent of the vote, and the mostly Kurdish HDP took 13 percent. In November, the AKP upped its win to 49 percent, and the HDP declined to 10 percent. The elections chaos came amid growing turmoil inside Turkey. In January 2015, Diana Ramazova, the widow of an ISIS fighter, blew herself up in Istanbul near the Blue Mosque, killing one person. In June, a bombing targeted an HDP rally in Diyarbakir, and in July, thirty-four members of a Kurdish youth group were murdered by an ISIS suicide bomber in Suruc. By targeting Kurds in Turkey, ISIS was bringing its war to Turkish soil. It was targeting Kurds because ISIS had been driven back from the Syrian city of Kobani across the border by Kurdish fighters. In August 2016, ISIS would target a Kurdish wedding in Gaziantep. ISIS also targeted Turkish soldiers in a shooting in Elbeyli near Kilis, killing one soldier on July 23.

As ISIS ramped up its campaign, the cease-fire between Turkey and the PKK began to fall apart. In the summer and fall of 2015, Turkish police were targeted in Diyarbakir, and a cease-fire between Turkey and the PKK fell apart. After a second brief cease-fire in the lead-up to the November 1 elections, the PKK declared the cease-fire at an end.

Turkey responded to the escalations in July with air strikes against PKK targets in Iraq and against ISIS in Syria. It was dubbed Operation Martyr Yalcin. Erdogan called Washington. "In our phone call with Obama, we reiterated our determination in the struggle against the separatist organization [PKK] and the Islamic State," Erdogan told reporters.[19] Then Ankara called a NATO emergency meeting on July 28. It claimed it was now fighting against both ISIS and the PKK and wanted NATO solidarity under Article 4 of the alliance's treaty, according to Turkish foreign minister Mevlut Cavusoglu.

Turkey also began work on a 764-kilometer fence along the border with Syria. Turkey and Syria share a 911-kilometer border. The wall reduced smuggling and illegal border crossings. At one of the first phases of the wall, built near Kilis, the number of smuggling events was estimated to drop from several thousand to seventy-seven in 2016. The wall included barbed wire, observation towers and floodlights. Each section of concrete was supposed to be two meters wide, three meters high and weigh seven tons. "No problems with our neighbors" had become a policy of building one of the largest walls in the world.

Chapter 2
The Bubble

Dubai Interlude

In December 2014, Muath al-Kassabeh, a Jordanian F-16 pilot, was conducting an air raid in Syria against ISIS when his plane crashed.[20] Captured by ISIS, he was placed in a cage and burned alive on video. "The blood of the martyr will not be in vain and the response of Jordan and its army after what happened to our dear son will be severe," King Abdullah said in a statement as he flew back from a visit to the US on February 4.[21] He ordered ramped-up air strikes against ISIS the same day. I flew into Jordan a month later.

In 2013, Queen Alia International Airport opened its snazzy new $750 million terminal. It has two concourses and in the middle a food court with Starbucks and Popeyes chicken. The venders sell Bedouin kaffiyehs and watches. While awaiting the Emirates flight to Dubai in March 2015, I popped into one of the kiosks that sell magazines and cigarettes. Up against one wall were the usual offerings from *National Geographic*, *Time* and others. Intermixed among them were headlines about ISIS and the battle for Kirkuk in Iraq. The headlines were a reminder that the kingdom was still in mourning over the death of the pilot, and air strikes were ongoing. Jordan, like Turkey, was a frontline state of the Syrian civil war. A million refugees fled across the border from Syria after 2012, leading to an unprecedented crisis. Tourism declined by more than 40 percent as foreigners feared that ISIS might strike the kingdom. At the baptism site on the Jordan River, the numbers fell from twenty-five thousand in 2010 to only three thousand visitors in 2015.[22] The kingdom was on edge.

From Queen Alia, I flew over Saudi Arabia to the United Arab Emirates to attend the Emirates Literature Festival, then in its seventh year. Located at the Intercontinental Hotel in Dubai, the festival seemed far removed from the region's problems. Bathers enjoyed time in a pool overhanging the main venue. In the distance the giant Burj Khalifa, since 2008 the tallest structure in the world, could be seen through the haze. Foreign workers from southern Asia relaxed on the lawn.

Dubai was on edge in 2015. Local Emiratis spoke with pride of their government and its moderate course in the Middle East. But they were concerned about neighboring Qatar and its support for the Muslim Brotherhood and Hamas: it was flirting with Sunni extremism. Locals also felt that their system of government, a monarchy, was a good bulwark against the extremism sweeping Iraq and Syria and the chaos in the region. "This is the problem with democracy – it can also bring with it that chaos; the way we are now, the government can contain the threat. Political conflict produces instability," one woman said.

The keynote speaker at the literature festival in 2015 was Nawal El Saadawi, the elderly Egyptian author and former prisoner. She spoke passionately about the need to be critical of governments. "I am always against the government, wherever I am in the world; when I was in the USA, I was against the government. If I were in Dubai, I would be against the government here." She said she had been censored throughout the Middle East. "Maybe it's only Dubai that can tolerate me and invite me.[23] I went to Doha, and I spoke against the government there, and I'm never allowed to enter again. The same in Saudi, Kuwait, Bahrain." She said she had been escorted by police from Bahrain, taken to the airport and sent on her way. The crowd, many of them wearing the traditional Emirati kandura robes, swooned. One woman spoke and praised the Egyptian author, saying her books were influencing people's lives locally.

While Saadawi was speaking, the crimes of ISIS were ongoing in Iraq and Syria. In an April 2015 video, ISIS took sledgehammers to Hatra in Iraq. It destroyed the gates of the ancient city of Nineveh. It destroyed St. Elijah's monastery and the Mar Gorgis monastery in Mosul in March 2015. Then it blew up the fourth-century Mar Behnam monastery in the Nineveh Plains. It also demolished sculptures in Mosul's museum. It ransacked and destroyed parts of the three-thousand-year-old city of

Nimrud. In August 2015, ISIS would blow up the temple of Baal Shamin in Palmyra. Yet as it was destroying culture, the Gulf was building culture. In Abu Dhabi, a new Louvre was being constructed. It would eventually open in late 2017.

Although ISIS did not conquer the great historic centers of the Arab world – Damascus, Baghdad and Cairo – its destruction of culture and history represented a fundamental break with the past. Thousands of years of civilization were destroyed in a few months in 2015. Minority groups that held the heritage of the ancient Assyrian and Chaldean empires and were part of the mosaic of the region were forced into exile, sealing the fate that had slowly caused attrition among them over the last decades. But in the Gulf, there was optimism and forward thinking. This was partly a facade painting over monarchies that were illiberal. In many ways, Dubai and Abu Dhabi feel like a bubble of what Alan Greenspan had once called "irrational exuberance," referring to the United States during the dot-com bubble of the 1990s. They are made possible by extreme wealth provided through oil and gas revenue, and this has generated opulence and decadence. It also overshadows brutalities, including human rights abuses of foreign workers and widespread hypocrisy in which an officially conservative kingdom tolerates human trafficking in women. But compared to the troubles affecting the region, the effort to build universities and museums while museums and universities and libraries were being burned and shuttered in Mosul and Raqqa was symbolic.

Iraq, Spring 2015

In the spring of 2015, ISIS put a bounty on the heads of foreigners in Iraq.[24] That's the first thing locals in Erbil, the capital of the Kurdistan Regional Government, told us when we landed. It added to the doubts about the trip. Back in Jerusalem, my wife was not sure about the idea to go cover the war against ISIS in Iraq. "I don't accept that my husband will end up on video in an orange jumpsuit," she said, referring to the brutal videos ISIS released of its executions of hostages. James Foley, Steven Sotloff and others had been killed in the fall of 2014. John Cantlie was still a prisoner of ISIS.

I reached out to friends who knew about Kurdistan. Sherkoh Abbas, a Syrian Kurdish leader who was president of the Kurdish National Assembly of Syria, put me in touch with several locals, including a man named Zach Huff, an American he recommended we meet in Erbil. I searched Instagram and Twitter for local Kurds and foreigners who were present. Itai Anghel, an Israeli reporter, had come back from Syria and recommended the trip. An American foreign volunteer and an Italian, who were training Kurdish anti-ISIS fighters, spoke to me via Skype. They were down in Kirkuk, south of Erbil. I said I'd try to come meet their unit on the front line. In Dohuk, I found Vager Saadullah, a local journalist and fixer who had written for the websites Al-Monitor, Middle East Eye and War Is Boring. He said he could get us to a frontline position near Mosul Dam. Mosul Dam had been the site of a major battle in August 2014 where the tide had turned against ISIS. Laura Kelly, my colleague at the *Jerusalem Post*, said she would come. Based on those contacts, we decided to risk it.

I felt that this war unfolding in northern Iraq had to be seen and documented. The crimes ISIS had committed in 2014 against Yazidis – raping and selling women, machine-gunning men – were horrific. Between June and August, ISIS carried out numerous atrocities. It massacred fifteen hundred Shi'ite cadets at Camp Speicher and slaughtered hundreds of Shi'ite prisoners on June 10. It had ethnically cleansed Christians from the Nineveh Plains, devastating Hamdaniyeh (Qaraqosh), the largest Christian town in the area. Then it turned its sights on the Yazidis. Some of the videos of the massacres were widely shared in the fall of 2014. Social media such as Twitter and Facebook made no attempt to hide them. We'd heard stories of heroic Kurdish fighters who had stopped ISIS as it advanced on their territory. They reminded me of something like the British, standing alone against Nazi Germany. I felt a duty to go to Iraq and be with the people who were standing against this incredible evil, this new Nazism, if that's what it was.

Flying into Iraq in June 2015 from Jordan, the Royal Jordanian airliner had to pass over large swaths of Anbar Province controlled by ISIS. It made an arc south of Mosul and landed at the new international airport. Zach Huff, the American who had lived in Erbil for seven months, met us at four in the morning. I was traveling with Kelly. It was our first time in Iraq. The Kurdistan region and its autonomous government advertises itself as "the other Iraq," safer and cleaner.

Our first stop was the Harsham Internally Displaced Persons and Refugee Camp that had been set up in September 2014, just outside Erbil. Located next to some new high-rises, the camp consisted of 299 caravans and huts, with a main entrance manned by a group called ACTED. The caravan housing was laid out in a grid. According to a map at the entrance to the small camp, there were 271 families and 1,432 people there. They were a cross section of Sunni Arabs from neighboring areas who had fled ISIS. A full 531 of the residents were from Mosul. Others came from towns in Nineveh Province such as Sinjar and Hamdaniyeh, and from provinces farther away such as Salahadin and Anbar. "When the disaster ends, they will go back," said one of the men.

The camp had its own bakery, and a primary school was scheduled to open in September. Latrines, bits of whose sewage flowed down past the new high-rises, had signs urging people to use the toilets rather than defecate outside. Signs of other donors, such as the Norwegian Refugee Council and the Barzani Charity Foundation, adorned walls of the entrance. One caravan held a "child-friendly space," and UNICEF was scheduled to build a school in July. The men worked outside the camp in what jobs they could get. One man from Diyala Province said he dreamed of going home. There was little contact with their family members living under ISIS control. "The phone network is down in Mosul."

According to the Kurdistan Regional Government, there were more than two million refugees and internally displaced persons in the Kurdish region in 2015, most of whom had fled ISIS. Others had fled from Syria or Iran. They numbered about 35 percent of the Kurdistan region's population by 2015.[25] The Kurdish region, which had once been poor and ravaged by Saddam Hussein, was now hosting people. Kurds who had spent half their lives as refugees in Iran or Turkey, fleeing Saddam's genocidal Anfal campaign in the 1980s, in which thousands of villages were destroyed, were now the hosts. How quickly history had changed in just decades.

After the camp, we toured Erbil. In Ainkawa, the mostly Christian part of town, popular with expats, there was a Quiznos, a Hardee's and a Pizza Hut. It could have been Tucson, Arizona. The road to the US consulate was blocked with concrete. In April, just two months earlier, a car bomb had targeted it. We passed a Chaldean church, shops selling Tuborg beer and then Sami Abdalrahman Park, the local parliament and down to the historic Citadel in the center of town. Erbil is built in concentric circles around the eight-thousand-year-old Citadel, which is a UNESCO World Heritage Site. Sitting on top of a large earthen cone, the Citadel dominates the city center and overlooks a pretty park that has fountains. It was hot in Erbil in June, and walking in the humid air brought out the sweat.

While parts of Erbil were modern with wide avenues, down by the Citadel, life was a bit simpler. The older parts of Erbil are run-down and evoke a feeling of any desert-like Third World country, dusty, peeled paint and architecture similar to what one finds throughout the Middle East, with cement buildings and single-family homes abutting one another making up the older parts, while the modern areas had apartments. Men with trollies pushed giant blocks of ice. Money changers held stacks of cash the size of toaster ovens. Not far from the Citadel, in an alley of one of the old markets, was a gun repair shop. Antique weapons and rifles dotted the walls. It is a reminder that many of the Peshmerga or local soldiers outfit themselves before going to battle ISIS. There was a whole street in Erbil devoted to selling surplus military equipment, including US Army body armor with the names of the former owners still inscribed. One I picked up said it was protection against up to 7.62 mm rounds. It had been produced in 2005 by Ceradyne, a subsidiary of 3M. The green body armor plate had "DeLucia" written on it and said it was "good for six months only." It had obviously outlived its "good" period by 2014.

We found our hotel, located on one of the big circular streets called 100 Meter Road. It was a simple affair, several stories high, and barely looked like a hotel from outside. Inside wasn't much better. There was an eating area of a dozen tables off to one side, a buffet and then stairs leading up to the rooms. My room had a window looking onto a back alley. It was small. There was no TV, but there was a prayer rug.

In the morning when I went downstairs for breakfast, a large man at a corner table shouted, "Heloooooo!" He had this way of rolling out the greeting with a guttural sound. "Who are you?" he wondered. He was a professor at a local university. He had fled Mosul when ISIS arrived and was living at the hotel, which it turned out was run by other Moslawis, the people of Mosul. He said that his five sons had stayed behind. They needed work and didn't want ISIS to take their homes if they fled. They were educated, including engineers, and ISIS needed men like that to run its new state. He spoke to them frequently, he said. Of course ISIS was cruel, but it was one evil among many, he thought. It seemed strange talking to this elderly man who was in contact with men inside the ISIS "caliphate." What about the bounty on the heads of foreigners? With one call, he could give us up. I wanted to leave the hotel.

So we went to see a man nicknamed "the professor," a Syrian Kurdish intellectual who was said to be a former adviser to the former prime minister of the Kurdistan region, Barham Salih. The professor lived in a middle-class neighborhood, his electricity kept on with a generator. Generators were everywhere in Erbil because of frequent power outages. Inside the house he had a framed picture of *Charlie Hebdo*, one of the issues that had offended some in Europe. In January, terrorists had attacked the magazine's offices in Paris, murdering twelve. The professor's decision to get a copy was a sign of defiance against Islamists.

In June 2015, a year after ISIS had arrived on the border of Kurdistan, many Kurds had a pragmatic and long-term view. Although they were holding the line against ISIS, they repeated the old saying "Kurds have no friends but the mountains." The professor agreed. The Kurdish academic had a prophecy for the future. "Joining Syria and Iraq is a utopian idea. The future is in Turkey, what happens there. Assad will survive. This conflict will continue for many years. The Islamists will grow." He also argued that many Sunni Arabs in the neighboring area secretly supported ISIS. "It didn't come from a vacuum; it is an Arab mentality and their culture. ISIS is like Nasser's Arab nationalism or Ba'athism of today," he said, drawing parallels with history. "It is a new Islamist age."

Chapter 3
The Eastern Front

The Road to Dohuk

Erbil is about 360 kilometers north of Baghdad and two hundred kilometers from the Turkish border at Zakho. It has a population of almost 1.3 million people and was the fourth-largest city in Iraq after Baghdad, Basra and Mosul. After ISIS conquered Mosul, Erbil probably became the third-largest city in the country. It had been named the Capital of Arab Tourism for 2014. It was plowing $1 billion into new hotels and hoped to welcome three million visitors. Unsurprisingly, the tourists vanished once ISIS came knocking on the door of Kurdistan. At one point in 2014, the extremists were just two dozen kilometers from Erbil on the road from Makhmur. The threat motivated Obama to order air strikes on August 7, 2014.

Many parts of the city are new, including the airport, which opened in 2010. There are a lot of signs of Turkish investment, which is no surprise, as Turkey is the main trading partner of the Kurdistan region. When ISIS attacked in August 2014, the region was mostly cut off from the rest of Iraq. The road to Kirkuk and Baghdad was threatened. So the Kurdistan Regional Government (KRG) began exporting its oil to the north, and Turkish investment poured in. But an economic crisis followed, and Baghdad cut the KRG's budget, preferring to use the money for its own battle against ISIS. Civil servants went unpaid for months.

The facade of a flourishing economy in the city and its rhythms continued. Its ample nightlife in the Christian area of town flourished. Foreign reporters and foreign contractors poured in. The airport serviced

27

around five thousand passengers a day on fifty flights, for a total of around 150,000 a month.[26] Many Westerners enjoyed visas on arrival, whereas Baghdad's visa process was lengthy.

On June 12, 2015, Kelly and I got a taxi heading for Dohuk. Since the ISIS advance, the road to the north had changed. In 2013, the KRG had decided to ring the southern and western parts of Erbil with a massive trench, eventually extending two hundred kilometers. This was a World War I–style fortification to fight an enemy that combined terror with jihadist zeal. But the trench would effectively make it so car bombs couldn't get in the city without going through a checkpoint. It would be two-meters deep and three wide. Checkpoints and strongpoints would line it every 250 meters, and tens of thousands of Peshmerga would be sent to man the wall.

The arrival of ISIS disrupted these plans. ISIS cut through defensive barriers in Nineveh, striking toward the Kurdish cities. Stopped at Makhmur, ISIS had also advanced toward Kalak on the Great Zab River northwest of Erbil. To get to Dohuk in June, we headed north toward this battlefield. By then ISIS had been pushed back. Our taxi driver recalled how Masoud Barzani, the KRG's president, whose Kurdistan Democratic Party has dominated Kurdish politics alongside its rival Jalal Talabani's Patriotic Union of Kurdistan, had even called Iran for help in August. The US was too slow to respond, and the Kurds needed help. The Iranians had sent help, as they did throughout Iraq, to counter ISIS.

The drive north from Erbil covers flat plains that spread out toward Mosul to the northwest and toward the mountains to the northeast. It's a long, boring road, interrupted here and there by checkpoints with Peshmerga men, their AK-47s slung over their shoulders, asking for IDs. Americans always get a smile. Near Kalak there is a large metal statue of a fish, evidently because the town is known for fish. A local shawarma shop, however, belies the fish mongering. The meat is good, too. We traveled past Kalak and toward another dusty town called Bardarash. Here the two-lane highway became clogged with Turkish trucks. Endless lines of trucks became our companions, some of them pulled off on the side of the road. One had "Gazprom" printed on the side, the oil giant from Russia. There were oil fires in the distance. The road was dotted with memorials to fallen Peshmerga. Eventually the plains give away to foothills in the distance near the Yazidi district of Shekhan. The road improves and crosses up into a mountain pass. Signs warn that the speed limit is monitored by radar, but we never saw a police car. And then laid out below the road is Dohuk.

Dohuk was built in a valley. In the 1980s it was a small town, but by 2014, it had some 250,000 people in it, with apartments and hotels stretching out along a valley. On both sides are pretty, bare mountains, dotted with short trees and bushes. Some of the people there were IDPs (internally displaced persons) from Mosul and Sinjar, including Christians, Arabs and Yazidis who had settled in Dohuk since 2014, swelling its population. Our taxi dropped us at Park Azadi, "Freedom Park," and we waited for our contact, Vager Saadullah, to pick us up. He came soon enough with his own car. Saadullah was born near the historic city of Amedi and is an intense Kurdish patriot. His family had suffered under Saddam and he grew up as a refugee in Turkey before returning in 1992. His family had moved to Dereluk in the mountains and then to Dohuk in 2006. Conflict didn't spare his village, because up near the Turkish border the PKK was present, and the Turkish army had established a string of bases inside Iraq.

A former journalist, he took up being a fixer for the money after 2014. For several hundred dollars a day, he was helping journalists arrange meetings, driving them and translating. "You want some food," he suggested upon meeting us.

So we drove to have some pita with meat and then took a tour above the city to see Dohuk Dam. Built in 1988, the sixty-meter-high dam is perched above the city. Next to the dam is a kind of coffee shop and small amusement park. It could be Switzerland, if it weren't Iraq. This part of the Kurdish region, with its mountain air and protected by the hills on all sides, seemed far removed from the war. But Saadullah said that the war had come so close in August 2014 that people began to flee to the mountains, as they had when fleeing Saddam or other enemies. "I decided to become a sniper," he recalled. But in the end ISIS didn't lay siege to the city, and the people stayed on. Instead the Peshmerga reinforcements, bolstered by US airpower, checked the enemy advance twenty kilometers south of the city, on the plains that overlook Mosul.

According to Saadullah, there were some one million IDPs now living around Dohuk, and the city itself had 500,000 residents. There was a lot of Turkish influence here, he said. "Before the war you couldn't get a hotel, there were so many tourists." Northern Kurdistan is more conservative than some areas like Erbil or Sulaymaniyah. The Islamic parties polled 16 percent in the last elections, said Saadullah. "Western tourists are afraid to come here because it is called 'Iraq.' Our dream is independence, and we will have a better name for ourselves. I don't want to emigrate; I want to serve my people here." Other Kurds we met said they looked forward to the day when they could burn their Iraqi passports. "We waited a long time for independence and have thousands of martyrs," said Saadullah.

After leaving Dohuk, the road to Mosul reaches a small pass before continuing down toward Nineveh Plains. There were checkpoints along the way, manned by Peshmerga in mismatched uniforms. Some wore American-style surplus fatigues, others the traditional Kurdish clothing, baggy pants and shirt in camouflage colors. An escort jumped in the car to take us into the Christian village of Telskuf, thirty-five kilometers from Mosul. "I've been serving in the Peshmerga since the 1980s," he said. This man, now in his fifties, had spent his whole life at war. "I lost thirty-three family members during the Anfal campaign."

In Telskuf, the Peshmerga had commandeered one of the houses, a two-story bungalow. In one room the local commanders were seated to greet us. They came in all shapes and sizes, fat, tall, in their forties and fifties. In the corner were a small Kurdish flag and a statue of the Virgin Mary. This had been the home of a Christian family. When it was liberated, it became the headquarters of the unit. "Since August 2014, our men have been here," the commander said. After several rounds of tea, always a requirement when meeting Kurds, he offered to take us to his front line.

After a short drive, past buildings and walls pockmarked with mortar fragments, we reached the berm. Using bulldozers, the Kurds had built up a long berm stretching from Telskuf toward the south. Every hundred or so meters, they put sandbagged positions, a few tents for sleeping quarters, a latrine and, if they could find it, some sort of concrete roof over a shed to hide from mortar fire. This was a First World War battle-field being fought intermittently with twenty-first-century technology.

The men could even listen to ISIS communications. It was also a static battlefield, another commonality with the Great War. After its initial advance in August 2014, ISIS had been largely checked and stopped. For three years, the front line remained mostly the same over hundreds of kilometers. It would take ISIS years to lose what it had conquered in mere months in 2014. Mosul, which fell in a day, would take the better part of a year to be recaptured. In the waning days of 2015, ISIS was still a menace to Iraq and could carry out limited offensives.

"Last time they came at us, they brought ladders," said one of the fighters, beaming with pride. He showed a photo on his phone of two dead men in black. He had shot them as they came. Then his men went out and burned the bodies. These men were serving twenty days at home and ten days on the line. They were all volunteers with families and regular jobs. They had a mix of rifles, mostly AK-47s and some Soviet-era Dragunov sniper rifles. These they held in particular pride. Each position had a DShk, a heavy machine gun that first saw action in 1938 with the Red Army.

For the fighters, the war on ISIS was just the latest in a long string of wars. "In the 1970s we fought Saddam with the help of the US and Israel and Iran," some of the older men remembered. "But the USA and Kissinger betrayed us in 1975." Another man, wearing a cowboy hat, chimed in. "Remember, we have no friends but the mountains." And a third man, large and fat, reminded his comrades how in 1946 the Kurdish Republic of Mahabad in Iran had been betrayed by the Soviets. "Now we are independent in all but name." This was the real story here at the end of this front line, in the middle of nowhere, in the quiet afternoon. As ISIS slept and fires burned from oil-soaked tires that it had lit to avoid being seen by coalition drones and aircraft, the Kurdish men were enjoying independence. There were no Iraqi flags here. In fact, from Erbil to Dohuk there were no Iraqi flags. This wasn't Iraq, in their view. I looked through the sights of the Dragunov at the ISIS position. "You see there, that is a monastery," one of the men said. We were looking out at Christian villages in the distance. This was once a peaceful farming area, now riven and scarred by war.

But what kind of war? I'd expected to be fearful and in a bunker worried about ISIS. But the famous war machine was nowhere to be seen. A few mortar shells a day was all that hit the position, the men said. ISIS attacked at night, or sometimes under cover of fog. But the men ISIS was sending were not veteran fighters; they were zealous new recruits, foreigners. Some looked Chinese, the Kurds said. These were the Uighurs who had joined up. Unlike the famous Chechan snipers Kurds had faced in Mahmur in 2014 or that Syrian Kurdish YPG fighters were facing in Kobani in 2015, the ISIS fighters at the front line near Telskuf were its second-rate men. This was because ISIS was busy fighting near Ramadi and other areas in Iraq.

The Kurds had no interest in moving forward. They had defended their land and built a front line. Now they would defend it. They had one request. "Give us more MILAN anti-tank weapons." This was because their position had nothing that could penetrate the "Mad Max" armored vehicles that ISIS built in its factories near Mosul. These vehicles are often called vehicle-borne improvised explosive devices (VBIEDs) by the US military. "The problem we face here is that their [ISIS] fighters want to die, and we want to live," said one of the Kurdish men as we left, pointing out the stark contrast between the forces arrayed against each other.

A short drive back to the HQ brought us to Deputy Division Commander Sardar Karim. "Our morale will improve now that you are here," he said. But it didn't appear his men needed prodding from us. "Most of our commanders fought Saddam, so that makes us different." He recalled how his men had liberated Kurdistan in the 1990s. Now his Peshmerga had normal full units, four brigades of a thousand men each and divisions strung out from here to Erbil along a thousand kilometers of front. "In those days in the mountains, we stood against a very powerful regime which had help from the Arab and Western countries. We were alone, but we did not give up. They used poison gas. But we never gave up our rights."

The men reminisced about the old days, when they had no weapons or armored vehicles. Now the unit had a captured Humvee that they had taken off ISIS at the battle of Mosul Dam. ISIS had captured it from the Iraqi army in June 2014. "In August we were fighting and [KRG] President [Masoud] Barzani came here to lead from the front as a commander. We reorganized and fought. We knew the ISIS tactics, and we held for three days until the Americans came," recalled the commander. Now the

Kurds were confident and felt they had more experience. The thousands of vehicles ISIS had captured from the Iraqi and Syrian armies had been destroyed by US-led airpower. The Kurds had also just begun to receive some foreign weapons. The commander said he had some that had come from Bulgaria. "Everyone knows we are not just fighting for ourselves but [for] the whole world, and we need their support." But the men were worried about Western support. "Why the US government's interest is more with the Arabs than the Kurds?" the commander asked. I had no answer. Although the men were confident in their position, they were concerned that ISIS had captured equipment from the Iraqi army in Ramadi. One officer alleged ISIS now had drones.

Next door to the Peshmerga was another house, now occupied by a Christian militia unit called the Nineveh Plains Forces. With a flag representing the "two rivers" of Iraq that is common among Assyrians, the men said they were Christian IDPs who had fled Mosul and Nineveh. Some had been living in Erbil and volunteered. For eight months they had been in Telskuf helping provide security in the Christian town. "The unit was formed as a regiment by the [KRG] Peshmerga Ministry after the war began, so we got volunteers and began training," said a commander who gave his name as Safaa Jajo. He was born in 1977. A strapping, fit man, he liked to pose with his rifle and the new scope he had bought.

With the Christians, the younger soldiers brought Arabic coffee instead of tea. The subtle differences. The commander also listened on his walkie-talkie to ISIS radio chatter. It was surreal.

The Christian volunteers were younger men, in contrast to the Peshmerga, who were almost all family men in their thirties and forties. They hoped that the "Americans" would change their "strategic plan" and seek to liberate the Christian towns of Nineveh Plains. For the Christian fighters, times were difficult. They complained of having to buy their own rifles and that their families were living as IDPs. "Before ISIS it was also bad in this area. We had no running water, and we suffered from Islamist attacks. There was terrorism against the US forces, and seventeen Christians were killed."

One of the most iconic and historic Christian villages in Nineveh is Al-Qosh, which sits at the foot of a ridge of mountains overlooking the plains around Mosul. Driving into it, we encountered the first Iraqi flags of the trip. The Nineveh Plains are technically outside the KRG, and this was "Iraq," but there were no federal forces in sight. The village is ancient, and there is a thousand-year-old synagogue that commemorates the tomb of the prophet Nahum. We went looking for it but ended up at one of the houses of the locals. It was adorned with statues of the Virgin Mary and Jesus, as well as a mural of the Twelve Disciples. Basima Safar, a middle-aged woman, said the house belonged to her and invited us in for a coffee. "I am a painter," she said. "I am still here," she said, gesturing toward the plains below and the front line a few kilometers away. She said that before ISIS, many tourists and journalists came to the town. No matter what happened, she said, she would remain.

Even the prophet Nahum probably couldn't find his own tomb in Al-Qosh, despite the stories about its fame. We searched and thought it was all in vain, until we found a nondescript, ruined building with a metal roof. The metal roof was actually some sort of scaffolding erected to protect the ruin from the elements. We made our way over a wall and into a courtyard of the old synagogue. It was mostly falling apart and full of rubble. Just barely visible inside was a masonry-encased green, shrouded block the size of a table. This was the "tomb" that people pray to. On one wall was a Hebrew inscription. Here in Iraq, where only a handful of Jews remained, we were seeing this ancient history of one of the diverse peoples that once made up the mosaic of Nineveh Plains. Jews once lived in places such as Erbil and Mosul, as well as in Baghdad and Fallujah. These were centers of Jewish learning and power in ancient times, home to the Babylonian Talmud. No more. Now, like the Christians cleansed by ISIS and the Yazidis slaughtered and raped, they were gone from this area. The ruined tomb was one of the only testimonies that Jews ever lived here.

After leaving the tomb, we drove down the road toward the Monastery of the Virgin Mary. Along the road was a large, square building with four circular turrets on each side. It looked like a fort, but made of modern concrete. "That was one of Saddam's posts," said Saadullah. In the 1980s, these forts had been constructed throughout northern Iraq as part of Saddam's suppression of the locals, especially in the Kurdish region. They were the heavy hand of government security, to which prisoners were disappeared to be tortured. Like ISIS, Saddam Hussein had sought to change the demographics of this area. His army had destroyed thousands of villages and collectivized other minorities such as Yazidis and Christians, placing them in planned villages. He had settled loyal Sunni Arabs in between the minority groups, to control them. Kurds call this "Arabization," and it still affects and haunts the politics of northern Iraq. The police forts were meant to make sure the locals didn't rebel.

Down from the fort was a pretty monastery with refurbished walls. "The abbey was founded in the period of Bishop Yasif Aoudo and Abbot Elisha al Duhoki, the general chairman of monks in 1858. The administration of the abbey decided to build a new abbey under the name of the Virgin Mary," said the plaque.

It said that the building was supposed to house a "large number" of monks who had lived in the seventh-century Rabban Hormizd Monastery on the mountain above. "It also helped the monks care for their sheep and their agricultural needs." Built on seven acres of land, the abbey contains a museum that was founded in 1974 and an orphanage built in 1950. The sun was getting lower in the sky, and we didn't have time to stay, so we moved on. After snapping a photo in front of a sign saying "Baghdad 440 km, Mosul 37 km," we drove back.

In Dohuk while waiting for a taxi, we met two men who served in the Peshmerga on the Nawaran front, south of Telskup. Both were husbands and fathers in their thirties. "Our main problem is the lack of heavy weapons," said the first man. "The Iraqi government receives weapons from the international community, and they give it as a gift to ISIS." This was the rumor and conspiracy in which many Kurds believed. How did ISIS get so many heavy weapons? they asked. ISIS had overrun arms depots and captured abandoned Iraqi equipment, but after almost a year of war, the men wondered how ISIS still had such weapons. "They got them when the Iraqi army abandoned Ramadi." The Peshmerga complained that they lacked ammunition and that ISIS used many disguises to attack. "They dress as women or use families as human shields." The Peshmerga said that their long front line was so under equipped that MILAN and other anti-tank weapons had to be shared among units. In one recent attack, the Peshmerga said they had lost eleven men to a suicide "uparmored" truck. These trucks look like something out of the *Mad Max* films, civilian vehicles converted to spread death and destruction.

The jihadists welded armored plates onto them, covered the windows and then packed them with explosives.

Lalish

The persecution and mass murder of Yazidis were the most gruesome of ISIS's long list of crimes. The Yazidi holy site of Lalish, located south of Dohuk, was on the tourist itinerary of northern Iraq before ISIS arrived. Now it had become a shelter for the persecuted people. To get to Lalish, we drove through hills and near Yazidi villages where small shops sold beer, a rarity in northern Iraq. At the entrance to the site, some Peshmerga with their AKs stood guard. In the distance were another Saddam-era fort and an oil fire, the future and the past of this region.

Luqman Mahmood, a local journalist and guide who took it upon himself to give tours of the area, sidled up to us. "There are 366 sites for burning candles here," he said, referring to places set for candles around the temples and walkways connecting them. Flowers were also strewn about to mark the New Year. "Yazidis have suffered seventy-four genocides in the last six hundred years," he said. "We get many foreign visitors here. The consul of Germany came here recently and the consuls of France and the US." According to Luqman, there were 700,000 Yazidis in Iraq in 2004. They include different castes – Pirs, Sheikhs and Murids. "Each marries only within their group." He claimed there were five thousand Yazidis still held by ISIS in 2015. He then gave details of the August 2014 genocide. "When ISIS came to one village, there were 184 people they caught. The people were told to convert. ISIS killed all the men and took all the girls. Now ISIS has three thousand of the most beautiful girls."

The temple complex of Lalish consisted of a series of low-lying buildings nestled among the trees, rocks and streams. In one temple there was a kind of spring, and women sat outside. The hills were dotted with tall stone cones that mark Yazidi sites. "This temple has the sun and moon on the doors of the tomb, because they are close to nature," Luqman attempted to explain. He said Yazidis believe that Noah's Ark came to rest on Mount Sinjar, several hours' drive to the west of Lalish. The mountain was where many Yazidis had fled in 2014 to seek shelter from ISIS. When Obama ordered air strikes, he had also ordered that humanitarian aid be delivered to the mountain. "A month ago we had six hundred families still living here who fled Sinjar," said the guide. In October 2014, around 200,000 Yazidis fled to this area. Now they were housed in IDP camps that dotted the countryside nearby. But at Lalish, the quiet and the trees embracing the temple seemed tranquil. The war and the suffering were nowhere to be seen.

At the time, one of the most recognizable voices in the community was Vian Dakhil, a Yazidi member of Iraq's parliament. On August 5, as ISIS was killing Yazidis, she wept while speaking to parliament in Baghdad. She implored the world to do something. Then, seven days later, she was on a helicopter piloted by Maj. Gen. Majid al-Tamimi, who had been airlifting Yazidis off Mount Sinjar. He overloaded his helicopter that day and crashed into the mountain. Dakhil was injured. Tamimi died. Four years later, a small monument would be built to him in northern Iraq, to commemorate his sacrifice.

In the dark days of 2015, I reached out to Dakhil. She spoke for twenty minutes describing the suffering Yazidis, 350,000 in IDP camps, six thousand missing. She said it was like a new Holocaust of her people. "I want recognition for what they did as a genocide. ISIS killed men and kidnapped women and killed girls and boys, separated children from mothers and did terrible things." Like so many Iraqis of her generation, she was scarred by war. She was born in 1974 in Sinjar; her family had to flee into exile to avoid Saddam Hussein's bulldozing of Yazidi villages. But before 2003 there was more security. After the US invasion, jihadists began terror attacks on Yazidis. It was a rehearsal for the attack of August 2014.

"When ISIS Came, We Were Happy"

Through the night we drove back to Erbil with a taxi driver who handled the car like a madman. He knew several words of English and place names in the US that he would shout with glee while blaring Kurdish music. Getting back to the hotel run by the men from Mosul was a welcome respite.

"Corruption is 100 percent in Iraq," said the elderly man who lived at the hotel. "Helllloooo." He was happy to see us again. Misbah Mahmoud al-Solamani said he had been born in Mosul in 1948. "It was good until

1998." He said that he was one of eight children who grew up without a telephone even during the years of Saddam, which he thought were better than today. "Iran has stood on its feet now," he said, arguing that the real winner from the chaos in the region was Iran's growing influence. "Dictatorship suits Iraq." Solamani spoke in short proverbs. "The Kurds do something for their people." Okay. "America may be right in the long term." Okay. "When US troops first came to Mosul there was cooperation for a few months, and they sat in the cafes and there was peace." But Solamani said that soon things changed dramatically. Then the man moved on to other themes. "In 1988, I had a car, and I used to drive out to Nimrud with friends." This appeared to be a reference to the fact that ISIS had destroyed Nimrud. It was probably a parable for Iraq in general. Iraq had been destroyed, he was saying. His life had been turned upside down, and now all he knew was a small corner table in this no-frills hotel in Erbil.

Like Solamani, the younger Sunni Arabs of Iraq also found their lives turned upside down. Mohammed, an IDP from Tikrit, had come to Erbil fleeing both ISIS and Shi'ite militias. In his early twenties, he was handsome and skinny, carefree and happy but living alone in a Kurdish city. He said that in battles for Tirkit between the Iraqi army and ISIS, the Shi'ite-led army used Sunni recruits just to sacrifice them at the front. During Saddam's time the Ba'ath Party had been led by Sunni Arabs, and the officer corps was made up of Sunni officers from towns like Tikrit, where Saddam was from.

In Tikrit, Mohamed said, the Shi'ite militias had banned Sunnis from entering Saddam Hussein's former palace. When ISIS arrived, it massacred Shi'ites in the old palace. This was the religious bloodletting, a new Thirty Years War–style slaughter in Mesopotamia. He recalled the years before ISIS came, when Iraq's leader Nouri al-Maliki became increasingly sectarian and pro-Iranian. "Sunnis joined the army in Tikrit to take care of their homes. But the Shi'ite[s] stole everything and burned the markets. When ISIS took over, they didn't steal or bomb," Mohamed said.

"When ISIS came, we were happy. They beheaded the Iraqi soldiers and police. Then the Iraqi army bombed Tikrit and harmed civilians aimlessly," Mohamed said. ISIS had come out of the American-run prisons for insurgents and found supporters among former Ba'ath members and foreign volunteers, he said. We sat for a narghile and took long drags on the apple tobacco. "Ninety percent think there is a hidden deal with the Iraqi government, so that the Shi'ite[s] will retake the cities." He said the Shi'ite militias were moving on Tikrit and that as they moved in, they were looting the houses and dividing them among the families of men ISIS had killed. "The Shi'ite[s] are building mosques, and the Sunni[s] will be a minority now." The Iranians had come to Iraq, he asserted.

Mohamed said that after fleeing Tikrit, he made his way to Samarra on the Tigris River. "There was a checkpoint, and there had been a Sunni guard there from Mosul. But the local colonel had been changed. We had known the officer, but then the Shi'ite militias came and killed the Iraqi army soldiers in September." The confusing killings seemed to indicate a cleansing of Sunni soldiers in the army by Shi'ite militias. "After that, no Sunni could join the army. They would accuse us of being ISIS. It was government policy." It was part of a larger pattern. "When Ramadi Sunni[s] tried to flee ISIS, they were killed by the Shi'ite[s]. There is a checkpoint run by Jaish al-Mahdi, Moqtada al-Sadr's army, and they kill Sunni[s]. So do Asaib Ahl al-Haq." They wear the black clothes and the green headband, said Mohamed.

In 2015, Mohamed still thought that ISIS posed a danger to Baghdad. He said that the major Sunni tribes such as the Dhullam might rebel against the government. But the IDP from Tikrit was still sure ISIS was worse for Sunnis, because it had massacred locals as well.

Chapter 4
The Long Road to Europe

Eastern Europe: The Refugees Arrive, September 2015
I peered into the fog. It was 5:23 a.m., and the train tracks stretched
into the distance. Cold. Gray. Rainy. Then shapes began to move in the
distance. It could have been a good setting for a Stephen King novel.[27]
The shapes were just bits of darkness in the fog. Then came the outline
of a man. A woman behind him carrying a bundle, a small baby wrapped
in a blanket. They trundled along. Solitary figures, some in groups that
looked like families. Young men and women mostly. Slowly they came.
There were more and more. They passed my car, parked next to the
tracks, and continued on their way along the empty railway line toward
the Hungarian border.

The shadows in the fog were some of the hundred thousand migrants
crossing into Europe that month. Most had come via inflatable raft from
Turkey. They were part of an unprecedented migration of people from
the Middle East, Asia and Africa. After years of war in Syria and Iraq,
these people knew they wouldn't be going home, and they wanted a new
life. In 2015, around 400,000 Syrians crossed into the EU seeking asylum.
There were also almost 180,000 Afghans and 120,000 Iraqis. Thousands
died en route, with the International Organization for Migration esti-
mating 2,926 had drowned by September 2015.[28] One of those was
three-year-old Alan Kurdi. He was born in Kobani, in eastern Syria. On
September 2, 2015, his father took him to board a smuggler's boat near
Bodrum, Turkey. They were destined for the Greek island of Kos, but the
boat overturned, and the boy drowned. Photographs of the dead boy's

body, washed up in Turkey, made headlines around the world. Seven days later, I landed in Thessaloniki, Greece.

I wanted to trace the migrant route to Hungary from Greece. It wasn't difficult. At the Greek border town of Idomeni, thousands of refugees were trudging through a field to get to Macedonia. They didn't try hiding from border guards. Médecins Sans Frontières had set up caravans and aid stations for them. Signs said, "Toilets, showers and drinkable water." They were following the rail line north. Nearby was an official border crossing along the E75 highway. But the actual way north was a kilometer north of the official crossing. Across the Vardar River, more like a stream, the migrants were forming up in columns. The Greek police directed them into groups of forty. Then the police escorted them to the border, where they were sent across an old bridge into the Republic of Macedonia.

After driving the legal route around to Macedonia's Gevgelija, I found the migrants on the other side. Here the Macedonian military had been deployed and was trying to control the flow of people. A huge jam was created on the bridge, with the Greek police funneling more people in and the Macedonian army trying to arrange buses and taxis north. Gevgelija had been a gambling town popular during the Cold War. Now it was popular for aid workers and migrants. The police were nonplussed, but they looked on bemused. As long as the people moved north, it was fine.

The refugees were fleeing war in Syria and Iraq. After years of conflict, they realized they would probably never go home. They had no life in Turkey. For some of the minorities, such as Kurds and Yazidis, it was about fleeing to escape ISIS. The Yazidis found it especially difficult, because they faced continued persecution along the way and often had to hide their religious identity. One Kurdish man I spoke to said he had been an artist in Aleppo before the war. The war had come, and Aleppo became divided between the regime and the increasingly extremist rebel groups. Eventually, with his wife, he escaped to Turkey. Now he would make his way north to Sweden, he said, where there were Kurdish distant relatives.

Over the next days I made my own way north, first to Serbia, where the refugees crowded into the Albanian-majority town of Presevo that is in Serbia but which sits on the border where Kosovo, Albania and Macedonia meet. For the refugees, the familiar sight of Turkish-style minarets in the Albanian town must have seemed strange in this European landscape.

Crossing Serbia, they were dumped near the Hungarian border by buses. Some walked the whole way if they couldn't afford or find transportation. At the Hungarian border, they congregated at the border town of Backi Vinogradi. This was the wine-growing region in Serbia. It was also a Hungarian-speaking area. Signs pointed across the border to Asotthalom in Hungary. But Hungary was building a large border fence to keep the refugees out, and they had to go via another Serbian town called Horgos to cross to Roszke in Hungary. This is where I ran into the figures in the fog. I'd slept in the car the night before and was stiff and tired. Some Afghan asylum seekers were warming themselves by a fire they had kindled in the old railway station. They smiled and laughed. One who said his name was Mahdi Sadat had come across a whole continent to get here. "They don't have anything halal in the store," he said.

I joined a group of migrants to make the last kilometer into Hungary. Some members of the Roma minority sold cigarettes and water along the tracks. In the forest there were people camping, getting up to make the final crossing to the EU in the morning. Once we reached the Hungarian side, the massive fence with razor wire was clearly visible. The crews were about to close it and cut off this railway route. Until then the Hungarian police were managing a makeshift camp in a field of mud. They were sending the migrants north. According to the local UNHCR post, around two thousand people had crossed on September 12, and they expected at least five thousand by day's end. Many of the people crossing were from Aleppo in Syria, a city that once had three million residents and was now reduced in part to ruin.

Across Europe there were salacious stories about the refugees. Headlines portrayed them in biblical and natural disaster-like terms, a "flood," a "torrent" or a "tide." Concerns about terror and xenophobia, about mass rape and Islamic "infiltration." Headlines claimed many of those coming were young men. Chris Matthews, the US TV show host, mocked the migrants in November 2015.[29] "Let me finish tonight with two numbers that don't make sense," he said. "The first number is four, the number of Syrians we Americans have trained and recruited to fight ISIS. Hold on to that number. The other number is four million. That's how many Syrian refugees there are, including all the able-bodied men we've seen on board boats to Europe." Matthews saw something sinister in the numbers. "Four million fleeing ISIS and Assad and just four trained to fight. Are just one in a million willing to fight for Syria? Is that the deal? Would just one in a million be willing to fight for our country if it were taken from us? There are dread implications. It signals ISIS is taking the country from people who would rather live in the West."

Matthews implied these refugees were cowards. But the ones I met were not cowards. And they were not all men. I gave a lift in the rental car to women and children. I gave teenage boys dry socks. The men from Syria wanted to escape the war. ISIS had drawn its claws across the countryside and uprooted these people. Some had already spent time fighting. Some of the men had fought alongside the Syrian rebels. Some were minorities, like Yazidis, their villages systematically dynamited by ISIS, their temples torn down, their sisters sold into slavery. They'd hoped the international community would come, but the aid was too late. Among the Kurds, many had stayed to fight, joining the YPG as it held stubbornly on to Kobani, under siege, fighting to the last. But not every man can be a fighter. Many had chosen a different path and risked life on board small rafts to get to Europe.

The Emerging ISIS Threat
Concerns about ISIS infiltrating the migrant wave were borne out. Already in January 2015, Amedy Coulibaly had made a video with an ISIS flag before attacking a kosher supermarket in Paris in the wake of the *Charlie Hebdo* attacks. In February, a gunman fired shots at a synagogue and allegedly swore allegiance to ISIS leader Abu Bakr al-Baghdadi. In June a man beheaded his boss in France. In November 2015, terrorists killed 130 in Paris. Some had been in Greece before. Abdelhamid Abaaoud had been directing a cell in Athens. Another attacker blew himself up at the Stade de France. He had faked a Syrian passport and claimed to be from Idlib when he arrived in Greece. He had arrived on the island of Leros in October 2015. In March 2016, ISIS would strike

Brussels, killing thirty-two. In July, a French-Tunisian would drive a truck into a crowd in Nice, killing eighty-four.

In general, though, the massive number of migrants didn't produce a wave of terror that was not already percolating. The terror networks and radicalization had already produced five thousand ISIS members and tens of thousands of supporters in Europe. If anything, the millions of people seeking shelter in Europe from ISIS and Assad were fleeing extremism that had, in part, been exported from Europe by extremist preachers.

For most of 2015, the world had been on the defensive against ISIS, holding the line. In March, Iraq had launched a major operation to retake Tikrit. But ISIS responded by going global. In Sinai, the jihadist group known as Ansar Beit al-Maqdis swore allegiance to ISIS under the name Wilayat Sinai or "Sinai Province." In July, it carried out a major attack on a police station at Sheikhd Zuweid in north Sinai. Two dozen Egyptian police were killed, as were up to a hundred ISIS fighters. The extremists grew bolder, allegedly downing the Russian Metrojet 9268 on October 31, killing 224 people. President Abdel Fatah al-Sisi vowed to defeat the jihadists.

One place they were being defeated was in northern Iraq's Kirkuk Province.

Chapter 5
Securing Kirkuk

Iraq in a Microcosm

One wall of the police headquarters in Kirkuk is decorated with faces.[30] They are the two hundred officers who have died fighting terror since 2003. Terrorists exploited the divisions in the population in Kirkuk. An ancient city, it is claimed by both Baghdad and the KRG, and the Iraqi Constitution of 2005 was supposed to lead to a final status in which the oil-rich province would end up with either the federal government or the autonomous region. Instead it remained in limbo, its diverse population of Turkmen, Arabs and Kurds living together in tension.

Terror came to the city in 2004, when the Ansar al-Sunna group blew up the Rahimawa police station, killing thirteen. In 2005, a truck bomb targeted the Patriotic Union of Kurdistan (PUK) offices, killing four. Abu Musab al-Zarqawi's al Qaeda was blamed along with a small Islamist Kurdish group called Ansar al-Islam. In 2009, a car bomb killed forty, and a series of bombings in July 2011 killed ten. When the Iraqi army fled Kirkuk in June 2014, as part of its retreat from Mosul and other Sunni areas, the Peshmerga filled the vacuum. For a while the city looked like it might fall to the jihadists, who were just a few kilometers away. Instead, hard men with years of experience fighting stepped in to crush ISIS.

Brig. Gen. Sarhad Qadir, the director of Kirkuk's suburban police, was instrumental in ridding Kirkuk of ISIS and turning it into a safe and quiet city, firmly in the hands of the Kurds in 2015. Something of a legend, he was wounded fourteen times and prides himself on showing up first at the scene of terror attacks. His office inside the sprawling walled police

HQ compound is full of awards and letters of thanks from US forces. Qadir was born in Kikruk but lived outside the city much of his life, returning in 2003 once Saddam's forces were gone. A Peshmerga fighter since 1982, he studied in a security college in Erbil after 1992. A former head of security in Kirkuk, he also helped lead security operations in Daquq, Dibes, Hawija and other areas. His administration controlled 250 villages and sixteen towns, he said. There are more than 500,000 people under his police jurisdiction. An old rifle on the wall is a reminder of Qadir's days as a resistance fighter against Saddam. An Iraqi flag and a Kurdish flag lined Qadir's desk.

"Kirkuk is like Iraq in a microcosm," he said, sitting at the giant desk. "It has Arabs, Turkmen and is important for Kurds. It is important politically and militarily." Qadir's desk has two phones, and they rang throughout the meeting. "One problem we have here is intelligence agencies from neighboring countries which try to make problems in Kirkuk." This is a reference to Turkey and Iran. In 2003, Turkish intelligence agents were detained by US forces, accused of a plot, in an incident that soured relations between Washington and Ankara.

Qadir is proud of his record fighting terror. "Before 2014, we had Ansar al-Islam, Ansar al-Sunna, al Qaeda and Naqshabandi." In 2015, he said that there were still cells of these groups as well as former Ba'athists and members of other groups such as Jaish Mohammed, and Jaish Mujahideen. In his view, they have all been defeated. "In 2006, I captured an al Qaeda leader who Osama bin Laden had personally sent to cause problems. Because if you defeat security in Kirkuk, then you hurt the Americans. If you can undermine them, then you can destroy Iraq." In Qadir's telling, Kirkuk is the key to the whole country. Because it sits on the rift between Baghdad and the north, a kind of fault line between the Sunni Arabs, Shi'ites and the Kurds, it can set the country aflame.

"Daesh has attacked the city fourteen times. They tried to control Kirkuk for its oil and its electric power station," the police commander said. "Protecting the city was not easy; when they first attacked, we had no allies. Many were killed. We suffered twenty-nine martyrs in that battle, and 270 members of my team have been murdered by terrorists overall. We sacrificed a lot to protect the communities here and sacrifice our lives for the city."

In 2015, when ISIS still seemed strong, Qadir was convinced it was already weakened. "They cannot attack," he said. He mocked Europe's fear of terror. "They had one attack in Paris; we had seven car bombs here." The police commander said he worked for the safety of all the communities in the city, but as a patriotic Kurd who still kept his old rifle on the wall, he was rooted in the tragic history of the city. "If it wasn't for Kirkuk, there would not have been Anfal," he said. Barzani and the Kurds had held out for autonomy in Kirkuk in the 1970s, and Saddam's wrath was the chemical weapons campaign and ethnic cleansing that followed in the 1980s.

Qadir said in 2015 that he didn't want any other militias in the city. He had banned the Shi'ite Hashd al-Sha'abi from Kirkuk, but said they were present south of the city in Taza and Tuz Khurmatu, where there had been clashes with the Peshmerga. "The Iraqi police left their posts, and the people gathered around the Hashd, and they have their youth with them and protect their people. My police are in Taza District as well, and we don't have a problem." He said that the local Popular Mobilization Units were Shi'ite Turkmen and others, and it was natural they had filled the vacuum left by the authorities fleeing.

Qadir was a close friend of the Americans after 2003. He said that the city's problem began with the US withdrawal in 2011. "If they had not left, then what's going on in Iraq would not have happened. Kirkuk deserves more American presence."

Like many Iraqis, the police commander was surprised to find so many foreigners in ISIS. "We killed a lot of foreign terrorists. British, Turkish, even Iranians and Americans. We have even killed Chinese. And we arrested a lot of them. I'm surprised how ISIS gathered all these nationalities, and they decided to come here to kill themselves and kill other people." He said the foreign terrorists who died in attacks are buried by the municipality. "I ask them to treat the bodies humanely and not insult them." Others that were captured were being held nearby. One of the ISIS suspects was brought into the room at one point, shackled, and sat down on a couch. He was tired, staring at the ground. He had signed a confession, and a copy was brought over. Qadir was coy on the methods used to extract the confession and other details of how prisoners were treated. The prisoners were a burden, especially the foreign fighters.

For him ISIS was "against humanity and everyone," but he admired its men's tenacity and bravery. "There is less appeal than last year, and air strikes have killed many of them. In those areas they control, the people no longer support them, but they can't resist." But he pointed out a difference between the US-led coalition against Saddam and that against ISIS. "The international coalition bombed Saddam two thousand times in twenty-four hours. In seven months they didn't bombard ISIS that much." His estimate was slightly low. By August 2015, the US-led coalition had conducted six thousand air strikes in Iraq and Syria.[31] A total of 22,478 weapons, consisting of bombs and missiles and other types of ordnance, had been dropped on Iraq and Syria between the beginning of operations in August 2014 and August 2015. But shock and awe this campaign was not; it was a slow, grinding war.[32]

To see how grinding, we drove out of Kirkuk. The city is about an hour's drive south of Erbil and it is located on a dry plain with small hills to the west. There are dried riverbeds and signs of irrigated fields that fell fallow during the war. As we drove out toward the line of hills that marked the Kurdish defense line overlooking the Hawija District, the signs of war became more evident. Shattered villages, pancaked houses, destroyed hamlets. Oil fires flared in the distance. Kirkuk produces hundreds of thousands of barrels a day and contains up to 6 percent of the world's oil reserves. There are nine billion barrels of oil under Kirkuk.

Holding the High Ground on the Front Line

To get to the front line, the road snakes up dry foothills, climbing slowly over one hillock and another, onto a ridgeline. Eventually the bunkers and sandbagged positions come into view: a long front line stretching into the horizon, made up of positions dug into the hillside. The Kurds hold the high ground. We come to a checkpoint with two Kurdish women in uniform. These are members of the Kurdistan Freedom Party, an Iranian exile group led by a flamboyant man named Hussein Yazdanpanah. Unlike many of the Peshmerga, who wear mismatching uniforms, the PAK all wear the same olive forest camp. Yazdanpanah's men are zealous.

A hero from the first days of the war, Yazdanpanah gained notoriety because of his resemblance to Stalin, with a raft of gray hair and stately mustache. But he's not like Stalin, he said. Hosting us and showing us around the front line, Yazdanpanah said that the real threat is not just ISIS but also Iran and its influence in Iraq. He predicted that eventually, when the war with ISIS is over, the Kurds will have to defend themselves against the Shi'ite militias. They will come north, he said. Like many Kurds, he compared the struggle they faced to the battles Jews faced to create Israel. "We are making a struggle for freedom and democracy here in Kurdistan, and the Hashd stands against that. It is like what happens in Israel, where the enemy wants to push Israel into the sea and denies the Holocaust."

Sitting for tea next to an open fire, the Kurdish commander explained what he was really fighting for. A passionate Kurdish warrior, he said that they've been fighting for independence for five hundred years. Founded in 1991, his party is secular and democratic and seeks a strategy of independence. He also supports Kurdish rights in neighboring areas, in Syria and Turkey as well as Iran. He called on the West to help Kurds stop Iran. Before taking leave of the front, which was quiet, Yazdanpanah called out, "Tell the West to send us weapons directly to the KRG, not via Baghdad, which takes them from us." The cleavages he sketched were clear. For many Kurds, Baghdad was so far away it might as well be on the moon. The war against ISIS was a kind of new war of independence, a way to prove themselves to the world. But they were worried; when it was over there would be another round.

The commander for the area overlooking Hawija, including Yazdanpanah's sector, was another Kurdish icon, Dr. Kemal Kirkuki. A former speaker of the Kurdistan Regional Government parliament and a politburo member of the Kurdistan Democratic Party (KDP), Kirkuki represented the kind of Renaissance man who had gone to the front in 2014. Born in 1954, he was a Peshmerga from age fourteen. He was imprisoned during the Saddam era. From the same generation of leaders as Qadir, for him the desire to serve at the front is connected to his other political roles. Politician and military commander go hand in hand in the KRG. This poses a problem, because it means many Peshmerga bases are also political entities, associated either with the PUK or the KDP. Although the KRG has a Peshmerga Affairs Ministry and was trying to reform its armed forces before 2014, the war had postponed all that. The

Peshmerga grew out of the independence struggle prior to 1991, and they were divided on party lines. In the 1990s, the KDP and PUK fought a brief civil war, and they have different orientations. The KDP is more pro-American and conservative. The PUK is more secular and closer to Iran and the United Kingdom. The PUK is also closer to the Kurdistan Workers' Party (PKK) and the Kurdish People's Protection Units (YPG). Many KDP people I met loathed the PKK, which some even called "a Kurdish version of ISIS, except Marxist."

All this party politics was not on Kirkuki's mind when I met him in December 2015. Wearing traditional Kurdish clothes, he sat at a desk, a large map of his sector on one wall. An orderly brought tea. Kirkuki said he commanded around twenty thousand men over forty-four kilometers of front line facing Hawija and other areas. Like other commanders, he said that when ISIS had arrived, the Iraqi army had abandoned its positions. "They left the keys in the vehicles and anti-tank weapons strewn around. Humvees, mortars and tanks. ISIS captured them all."

But Kirkuki's vision of the future was one in the making for the last hundred years.[33] "It is a century since Sykes-Picot. The problem of Iraq is that it was put together without Kurdish input and imposed on the Kurdish people." Because of this colonial-era structure, the Kurds suffered under Arab nationalism and the Ba'athism of Saddam Hussein. Some 182,000 were killed and 4,500 villages destroyed, he said. Kirkuki's solution is to carve Iraq into three countries: Kurdistan, Sunnistan and Shiastan. He argued that a united Iraq is always a danger to minorities. "One ethnicity or sect should not rule Iraq. The best choice is everyone in their own state." He said the UN gives people the right to this self-determination, and Kurds should take their rights. To get those rights, though, the KRG had one obstacle. "We have two million refugees and IDPs and we have limited resources. Our budget was cut by Baghdad." He suggested that the internally displaced persons should return home soon, lest they become a demographic or security threat.

Chapter 6
The Road to Sinjar

Archipelago of Refugee Camps

From Dohuk in northern Iraq's Kurdish region, there are two roads to Sinjar, where ISIS carried out genocide against Iraq's Yazidi minority.[34] The first road runs near Mosul Dam and then makes its way in a long arc around the Sinjar Mountains to Sinjar city. In 2015, it was dangerous and exposed to fire from ISIS. The second road begins as a large highway that runs north to the Turkish border at Zakho. Taking an exit, one heads west toward Sinjar along the Syrian border through the town of Rabiah. We chose the second.

The landscape along the way in winter is a mix of wet, muddy, caked earth. North of Dohuk there is a new, stately white building that marks the new campus of the American University of Dohuk. The roadside is sprinkled with bits of grass, like a dusting of green snow. The mountainous crags of the Kurd Mountains peer down from the east. The road is heavily trafficked by trucks, because the Duhok Province's government has so directed the thousands of mostly Turkish trucks that ply this route. This is Kurdistan's economic lifeline. After the ISIS invasion in 2014, much of Kurdistan was cut off from the Arab areas around Mosul to the east and also from Baghdad to the south. The roads became unsafe, and a disagreement with Baghdad about oil exports led the trade to shift to Turkey via the KRG's own pipeline. Hundreds of thousands of barrels a day flowed to Turkey. Baghdad cut the KRG's budget in retaliation, and the KRG became more economically independent but also more dependent on Ankara. Kurdistan had been tied to Turkey before, during the years of Saddam when many refugees fled to Turkey. "It used to take eleven hours to drive to Erbil, the capital of the Kurdish Regional Government. Now it takes two," explained Vager Saadullah, who accompanied me to Sinjar. He had helped me get to Telskuf earlier in 2015 and became my companion on the lonely road to where ISIS committed its crimes. Originally he was just my fixer, hired to help drive and translate, but eventually we became close friends.

As we meandered northwest, there were sparsely populated little villages. One of them is Christian Assyrian; others are Kurdish, part of the diversity of northern Iraq. This is the mosaic that survived the ISIS assault. Signs directed us toward "Shingal," the Kurdish name for Sinjar. The name refers both to the mountain and to the eponymous city below. As we drove, the road abruptly curved, and rows of white tarps and caravans came into view. They lined a valley, and between them were people, women and children, walking and playing.

"This is the largest refugee camp for Yazidi refugees," said Saadullah. In 2015, there were twenty thousand people at this particular camp, refugees from villages around Sinjar. It was one of many similar camps in the area. Most of the Yazidis who fled didn't go back, even after liberation, and in 2018 they were still there, living on the margins, forgotten by history and the international community. On the sides of the road some men made a living by selling chickens or other foodstuffs. In 2015, little girls hawked $5 phone cards from Korek Telecom, the national carrier of Kurdistan.

We stopped and sought to buy three chickens to bring to people in Sinjar. They were 20,000 dinars, roughly $20, for seven kilos: $3 a kilo. The chickens were kept in the back of a truck with a UNHCR logo on the tarp, but these sellers were not UN workers. The young son of the salesman butchered one of the chickens by the side of the road. These refugees said they were from villages that are still occupied by ISIS or that are close enough to the front line that they cannot go back. The hope of the KRG government was that once Sinjar was liberated, the 200,000 or so Yazidi refugees would return. In December 2015, the refugees were still in the camps, afraid to go back.

We drove on and came to a purpose-built bridge over the Tigris River. Those rivers, the Tigris and Euphrates, which gave birth to Near Eastern civilizations, conjure up feelings of greatness and beauty. Babylon,

Sumer, Akkad, Assyria, the great ancient empires now laid waste. The river itself is muddy, utilitarian, not grand. The bridge is like so much of the construction here: a kind of gray, made from cement blocks. An abandoned building was on the far bank. Overlooking the bridge is a Peshmerga checkpoint. Just up the river is the boat crossing to Syria. The old land border crossing was closed at Rabiah in 2014, and those entering Syria are obliged to take a boat. On the other side in Syria, the Kurdish People's Protection Units (YPG) was in charge, having liberated the area from ISIS and created an autonomous region. But the YPG is closely connected to the Kurdistan Worker's Party (PKK), and the PKK has very bad relations with the KDP, which is in charge in Erbil. So the KRG and YPG officials didn't seem to get along on both sides of this border. Even though these two Kurdish entities existed as neighbors, there was no open border.

The road to Sinjar winds its way up a hill, at the top of which is a small kiosk and checkpoint. "This was the farthest extent of ISIS advance; they almost got to the Tigris," said Saadullah. In August 2014, ISIS had swept into this area, surprising Peshmerga defenses and overrunning villages. Entering this borderland, having passed the refugee camp, is like retracing the trauma and genocide of the Yazidis in reverse. It is to follow the Kurdish liberation of these areas as well. After the initial reverses in early August 2014, a reinvigorated Kurdish force swept ISIS from this high ground overlooking the river and pushed it back to the Sinjar Mountains. The Kurds returned to their villages, such as one whose sign indicated it was called Shebane. It's still a poor village, but the Kurdish and PDK and PUK flags fly, representatives of the two main political parties of Kurdistan. The houses are a dull gray cement.

It was "Kurdish Flag Day," the seventeenth of December, as we drove on. Kids were selling flags throughout Kurdistan. At one store, flags mixed with military uniforms. Many young men wore camouflage, because either they were already in the security forces or they wanted to be. Women dressed in long, flowing gowns, the traditional outfit. Others wore uniforms, a reminder of the numerous women who serve in the Kurdish forces.

This is a war of contrasts. A contrast between Kurdistan, where there are churches and Yazidis and women dress as they please and restaurants serve alcohol, and the strict, Manichaean world of Daesh, as ISIS is called locally.

When ISIS swept into Iraq, it exploited the Sunni Arab resentment of the Baghdad government's Shi'ite-dominated halls of power. There had been perennial insurgency among Sunnis since the fall of Saddam, through a brutal terror campaign first run by al Qaeda and then by ISIS. Few understood in 2014 that ISIS was not just an ordinary brutal extremist movement, but that it would mean total ethnic cleansing of minorities and eventually genocide.

There used to be wheat on these fields leading to Sinjar, said locals. But the villages are deserted. One village along the road had been an Arab village, but the locals said it collaborated with ISIS, and when the Peshmerga retook it, the people fled. It is a ghost town now, and many buildings were destroyed. It wasn't clear if they had been destroyed in fighting or afterwards to ensure the residents did not come back. Along the road one can see forts that Saddam Hussein built during the 1980s.

This is a landscape of death, I thought. The lonely road to Sinjar is a straight line. The metal pylons to some power lines are broken in half or droop like giraffes eating from the ground. It looks like a post-apocalyptic world. Houses that were once stately farms on both sides of the road are abandoned; some of their roofs are destroyed. The abandoned Iraqi army checkpoints here are decorated with graffiti from wars gone by. Some have Iraqi flags on them, crossed out now. Others have graffiti noting that the Rojava Peshmerga, Kurds from Syria who are connected to the KDP, are manning these checkpoints. They are unable to operate in Syria because the YPG, the most powerful Kurdish group there, does not let them. The political rivalry with the YPG is rooted in the KDP-PKK rivalry. The PKK has branches in Turkey, Syria, Iran and Iraq. The KDP also has influence in all four countries. These are the two pan-Kurdish parties and political traditions.

Passing through Rabiah, we found the town partly in ruins. Here and there Arab men pasture sheep or a family squats in a courtyard. Some boys play with a fire kindled on the ground. A large hospital building dominates the skyline, its walls blown in and roof partially collapsed. The monumental building was the site of a large battle during fighting between Peshmerga and ISIS in the town in the fall of 2014. The central hospital in Rabiah was occupied by foreign volunteers for ISIS. Around sixty Kurds died to liberate it.

Most of this city was heavily damaged in fighting in August and September 2014. One road leads from Rabiah to Mosul Dam and passes through several Arab villages mostly inhabited by the Shammer tribe. According to the Yazidi and Kurdish Peshmerga, the Shammer did not collaborate with ISIS, and when the war passed through here and ISIS was defeated, the tribe stayed in its villages. In those places where there are Shammer, one sees signs of some bit of normal civilian life. Kids play soccer next to a burned-out car. Men chat by the roadside. But life here has obviously become wretched. People take water from wells; there is no business to be done. Shepherds take their flocks out, even in the abandoned city. A fat, white cow eats from an oil drum used as a trash can by Peshmerga who are keeping watch on the border. To the north, the sun's rays lighting the buildings, are factories in Syria. This was once an area of commerce and production. The war fell hard on those large institutional buildings that could be used for defense.

As we pass onward, the terrain seems more scarred by war. Abandoned sandbagged military positions dot the landscape. Twisted and broken metal objects, junk and rebar, are in piles, part of what was once a series of shops on the side of the street. The road is guarded by Kurdish checkpoints every few kilometers. Many of the Yazidi residents of this area had not returned in December 2015; most of them would not return over the following years, either.

Along the way, I spoke with some of the Rojava Peshmerga. Rojava is the Kurdish name for eastern Syria. Erbil had sent them to guard this lonely landscape, the closest they can get to their homes in Syria. "There was the Kurdish National Assembly that was for Syrian Kurds from Rojava who wanted to fight the Syrian regime," one of their officers said over tea. The PYD, the political wing of the YPG, did not let them enter Syria, and they claimed the YPG has a Stalinist mentality. They also argued that the YPG received weapons from the Assad regime. So they ended up in northern Iraq, guarding checkpoints along a long, cold, lonely road that runs to Sinjar, in the shadow of the ISIS genocide.

The Rojava commander said that the Yazidis he has seen fear to come back. Many a Yazidi plies the road taking stuff out of Sinjar but not returning to stay. He personally saw a mass grave of seventy-four bodies when his unit helped to liberate a village. There is no electricity in the area except by generator. Many of these men resent the Arabs who joined ISIS and who now want to come back. Along the road we saw several Arabs pasturing sheep, but only some have returned to these villages. The return of the Arab tribes to this area is something the Yazidis in the town of Snune said they feared. The days of some sort of coexistence with Arab neighbors are over. They don't trust the Arabs, who they say celebrated the arrival of ISIS. Many Yazidi survivors of the genocide, including women who were enslaved, recalled how their neighbors turned on them. Some of the men who purchased and raped them had once lived next door in Arab villages.

The main street in Snune, north of Mount Sinjar, was once intended to be redone as a stately thoroughfare. The town is part of an area disputed between the KRG and Baghdad's central government. The KRG had invested money before 2014 in pretty, tall, white street lights, decorated with gold emblems at the base. The lights are still there, but most of the town is in varying states of ruin. A thriving market does business selling to Peshmerga soldiers. Most of the people in this Yazidi district that numbered more than ten thousand have not returned.

The owner of one of the shops, Adar, a long black coat wrapped around his shoulders, said he came back the day the village was liberated in December 2014. He recalled vividly that August 3, 2014, when the people packed what they could into cars and fled. "We knew what ISIS will do; they had killed people in Mosul." They had seen their people fleeing Sinjar and knew that these villages would fall as well, as ISIS swept north of the mountain. In August 2014, the Kurdish YPG coming from Syria, with help from Western airpower, was able to rescue Yazidis trapped on the mountain. In December the Kurdish forces were able to retake the area, and on the seventeenth of December, Adar came back. "Many people did not; there is no school, no electricity, the water is bad, there are no services."[35]

At Sharf a-Din, a local shrine and pilgrimage site, photos of martyrs from the war adorned the site. I watched as a man climbed up to the cylindrical steeple that marks the shrine so he could take a selfie. These cylindrical-style temples mark the landscape in this region of northern

Iraq. North of Erbil as one enters the Yazidi villages on the way to Dohuk, they are visible from the road. In Sinjar they were once common. This style of construction is integral to the history and culture of Iraq and the Kurdish region. The ancient Nabi Yunus Mosque in Mosul incorporated the same cylinder on its roof, alongside a minaret, a testament to the way different faiths have shared the region. But ISIS systematically tried to erase Yazidi holy sites, just as it sought to commit genocide against the people. It blew up shrines and demolished them. Sharf a-Din survived because of the dogged defense led by a man named Qasim Shesho.

Nearby is the house of the famed commander. When we went there, the Peshmerga guarded the compound, which also seemed to double as Shesho's command post. The yard was strewn with Humvees and various other vehicles with mounted weapons. It's a strange sight in a small village with a religious shrine. But it represents what ISIS wrought on this district and the changes it caused. Many thousands of Yazidis joined the Peshmerga and also the PKK or local units called the Ezidkhan Protection Forces (HPE), and have trained in war. The whole Yazidi district was festooned with checkpoints and military camps. I saw no civilian life. Those who learned war earlier in life, such as Shesho, proved prescient. As the quote attributed to Trotsky is commonly paraphrased, "You may not be interested in war, but war is interested in you."

Shesho's life seems to have been something made for a movie. A former prisoner of Saddam, he was a kind of mountain warlord and bandit, assassinating Ba'athist officers before fleeing abroad. After 1991, he settled down and became a local political figure. In 2014, he took up arms again to fight ISIS. When the Kurdish Peshmerga fled, he held on with just seventeen men to defend the shrine. He resolved to die fighting, but although ISIS attacked, he survived. Eventually his seventeen followers grew to thousands, and he helped to liberate Sinjar. His son Yassir Kasim Khalaf Shesho, who was living in Germany, came back to defend the shrine. When I met him, he proudly showed off the M-16 rifle that his fighters had acquired.

Driving from his compound up the mountain, we passed a cemetery for PKK and YPG fighters who helped to save the Yazidis from ISIS. A concrete-walled base along the road was occupied by the YPG and PKK forces from Syria, a giant poster of Abdullah Ocalan, the imprisoned

Kurdish leader in Turkey, affixed on the hillside above. At night these giant posters were illuminated by lights, an oddity in an area where electricity is rare and everything runs by generator. The Turkish air force would bomb this cemetery in April 2017.

Mount Sinjar

Ascending the mountain, a short drive after leaving Sinjar city, is a long, slow process with unending bends in the road. Along the way are thousands of tents and makeshift houses inhabited by Yazidis. There are only a few signs of international organizations. A Red Crescent tent, a few UNHCR tarps and a sign reading "Mission East." These people have been abandoned by the world. There were also competing interests at play on the mountain: the Kurdistan Regional Government's ruling party, the KDP, has several Peshmerga posts along the road, as do the YPG and the PKK, the Kurdish organizations that operate Syria and Turkey. In October 2017, the Peshmerga would abandon the area to the Iraqi army, and in April 2018, the PKK would leave after Turkish threats. When we drove up the mountain, that future didn't seem possible; the Peshmerga were firmly in control.

The mountain is beautiful. Its rising fins of stone reveal a tortured geological history. The mountain was a crucible in 2014 through which more than 100,000 Yazidi people fled ISIS. It was a place of both refuge and starvation. Here the Yazidis who wished to remain close to their lands and within sight of the plains around Sinjar and Snune stayed to fight and die in the mountains. A year and a half later, the results of that epic struggle could be seen. The cars that passed were full of men in varying uniforms. Like many of the Peshmerga, they buy their military equipment from local stores. Their AK-47s are aging, and they complain they are substandard.

Standing near the summit of Mount Sinjar was a newly built monument: a replica of a pickup truck with a twin-mounted DShK machine gun on the back. It overlooks a snake-like road that stretches down toward Sinjar city. It was at this spot that Qasim Dorbu, a Yazidi fighter, defended the mountain on August 3, 2014, when ISIS swept across the plains below. A plaque said he saved thousands of Yazidi refugees' lives by his stubborn defense. ISIS could not break through and remained below the summit, to be pushed back by Kurdish forces in December of 2014. Nearby was a health clinic run by a Kurdish woman that helps to serve the needs of the twenty thousand Yazidi IDPs who sought shelter on the mountain. Their tents and huts dot the landscape on the road north of the summit.

The visible stain of the crimes against the Yazidi could be seen along the roads leading to the summit. Colorful clothes left behind by the fleeing people were everywhere, as were the cars that they abandoned. It was like an open air museum of suffering and genocide.

Sheikh Naser Basha Khalaf provided an example of this transformation from victimized society of a peaceful, poverty-stricken minority to an armed organization, taking their future in their own hands. On one shoulder he slung his $5,000 Russian sniper rifle, and around his belt he wore a silver-handled revolver.

Sheikh Naser comes from a well-known family in Sinjar who have the status of sheikhs in the Yazidi faith and leaders of the Yazidi tribes. A local leader and media officer in a local party branch of the Kurdistan Democratic Party, he has the role of a community and religious leader as well as a politician.

In December 2015, the Yazidis ran the intelligence office in Sinjar and the municipality, and had thousands of their Peshmerga strung out over the mountain and on the front line against ISIS. There were also members of the YPG and local affiliates, their triangular flags fluttering their vehicles. The two groups coexisted uneasily, both fighting ISIS but suspicious of each other. Like the Jewish refugees from Nazi Germany who returned to Central Europe with the various Allied and Soviet armies, these Yazidi men and some women who joined different fighting units went through a horrid crucible to see the future in this region.

It's hard to describe a landscape so torn and broken. Leaving the mountain behind, one sees the terraces and old stone houses at its base. This area was once disputed between the Baghdad-based federal government and the Kurdistan region. Then it came firmly into the hands of the Kurds, whose checkpoints are in every locality, whose flags fly from the homes. It is a sign of how the rise of ISIS created a firm determination in the KRG and its unified forces that these disputed regions would be finally taken and administered. At the time, I jotted down in my notes,

"There is no way for the Baghdad government to get to these areas. ISIS occupies the area between Sinjar and Baghdad."

The Kurds and Yazidis say they no longer trust the Arabs here, who supported ISIS. The genocide committed against the Yazidis, and the speed with which ISIS conquered this area, hardened the view that most of these Arabs who once lived here should not return. Local people recall how their neighbors turned on them, how they hoisted the black flag, and how Iraqi troops melted away and left behind weapons for ISIS that were used to deadly effect against the Kurds and Yazidis.

There are other forces at work as well. Many Kurds argue that Saddam tried to "Arabize" the land around Sinjar and brought in many Arabs to live in villages nearby and destroyed Kurdish and Yazidi villages. Many Yazidi tribes were collectived and placed in planned villages around Sinjar. The genocide in 2014 represented the continuation of a cycle that had begun under Saddam of removing them from the land and pitting them against Arab neighbors. The reversal of this trend came in 2015, when Arabs fled and Kurds came to control Sinjar. But Yazidis remained victims, unable to return from IDP camps and still living marginal lives on the mountain. Kurds did not move into the abandoned villages or rebuild them. The ruined villages were left as a kind of museum of this most brutal of wars and a reminder how powerful ISIS was.

Chapter 7
The Hell of Sinjar

Slavery and Extermination
"They killed old women, men and children here. They blindfolded them and shot them with bullets from AK-47s and M-16s." Sheikh Naser Basha Khalaf holds up two rusty bullet casings he has plucked from a mound of dirt. Sheikh Naser was one of those Yazidi men who fled ISIS for Mount Sinjar, which overlooks the long, flat plain in northern Iraq. A local politician and community leader in liberated Sinjar, in November 2015 he began working to uncover mass graves of Yazidi people murdered by ISIS in August 2014.

After the initial ISIS advance in August, the Peshmerga began a long slog to push the extremists back. On Mount Sinjar, members of the PKK and the YPG had stayed behind and fought alongside the Yazidis against ISIS. The YPG had helped to save hundreds of thousands of the minority by carving out a corridor to Syria in 2014. US air strikes had helped stop the enemy. But thousands of women had been herded together in villages in the valley below the mountain. They had been selected and then transported to Tal Afar, Mosul and Syria to be sold and raped. They were systematically photographed and given new names. Their stories are too shocking to read again and again.

One woman told *The Guardian* that she was taken to a house in Raqqa that had been taken over by an ISIS fighter. He "kept her as his slave, then sold her on after four months to another ISIS fighter. He found her disobedient and sold her on straight away to a fighter of only eighteen, who lived at a compound of Libyan fighters near Deir ez-Zor in eastern

Syria. Many Yazidi girls were being held in the same compound of 100 to 200 caravans," the account notes.[36] "The women and girls were chained, beaten, raped and passed around like animals between the men. At the edge of the compound, a barbed-wire fence prevented them from escaping. The stories of privation and torture suffered by Yazidi women in this compound are some of the worst in a catalogue of abuses."

Unlike in the Holocaust, during which information about the extermination camps was not public, and the Allied powers had scant information about the genocide taking place, the Yazidi genocide took place in real time and was often posted on social media in videos and accounts. On September 7, 2014, *The Independent* reported that it had been able to speak to a Yazidi woman being held in a house by ISIS. "To hurt us even more they told us to describe in detail to our parents what they are doing. They laugh at us because they think they are invincible. They consider themselves supermen," the woman said.[37] "But they are people without a heart. Our torturers do not even spare the women who have small children with them. Nor do they spare the girls, some of our group are not even 13 years old. Some of them will no longer say a word," the seventeen-year-old told the journalist. "Women are raped on the top floor of the building in three rooms. The girls and women were abused up to three times a day by different groups of men." The account noted that "British extremists fighting in Syria and Iraq have boasted on Twitter and other social media that Yazidi women had been kidnapped and used as 'slave girls.'"

The initial shock of ISIS crimes and the presence of thousands of foreign fighters, including many from Europe, spurred the international community to act. It helped prod Obama to begin the campaign and helped bring together a massive coalition that would eventually number seventy-nine members. However, within a year and a half of the worst of the crimes, the international community would largely forget the genocide and the reasons that brought the coalition to Iraq and Syria. The defeat of ISIS remained a priority, but the victims of ISIS did not.

Eventually there were fewer accounts of rape, and abuse declined as media took less and less of an interest, and the number of survivors who were able to escape declined. Accounts like the one at Alternet. com in September 2017 about the role of women in abusing Yazidi slaves were rare. One woman told Rania Khalek that she had been raped by an ISIS fighter nicknamed Abu Qutada, whose wife helped rape the woman named Seeham. Abu Qutada's wife also "forced her to clean their four-story house from top to bottom every day. Abu Qutada's wife would invite her female friends to join her in taunting Seeham as she cleaned."[38] The victim recalled that "she forced me to clean the entrance to the neighbor's flat and she forced me to clean her and her neighbors' shoes. They would make fun of me while I cleaned." Some Yazidis were trafficked abroad. Two and a half years after the genocide had begun, Yazidi victims were still being found. In December 2017, a Yazidi woman was found in Turkey. How she had ended up there – whether she had been trafficked or fled there as a refugee after escaping – was unclear. However, the first stage in achieving justice was to liberate the areas where the genocide happened.

In November 2015, the Peshmerga launched an offensive into Sinjar city and pushed ISIS back so that the entire area of Mount Sinjar and the landscape around it to the north and to the south came under Kurdish control. Two dozen mass graves were found, on both sides of the mountain. Eventually, sixty-nine in total would be located around Sinjar, of some two hundred across Iraq that contained victims of ISIS. I arrived soon after several had been discovered in Sinjar, to see the genocide up close. It was like driving into Europe in 1945, I thought. Like seeing the liberation and the Nazi crimes, on a much smaller scale. We drove in at night and spent the evening with a demining team that was living in civilian houses near Sinjar. In the morning, we drove into Sinjar. The city was in ruins, and most of it had not been cleared of IEDs. So we stayed on one marked road, with rubble and destruction on all sides. It reminded me of something out of the Second World War, but that's because all war ruins seem to look the same. The more I saw, the more I realized that. A small shop run by a Yazidi man who had returned sold beer. I drank one, even though it was ten in the morning, to steel my nerves for the day ahead. I dreaded seeing the aftermath of genocide.

We met Sheikh Naser at his makeshift headquarters, an old municipal building. In the courtyard was an American Humvee, turned over and with its innards ripped out. It must have been hit by an air strike. After tea and greeting his staff, Sheikh Naser and a guard holding an AK-47 jumped into a pickup truck. The Peshmerga with the rifle crouched in the back, on lookout. We drove out of the city through more streets strewn with rubble, ruined city blocks, blown-up gas stations and old HESCO blast walls from the years when the Americans had been here. There was still ISIS graffiti around. Outside the city, we came to a mound of dirt.

The New Killing Fields

This is a beautiful landscape, framed by the great, long Mount Sinjar. But now the area feels like a "cancer," said Sheikh Naser. Around 300,000 Yazidi people are refugees, thirty-six hundred women are held as sex slaves by ISIS, and more than a thousand men and elderly women were gunned down. After crossing an earthen berm, we come to an ordinary field of sparse grass. To most of us it wouldn't look abnormal. But a close look at a mound of earth reveals the horror. Bones stick out from the ground, dry and bleached in the sun. "After they were killed, they were buried with a bulldozer, but dogs dug up the bones, and rains washed them." Women's clothing pokes up from the ground. Blindfolds. A lone human skull, with a bullet hole in it. A jawbone sits next to a purple soccer jersey a teenager might have worn. Sheikh Naser Basha Khalaf points to matted hair, human hair from a woman, twisted between rocks.

To come face to face with genocide is unimaginable. My parents told me, "Never again." They told us in university about human rights. But it was a lie. In my lifetime we sat through the genocide in Rwanda, the ethnic-cleansing in the Balkans, the genocide in Darfur. ISIS broadcast its mass killings on social media, and its members bragged of selling women on Twitter. Here in the killing fields of Sinjar, the bones of those killed in 2014 sit on the surface. Human hair pokes through grass that has grown on the bodies. Skull fragments. Bullet casings. A teenager's soccer jersey that says "Emirates" on it. The clothes people wore when they were murdered are there. The blindfolds they wore could be seen. The Iraqi ID badges have been recovered. No international investigators are here. No NGOs are working here to protect the human remains. The world was silent again. These lives could have been saved. To see the bones sitting there causes anger and rage. How could the Western powers with all their technology, all their drones, their EU Parliament and councils of human rights and international criminal courts, do nothing? Drones surely could see this happening in real time, and ISIS videoed it and broadcasted it at the time. ISIS didn't try to hide the mass graves. It just bulldozed the bodies. Sheikh Nasir, who had escaped to the mountain in August 2014, said he and his men could see the bulldozers making the graves. Later, wild animals dug up the bodies, and the bones were strewn about. Bleached by the sun.

We drove to a second mass grave, slightly smaller. This one was southeast of Sinjar city, in a field near the earthen berm that marked the new front line with ISIS. In a slightly damp field, with new grass poking from the earth, the grave was also near a dry streambed. It had been taped off with red caution tape, like a crime scene, which it was. The Peshmerga pointed to several Iraqi police badges in the grave. Some of the Yazidis had worked for a local security force before being murdered. One man showed me on his phone that he had found IDs of the Yazidi men killed here, when they first discovered the grave in early December 2015.

I was one of the first foreigners to see it. I snapped as many photos as I could. But there was something surreal here. As bones stuck out from the earth and the men spoke of the IDs they had found, there was a lack of professional documentation. Where were the NGOs? Where were the experts from the International Criminal Court? Where were the local courts and forensics? Iraq is a poor country, and there was a war just a kilometer away, but it seemed like someone should care more about documenting these crimes immediately upon discovery. The Nuremberg trials began in November 1945, eleven months after Auschwitz was liberated. But the evidence collection, interrogations and documentation of the Holocaust took place almost immediately, to the extent that the liberating powers could. That was in 1945 with rudimentary techniques and with millions of victims.

In Sinjar in December 2015, there were a limited number of sites of mass graves. Survivors such as Nadia Murad had told the details of how ISIS had rounded up people. And there were seventy countries involved in fighting ISIS. Yet not one of them had sent a team to investigate. The entire time I spent in Sinjar, and from what I heard about the time before and after, no international teams or professionals or academics or researchers or basically anyone came to document the graves. By 2018, it was even harder to get into Sinjar than in 2015. Alissa Rubin, who went there for the *New York Times* in April 2018, described a gauntlet of checkpoints, including the Iraqi army and various Shi'ite militias.[39] Although small nonprofits such as Yazda, which focuses on advocacy, aid and relief for Yazidis, did publish maps and accounts of the genocide, it was done with limited resources and access. The international community that met in Kuwait to pledge money to reconstruct Iraq in early 2018 never mentioned Sinjar. Although the International Commission on Missing Persons came to the Sinjar region, work to excavate the mass graves and identify remains moved at a snail's pace, with an announcement in March 2019 that one grave near Kocho might be unearthed with UN support.

The reason the coalition had been formed was forgotten. It didn't focus on liberating Yazidis or documenting crimes against them or locating missing people. By speaking to me, the local Yazidis thought they could bring awareness to their plight and the genocide. I felt guilty that although the world knew the harrowing details, so little was done afterwards to help people or document the crimes or find missing people.

What kind of people are these ISIS members who lined up elderly women they deemed too old to sell or rape and shot them in the back of the head? It was an attempt to exterminate a community, a genocide in our time. Sheikh Nasir said he expected to find more than twenty additional mass graves. Seventeen had been found by December 2015. The uncovering of the depredations of ISIS had only begun.

As we left the mass graves and drove back to Sinjar city, past the ruin and destruction, it was clear that there was a major vacuum in northern Iraq. A gap of people, of missing communities, cleansed and destroyed by ISIS. The whole area had been ruined, the people driven either onto the mountain or into IDP camps. There were few if any resources to help them. As we made our way up Mount Sinjar again to leave, the clothes the Yazidis left by the side of the road in 2014 were still visible. On the side of the mountain was a bench where young couples might once have driven to watch the shadows gather at sunset. There would be no more young couples here, in this beautiful setting turned into a kind of hell.

Part II
The War against Chaos, 2016

"Two caliphates fall, Mosul survives. We are Ottomans." My grandmother said this in 1996, she came from an old Mosul family that lived in Bab Lagash neighborhood

– Tweet by Mosul Eye, March 17, 2017

Chapter 8
By, with and Through

From Generation 9/11 to Generation Surge

"I was surprised at how quickly ISIS took over part of the country," Lt. Col. John Hawbaker remembers thinking in 2014.[40] Like so many of the US officers who returned to Iraq to fight ISIS, he had many years of experience in the country.[41] This was America's generation that had led the "surge" in 2005–2006. Hawbaker, a commander in the 73rd Cavalry Regiment of the 82nd Airborne Division, had been in Anbar and Baghdad in 2005–2006. He returned to fight in the battles around Mosul in 2017.

American and Iraqi history have been closely intertwined since George H.W. Bush chose to take a stand against Saddam Hussein's aggression in Kuwait in 1990. The shared history grew with the 2003 invasion and the surge. "We were doing counterinsurgency under US leadership" is how Hawbaker characterized the difference between 2005 and the anti-ISIS war. "The difference now is that the Iraqi Security Forces conducts a fight, not as a counterinsurgency but against a conventional force."

For many Americans, the return to Iraq was to familiar and intimate territory. Tal Afar, where ISIS had begun its campaign of murder and ethnic-cleansing, attacking Shi'ite Muslims in June and then Yazidis in August, had been in the spotlight before.

H. R. McMaster, national security adviser under Trump, gained fame as a US Army general for defeating the Iraqi insurgency in Tal Afar in 2005, providing what some thought was a model for the US surge that

69

reduced the insurgency. We now know that McMaster's fears about the future were correct. "One of the big grievances in Tal Afar was that we have a Shi'ite-dominated, Iranian-influenced government in Baghdad," he told PBS in 2007.[42] In another interview, he said the US needed to "develop institutions that can survive and that will operate in a way that is at least congruent with our interests."[43] Throughout the region, a generation of leaders arrived on the scene in 2014 with different agendas as the disaster of ISIS unfolded.

Throughout the war, the players were those who had been carved out of the post-9/11 Middle East. Bashar al-Assad was born in 1965, and the rebellion in 2011 was his first major test in a decade in power. Gone was the old guard: Muammar Gaddafi, Hosni Mubarak, Ali Abdullah Saleh of Yemen. The younger generation was in power. General Abdel Fatah al-Sisi led the military into power in Egypt in 2013 after two years of cha- otic rule by the transitional government and the Muslim Brotherhood. Like Sisi, Erdogan was born in 1954. Since he was first elected prime minister in 2003, he has dominated Turkey. Iraq's Haider Abadi was born in 1952, while his political ally Hadi al-Amiri of the Badr Organization was born in 1954. Abu Mahdi al-Muhandis, the Shi'ite militia leader, was born in 1954. Qais al-Khazali, a member of the younger up-and-coming generation, was born in 1974, and Muqtada al-Sadr in 1973.

In the Kurdish region, the new generation of leaders was similar. KRG prime minister Nechirvan Barzani was born in 1966, while his cousin Masrour Barzani, who handled security, was born in 1969. Deputy Prime Minister Qubad Talabani was born in 1977. In the rest of the region there was the same pattern. Jordan's King Abdullah was born in 1962. Saudi Arabia's Crown Prince Mohammed bin Salman was born in 1982, and Qatar's Emir Tamim Bin Hamid al-Thani was born in 1980. Iran's Hassan Rouhani was one of the few older men left, born in 1948, a year before Israel's Benjamin Netanyahu. In Lebanon, President Michel Aoun was born in 1935, while Hezbollah's Hassan Nasrallah was born in 1960. The leader of ISIS, the scourge of the region, Abu Bakr al-Baghdadi, was born in 1971.

What unites these men is that Arab nationalism, which appealed to the 1950s generation, is now an ossified concept. A more sectarian Middle East, living in the shadow of the Islamic Revolution in Iran in

1979 and the Afghanistan jihad of the 1980s, was the one these men knew. Although some of them might have rejected the sectarianism that sees the region through the eyes of Shi'ite and Sunni, they could not ignore the reality that this rhetoric was on the rise and creating cleavages in their societies. Countries were increasingly divided along religious and ethnic lines. ISIS was the extreme end of this spectrum.

In Iraq, the US and its allies tried to rebuild and reconstruct the country. The US led an invasion of Iraq in March 2003. In April, the statue of Saddam was yanked down in Baghdad's Firdos Square, symbolizing the end of his brutal rule and the start of a new era. They encouraged a new constitution in 2005. But they couldn't prevent the rise of sectarian, Shi'ite-dominated politics. Obama's administration, looking to draw down troops by 2011, had supported the rise of Nouri al-Maliki. Emma Sky, who advised US general Ray Odierno in Iraq from 2007 to 2010, claimed the US abandoned democracy as it embraced Maliki. At *Foreign Affairs*, she wrote that "when Iraqiya, the nationalist, non-sectarian political party led by Ayad Allawi, narrowly defeated the Dawa Party led by Nouri al-Maliki, the incumbent Prime Minister, the Obama administration failed to uphold the right of the winning bloc to have the first go at forming a government. Instead it signaled its desire to keep Maliki in power, despite the stipulation of the Iraqi constitution and the objections of Iraqi politicians."[44]

What might have saved Iraq in 2014 was a functioning army. Lt. Col. James Downing of the US 82nd Airborne, an adviser to Iraq's 15th Division in the 2017 battle for Tal Afar, recalled the troubles faced after 2003. The US Coalition Provisional Authority under Paul Bremer had dissolved the Iraqi Armed Forces in May 2003, sending around 350,000 men packing. When the US and its allies sought to rebuild, they initially called it the Iraqi Civil Defense Corp, and later the Iraqi National Guard. "They became the [new] Iraqi army by the time I left," recalled Downing.

Downing first arrived in Iraq as a captain in the 1st Cavalry Division, when it deployed to the country in early 2004. "When you look at 2004, there is a period from the major ground conflict of 2003 to spring 2004 where not much happened except reconstruction." His armored division was busy aiding in the rebuilding of Baghdad. While rebuilding the security forces, they spent 90 percent of their time concentrating on infrastructure tasks. Over fourteen months, the United States planted the seeds for an Iraqi special forces unit that would eventually be called the Golden Division or the Iraqi Special Operations Forces (ISOF).

However, the Iraqi insurgency was bubbling up as well in 2004. In March, a convoy of US military contractors was attacked in Fallujah. Their bodies were mutilated. Months later, the United States assembled thirteen thousand men to take back the city. But the insurgency grew and set down roots, learning from its mistakes. It learned to plant improvised explosive devices. "In 2004, we were talking about very rudimentary and not well concealed IEDs triggered mostly by the victim," said Downing. "They evolved rapidly to remotely operated, using cell phones and booby traps." By the time he came back in 2006 for the surge, al Qaeda in Iraq had perfected its networks. Parts of the country were ungoverned spaces where Sunni jihadists operated openly.

Eventually the United States increased its troop levels from 130,000 to 150,000, to put down the insurgents. "I switched to be a company commander and then from November 2006 to February 2008 I operated all over Iraq, mainly targeting extremist organizations such as al Qaeda and the Islamic State of Iraq," said Downing. Al Qaeda leader Abu Musab al-Zarqawi was killed in June 2006 when F-16s dropped two five-hundred-pound bombs on his safe house near Baqubah. US forces faced tough battles throughout the country. "We would air assault in and go over their defensive IEDs and attack them in their sanctuaries," Downing recalled. Foreign fighters began to make their first major appearance.

"It was very security dependent, so in more secure areas the ratio [of Iraqis to Americans] would be a much lower number of US to our Iraqi counterparts, and in those areas with higher threat, more coalition forces." The Iraqis began to improve. He described this as the "seeds" the US planted back then. Sunni tribal allies played a key role as well. They would later be alienated, which helped ISIS gain a foothold by 2013.

"I was surprised at that rapid level of advance," Downing said.[45] "We didn't know at that time we would be asked to assist. I was not surprised when the Iraqi government asked us to help." He returned in January 2017, to face the new kind of enemy that ISIS had become: a more conventional force that was able to fight and hold urban and rural areas. Rising to the challenge to defeat ISIS was a costly lesson.

By 2010, the US had spent around $49 billion for reconstruction, according to a report Curt Tarnoff presented to the Congressional Research Service. The report noted that by April 2009, there were 645,000 Iraqi security forces (ISF) members, including thirteen infantry divisions.[46] Most of the money the United States spent went to training, but even after 2008, only 67 percent of the ISF was able to plan or execute operations. They still needed US assistance. And turnover was high, with up to 60 percent of police leaving the force.

Up until the Iraqi army fled from ISIS, it had bought $18.5 billion worth of equipment from the United States. It received Foreign Military Financing (FMF) and Excess Defense Articles (EDA) grants, overseen by the US Department of State. There were also Built Partner Capacity grants from the US Department of Defense. This was funneled through the Iraq Security Forces Funding until 2012, and then the Iraq Train and Equip Fund.

Initially the United States thought it could rush more equipment to Iraq to defeat ISIS. According to the US State Department, in 2014, the FMF began to redirect counterterrorism funds to Iraq. Hellfire missiles, 2.75-inch rockets, tank ammunition and small arms poured in. "The funds were critical to the Iraqi effort to blunt ISIL's advance," a January 2017 report said.[47] Three hundred mine-resistant ambush protected armored vehicles (MRAPS) came under the EDA, and M1A1 Abrams tanks and Cessna attack aircraft arrived as well. According to the State Department, there were also howitzers, armored tactical vehicles, OH-58 helicopters, and Humvees (HMMWVS). "In 2014, the President used his drawdown authority to grant Iraq $25 million worth of defense articles and services directly from U.S. defense inventories."[48] Anti-IED equipment was rushed to Baghdad as well as 326 Bangalore torpedoes, two hundred anti-personnel obstacle breaching systems and a thousand AT-4 anti-tank weapons. Congress rushed through $1.6 billion for the Iraqi Train and Equip Fund (ITEF).

The US Combined Joint Task Force – Operation Inherent Resolve was designated in October 15, 2014, to reflect the "commitment of the us and partner nations in the region and around the globe to eliminate the terrorist group ISIS and the threat they pose to Iraq, the region and the wider international community."[49] Through the coalition, the us was helping to lead combat operations against ISIS.

By August 2015, the United States said it had sent twelve hundred transportation vehicles and twenty thousand small arms to Iraq.[50] Two thousand more AT-4 anti-tank weapons had been sent, along with twenty-nine light armored vehicles. It took over a hundred airlifts to get the equipment there. The coalition was also providing the Kurds eight million rounds of ammunition, small arms, machine guns and mortars by 2015.

However, the us-led coalition quickly realized that it would need to do more. The Iraqi army was shattered. It survived with just a handful of decent units. One of these was the Counter Terrorism Service of Iraq's Special Operations Forces (ISOF). The so-called Golden Division had its origins in 2003, when the us wanted to create an elite and independent counterterror unit.[51] Trained by the Americans in anti-terror operations, it only had 1,824 men in 2007, according to a study by David Witty for the Brookings Institution's Center for Middle East Policy. Eventually it would grow to ten thousand men. It had high morale and was officially nonsectarian, including Sunni Arabs and Kurds as well as Shi'ites. Its commanding officer, Fazil Barwari, was Kurdish. At Tikrit, Samarra, Baiji and the gates of Baghdad it helped check ISIS and push the black flag back.

The Sunni cities fell to ISIS one after another in 2014. Fallujah fell first in January. But at the time the extremists were seen as simply "a new al Qaeda" or "insurgents." But the insurgency was different from before. On June 10, they rumbled into Mosul in an unprecedented blitzkrieg. Mosul had been run by the Nujaifi family, an old Sunni Arab family from northern Iraq that has close connections to Turkey. Atheel al-Nujaifi had campaigned as head of the al-Hadba bloc in the 2009 elections against the Kurds. Nujaifi clung on to ideas of establishing a "Sunni army" to fight ISIS as Iraq fractured. Yet there were no Sunnis to be found. Lt. Gen. Mahdi Gharrawi, the Iraqi security commander of Nineveh, sought to curb the debacle.[52] He had tried to stem the rise of ISIS in the lead-up to the eventual ISIS offensive, by seeking out sleeper cells, fighting terrorism.

He'd even succeeded in a June 4 raid on an ISIS leader's house in Mosul. Eventually Nujaifi, Gharrawi and the rest of the leaders of Mosul fled to the east of the city and then toward the Kurdistan region.

At Nuri Mosque in Mosul, Abu-Bakr al-Baghdadi came to declare the caliphate. The main imam, Omar al-Hilali, told *Rudaw* that after a week of curfew in the city, ISIS came to the mosque. "They decided the caliphate in the mosque nearly a month after they came to the area. People were thirsty for change at the time. Hence they felt peace and security, enthusiastically welcoming it. Al-Baghdadi only declared the caliphate in his speech, showing the world that a caliphate was declared."[53] Soon the executions began. Then ISIS attacked Sinjar and threatened Erbil and Baghdad.

On August 7, Obama appeared on television to announce that he had ordered military action against the extremists. "We intend to stay vigilant and take action if these terrorist forces threaten our personnel or facilities anywhere in Iraq, including our consulate in Erbil and our embassy in Baghdad. We're also providing urgent assistance to Iraqi government and Kurdish forces so they can more effectively wage the fight against ISIL," the US president said.[54] He also emphasized the importance of stopping genocide. "Second, at the request of the Iraqi government – we've begun operations to help save Iraqi civilians stranded on the mountain. As ISIL has marched across Iraq, it has waged a ruthless campaign against innocent Iraqis. And these terrorists have been especially barbaric toward religious minorities, including Christian and Yezidis, a small and ancient religious sect. Countless Iraqis have been displaced. And chilling reports describe ISIL militants rounding up families, conducting mass executions, and enslaving Yezidi women."

His policy was clear. "I've said before, the United States cannot and should not intervene every time there's a crisis in the world. So let me be clear about why we must act, and act now. When we face a situation like we do on that mountain – with innocent people facing the prospect of violence on a horrific scale, when we have a mandate to help – in this case, a request from the Iraqi government – and when we have the unique capabilities to help avert a massacre, then I believe the United States of America cannot turn a blind eye. We can act, carefully and responsibly, to prevent a potential act of genocide."

Tactics and Strategy

The US air strikes helped to turn the tide. Tikrit was liberated in March 2015, and parts of Sinjar were recaptured in November 2015. Ramadi was retaken in December 2015. In June, Fallujah was liberated. The US had carried out two hundred air strikes by September 2016. Twelve teams of US advisers arrived: seven around Baghdad and five near Erbil. The US sought to defend major dams, at Haditha and north of Mosul.[55] The US also sought to retake the oil refineries at Baiji that ISIS was using as a source of income. By the end of 2014, a total of 1,371 air strikes had been carried out, of which 572 were in Syria.[56] In Syria, the US initially helped the Kurds hold out in Kobani. One year into the coalition's war, thirty-three hundred US troops had been deployed alongside twelve hundred other coalition members. A total of 10,684 targets had been hit, and ISIS had lost 30 percent of its territory, some seventeen thousand square kilometers. Around fifty US special forces operators were active near the front, Defense Secretary Ash Carter told the House Armed Services Committee. "These special operators will over time be able to conduct raids, free hostages, gather intelligence and capture ISIL leaders."[57] The first US combat death came in October 2015, when Master Sergeant Joshua Wheeler of Delta Force was killed near Hawija. He was part of a unit of at least thirty men.

In March, Staff Sergeant Louis Cardin of the 26th Marine Expeditionary Unit was killed near Makhmur. In May 2016, a US Navy SEAL was killed in battle at Tel Skuf, the front line I had been at in June 2015. US special forces were embedded with the Iraqis and Peshmerga who led the operations. Commanders said the forces would not conduct missions on their own. Yet the number of soldiers kept increasing, to 4,087 in April 2016. Near Qayarrah, they established a forward base at a former air base called Q West. This was in addition to the artillery fire base near Makhmur known as Fire Base Bell.[58]

The story of Fire Base Bell encapsulated the limited footprint of US involvement. Located near the road that runs from Erbil to Makhmur, it wasn't far from another US base called Camp Swift. Swift was located in a compound with the Iraqi army on one side and Peshmerga on the other. It marked the dividing line between the Iraqi forces and the Kurds. Fire Base Bell, however, was a wholly American affair. Consisting of two

M777A2 howitzers and two 120 mm mortar systems, it was called Task Force Spartan and included two hundred Marines from the 26th Marine Expeditionary Unit.

The Marines began preparing for deployment in December 2016. The first eighty artillerymen, eighty riflemen and twenty engineers arrived in Kuwait in February. They trained for a month and then moved up to Makhmur. Fire Base Bell was carved out of an existing complex named Karasoar. By July, when the unit left, they had fired two thousand rounds in 486 missions.[59]

The coalition's war that unfolded from August 2014 to the spring of 2016 was not just a war on ISIS. Eventually seventy-nine countries and groups would join the US-led coalition, the largest ever brought together in history, with more firepower at its disposal than all sides of the Second World War put together. However, the firepower brought to the front line looked nothing like in previous wars. It was targeted and precise. It was also public. The coalition had a Facebook account and several Twitter accounts. It published daily strike updates. You could follow the war almost in real time, not only on the coalition's website, but also on other platforms such as the ISIS Live UA map.

Unlike previous anti-insurgency campaigns, this one was fought in the open. But at the same time, the US effort was being transformed. The conflict wasn't just the forever war of Afghanistan. The war in Iraq and Syria and the slow mission-creep taking place was also expanding into Yemen, Somalia, Africa, Asia. Much of this was a war against terrorism, including ISIS. Sometimes it also targeted older organizations, such as al Qaeda. Often it involved both groups, which were increasingly overlapping, such as those that emerged in Niger. These groups were growing and spreading chaos. The leftovers of the Libyan war spread weapons into Mali and south into Nigeria and Niger. The long-term effects also resulted in terror attacks in Burkina Faso, Cameroon and neighboring states. Terror spread across Somalia as well, and Yemen sank into a brutal civil war. Eventually the Saudis would lead a coalition of Gulf states to fight Iranian-backed Houthi rebels in Yemen. This was somewhat peripheral to ISIS, but ISIS was making inroads in Asia and had recruiting tentacles throughout the world, from Bangladesh to Indonesia and the Carribean.

The United States never articulated a broad strategy, but its tactic was to battle chaos. In May 2017 testimony to the House Armed Services Committee, General Raymond Thomas III, the commander of the United States Special Operations Command (SOCOM), claimed that US special forces were deployed to eighty countries. He had eight thousand out of fifty-six thousand men posted to forward bases.[60]

This was a war on chaos. Since 9/11, the US had faced numerous security challenges, none of which it had defeated. Instead these challenges festered, and the US commitment to training local partner forces and helping them counter terror had to grow as well. The war on ISIS was the most visible part of this massive war on chaos. Clearly the concepts of counterinsurgency (COIN), so popular during the surge, had not borne success. In addition, books such as *The Pentagon's New Map: War and Peace in the Twenty-First Century* (2004), which divided the world into the nonfunctioning core and the rest, were still relevant. Defeating ISIS would, in theory, bring stability to the region. The problem with US strategy as it moved toward the waning days of the Obama administration was that it never had a real endgame. It had no long-term strategy. The Obama team never sketched one out, and Trump was openly critical of Obama's anti-ISIS strategy. During the 2016 election campaign, the Republican frequently critiqued the Obama administration regarding ISIS.

During Trump's October 2016 debate against Hillary Clinton, he said he would "knock the hell out of ISIS. ISIS happened a number of years ago in a vacuum that was left because of bad judgment. And I will tell you, I will take care of ISIS."[61] Clinton responded that she intended to defeat ISIS. "To do so in a coalition with majority Muslim nations. Right now, a lot of those nations are hearing what Donald says and wondering, why should we cooperate with the Americans? And this is a gift to ISIS and the terrorists, violent jihadist terrorists." Trump thought maybe he could work with Vladimir Putin to defeat the extremists. "We could fight ISIS together." He also blamed Clinton and Obama for ISIS. "Whether you like it or not, the way they got out of Iraq, the vacuum they've left, that's why ISIS formed in the first place. They started from that little area, and now they're in 32 different nations, Hillary. Congratulations. Great job."

The war against chaos that US special forces were waging had no

coherent strategy in Washington as 2016 continued. The Obama administration was wrapping up its time in office, and the Trump administration
would take time to get on the ground. Generals and commanders
such as Sean MacFarland, Joseph Dunford, Joseph Votel and Steven
Townsend would continue the slog toward Mosul and Raqqa.[62] The
anti-ISIS coalition would be held together by Brett McGurk, the envoy
whom Obama had appointed in 2015. McGurk had a complex view of
the region, one that blended an understanding of Iran's interests with his
own plan to get Saudi Arabia and Iraq back on track. The Obama administration was busy cementing its Iran deal and didn't want to antagonize
Tehran. For US policy makers such as McGurk, that means waging an
anti-ISIS war but doing it carefully. Many things conspired to undo that,
including Saudi-Iraq tensions over the Saudi ambassador to Baghdad.
Saudi-Qatar tensions were also increasing. Iraq and Iran were also angry
at the presence of Turkish soldiers in northern Iraq. And the region was
watching with concern the growth of Kurdish power in Iraq and Syria.
Increasingly, Turkey was a linchpin in this complex problem.

Chapter 9
Turkey's Bad Memories

Kilis, February 2016

The Turkish border town of Kilis has a small college campus called Kilis 7 Aralik University.[63] On the way back from narghile at an outdoor café, some Turkish female students chatted. Their hair blew in the slightly cool evening air. Then came the "boom," "boom," "boom." The students asked us what it was. "Outgoing artillery," Muhammad Misto, a Syrian journalist based in Turkey, said. Turkey had brought up T-155 Firtina self-propelled guns in late 2015 and hidden them in a field near the town. These are mobile artillery that look like tanks, with treads and a larger gun on the turret. In February 2016, they fired several 155 mm rounds a night into Syria. It gave the town the feeling of being on the front line. A rocket fired by ISIS from Syria had hit a local school in January, so in many ways the town was on the front.

Kilis was one of the main way stations into Syria during the Syria conflict. At the modern Olea Hotel in central Kilis, people whispered about ISIS spies and networks and PKK terror threat. TV shows blurred images of smoking, part of an Islamist cultural change in traditionally secular Turkey. The minibar didn't have alcohol. The hotel said it was at full occupancy. "Journalists and intelligence agents," whispered the night manager.

Refugees came through the town to get away from the fighting. Syrian rebels transited the town to defend areas on the other side of the border. In February 2016, when I arrived, the rebels were still trying to hold

Aleppo. The vicious battle for Aleppo would continue throughout 2016, until the last rebels left the city in December.

ISIS was on one side of the border. A great border wall was being constructed, and massive trucks carrying equally massive concrete segments of wall made their way north and south of the town. They were sealing off the border from ISIS on one side, and toward Afrin, from the YPG.

Because Kilis was a center of aid for refugees, a large presence of organizations had grown up around it. The AFAD, a large Turkish government charity, ran camps near the town. There were around 120,000 Syrian refugees near Kilis, out of a total of some three million in Turkey altogether. At the local AFAD office, a bust of Ataturk stared down on the workers in their neon-orange jackets. A poster showed the drawing of a hand with a Turkish flag helping a Syrian hand sticking out from rubble. The support for refugees overshadowed a larger dilemma unfolding at the border.

Turkey was already contemplating an operation on the other side of the wall, into Afrin Province and into Jarabulus city to clear ISIS and the YPG from the border. Ankara feared the YPG, which it viewed as the same as the PKK, would "link up" with US-backed elements of the Syrian Democratic Forces coming from eastern Syria. Tensions were high.

The concerns along the border near Kilis were a boomerang effect of the rise and fall of ISIS. When ISIS was growing in Syria, it had taken territory and some fighters from the Syrian rebellion. Turkey was not only host to Syrian refugees but also sympathetic to the rebellion. However, as the opposition groups fractured and ISIS grew, it took the wind from the sails of the rebels against the Assad regime. Soon the rebels were fighting not only each other but also ISIS. Volunteers for ISIS passed through Turkey. In October 2015, an ISIS bombing in Ankara killed 109 people. Many of the victims had been engaged in a peace march that opposed Turkey's war with the PKK. It wasn't clear whether the ISIS bombing was targeting only Turkey or was part of the broader ISIS war in Syria against the YPG. ISIS also targeted a Kurdish wedding in Turkey in August 2016, killing fifty-seven people. For Turkey, the conflict in Syria was on both sides of the border.

Western policy makers became increasingly concerned that the

Syrian rebellion was becoming more fractured and jihadist, and less of a likely alternative force to lead a democratic Syria. When journalists were kidnapped and later beheaded by ISIS, Syria became synonymous with a tragic quagmire of death and killing. Soon some in the West saw the alternative to Assad as just as bad. Turkey didn't share this view, but it was concerned about the reverberations from ISIS. Early on, it had not taken this threat seriously, preferring to focus on Assad. When the cease-fire with the PKK fell apart, Turkey began to view the Kurdish YPG as a threat equal to that of the PKK. It believed the two organizations were the same.

When the YPG was smaller and under siege in Kobani in 2014 and 2015, Turkey could ignore it. But once the Obama administration began to send small arms to the YPG and to use air strikes to support its war on ISIS, Ankara saw a problem developing. At the same time, the Obama administration's role in the Geneva process opposing Assad shifted energy toward building the massive coalition against ISIS. Programs run by the CIA to arm rebel groups in Syria were reduced, and the US Congress and commentators began to question whether they had been effective in the first place.

Turkey sought to step into the vacuum. It wanted to bolster the rebels and began working with a plethora of groups, many of which had rear echelons on Turkish soil. These included groups such as Faylaq al-Sham, which became increasingly a client of Turkey. Other groups such as Sultan Murad, Nur ed Din al-Zinki and Ahrar al-Sham had good relations with Ankara. Turkey facilitated the shifting of rebel forces from their salient in Idlib to Kilis and thence on toward Aleppo. Ankara didn't want Aleppo to fall to the pro-Assad forces. At the same time, it wanted to weaken ISIS on the border and the YPG. This was the context I drove into in the early months of 2016. The war on ISIS had boomeranged and the troubles on the border were growing.

After receiving permission to enter the refugee camp on the border, Mohammed and I drove the short ride down to the border. The border area was a hive of activity, with Syrian families crossing back and forth, trucks with aid going into Syria and journalists hovering around. A large gate framed the road. The crossing was called Bab al-Salam in Arabic. The words "Oncupinar Gumruk Kapisi" were printed above it, a reference to it being a "customs gate." To the left were a fence and white caravans, marking the refugee camp. The camp had a capacity of thirteen thousand people and was laid out in a planned manner with caravans and community buildings. Syrian women in one of the communal buildings worked in textiles. After getting our "guest" badges and being searched for weapons, we entered the camp. On the concrete walls of the entrance there were murals, Syrian flags, a Quranic verse and photos from the days when the camp was constructed. The camp had recently experimented with two-story living quarters, the first of their kind, according to the locals. The camp also had a school, and kids were learning Turkish. In the same large building housing the textile factory for women, there was an artists' collective.

In a classroom, men painted photos of bombed-out villages. At the end of a hallway, beyond the room with the painters, was a large room with looms for weaving. A woman in a white head scarf introduced herself as Bushra, a refugee from Syria. She said that in 2012, the Syrian army had bombed her village near Kfar Rambeh in Idlib Province. She fled to Aleppo and then to Turkey. She said most of the refugees had similar stories. They were also almost all Sunni Arabs from northern Syria. Very few Kurds, she estimated only 5 percent of the camp, had come here to stay. "They prefer to move on toward Europe." It reminded me of Alan Kurdi, the boy who had drowned, and the Kurds I had met on the refugee roads of Eastern Europe.

The refugee camp only provided work for a small number of women. Others chose to go into Kilis to take low-paying jobs in factories. Some stayed at the camp for safety and comfort. "Those here are lucky, really," said Ayla Cimen, a forty-eight-year-old volunteer who helps run the weaving salon. "They have everything here. At other camps they don't have everything like we do here." She was pessimistic about the international community's ability to help. "They come and look around and don't come back," she said of Western NGOs.

The Changing Face of Syria's Revolution

The Syrians were setting down roots in Turkey. Kids were learning Turkish, and teenagers were integrating into society. But the sounds of war could be heard in the distance. "We hear artillery and conflict at night, and we are afraid," Bushra said. Many of the women in the camp had husbands, some of whom were still on the other side. "Many of the women who come here are tired of war, and some are psychologically damaged; you can see it on their faces." The refugee camp had now become a home for many, and life was going on. There were weddings weekly. Seventy-five students from the camp had enrolled at the local university. Politics was never far away from the discussion. In the Turkish narrative on the border, the Syrians were being welcomed and "Turkey and Syria are one," some said. The Syrians shared concerns about the fate of their villages on the other side. "How did Hezbollah get so strong and take over Syria?" one of the refugees wondered.

One of the men making paintings at the camp was more cynical than Bushra. Named Hassan was disappointed at Turkey's "cowardice" for not intervening in Syria. He argued that once the Russians had intervened more heavily in 2015, Turkey was left with fewer choices. "Syrians began to feel sympathy for ISIS; they were angry at the world['s] silence, and that's crazy," the man said. "It's crazy the world would allow this." He argued that ISIS was creating a new generation of believers in the last years, indoctrinated since childhood. They were ready to fight to the death now. "Maybe America is not interested or has a plan for Syria. In a few years, these kids will grow up and be a danger to the world; they will go everywhere."

The Russian role was creating a new situation in Syria. In late November, Turkey had downed a Russian Sukhoi Su-24 warplane near the border. With the rebellion being slowly defeated and the United States focusing on the war on ISIS, there were concerns that ISIS could take advantage of the weakening of the rebels to launch an offensive. "They were in a bad situation a month ago, but now they are relaxing," Hassan said. Turkey's concerns about ISIS had led to a harsher situation at the frontier. "Crossing the border now means death; the instructions are to shoot on sight anyone crossing illegally," the Syrian artist said. The rise of ISIS also led to conspiracy theories and questions. Some blamed the US for ISIS success. They wondered how ISIS had put down roots in Raqqa, which they said had not been religious before the war, while religious areas such as Hama and Idlib had not fallen to ISIS. The Syrians were pessimistic about military support. They said Saudi Arabia was fickle and that they wanted antiaircraft weapons to stop the Syrian regime's warplanes.

Driving back from the border, we stopped at a warehouse run by the Turkish aid organization IHH. The impressive project was well organized to aid IDPs on the other side of the border. IHH is a religious organization, and its 365 local volunteers were mostly pious Muslim men from Syria. "We begin with tents and mattresses for the IDPs," said one of the volunteers. A hundred thousand pieces of bread, twenty-five thousand hot meals, twenty-five hundred biscuits were heading to Syria daily. In addition, twenty-five thousand bags of diapers, twenty thousand blankets and twenty-five hundred tents had been given.

In one large kitchen, kept perfectly clean, a man carved up the carcass of a sheep. Another man in a green tunic stirred a giant cauldron of soup. Turkey's success at organizing this aid on a government and private level was impressive. It had found a way to take in millions of refugees without the resulting social problems. But there was concern that if the war against the Assad regime was seen to be lost, these refugees would have nowhere to go back to. Because Turkey had played such a key role in supporting the rebellion, it now faced a catch-22. It had to keep supporting the rebellion to not be seen as selling it out. Meanwhile, the rebels increasingly became dependent on Turkey.

After spending time in Kilis, I decided to drive along the border through Turkey's Hatay Province to the other large Syria-Turkey border crossing at Reyhanli. Called Bab al-Hawa, it was the main entrance to Idlib Province. Around 300,000 Syrian refugees had fled to Hatay since 2011 through Reyhanli. Considered a conservative town, Reyhanli, with ninety thousand residents, had suffered a terror attack in 2013 due to the war and was also on edge. To get to Reyhanli, the highway from Kilis followed the border with Afrin. The rolling hills were pretty. For Turkey, the area across the border was held by terrorists, but all seemed quiet. Military patrol vehicles passed us several times, and at one point we overtook an entire Turkish military convoy. "They no longer stop at stoplights due to the PKK terror threat," said a local man. We stopped to look at the border. Bulldozers and construction vehicles were carving out a patrol road and a wall.

Hatay Province held a diverse cross section of Turkey. It had many

Arabs and Alawites. Originally assigned to Syria after the First World War, it had been conquered by Turkey after a referendum. Culturally, it still felt connected to Syria and Lebanon. It was also home to Antioch, the ancient city that was an important Christian center for centuries.

The border with Syria, like in Kilis, was just a short drive from Reyhanli. Men with beards and women in niqab waited to cross into Syria. There were dozens of trucks run by local NGOs, with Turkish and Arabic written on signs affixed to them, that were preparing to bring food into Idlib. Like Kilis, the border area at Reyhanli had become the rear area of the rebellion. It was the lifeline, and increasingly it was totally reliant on Turkey for what would come next.

Several hours east from Kilis, the Turkish town of Suruc had played the same role for the Kurdish city of Kobani that Kilis had for its border area. Many Kurds had congregated to support their comrades on the other side. In July 2015, an ISIS terror attack in the city murdered thirty-four mostly young Kurdish activists.

In 2016, I paused before entering Suruc. A large refugee camp stretched into the distance, not far from the Syrian border. Families and kids picnicked in the grass and among rocks at the entrance. There was a small makeshift market near the entrance. A large Turkish flag fluttered above. People sold old clothes. Women hawked tomatoes, oranges and lettuce. The refugees congregated in little groups in the dry field that was dusted by bits of grass. A sign on the road read "AFAD Suruc Cadirkent Konaklama Tesisi," a reference to the AFAD's accomodations at the Suruc refugee camp. An aerial photo posted on the camp's Facebook page shows more than eight thousand buildings within the camp, housing thousands of people.

A former student from Manbij in Syria named Deniz said he had fled through Kobani in 2014. ISIS had taken his city, and he wanted to go to Europe but didn't have the finances. Many others shared similar stories. They had fled the ruins of Kobani and villages that had been ravaged by ISIS in Syria. Unlike with the mostly Arab Syrians in Kilis, there was no sense of brotherhood here. No paintings of Syrian flags. The Kurds were tolerated guests, but Turkey was on alert for the PKK and viewed Syrian Kurds with suspicion. The men said they didn't see how they could return to Syria with the privation there and the ongoing war.

Kobani had been devastated in 2014 and early 2015. Syria's Kurdish area was increasingly isolated. Its border with Turkey was being cut off with a wall. Its border with Iraq was mostly closed, with a small crossing at Faysh-Khabur into the KRG, where boats plied the river to bring people and goods back and forth.

As one drives back from Suruc to Gaziantep, the road crosses the Euphrates at a town called Birecik. Like many ancient towns in Turkey, it played a role in the Roman history of the region and later as a Christian bishopric. It took part in early Church councils. Later the city was the center of a massacre of Armenians in 1895. The ancient Roman part of the city was submerged by a dam built in 2000. Today this rich history seems gone. As I drove across the massive, dam-bloated Euphrates, it seemed odd that this water would flow south into ISIS territory, past Raqqa and then to Iraq. As ISIS had flowed into Syria and Iraq, so the river followed it.

After Birecik, I drove back toward Kilis. There were rumors that refugees had broken through the border at Elbeyli, and I sought to drive down to see. Through olive groves and rolling hills, the road passed towns with posters of MHP, a far-right nationalist party. As I neared the border, there was a Turkish army checkpoint. The men waved my car over. Some Syrian refugees were walking along the road. The soldiers were jumpy and angry. They didn't speak English, but they made it clear they wanted to rifle through my bag and car. I let them. Eventually one of the commanders, more round-headed than his younger soldiers, came over. He asked in Arabic if I was a journalist. "No, just trying to get to Gaziantep Airport." He looked at my US passport and then waved me through. Whatever was happening near the border, after the checkpoint, was being kept quiet. As I drove back toward Kilis, there were more checkpoints being erected.

Turkey was on edge. The rising populism of the government, the internal war on the PKK, the ISIS attacks, the millions of refugees, the military moves along the border – all of it combined to make the country of eighty million seem like it was walking a tightrope. Erdogan wanted more power and constitutional changes. Anger at the US and the West was growing. More journalists were being detained. What was clear was just how large the long-term effect of ISIS and the war against it would be. Turkey's role in the region had gone through phases. First, it was "No problem with our neighbors," then it was experiments with "neo-Ottomanism" and then it was widening involvement in the Syrian war. It had experimented with turning a blind eye as thousands crossed the border into Syria to support the rebels. The era of lawlessness was ending, and it was clamping down on the border. Ahmet Davutoglu, the foreign minister-turned prime minister, left office in May 2016. Once he was gone, there would be little constraint on Erdogan and the close team around him, including Ibrahim Kalin and Intelligence chief Hakan Fidan. As I settled in at the smoking lounge on the second floor of Gaziantep's small airport in February 2016, the worst for Ankara was yet to come.

Chapter 10
ISIS Comes to Africa

Senegal, a Key to Security in West Africa

"We are on our toes," said former Senegalese prime minister Aminata Touré in March 2016, speaking at her beautiful villa in downtown Dakar. Relaxing on her couch in a long, lemon-tinted dress covered with geometric shapes, she discussed her country's challenges. "We are surrounded by countries with troubles; Mali, Guinea-Bissau is shaky, it is not an easy environment. We are alert about security."[64]

In February 2016, the Senegalese woke up to a disturbing story. A medical student named Sadio Gassama had left his studies and work and traveled to fight alongside ISIS in Libya. Born in southern Senegal's Casamance region, he became symbolic of a small but troubling group of young men joining the extremists. These were not men from impoverished backgrounds, but educated men. That worried Senegal.

Abdou Cisse, a journalist who kept track of locals going to fight for ISIS, told France 24 that the tentacles of ISIS propaganda first penetrated the country in 2015. "Several of these Senegalese media users who have open profiles started posting a lot more," he recalled in 2016.[65] "I'd say there are at least a dozen Senegalese now fighting with ISIS groups. Some of them have jobs that prove they are well educated, maybe even affluent – there are doctors and teachers among them. Others studied in reputed universities." The men who had left soon began posting propaganda on local social media. "I noticed they wrote in a very literary style, without any spelling or grammar mistakes." The men wrote in French, the common language of Senegal.

The Senegalese ended up in Libya, rather than Syria and Iraq, because it was closer and because the route to Syria had been closed by Turkey's border wall. Libya had fallen into civil war in 2011, and ISIS put down roots. In February, ISIS murdered twenty-one Coptic Egyptians, and in April 2015, they murdered dozens of Ethiopian Christian migrants.

In Senegal and West Africa, the draw of jihadist extremism led to locals joining a variety of groups. Boko Haram in Nigeria began to extend its influence across borders in Niger, Cameroon and Chad. It exploited the weak states across the Sahel, in a band of countries extending from Ethiopia and Somalia in the east all the way to Senegal via Mali and Burkina Faso in the west. In 2012, Nigeria expert Jean Herskovits had argued in the *New York Times* that there was "no proof a well-organized, ideologically coherent terrorist group called Boko Haram even exists today. Evidence suggests instead that, while the original core of the group remains active, criminal gangs have adopted the name Boko Haram."[66] In March 2015, Boko Haram swore allegiance to ISIS, and its terror attacks and kidnappings of hundreds of young women, mirroring ISIS assaults on Yazidis, made clear it posed a major threat.

Senegal and West Africa also found themselves on the front line against al Qaeda–affiliated al-Mouabitoun and al Qaeda in the Islamic Maghreb (AQIM). In 2012, jihadists from Ansar Dine had taken over the historic Malian city of Timbuktu and destroyed its shrines and ancient history. Other jihadists from the Movement for Oneness and Jihad in West Africa (MUJAO) took over the city of Gao. Eventually these groups threatened the southern part of the country and Mali's capital Bamako. France intervened in January 2013 with Operation Serval, sending thousands of troops to Mali. Troops from Mali, Chad, Nigeria, Burkina Faso, Senegal and Togo joined the operation. In 2014, France launched a second operation, dubbed Barkhane, alongside Mauratania, Niger, Mali, Chad and Burkina Faso, to defeat the jihadist groups. These became known as the G5 Sahel countries, and eventually thirteen thousand peacekeepers were sent to Mali. Initial successes pushed AQIM and the other groups back, but their leaders, such as Mokhtar Belmokhtar, survived. The campaign in Mali, like the US-led coalition's efforts against Syria, succeeded in rolling back the extremists.

As the ground campaign settled in, ISIS, AQIM and Boko Haram expanded their attacks to other neighboring countries. AQIM carried out attacks in Burkina Faso and Ivory Coast. To shore up the Sahel's defenses, the Americans began upping their commitment. In May 2017, Brig. Gen. Donald C. Bolduc of US Special Operation Command Africa told the *New Yorker* that the Pentagon's "biggest fear in Africa was the spread of ISIS, that the group would stake a hold in a remote or weakly governed area and use that territory as a base from which to expand."[67] Somalia, northern Nigeria and Mali were mentioned. This was the zone that scared the Americans. An ungoverned space.

ISIS fighters in this area came from Chad, Ghana, Senegal and Nigeria. In Libya, thousands had joined ISIS. Senegal, a stable and democratic country, increasingly became the linchpin for securing West Africa, a model that could be built on. Senegal was also the center of operations in West Africa for international organizations and NGOs. A member of the Trans-Saharan Counterterrorism Initiative, it was also a host country of the US Africa Command (AFRICOM) and Operation Flintlock, an important annual counterterror joint exercise with US allies in the Sahel. And Senegal contributed troops to UN missions such as the Multidimensional Integrated Stabilization Mission in Mali (MINUSMA).

If Senegal was a kind of linchpin to West African security and confronting ISIS in West Africa, then its capital Dakar was the eye of the pin. From the air, Dakar looks like an anvil; it juts into the sea. Just off the coast is the fortress island of Goree, colonized by Europeans after 1444, which saw millions of slaves sent to the New World. It is a tourist site now and has been visited by numerous world leaders, including Nelson Mandela and Barack Obama. Dakar itself is laid out across the anvil-like geography. At the southern tip, near Goree, are the port and the most built-up part of the city, which is home to around a million people. A coastal road called Route de la Corniche leads past the armed forces museum and Cheikh Anta Diop University, the largest in Senegal, home to sixty thousand students.

Down the coast, in the Oakum neighborhood, is the giant Mosque of the Divine, constructed in the 1970s with two iconic large minarets toped with stacked domes. The green, onion-like domes, and the black and white structure that is made up of curved triangular windows, feels very local; it blends into the African landscape. It is one of several grand mosques that look like nothing one sees in the Middle East or North Africa. Also in Oakum, which was once a small village, is another pillar of Dakar, the giant African Renaissance Monument, completed in 2010. It shows a fifty-meter-tall, bare-chested man, holding a young child and woman and pointing west. Built by a North Korean firm, it has all the subtlety one would expect. The contrasts among the bustling city center near the port, the island of slaves at Goree, the university, the giant monument and the beautiful mosque present the mosaic of what Dakar means to Senegal and to West Africa. With the exception of Ivory Coast's Abidjan, which is the largest port in this part of Western Africa and has a population of eight million, Dakar is the most important city in the region. It is the cultural capital of West Africa. Senegal is one of seven countries in sub-Saharan Africa in which more than half the population has electricity.

One of the first people I spoke to in Dakar was the Israeli ambassador, Paul Hirschson. "Dakar is Africa in one city, the development and the problems," he said. He contrasts Senegalese culture with neighboring Mali and Mauritania, both of which are more influenced by Arab North Africa. Dakar is also a contrast with the interior. Annual wages in Dakar often reach $5,000, ten to twenty times what people outside the city make. In fact a short drive outside the city into the rolling landscape filled with giant baobab trees presents a major change. Where Dakar is modern, the rest of the country is rural, and life is simple. It is easy to understand why securing the borders of countries like this is tough, where large tribes transcend borders and weak states erode one another.

The Western Front

"Terrorism is a huge issue in Mali and Burkina Faso, and some media say the next target is Senegal," Hirschson said. "We pray it doesn't come true, but thanks to our geographic position and that it is a well-known country, they do all that is possible to prevent an attack." Dakar had once hosted the iconic Dakar Rally. It was canceled in 2008. The clouds of war hang on the horizon. Tourism has declined. Security at hotels like the Radison Blu on the coast has been increased. The Radison Blu in Bamako had been targeted in November 2015, killing twenty, and hotels were especially on edge when I was in the country. A terror attack in

Ouagadougou in Burkina Faso in January 2016 killed thirty, and in the Ivory Coast at Grand-Bassam on March 13, gunmen targeted a resort on the beach, killing sixteen. AQIM took credit for the latter attack.

But Senegalese tend to emphasize that they will weather the threats because of the unique blend of Islam and local traditions in the country, including large Sufi brotherhoods. Local imams stress coexistence and seek to celebrate Christian holidays, even though only 5 percent of the country is Christian. One imam, whose association of Senegalese religious leaders represents thirteen hundred imams, said that every country has extremism. "We don't have an issue with young people attracted to extremism via social media. Many of the people are not connected to these media though, so that is one reason. Illiteracy means that we don't face as much of a problem. If we solve illiteracy, then we [will have a bigger problem]." This was one of the ironies of ISIS and global jihadists movements. They preyed on the middle class, more than on the illiterate poor and traditional. "Those who speak French are more attracted to extremism in Senegal," the imam said. What about those Senegalese who travel to France? "We have no tolerance for extremism among them, zero percent. We encourage imams to work with families and work against this." What Senegal's success showed was that a strong state with a national ethos and local tradition was a bulwark against ISIS.

Other Senegalese I spoke to agreed with this assessment. "We don't allow radical Islam to penetrate due to our synergy," one woman said. "I read about a meeting of extremists here, and one man said it was difficult to get weapons. When we realize someone is speaking extremist, people will fight against it and police will investigate." She believed that ISIS could not recruit in the country. "We don't have that mentality. But poverty could be our weakest link. Extremists may fund schools for children, so we must guard against that and be careful."

Senegal is at the heart of military air traffic heading to Mali. Senegalese troops are often deeply involved in operations. It has what is considered one of the dependable West African armies – a country that has thriving democracy and has never had a coup. In January 2017, Senegal even sent its army to restore democracy in neighboring Gambia after Yahya Jammeh refused to concede electoral defeat.

Senegal had adopted a NATO framework for its army and sought to knit it into Western military cooperation, with constant training and promotions for merit as opposed to tribal, political or family connections. In general Senegalese were optimistic. But they weren't taking any chances. The military base near the historic lighthouse in Dakar had built a security fence around its barracks and given flak jackets to soldiers. A wall was being built. More money was being devoted to security by the government.

"Economics is the main issue we are dealing with," said Touré, who was prime minister from 2013 to 2014. But regional instability was also a major concern. The two were connected. "We are trying to improve the standard of living for the whole population. We face development challenges, but we are making inroads in education. We now have universal education for girls and boys." A new law ensuring gender equality also meant the country had one of the highest percentages of women in parliament.

One of the issues facing the region was the fact that many people lack travel documents, and similar languages and cultures mean people cross borders freely without being documented. "There is a problem in handling security in such a situation," said Touré.

Professor Ibrahim Thioub, the rector of the University Cheikh Anta Diop, was also confident that Senegal would weather West Africa's storm. The colonial powers that preyed on Senegal in the nineteenth century radicalized local people. "To respond, some young people raised the banner of jihad and decided to face the predatory regime of Europeans. From the eighteenth to nineteenth centuries, there were many jihads," he said in his office on the sprawling university campus, located on the second floor of a run-down building. The aging academic said the resistance to colonialism led to the rise of Sufi brotherhoods in Senegal that still determine much of the country's culture and politics. "They said the problem was not to fight for power of material goods, but to make the greater jihad, not killing other people, but to kill the passion in yourself, to kill the expectation of power. You are the enemy of yourself and fight against material desire to get access to the light of God." He said this concept led to the creation of a unique culture in Senegal and a kind of "new citizens" with a hunger for education in the country.

After leaving the university, I took a walk back toward the city.

Fishermen uncoiled nets from their colorful boats. Artists displayed tall, black figurines for sale. Wooden figures painted as African policemen, doctors and farmers. A large mural showed black civil rights leaders, including Martin Luther King Jr. It was evidence of the blend of African orientation that affects Senegal deeply.

"I think they base their security in Senegal on a relatively good network of informers," said Ambassador Hirschson over dinner at a local restaurant. As he ate shrimp and salad, he said that a lot of what makes Senegal successful is "informal security. Communities throughout the country identify someone as behaving suspiciously – they will pass it on. It goes through religious and traditional leaders. There is social solidarity and a well-established relationship between the state authorities and local communities." The history of functioning democracy and social solidarity had cut the rise of extremism. "People on the whole feel a commitment to the state and a collective society." This commitment had led to the arrest of Imam Babacar Dianko in the eastern Senegal town of Kedougou. He was a Senegalese preacher alleged to be linked to MUJAO.

But beyond the sphere that Senegal had created, its multilayered culture of Brotherhoods and religious leaders and state partnering with community, the coordination with neighboring states was weaker. In a sense Senegal is the spearhead of the war against chaos that underpinned the age of ISIS, but it's not clear its model can be replicated. A local security expert sketched out the Sahel, three hundred million people across a huge part of Africa. "Two hundred million don't have national documentation." Without national documentation or a cohesive national culture, the state's ability to stop people crossing borders was eroded. This affected other states in the region. "I think in Mali there is a particular problem because national solidarity has collapsed." The Tuareg rebellion that threatened northern Mali had created the vacuum for jihadists to enter. Guns from Libya flowed across borders and empowered the jihadists, just as ISIS had raided the depots of the Syrian and Iraqi army. "After Bamako, Senegal is frightened, and after Ougadougou, they are very frightened. The radicals are out there, and they will just wait," the security expert said.

In August 2016, Senegalese authorities detained an alleged terrorist at an airport. A French-born man of Senegalese descent, he was accused of being linked to fighters in Iraq and Syria. In February 2017, two Malian nationals were detained in Dakar by the counterterror police. They were accused of being part of Al-Mourabitoun. Ould Nouini, one of those caught, was accused of being linked to the Grand Bassam attack in Ivory Coast. And twenty-five hundred kilometers to the east, ISIS members were planning a more brazen attack on US forces training troops in Niger.

Chapter 11
Europe Confronts Terror

Weathering the Storm

Over a thousand decision makers, intelligence and defense officials, and police experts arrived in the Israeli seaside town of Herzliya in September 2017 to attend the seventeenth annual International Institute for Counter-Terrorism World Summit on Counter-Terrorism.[68] Hosted at the Sharon Hotel, the guests mingled amid a buffet and looked out on the Mediterranean. The breeze was warm. Israel is a leader in counterterror strategies, learned from many decades fighting the phenomenon. Over the years since September 11, its strategies have become more recognized in Europe and the world, as many countries face similar threats.

Until recently many European countries had fought terror but generally saw it as a foreign threat. This was particularly true when it came to the Israel-Arab conflict. Terrorists used Europe as a base to attack others, not to attack European targets. Because of that, countering terror was not seen as something that meant dealing with local, indigenous terror cells. However, by 2017, things had changed.

"Our storm flags are up," said Piet de Klerk, ambassador at large and special envoy for counterterrorism at the Foreign Ministry of the Netherlands.[69] He was one of many experts discussing the growing terror threat in the world and how threats were changing over time, because of factors including mass migration, cyberterror and the slow defeat of ISIS in Iraq and Syria. "No individual is born a terrorist," said de Klerk, to a large hall full of mostly men in suits. He said Muslim countries were an ally in the war on terror.

It didn't seem that way in 2014, when thousands of ISIS supporters left Europe to go fight in Syria and Iraq. The International Centre for the Study of Radicalisation and Political Violence estimated that twelve hundred ISIS volunteers had come from France by January 2016.[70] The UK and Germany had allowed six hundred each to go. According to the report, Belgium had the most ISIS fighters per capita, forty out of every million residents, or 440 people. Denmark and Sweden had produced their fair share with an estimated 150 each.

Of the five thousand ISIS members who left Europe to commit genocide and terror in Iraq and Syria, around 30 percent were estimated to have returned by July 2016. The profile of the ISIS volunteers was not clear and simple, either. Although some were young men of immigrant background, some 40 percent were women in the Netherlands, and 20 percent were women in Germany and Finland. Some were converts. The fighters were also criminals, dropouts and drug users. A NATO policy paper from July 2017 argued that "returning foreign fighters clearly present the next major challenge to policy makers in tackling the ever-evolving foreign fighters phenomenon." It estimated there were still fifteen thousand foreign volunteers fighting in 2016. These were from Europe and other countries as well, such as the Russian Federation.

The EU was slow to recognize the threat or to seek to interdict the flow of fighters. Among women jihadists, the number arrested in 2013 was six, while it rose to fifty-two in 2014, and to 218 in 2015. Before ISIS began attacks in Europe, some states even tried rehabilitation for fighters, who might have committed grievous crimes. Denmark experimented with an "innovative" program that offered gym memberships rather than prosecution. But the increasing evidence of crimes by European jihadists made such programs rare after 2014. The horrific accounts of torture and beheading by groups such as the British ISIS members dubbed "the Beatles" led to revulsion back home.[71] One of them named Mohammed Emwazi was allegedly killed in 2016. Another suspect was Alexander Kotey, a convert from West London. A third suspect was El Shafee Elsheikh, a British citizen of Sudanese descent. The "Beatles" were accused of helping to guard ISIS hostages, and of torturing and beheading several, including James Foley, Steven Sotloff, Peter Kassig, David Haines, Alan Henning, Haduna Yukawa and Kenji Goto, most of whom were killed in 2014.

Brussels, March 2016

I happened to have landed in Brussels a week before the March 22 Brussels terror attacks. Even then Brussels seemed on edge. At the Gare de Bruxelles-Nord, armed soldiers were on patrol, and an NGO raised money for Syria. Migrants lined up for food. The large, cavernous train station had its share of food shops serving baguettes and meat. But just outside was the red-light district. Girls stood in the windows in their underwear looking for clients, talking to each other. The brothels on Rue d'Aerschot had names like Le Berry and Alexandra. Men wandered by in the early morning hours. They were a diverse mix, representative of Brussels. Around the corner on Rue de Brabant was a primarily immigrant neighborhood with Dubai Market, an import-export shop, and Durmaz Men's Wearhouse. Within just a hundred meters were the most European of things: women walking back and forth mostly nude in windows selling themselves, and a new immigrant neighborhood. The men who sought to go to Syria and live in the "caliphate" sought to leave these dreary brick neighborhoods behind. But they also wanted a brothel of their own, with promises of Yazidi sex slaves and the villas abandoned by those who had fled ISIS.

The attacks that came a few days after I arrived in Brussels, once I had fortuitously left, included three coordinated bombings: two targeting the airport in Zaventem, and one in the Maalbeek metro station. Thirty-two people were killed. They were some of several ISIS attacks that rocked Europe. The attacks were carried out by several men whose lives were linked directly to the rise and fall of ISIS.

Najim Laachraoui was born in Morocco but raised in Brussels. He studied engineering and even worked at Brussels Airport. He traveled to Syria in 2013 and allegedly joined ISIS after having served with Jabhat al Nusra, part of a wave of supporters of the Syrian rebels who went over the jihadists. He was wounded in a battle in Deir ez-Zor. Returning to Europe, he was linked to the November 2015 attacks in Paris but evaded arrest. He died in the March 22 suicide bombing.

A second member of the cell was born in Brussels. A career criminal, he had been arrested for possessing weapons and kidnapping in the past. Later he was investigated for ties to terror, before eventually dying in the March attack.

A third member of the cell, Ibrahim El Bakraoui, was also born in Brussels. He was also involved in criminal activity, once shooting at police in 2010. He was arrested in Turkey in June 2015, as Ankara cracked down on suspected ISIS supporters, and was deported to the Netherlands.[72] He was investigated and released. He also died in a bombing.

A fourth member of the group was thought to have fought in Syria, and his brother died fighting in Syria. Another man from Sweden linked to the group had fought in Deir ez-Zor with ISIS. He returned to Europe via Leros in Greece as a migrant and was arrested for his role in the Brussels attacks.

Europe has greatly expanded its efforts against terror. This doesn't just mean deploying soldiers on the streets, but also greater interagency cooperation in trying to confront radicalization and dealing with returning jihadists. Luc Van Der Taelen of the Counter-Terrorism Unit of the Federal Police in Belgium said in 2017 that Europe's approach had changed.[73] Open borders are a challenge for Europe, and the EU thinks terror will continue to be a threat.

Dr. Magnus Ranstrop of the National Defense College in Sweden also sees the returning jihadists as a major problem.[74] At the Herzliya hotel, he said there were as many as 460 minors who might return and need to be reintegrated into the EU, children of the extremists who joined ISIS. The milieu in European countries includes segregation, and majority-migrant neighborhoods include hate preachers. The speakers who came to Herzliya also sought to stress that most ISIS members were not truly pious or knowledgeable of religion. This is contradicted by reports from ISIS victims who recalled them praying before they raped women and having a clear code of genocidal conduct.

Europe's long wake-up to the ISIS threat was part of a larger process. It had begun with attacks after 9/11 such as the Madrid attacks in 2004 that killed 192, the London bombings on 7/7 in 2005 that killed fifty-six, and various individual murders, such as that of Theo van Gogh in Amsterdam in 2004. Then there were the Toulouse and Montauban attacks in 2012 that killed seven, including students and a teacher from a Jewish school. Then came the attack on *Charlie Hebdo* in January 2015. In many ways the attacks of 2015 and 2016 were a unique wave. The attackers tended to be lone wolves, such as the man who drove his truck into a crowd in Nice in July, killing eighty-six. There was an attack in Stockholm in April 2017, which killed five. In London in 2017, there was an attack on Westminster in March, then one on London Bridge in June and an attempted bombing of the Underground in September. In addition, a right-wing extremist tried to kill worshipers at Finsbury Mosque in June, murdering one.

The blowback from the rise of ISIS helped to boost right-wing and euroskeptic parties in the EU. The British voted for Brexit in June 2016, partly due to a desire to close their borders. In French regional elections in 2015, the far-right National Front led by Marine Le Pen won 27 percent of the vote, garnering six million ballots. In the presidential election in 2017, she made it through to the final round and took ten million votes to Emmanuel Macron's twenty million. In the Dutch general elections in 2017, Geert Wilders's Freedom Party came in second with 13 percent. The Alternative for Germany party has also grown rapidly, winning double digit percentages in 2016 state elections and receiving millions of votes in the 2017 federal election. In Austria, Norway, Sweden, Finland and Italy, the far right is on the rise. A 2016 Pew Research Survey found that half of those surveyed in Europe felt migrants increased the threat of terror. In Germany, 61 percent thought so, and in the UK, 51 percent.[75]

As fear was rising, the social media giants that had provided platforms for extremists in 2014 to share their videos of mass murder and their recruitment calls finally decided to crack down. By February 2016, Twitter said it had deleted 125,000 ISIS-related or affiliated accounts. By August, it had suspended 235,000. Next the numbers grew to 377,000, and then to 935,000 by September.[76] Facebook and YouTube also sought to remove extremist content. But the problem was much deeper; the extremists had gone deeper online to hide, into Signal, Telegram and other apps. The huge number of ISIS accounts that were suspended shows how broad the problem was. It also illustrates how long it had taken social media to understand that terrorists and extremists were exploiting their networks to grow. The rise of ISIS was integrally linked to social media. Al Qaeda had spread slowly, using disks and VHS tapes. It had to invite journalists for interviews. ISIS had exploded onto the scene largely because of modern technology. It was a creature of modern times, as David Patrikarakos had helped to show in his 2017 book *War in 140 Characters: How Social Media Is Reshaping Conflict in the Twenty-First Century.*

The result of just several years of the rise and decline of ISIS was a more fearful and a more radicalized Europe. Even as the Iraqi army, Kurdish fighters and the US-led coalition were greasing up the rifles and tanks for the final push to destroy the caliphate, its long-term effects were being felt worldwide.

Part III

The Struggle for Iraq, 2016

"How would you rate American, Russian and Iranian policies in Iraq?"

"It's like this. If you work on a project with the US, they ask you for a progress report in three months. The Russians want it in six months. For Iran, it's ten years."

– Conversation heard in Iraq's Kurdistan region,
Tanya Goudsouzian on Twitter, February 2019

Chapter 12
The Road to Qayarrah

Waiting Game

In the third week of March 2016, US Marine Corps Task Force Spartan let loose its howitzers, targeting ISIS positions in six villages near the Tigris River, south of Mosul.[77] Under cover of the artillery fire, Iraqi army units moved forward to take the villages, in the first stage of an operation they hoped would bring them to the gates of Mosul. Rain and cloudy weather, a rarity in the flat plains around the city, slowed the advance. Iraqi defense minister Khaled al-Obeidi came north and toured Makhmour, a town near the front. Things were not going as planned. "Yes, that's right," he told reporters. "At the beginning the operation was slow, and that was because we were not familiar with the area. We want to start the operation slowly to see what kind of tactics [the enemy] use against us."[78]

The long convoy of Iraqi army vehicles supporting the tiptoe toward Mosul stretched back to Makhmour, and even back to Baghdad, 350 kilometers to the south. Symbolically, Iraq's military tradition also stretched back in time, to Saddam Hussein, to the Republican Guard, George W. Bush's weapons of mass destruction, sanctions, Kuwait, the Iran-Iraq War, the Al-Faw Peninsula, Anfal and Halabja. It stretched back to Kirkuk in the 1970s, the 1959 uprising in Mosul, King Faisal II, the massacres of the Assyrian Levies, the British "butcher and bolt" during the 1920 rebellion, the siege of Kut, Nader Shah's invasion in 1743, the Mongols sacking Baghdad in 1258, Saladin, Babylon, and Abraham living in Ur breaking his father's idols.

Every war stretches back in time and is informed by the past. This isn't just about strategy and tactics, it's about how the soldiers perceive themselves and stereotype their enemy. And wars stretch forward to what will come after. Carl von Clausewitz wrote that war "is not merely an act of policy, but a true political instrument, a continuation of political intercourse carried on with other means.[79] What remains peculiar to war is simply the peculiar nature of its means." The battle for Mosul that began to unfold in the spring of 2016 was a war, but it was also a political battle for the future of Iraq. That battle was being waged in Baghdad and Erbil as well as in Washington and Tehran. Iraq may have been a broken country, partially ruined, covered over in dust and poverty, a weak or failed state, but it was a door to the Middle East. The depredations that ISIS carried out in 2014 had brought the whole world to Iraq as part of what was then the seventy-nine-member coalition. It would bring much of the world to the battle for Mosul. Mosul would be the hinge on which the door was shut on ISIS.

The Most Dangerous Safe Dam in the World

July 14 is still a public holiday in Iraq, in memory of the revolution of 1958. The coup that year resulted in the killing of Faisal II, the king of the country. The longtime prime minister, Nuri al-Said, was also killed. The country became a republic under Abd al-Karim Qasim, an Arab nationalist who modeled himself after Egypt's Gamal Abdel Nasser. Eventually Saddam Hussein's Ba'athism rose to power, leaving deep scars on the nation. Much has changed since then, and Iraq has gone through new revolutions and conflagrations, but memories of 1959 are still enshrined in the holiday, even if many people on the street can't explain why.

I got up early in Erbil that day. After a breakfast of a bit of yogurt, a hard-boiled egg and some pita-like bread, I met with Col. Dilshad Mawlud, a Peshmerga officer who also served as a media officer for the Kurdistan Regional Government, and journalist Laura Kelly, my colleague. Together we drove north from Erbil to see Iraq's most dangerous dam. Called Mosul Dam, it was built in 1981, upriver from Mosul. ISIS had captured the dam for two weeks in 2014, and the fighting led to fears that it might be destroyed. The US Army Corps of Engineers had called it the "most dangerous dam in the world" in 2006. After ISIS was pushed back a few kilometers, a team of Italians was sent to examine the dam. Their work was guarded by Peshmerga.

Stories of the dam's imminent collapse read like biblical accounts of the flood. A massive wave of water would sweep down the Tigris and destroy Mosul. If it were to collapse, millions of people downriver could be threatened. When newspapers didn't have much to print about the war in Iraq that didn't seem repetitive, they would write about Mosul Dam. We wanted to see for ourselves this natural disaster that was about to happen.

The dam was one of the strange oddities of the war. It was still supplying electricity downriver to Mosul. While Peshmerga and Iraqi army positions facing ISIS lacked electricity and resorted to using generators for just a few hours a day, ISIS was relaxing with air conditioning. The excuse for keeping the electricity flowing was that ISIS was holding cities like Mosul and their millions of civilians hostage, so cutting the power would harm ordinary Iraqis. The goal was to liberate, not starve, the people.

The dam was laid out beneath a beautiful blue lake that had formed above it. The water looked unnatural, as dam lakes always do, as if it were computer-generated imagery in some badly made movie about water on Mars. To reach the dam, the road from Erbil bisects the old highway that used to connect Mosul with Dohuk. Then it snakes its way among small villages in the desert that were damaged in the battles of 2014. The landscape is deserted. Eventually the road ascends a small hill, and the dam and lake are laid out below.

There is a dusty and dingy little town near the dam. It too was uninhabited, except for one shop. We picked up ice cream snacks and water. None of the engineers could be found; they were apparently off for the holiday. Old water tanks and equipment, rusted under the beating sun, were scattered around the northern entrance to the dam. A giant white wall had been decorated with a Kurdish flag. The stories about the instability of the dam seemed far-fetched. The water level of the reservoir was low and the spillway dry. Vager Saadullah, the journalist and fixer, who lived in Dohuk and used to take his family for picnics at the dam before 2014, said that years ago he had been picnicking and spoken with a local man who was also enjoying a sandwich next to the picturesque lake behind the dam.

"The say it's the most dangerous dam in the world," Saadullah recalled mentioning.

"Yes, they've been saying it for years. I've worked at the dam since the 1990s," the man said.

Saadullah's story was meant in part in jest. The dam has always been unsafe, and rumors of its imminent demise might be exaggerated. After looking over the glassy water, we got back in Dilshad's white Toyota Land Cruiser.

Leaving Mosul Dam, we again drove through the battlefields of 2014. Houses in small villages were flattened. A US Army Blackhawk fluttered along on the horizon. This sector was seeing some kind of activity. US special forces, unseen and unwilling to give interviews, were operating in the area. Smoke was rising from ISIS positions a mile away. "Mortars fall here sometimes," said Dilshad.

The Peshmerga had tasked the guarding of the dam to a unit of women recruited from among Kurds from Rojava. Many Syrian Kurds had fled to Iraq over the years. Prior to 2011, around 150,000 Kurds in Syria lacked citizenship and faced oppression from the Assad regime. They had come to the Kurdistan Regional Government, sometimes as stateless people. Later, more poured in because of privation in eastern Syria after the civil war began. Some of them were Kurdistan Democratic Party supporters, and that put them at odds with the Kurdish People's Protection Units (YPG) who ran the area of eastern Syria known as Rojava that borders northern Iraq. The women guarding the dam were therefore victims of this history, of Assad's oppression and of Kurdish political infighting. They had joined the Peshmerga out of a desire to serve alongside men and do something in the war.

The women showed us around their base. It was simple, consisting of a few small buildings and caravans, including sleeping quarters and a storage shed for their weapons and supplies. In a kitchen, two of the soldiers were cooking rice and beans for lunch. They asked if we could snap some photos of them, and we walked to a small wall overlooking the road. One of the women posed with her AK-47. The others smiled and joked with Kelly. They didn't speak English, and we didn't speak Kurdish, but the enjoyment was mutual. War brings people together.

The Kurdish women watched over the road, AK-47s slung over their backs. This was one of numerous Kurdish women's units that had sprung up during the war, part of a larger trend of women serving in Kurdish forces. Among the YPG, across the border in Syria, thousands of women had joined the war against ISIS. Many women fought in the ranks of the PKK in Turkey as well. It was a stark contrast to the ISIS enemy on the other side, where women were forced to wear black abayas, living mostly unseen lives now. It was also a stark contrast with the Shi'ite militias coming north from Baghdad to fight ISIS. Their model was also religious, inspired by the Islamic Revolutionary Guard Corps of Iran that many of the militia leaders had served in during the 1980s. In short, the three large communities of Iraq had taken different paths symbolized in some way by women's participation in the conflict; Sunni Arab areas fell under ISIS, Shi'ite areas came under Iranian influence while the Kurds grasped for autonomy and independence.

Bashiqa

From Mosul Dam we drove south again, passing the front line at Telskuf where I'd been in June 2015. In the distance a mountain loomed. It stood guard over a front line called Bashiqa, after the town below it. The Kurds had transformed the escarpment above the town into a long defensive line with the usual sandbagged positions carved out by bulldozers.

The area was deserted, except for the Kurdish fighters. Below, in Bashiqa, the former Yazidi town was mostly uninhabited. So we could get to the front line, the local general Bahram Yassin had sent a jeep to pick us up. Dilshad, resplendent in his green fatigues, waved goodbye and passed us off to another group of Peshmerga in a gray SUV. The men wedged their rifles between the front seats and took off for the front.

Since 2015, the Turkish army had quietly built a secret military base on the dirt road leading to the Bashiqa front. The base housed a group of Sunni Arab fighters the Turks were training. Closer to the front, another Turkish base housed several armored vehicles and artillery. The Turkish agenda here wasn't clear. Turkey's ruling party, the AKP, enjoyed relatively warm relations with the KDP. Most of the Kurdish region's oil flowed through Turkey to the sea. Turkey used this as leverage to embark on a plan to train Sunni Arabs who had fled Mosul, with the hope that when ISIS was defeated, Turkish influence would imprint itself on the liberated city. Turkey's war effort was only loosely related to the larger US-led coalition. We were eager to find out about this secret war within the larger war, but the Peshmerga driving didn't speak English, and there was no interpreter.

We drove past the Turkish base. No Turkish flag hung, just an Iraqi flag, an oddity in this landscape of Kurdish flags everywhere. Earthen embankments, checkpoints at the entrance and concrete barriers surrounded the Turkish base. We drove on, up a cranky dirt road, where potholes had eroded into deep grooves. Eventually the road seemed to become part of a dry streambed. The Kurdish driver downshifted and pushed on. His G-3 rifle jumped with every pothole. Eventually we reached a height of land that formed a ridgeline, and a straight road navigated the ridge.

When we arrived near the front line, the men drove into a cul-de-sac. On one side was an embankment, with concrete blocks to reinforce it. Rusted tubes that had once been rockets fired by ISIS decorated the area near the blocks. Below the embankment was a series of disconnected structures. This was General Yassin's headquarters. A large, one-story concrete building made from blocks was his housing. A caravan adjoined it, and two more caravans, one a latrine, were at the other side of the compound. A large open tent was a greeting hall for visitors, and it was filled with Peshmerga seated in a large U-shape around a long table, the kind one might bring on a camping trip. Two light-skinned Western volunteers stood out in the crowd of Kurdish men; one was a volunteer medic from the US, and he sat next to the general. The Kurds were excited to have more guests. Yassin had turned his command post into a hodgepodge of travelers and hangers-on. Journalists, volunteers and others came and went during our time there.

"We are only eight hundred meters from ISIS," the general said, greeting us with tea and water in little disposable plastic cups, the kind you get on an airplane. "ISIS wants to attack at all times. They are not respectful; we must be ready," he said. The general had a square jaw and handsome face slightly pockmarked from acne, less rugged and more boyish than some of the Peshmerga we'd seen before. He had no facial hair. The general had been holding this line since 2014. He said ISIS had tried to use vehicular bombs, driving up the road toward the headquarters from Bashiqa below. "They used a Humvee once." Like many of the Peshmerga, the officers had been fighting various enemies for decades, from Saddam Hussein in the 1980s to insurgents in the 2000s, to ISIS.

Refugees were arriving daily, fleeing ISIS. The general said the enemy frequently used them as cover to attack. We were interested in the Turkish base to his rear and the rumors that there was a Sunni Arab force training there called Hashd al-Watani. The general pointed to a rotund Kurdish officer on his staff, his liaison with the Turks. He appreciated the Turkish fire support against ISIS but thought the Arabs at the base were not a promising force. "They are not good fighters; they are weak. But they are near us. The Turkish army has trained them, and that's why. They sent two hundred Hashd to take a village, and they couldn't succeed. They just come for the salary."

Like many Kurds, the general wanted a referendum and an independent state for his people. "This is our Kurdish land, and we won't go anywhere. I was a refugee in Iran for twenty years after 1975. So I won't ever leave again." He described the sacrifice of his men and said it had given them a right to a home like all peoples. "We have a different language and lived under dictatorship." He supported a referendum for independence. "Iraq has violated the rules; the contracts with the government have been broken. Now Iraq will be three parts: a Shi'ite state, a Sunni country and a Kurdish one. We cannot live together. The president [of the KRG Masoud Barzani] told [then-Iraqi prime minister Haider al-] Abadi we cannot live together. We want to make three parts and be good neighbors."

When the general was done discussing plans for Kurdistan, he showed us a large-scale model of the front line. It looked like the kind of school project students might build of a volcano, but it resembled the ridgeline front the Kurds were defending, and someone had even plunked down toy soldiers and a child's model jet plane to explain the positions. Here were the Peshmerga on the ridgeline and underneath ISIS, the general explained. The plane was supposed to represent the coalition air strikes. The Turkish fire-support base was marked as well. A row of villages at the bottom of the hill showed where many of the people fleeing ISIS would sneak through to get to Kurdish lines. They would come up the dry wadis at night. Some of them were members of the Shabak minority, an ethnic group that is Muslim and lives in the area. Unlike Yazidis, they were not seen as infidels by ISIS. However, as a minority group they were persecuted by Arabs.

A British volunteer named Alan Duncan stood with several of the Peshmerga.[80] He'd come to fight alongside the Kurds and lived at Bashiqa. A former marksman back in the UK, he used a Dragonov sniper rifle now. Jonathan Reith, the other foreigner, had come as a medic. He had EMT experience and lived in Michigan before. The horrific stories of ISIS abuses inspired him to come halfway around the world to help. Unlike some Western volunteers, who had fantasies of being fighters and heroes, he said that he recognized his medical training was more essential. "They need people who can train people in medical issues. [Foreign] fighters can stay home; if you want to come here to fight, then just stay the heck home." His arms were covered in tattoos, and he had a "medic" badge on his uniform. "There is no continuation of care here. A person gets a gunshot wound and you put a bandage on, and you need continuation of care, not putting them in a car and saying hope for the best; it's lack of resources. It's not about effort. If they had medically trained people, they could do more. We have forty kilometers of front line and one medic." There were no helicopters to evacuate the wounded. All they could do was drive them to the Kurdish town of Bardarash, twenty minutes down the road, where there was a clinic.

The men said that between the Turkish base and its tanks, as well as US air support, the front line was stable. As at most Kurdish front lines stretching over nine hundred kilometers in northern Iraq, there was no intention to push forward. Hold the line, wait for orders, was the mantra. Most of war was waiting around. But it wasn't all waiting. A plane could be heard in the distance, and there were IDPs on the way. The general said they had received information that a group of refugees would be coming tonight. In recent days, 102 children and their families had come through the lines.

Like most Peshmerga, the men at Bashiqa served ten days on the line and twenty days off. They had regular jobs back home. Mechanics, taxi drivers, laborers, shopkeepers. Their families relied on them. And like most Peshmerga, they brought a mix of uniforms to the front, some of which looked more civilian than military, just tan traditional Kurdish clothes that blended in well with the landscape. They brought their own AK-47s as well. Some wore sandals. Real boots cost several hundred dollars in the army surplus stores in Erbil. The men couldn't afford them. "They borrow money to fund their life here," said Duncan. "They might have three or five kids at home." Duncan also bought his own ammo. But he liked using the ammo. "I'm here to f--- with their heads," he said in his thick Scottish accent, describing taking potshots at ISIS.

The front line's most exposed position was called Lufa, and it was just eighteen kilometers from Mosul. To get to it, a supply truck made a run several times a day to bring water and food. The general gave us a pickup truck and sent a driver to take us down. Along with Duncan, we hopped in the back for the bumpy ride. After leaving the headquarters, we came to a fork in the road, which then snaked along down the mountain. Sitting in the back of the truck, hanging on as it jumped around, we suddenly felt exposed. The town of Bashiqa was laid out below, its streets and single-family homes clearly visible. There was nothing to stop mortar and sniper fire.

After a few minutes, we rolled into the forward position. A series of concrete squares, of the type that might be used to protect wire underground when building a bridge, were dug into a berm. Sandbags rounded out the top of the trenchline. The road we had driven on continued through the position and down toward Bashiqa. Before the war, civilians had used it. Now the Kurds had dug up the road to form a kind of moat in front of the line, so that no suicide trucks could drive up and into their area. Next to the first sandbagged position was another group of bunkers and sandbags held by a group of PAK soldiers from Yazdanpanah's unit whom I'd met before near Kirkuk. They waved as we arrived. Seeing them made things suddenly feel safer, and a bit like home. Anything familiar feels like home when one is so far away.

One of the bunkers, which was covered with a blue tarp, had been converted into a kitchen. A plump Kurdish man wearing a white undershirt was cooking up dinner in a large pot. Vegetables simmered in water.

Duncan ducked in as I watched the cooking and said he'd take us on a short tour. "We have no binoculars, and there is only one MILAN anti-tank missile up at the HQ." He said that if he had a "proper team," there would be a spotter and other specialists. "I was six years in Northern Ireland in the Royal Irish Regiment and six years in the Queen's Own after that." He explained why he had left the UK for this life on the front. "For me it was a combination of things that made me come out. It was a combination of everything – the inaction of the West – and it wasn't any one thing, in November 2014."

While we were talking, a small thud could be heard in the distance. "Incoming mortar." I wanted to duck into a bunker, but the men sat and smoked and sipped tea. They giggled at my desire for cover. The mortar shell hit behind us. Then there was a loud boom. "Outgoing Turkish artillery." Soon smoke filled a field down below. The Turks had found their target. This was the rhythm of life here.

As sunset came, some of the Kurds walked off to the side and prayed. They kneeled and faced Mecca. We had more tea. Then the supply truck came and dropped off dinner. Styrofoam to-go containers filled with rice. The man who had been cooking ladled some of his vegetable on top. Beans in a red sauce materialized as well. Dinner had never tasted so good. It had been a long day. Eventually I wanted to use the bathroom. "Take a piss over there," said Duncan, pointing across the road. As I ambled over, I had the distinct feeling that somewhere below an ISIS member was watching us. Soon the "thud, thud" of mortars could be heard. I zipped up and dashed back to the sandbags, trying not to run so the men wouldn't think I was a coward.

At night, after dinner, some of the squad of Peshmerga lay down on blankets on the dirt to sleep. They weren't concerned about mortars; they said they believed in God to protect them: "It's essential here." One of the men had a shortwave radio and would listen to the ISIS communications in the village below. So intimate, this war. One man took a position sitting on one of the bunkers, sandbags up to his chest, holding his AK and looking out into the night. Like most Peshmerga positions, this one had floodlights that had been installed in front of the line, ten meters from the sandbags. They projected down toward Bashiqa and in theory gave some sort of visual warning about an attack. But because of the nature of the terrain, with dry riverbeds on both sides and a road that leads down to the town, there were many crags and outcroppings that cast long shadows. Laura Kelly and I decided to walk over to the PAK fighters and see what their quarters looked like. We were greeted by their young commander, who showed us into one of the cinderblock bunkers. Inside, the air conditioning was humming, and it felt cooler but also swamp-like from all the wet air being pumped into the small space.

A group of Kurdish women in olive-drab uniforms was seated around the room. They didn't say much, but they were part of this company of PAK who had been at Bashiqa for more than a year defending against ISIS. They were Iranian Kurds like the rest of the PAK. Unlike the rest of the Peshmerga, they were in this war for the long haul, hoping to gain experience fighting ISIS and to one day use it to resist the ayatollahs.

Through a translator, one of the women said the situation in Iran was very difficult. "Iran is a dictatorship and aids terror all over the world; its regime is the enemy of the world, and Iran made all the problems. Iran and ISIS are the same." The women said that Iran was similar to Saddam's regime. "Before ISIS there was Saddam, and now Iran is making the Hashd al-Sha'abi." The claim that ISIS and Saddam's Ba'athist regime that carried out the Anfal genocide against Kurds are part of the same legacy is common in the Kurdish region. The view that the Shi'ite miliitas are the same as ISIS is also common. For many Kurds this explains the reticence to lead an attack on Mosul. They fear their Iraqi allies almost as much as ISIS, because they fear the influence of the militias once Mosul falls.

They were also more disciplined than the other Kurdish forces nearby, who were really civilians called up to hold the line. These women lived in a house beyond General Bahram's HQ, alongside the male fighters. This was home for them, and they had made it as nice as possible. They had a proper latrine out back that abutted a wadi. The sandbags were stacked lovingly, and a truck with a DShk heavy machine gun stood guard. Rocket-propelled grenades sat next to the bunker. ISIS would not break in without a fight. Outside, the mortar shells kept falling. Inside, the women tried as best they could to crack smiles. But things were tough here, and the war would go on and on.

I thought back to the First World War. My great-grandfather William

H. Hart had served with the 26th "Yankee" Division from 1917 to 1918. He had fought at Apremont, Seicheprey, Xivray-et-Marvoisin, Chateau Thierry, St. Mihiel and on the Meuse Argonne front. Names that now mean nothing. Xivray-et-Marvoisin, for instance, exists on French Wikipedia, but there is no mention of a battle there. "This section is incomplete," it says under the heading "History." Nameless men fought in a nameless battle there in 1918, as the tide turned against the German army and the Allies broke the back of the Spring Offensive. This war against ISIS, although it had many commonalities with the defeat of Nazism, also shared many qualities with the Great War. The long, nine hundred kilometers of trenchline, the waiting, the artillery; the waiting some more.

As we sat in that cinderblock bunker in 2016, one hundred years earlier men had sat in France watching across the line to their enemies. Of course the difference in death toll was staggering. ISIS held Mosul with at most ten thousand men. Although the Kurdish Peshmerga could field up to 200,000 men and the Iraqi forces included some 100,000 Shi'ite militiamen (the Popular Mobilization Units) and another 100,000 soldiers and police, the actual numbers put in the field in any given battle were quite small.

By June 2016, a total of 1,488 Peshmerga had been killed and 8,610 wounded.[81] The Iraqi army and PMU never released exact casualty figures, but they probably numbered more than ten thousand killed throughout the conflict. Tens of thousands of civilians would also lose their lives, and as the Mosul battle neared, the number would increase. By contrast, some twelve million died in the First World War on the Western Front, including four million French, two million British imperial soldiers and 286,000 Americans. Some nineteen thousand men lost their lives on the first day of the Battle of the Somme in 1916. So just a few days of fighting in the worst battles of the First World War killed more people than years of battle against ISIS.

Outside the bunker, the night air was still warm. ISIS was babbling on the radio, its men asking someone to "bring water and food." They too wanted dinner. "They hit a Turkish tank with an anti-tank missile," said one of the Peshmerga. He was referring to an April 2016 incident in which a Turkish M60 tank was damaged by an ISIS missile. Afterwards,

Turkey's retaliatory fire killed thirty-two ISIS members, according to reports. The US-led coalition was much more careful, Duncan said. We could see a car driving in Bashiqa in the distance, likely bringing food to the ISIS members who could be heard on the radio. "The coalition is too careful in taking out vehicles," he said. "ISIS uses civilians as shields." One of the concerns for the Peshmerga was that they had recently seen a bulldozer driving in Bashiqa. They feared ISIS was uparmoring it for use as a suicide vehicle. In the fog one morning, it had disappeared, and it hadn't been seen since. With only one MILAN anti-tank system, a five-minute drive up the road, the men were concerned.

On summer nights east of Mosul city, temperatures fall to around 80 degrees Fahrenheit. It's the only time that's relaxing and bearable, even for locals. On the front line, sitting on the Hesco barriers, we were cozy behind the floodlights that shone into the distance toward Islamic State. The sound of artillery shells striking the town of Bashiqa reverberated in the distance. "There's so much death and destruction coming between here and there," said Duncan. "It's so peaceful you can't imagine what's happening. It's surreal. You almost forget – it's so close to the end."

Back at headquarters, General Bahram was meeting with two members of a Peshmerga elite unit. They had come into camp to request permission to go up the line with their rifles and night vision, to see if they could ambush some ISIS members. After thanking them, the general said that he was glad we had gotten to see the Turks respond to the ISIS mortar fire. "They have saved a lot of Peshmerga lives here." He pushed back on the suggestion their presence was controversial. "There are no secrets here; ask the Americans. The Turks are very helpful."

Then the general turned in for the night. He gave us the use of one of the caravans. There was air conditioning, which was a welcome change from the hot day. There were no blankets or bedding, though, and we lay down on the hard floor.

Saddam's Army

The tall Turkish soldier led us to a caravan inside a military base near Bashiqa. Ringed with barbed wire, an earthen trench, concrete blocks, watch towers and trucks with mounted heavy machine guns, the base looked like it was hiding some sort of secret experiments. Security cameras were mounted around it. Massive concrete walls, ten meters high, marked the entrance, along with a large Iraqi flag. When the barrier at the entrance checkpoint is raised and the barbed wire rolled back, one may enter this sanctum.

We entered, cautiously, puzzled. Inside our air-conditioned SUV provided by General Bahram, we waited for permission to speak with the Arab army that Turkey was training to reconquer Mosul. Turkey's connections to Mosul go back to Ottoman times. In the 1920s, Ataturk's Turkey even thought of annexing part of northern Iraq. This was called the Mosul Question, and the province's status remained in doubt through the Treaty of Sèvres in 1920 and the Treaty of Lausanne in 1923. As the Ottoman Empire fell and modern Turkey emerged, its borders were not fully defined.

Eventually Mosul remained in British hands, but Turkish connections to leading families in Mosul continued. Turkey's main allies in Mosul were the Nujaifi family, including Osama Nujaifi and his political party, called the al-Hadba list, and Atheel Nujaifi, the head of a group called Hashd al-Watani. The political grouping they lead was sometimes called the Mutahidoun bloc, and it supported the "Nineveh five-year strategy," which called for a federal and autonomous Nineveh Province based around Mosul. Turkey's goals were less clear. It wanted influence in Mosul, and it wanted to help Sunni Arabs in the city. It had long also sought to protect Turkmen in the area, especially in Tal Afar and Kirkuk. The populist nationalism of Erdogan, combined with his religious bent, catered to desires to protect Sunnis, something Turkey was also doing in Syria.

The Bashiqa base was a manifestation of that, and no small investment. It was also closely linked to Turkey's good relations with the KDP in Erbil. Turkey maintained other bases in northern Iraq, along the Turkish border, to fight the PKK. But this was something different, as were its tanks overlooking Bashiqa. In December 2015, Baghdad had demanded Turkey withdraw and accused it of violating international law. But Baghdad's stance was not entirely consistent. In November 2015, Khalid al-Obeidi, the defense minister, had toured the area and posted on Twitter that he visited "the PMF training base in Zilikan" on November 27.[82] He also met Masrour Barzani, chancellor of KRG security. Obeidi said it related to operations to liberate Nineveh. Obeidi, a Sunni, clearly knew what the Turks were doing, since he had visited the base. In August 2016, he was sacked by Baghdad under a cloud of corruption allegations.

At the Turkish base everything was neat, modern and orderly. Clearly Turkey's NATO-affiliated army had built it. Inside the caravan, four large Iraqi men in uniforms sat drinking tea. One had an imposing mustache and sunglasses, like a character from a 1980s war film. Another was broad-shouldered, powerful and ruddy-faced, with suspicious eyes. A third was more fat and jovial. The last was also overweight, but more deliberate and plodding.

"We are from the old Iraqi army," he said.

You mean Nouri al-Malaki 's army that was defeated by ISIS in 2014?

"No, the older army."

Saddam's army?

"Yes."

Their eyes glistened a bit, as if with nostalgia. They said they had begun constructing the base in 2014, after Mosul fell to ISIS. General Sa'adi al-Obaidi, the man who said he was a leader of the group, said his men come from all backgrounds in Mosul, including Kurds, Shabaks, Christians, Sunnis, Yazidis and Shi'ites.[83] "These men are ready to attack Mosul. They also have more training – it's not finished yet." They had formed the Hashd al-Watani as a unit like the other "Popular Mobilization Forces," similar to the PMU. But they said they received no support from the federal government in Baghdad. "This camp was built by Atheel Nujaifi in difficult conditions, on his own initiative."

The men who had congregated around Nujaifi fled Mosul in 2014 and ended up in the Kurdish region. Nujaifi networked with the KDP and the Turks for support. He found willing officers in men who had once served in Saddam's forces as enlisted men in the 1980s and 1990s. The men were jaded by the decade and a half of chaos that followed the 2003 US invasion. For Kurds it had been a time of greater autonomy, but as for Mosul, the city had sunk into extremism, terror and insurgency. "The reason for the collapse of Maliki's army and the conquest of Ramadi by ISIS is the failure of the government. ISIS targeted Sunni areas like Fallujah." The government had mistreated the Sunnis, and they flocked to ISIS, the general said.

The men were fearful of Iranian influence. They said that Tehran has a major role in Baghdad and even "controls" events there. They looked fondly on the time under Saddam, when "Iran was afraid." They said now Iraq was under the "rule of Iran. Because of what Bush and Blair did, Saddam was overthrown and Iran entered."

Obaidi and his officers were upbeat. "We will do our duty in liberation, and then we will see. We don't know what will happen after this." They characterized themselves as soldiers without political ambition. Like the Kurds, they wanted more coalition support, more guns, weapons, armor. Asked about the Turkish role, they gave an instructive answer. "If the Turks don't understand the complexities here, how do you expect the Americans to?"

The officers sipped from their coffee, pausing for a moment to consider what would come next in the war. "We are preparing to go to Mosul. All of them are ready. They want to give their abilities and go into the city and kill Daesh, who killed their parents and brothers. They want their houses and cars back," said Obaidi. Some of the men had lived under ISIS control for several months in 2014, before fleeing. They characterized the extremists as foreigners and said they saw many French, Russians and Americans in their ranks.

Like the Peshmerga waiting for orders from Barzani, these men were also awaiting orders. "We can't decide; we are not connected to the operation leaders in Erbil. We are not decision makers, so we wait." Like the Peshmerga, they thought ISIS was mostly defeated and that its days in Iraq were numbered. Oddly, everyone seemed to think it was defeated, and yet it still controlled a quarter of the country.

In Qayarrah, where the Iraqi army was making slow process south of Mosul, the airfield called Q-West (Qayyarah Airfield West) had finally been taken on July 9. US defense secretary Ash Carter said that 560 more Americans would arrive to build up the forward base for liberating Mosul.[84] "We will retake Mosul, and the time to do it is now," the Hashd al-Watani officers agreed. "The people of Mosul don't like ISIS, and they are fighting ISIS. People have nothing to eat; it's like Deir ez-Zor in Syria." The men said they had heard that locals were raising the Iraqi flag in defiance of ISIS. But they also feared that a major battle for the city would lead it to ruin, like what happened in Fallujah and Ramadi. "We place in God's trust not to repeat these tragedies in Mosul. It is late in the day; we cannot repeat this problem in Mosul during the liberation action," Obaidi said.

Like the Shi'ite militias that had recruited Christians from Nineveh for their own unit called the Nineveh Plains Protection Units, the Sunni Hashd had its own Christian members. One of them came in to serve coffee and said he was from Hamdaniyeh, a large Christian town near Mosul that once had fifty thousand residents. They blamed the West for many of the tragedies in Iraq. "Hundreds of thousands have been killed."

The US in July was heading for elections, and the men wondered what a Trump presidency might bring. They didn't mind his anti-Muslim rhetoric; they thought the problem with the US was long-term. What would come in the future? *"Inshallah."* We shall see, they said.

The Villages on the Plain

In September 2009, the families of Wardak, a small village on the road to Mosul from Erbil, were sleeping on the roofs. They were keeping cool as summer turned to fall. The village was surrounded by berms put up by the Peshmerga to defend against al Qaeda. A river flowed through the village. After midnight, two trucks appeared on the road. Local security from the village knew what the trucks were: an attack. They fired at one and stopped the driver. But the other was able to drive into the village and detonate the vehicle, killing forty-three people.

The truck bomb was directed at this village because it was inhabited by Kakei (Kekei), a religious minority group that lives in northern Iraq and Iran. Like the Yazidis, they were seen as "infidels." The truck bomb was part of a series of mass attacks seeking to drive minorities out of the region. In 2007, al Qaeda had also carried out four major attacks against the Yazidi villages of Qahtaniyah and Jazeera, killing almost eight hundred people. In 2012, a car bomb targeted Shabaks in Mosul.

In 2014, ISIS carried out its own "final solution" that al Qaeda had set in motion, ethnically cleansing all the minorities from areas it conquered. Shi'ites in Tal Afar, Christians in Nineveh and Yazidis. Kakei in the area of Khazir also fled their villages. When we arrived there in the summer of 2016, an offensive had recently liberated the area. In May 2016, Peshmerga units had swept across a half dozen villages, pushing ISIS back toward Hamdaniyeh.

To get to Khazir, we followed the road from Erbil to Mosul. After securing permission from local Peshmerga officers, and an escort, we drove toward Mosul. There was a bridge over the Great Zab River, and then the road crossed next to a ruined bridge over the Khazir River. Before the war, some ten thousand Kakei had lived in the villages near the river. Now there were just several men from the villages to look after what remained. Most wore traditional Kurdish clothes and sported large, full mustaches. Some two thousand men from the minority community had joined the Peshmerga to help in the war.

The landscape was dry, and the buildings in the villages were damaged from the war. ISIS had carved out tunnels through the houses and underneath them so its fighters could move from one house to the next without being detected. The Kakei Peshmerga showed us how the houses were still dangerous from IEDs. ISIS had left behind traps and mines in many of the homes. On one road that stretched into the distance like a straight line, there was a building that had been destroyed, as if someone had picked up the roof and ripped the walls out of it. This had been a temple for the Kakei. Its green, triangular dome marked it as a holy site. ISIS had blown it up. Another holy site nearby called Said Qambr temple had also been desecrated. In the fading light, one of the Kakei Peshmerga kneeled down to pray in one of the damaged rooms, next to a tomb that was draped in a green flag. The graves outside the temple had also been destroyed. This temple had been targeted before, in 2004, the men said.

According to the Peshmerga, around fifteen hundred mines had been cleared since the villages were liberated. The local men, carrying AK-47s, and several with pistols tucked in their belts, said they wanted protection and wished to join the Kurdish region in the future. "Iraq has not been a good experience for us, even before ISIS," said one of the older men. The men said that most of the Kakei had escaped in 2014, but several had been killed by the extremists in a village called Talabad. Since then, many had been wounded by the IEDs. In one village named Kulbur, 40 percent of the homes were destroyed. The men said that ISIS had purposely destroyed their homes, as opposed to in Arab Sunni villages nearby.

ISIS had put a lot of work into its tunneling efforts. One of the tunnels was two thousand meters long. Inside it were small rooms for ISIS fighters to sleep in, tactical vests they had worn as fighters and food supplies. Outside the tunnels, ISIS had left graffiti on the walls. We poked our heads in one house. Through a courtyard of the one-floor residence there was a door to a room. The floor of the room was a gaping hole in the earth. It was dank and dark. This was one of the ISIS tunnels. We couldn't see into the pitch black, but Kelly and I thought we'd go into the tunnel anyway. After a few meters the dusty, noxious smell, and fear that ISIS might have left behind mines, encouraged us to climb back. We looked around the rest of the house. In another room, dirt from the tunneling had been piled. Holes had been made in the wall, so that fighters could leap from one house to another without going outside. This was what made removing ISIS from villages so difficult. They had planned for two years to face an offensive and prepared well for it.

A man with a stately mustache arrived. Dressed in a blue Kurdish-style outfit, with baggy pants, he said that his name was Ismail Hamid Silim, and he had been present during the 2009 bombing. "We don't trust the Iraqis anymore; we want to be a part of Kurdistan. We are a special minority group, and jihadists do not accept us, and they think they have a right to kill us, but we have a good relation with Christians." He said the international community should be doing more to repair the villages. "We need $2 million just to restore the electric infrastructure," he said.

"The ISIS plan was to destroy civil society and destroy the identity of our people. That is why they destroyed the houses and booby-trapped them. We have a very special religion; I am personally not religious, so I won't speak about it. Our religion believes in unity, and we respect others. We never did anything to others and never hurt others, and we believe in equality. We accept others." Silim was pointing to the tragedy of this conflict, a brutal war of ethnic-cleansing that had forever damaged Iraq and the region, destroying minority communities. Although the US had carried out air strikes in 2014 to stop the onslaught, since then it had largely ignored the need to repair the liberated areas. There was no investment, no international NGOs, no one to register the property damage or to account for it. It was as if a tree fell in the forest and no one heard it, so it didn't happen. ISIS had fallen on the Kakei villages in the plain, just a small example of the destruction it had wrought, and after liberation, no one had noticed.

Chapter 13
Marching Orders

The Peshmerga's New Clothes

The six men moved like a snake down the hill into a narrow valley. Each carried an M-16, and they wore matching tan uniforms. They moved slowly and deliberately. Red smoke billowed from two grenades that had been tossed on the hill in front of them. When they reached the bottom of the small valley, they split up and began advancing up the other side. They were practicing "bounding," moving as a squad in the field to confront an enemy.

The men were some of the five hundred undergoing an eight-week training program by the anti-ISIS coalition. By the summer of 2016, a total of eight thousand Peshmerga had been trained, out of a target of fifteen thousand. The US had outsourced the training to partner nations while it focused on rebuilding the Iraqi army. The Kurdistan Training Coordination Center, headquartered next to Erbil International Airport, supervised the training of the Kurds at four bases. It had around a thousand local and foreign personnel at its training locations. One base was located just outside Erbil, in a suburb called Bnaslawa. To get there we drove through a nondescript neighborhood until we got to its edge. There were some new apartment blocks being constructed that were used for urban-warfare training. Nearby was the entrance to a military base made up of several buildings housing classrooms. Beyond it were rolling hills. There, Italian, Dutch, Finnish, German, Hungarian, Norwegian, Swedish and British soldiers were trying to bring the Kurds up to the standards of a modern army. It was a challenge.

The Kurdish Peshmerga take their name from a word meaning "those who face death." Up until the 1990s, they had been an insurgent force. In the late 1960s and early 1970s, they had received support from the US and Israel in their war against Iraq's Ba'athists. In those years the shah of Iran, a key Western anti-communist ally, provided space in his country for logistical support. In 1975, that support ended in what Kurds see as a betrayal. In 1979, the shah was overthrown, and the Peshmerga could no longer find haven in Iran. Then came the Anfal genocide of the 1980s. Through all that, the Peshmerga remained a small force. But in 1991, it suddenly emerged, liberating towns and villages in northern Iraq. Its fighters came into Rania in early March and then took Dohuk. They eventually marched into Kirkuk and even considered taking Mosul as Saddam's army collapsed before them. Saddam was busy in the south fighting the US-led coalition and guarding against a Shi'ite rebellion.

Then came the 1990s. The Kurdish political factions – the Patriotic Union of Kurdistan and the Kurdistan Democratic Party – each had its own Peshmerga force. The PUK's was known as the 70th Division, and the KDP's was called the 80th Division. During a brief civil war, they turned their guns on each other, much as the Irish had in their civil war after independence from the UK in the 1920s. The growing pains of creating the Kurdistan Regional Government resulted in bloodshed. But eventually a unified government emerged. After 2003, the KRG received official status in the new Iraqi constitution, and the Peshmerga were supposed to become a more official force. But old habits and patronage die hard. They remained reliant on their political parties.

In 2010, the KRG created a Ministry of Peshmerga Affairs to finally reform the force.[85] The Gorran (Change) Movement, a party that had emerged in the Kurdistan region, sought to modernize the armed forces of the region. Dr. Kemal Kirkuki, the speaker of the KRG Parliament, told the Americans that "there had been progress in merging the KDP- and PUK-affiliated wings of the Peshmerga. However, a study by the Carnegie Endowment for International Peace in July 2014 said the reforms were only a "veneer." ISIS was already on the Iraqi border, and the ability to unify the Peshmerga was put aside. Only twelve of thirty-six Peshmerga brigades were unified under the Peshmerga Affairs Ministry; the rest still answered to their parties. This was clear on the front line, with most headquarters flying the KDP or PUK flags and many commanders wearing multiple hats, as politicians and as frontline commanders. Many commanders were personally loyal to either the KDP's Masoud Barzani or the PUK's Jalal Talabani.

Even the emergency of ISIS, however, did not prod the Kurdish leadership into change. According to Ali Hama Salih, a member of the KRG Parliament from Gorran, the KRG had tens of thousands of "ghost employees."[86] The whole region was hampered by a massive civil service, largesse made possible by oil sales. Although there were officially up to 250,000 Peshmerga, the actual numbers were lower due to the presence of so many "ghost" members, who in some cases might not exist or were collecting two salaries. Only forty thousand of these Peshmerga were under the unified command.

In October 2017, the Gorran Movement was still speaking about imagining a "Kurdistan with united Peshmerga forces, professional and unbiased following orders from one government, not two families."[87]

The coalition saw professionalizing the Peshmerga as a key goal during the war. By March 2017, the US State Department said it had trained eighteen thousand Peshmerga and seventy thousand Iraqi federal forces personnel. Training was only part of the project. Equipping them was the other part.[88]

As I drove out to Bnaslawa, one of the coalition trainers, who had served in Iraq after 2003, said that the failures against ISIS were due to the vacuum left when the US began to draw down troops in 2008. "We could have made this into a South Korea." What remained of South Korea in Iraq in 2016 was the training. The US footprint was small, and it was not intended to grow. The goal, according to the trainers, was just training, not telling the fighters what to do afterwards. "The idea is the Iraqis or Kurds make a plan. It may be bad to say, but our job is to say, 'Okay, it's their country.' We might see timelines as we see them because of our vast experience, but it's their country, so they have holidays and things," the trainer admitted. The remark about the holidays was apparently related to the fact that some of the trainees hadn't showed up for several exercises recently. Female Peshmerga, who were also being trained at Bnaslawa, hadn't shown up for several days.

The training was segmented so each partner force instructed the

Peshmerga in a different skill. Husky German soldiers taught Kurds how to use the Panzerfaust-3 shoulder-fired anti-tank weapon. Norwegians did small arms training. One of the American coalition personnel, who tagged along to see the training, was upbeat about its prospects. He contrasted it with experience training the Iraqi National Guard back in 2005. The current crop was infinitely better.

The coalition had devised a plethora of courses. For Panzerfausts, it was three-weeks long. There was a course in signals and a platoon-level infantry program that lasted six weeks. Company and battalion staff officers were in one classroom. Outside, men learned basic medical skills. In a field, others were learning to find IEDs with a hand-held metal detector. Men learned how to use 120 mm mortars in another classroom. Each trainer had to speak in his native language and then have it translated to the class. As they drew geometrics on the board, showing projectiles flying at the enemy, it wasn't clear whether the men understood.

The main challenge was that some of the Kurds came with combat experience, and they had to unlearn the way they had been doing things to take on the new methods. For instance, one young Peshmerga who had joined up at age seventeen said he'd fought ISIS since 2014. For him what was new was training with men in matching uniforms and receiving an M-16 and helmet as part of the drill. When it was all over, the men would be sent back to their units with the proper gear.

At the anti-IED training site, along a wadi, the coalition had plopped down a destroyed ISIS truck bomb. The uparmored vehicle had been encased in black metal plates. It had a plow on the front, and the back could be loaded with explosives. The driver side door was caved in. An RPG had killed the driver during a battle near Tal Afar. It had been brought down to Erbil to give a sense of the enemy.

As they stood in the baking 110-degree sun at Bnaslawa training base near Erbil in the Kurdistan region of Iraq, the experience of Ramadi was in the minds of the trainers helping the Kurds to learn skills from infantry tactics to use of mortars before being sent into the field. In one area, Kurdish Peshmerga, the armed forces of the Kurdistan Regional Government, were training to clear a dry riverbed so that an infantry column could pass through. Walking three abreast, the men swept the dirt and gravel for fake IEDs and marked the "safe" path.

"We learned from the experience in Ramadi," a tall British officer providing anti-IED instruction said.[89] "ISIS uses IEDs in unbelievable ways; they booby-trap houses to trap people inside; and 80 percent of anti-IED teams of Iraqi troops were lost. Our experts said they had never seen things like this before even in Afghanistan; the motivation of ISIS is destruction." As I'd see in Sinjar and the Kakei villages, ISIS intended to leave Iraq scorched and destroyed.

At a live-fire position, the trainers had built a mock-up of a typical Peshmerga trench line, with the kind of concrete and sandbagged bunkers I'd seen in Bashiqa. They were training the Kurds to defend a trench line, because that is what the men were used to doing.

The coalition was proud of its work. It had fielded two complete Kurdish brigades by the summer of 2016. These men now had radios, M-16s, Humvees, enough for twenty-five hundred fighters in each brigade. They had also given them MRAPS or Mine-Resistant Ambush Protected vehicles. In central Iraq, where the US was training a new Iraqi army, they were training whole divisions. So far fifteen brigades had been put in the field.

According to the coalition spokesman, around fifty MRAPS, eighty Humvees, fifteen mine-rollers and ambulances have been provided to the Kurds, valued at $150 million. In addition, "The US will spend $22 million to provide sustainment training and spare parts to help ensure the Peshmerga can maintain their equipment."[90]

On July 12, 2016, acting US assistant secretary of defense Elissa Slotkin signed a memorandum with the KRG that provides for direct funding of the Peshmerga without sending the money through Baghdad.[91] Prior to the deal, the Kurdish soldiers were often paid inconsistently due to a financial crisis, with some men on the line telling me that they received only two paychecks out of seven months of service. The KRG was trying to cut costs, and the $1.5 billion it was spending on the Peshmerga was a huge expense.

The training and finances were intended not only to help defeat ISIS but to provide the soil for stability to grow roots in thereafter.

An hour away in Qayarrah, the Iraqi army was still struggling, and the Americans had not been able to move into its base at Q-West. The coalition had wanted the Iraqi army to take Qarrayah before Fallujah. The

Iraqis were waiting for more trained units to arrive at the front, according to coalition personnel. Federal Police and Sunni tribal forces had to be trained to hold the ground the army would take. "It's not like they are US forces who are up and ready to go. So they have to move at their own pace," said a member of one of the units waiting for orders. The pace was slow. Even the best units, such as the Counter Terrorism Service Golden Division, were waiting for more men. Since it took eighteen months to train the elite counterterror forces, the Mosul operation would have to wait another two months to kick off.

While the Iraqi army and the Peshmerga waited for the orders to send in their newly trained forces, trouble was brewing with Iran.

The Iranian Front

On July 13, 1989, three Iranians arrived at an apartment on the outskirts of Vienna. Mohammed Jafar Sahraroudi, Hadji Moustafawi and their bodyguard, Amir Mansur Bozorgian, were there to negotiate with a Kurdish Iranian delegation. Inside the apartment were Dr. Abdul Rahman Ghassemlou, Abdullah Ghaderi-Azar and Fadhil Rassoul. Ghassemlou and Ghaderi-Azar were Iranian Kurds, but Rassoul was a professor from Iraq.[92] He was supposed to be mediating the meeting between the representatives of the Iranian regime and the members of the Democratic Party of Iranian Kurdistan (PDKI). Instead, the Iranians shot the Kurds at close range and then fled to the Iranian embassy. Austria, not wanting problems with the Islamic Republic, let the assassins quietly leave the country.

Twenty-seven years after the assassination, Laura Kelly and I went to meet the Iranian Kurds who were still challenging the regime. Iran in 2016 was at the height of its power. In Lebanon, its Hezbollah ally was the kingmaker in politics and was about to elect its ally Michel Aoun to the presidency. In Syria, the regime was increasingly reliant on Iranian advisers and pro-Iranian militias. In Iraq, the Popular Mobilization Units (PMU) now had 100,000 men under arms, directed by leaders such as Hadi al-Amiri and Abu Mahdi al-Muhandis, who had once fought alongside the Islamic Revolutionary Guard Corps in the 1980s. The Badr Organization ran the Iraqi Interior Ministry, which controlled the police. In November 2016, the PMU would become an official paramilitary force, and Iran's influence would grow even greater. With the Houthi rebellion in Yemen ongoing, Tehran increasingly appeared to control four other capital cities in the region: Beirut, Sanaa, Baghdad and Damascus.

Because Iran's influence stretched across Iraq to Syria and Lebanon, it stood to gain the most once ISIS was defeated. The only thing in its way was the Kurdistan Regional Government and the US-led coalition. To a lesser extent, Turkey and Israel were also challenging Iran's hegemony. However, Ankara had its own agenda in Iraq and Syria, and Israel was far away. Therefore any opposition to Iran in Iraq, such as that from Kurdish Iranian exile groups, had ramifications beyond the Kurdish region. These Kurdish Iranian groups wanted Western support and had opposed the Iran nuclear deal. The PDKI was the most prominent and oldest of them.

The PDKI's headquarters is near the city of Koya in northern Iraq. To get there we met an SUV with two armed Peshmerga and drove east from Erbil. Up through the hills, passing a sign that claimed the "Erbil Zoo" was being built nearby. On the south side of the Koya road, in the distance, was a large building on a hill. It was a martyr's monument for fallen Peshmerga. The road climbed and then spilled out into a large plain with hills on one side. Eventually it traversed a small dam and then came to a checkpoint. This was the dividing line between the KDP's Erbil Province and Sulaymaniyah Province. Large posters of PUK leader Jalal Talabani festooned the checkpoint's overhanging awning. We were in PUK land.

Just after the checkpoint, the road abruptly came to an intersection, and our SUV turned to the right. Small houses with sagging roofs made of metal lined the road. A sandbagged gate marked the entrance to what had once been a kind of refugee camp for Iranian Kurdish exiles. The area seemed deserted. Eventually several men in Kurdish clothes came out of one of the houses. This was the PDKI base, now fallen into disrepair and bordering on ruin. It looked more like an abandoned town in the American West than the heart of the resistance to the ayatollahs. In the 1990s, Iran had massed thousands of men on the border with Iraq and carried out air and artillery strikes against the Kurdish exiles living around Koya in places like this. Around two hundred PDKI members had been assassinated by Iranian intelligence since then.

The PDKI sees itself as the descendant party of the Kurds that declared the Republic of Mahabad in northwestern Iran in 1946 – the original Kurdish independence movement and Peshmerga. But in recent years, their party has been split in half, so that it has an offshoot group with similar origins called the KDP-I. There are other Iranian Kurdish groups as well, including the Kurdistan Free Life Party (PJAK), which is related to the PKK and the PAK, and another group called Komala.

At the meeting with Mustafa Hijri, the requisite tea course came. Then Hijri arrived, resplendent in a formal Kurdish outfit. He had been a teacher at Tehran University decades ago, he said. "After the Iran revolution and the Islamic Republic, I became a member in this party and supported democracy, but for the last thirty-seven years I've been in the leadership. When the KRG was founded, we stopped fighting Iran, because we didn't want them to have an excuse to fight KRG. We stopped that based on an agreement, so for twenty years, from 1992, they stopped fighting. In the last twenty years, we wanted to solve our issues through negotiations," he explained.

But negotiations have gone nowhere. There is increasing oppression of Kurds in Iran. In 2015, the regime was on the brink of signing the nuclear deal with the US, and the PDKI decided that now was the time to begin the resistance again. "We decided to send our Peshmerga fighters back to Iran. Last year when we sent back some Peshmerga, we ordered them not to fight if the Iranian army didn't attack them. Only do some partisan work with the people. Last year, the Iranian regime didn't attack our Peshmerga, so there was no conflict." Hijri said the lack of conflict was due to Tehran wanting to keep quiet before the nuclear deal was signed. After it was signed, Iran's regime began to attack the PDKI. "We decided to continue in these operations, and if Iran continues to attack us, we will move from just defending our men to defeat Iran, and we will go on the offensive. That is our plan now. We want to change from defense to offense."

For Hijri and his comrades, the goal is to create a federal, democratic Iran. But the chances for that seem distant, considering that Tehran is busy spreading its revolution in its near abroad, in Iraq, Syria and elsewhere. Iran is even recruiting Shi'ites from Pakistan and Afghanistan to fight in Syria. Iran's attempt to connect conflicts from Lebanon to

Afghanistan is part of the boomerang effect from ISIS. Its rise gave Iran an excuse to fill in the vacuum as ISIS was defeated. In Syria, it used the regime, pressing toward Deir ez-Zor. In Iraq, it worked through the PMU. In Lebanon, Hezbollah also grew in strength, arguing that it was a "shield" and "defender" of Lebanon against "takfiri jihadists," a term used for ISIS.

The reality was that Hezbollah intervened in the Syrian civil war in 2012 at the request of Assad. The Syrian regime, which had occupied Lebanon from the 1970s to 2006, now found itself occupied by foreign forces it was relying on. Tiny Hezbollah suddenly was at the forefront of numerous conflicts, its cadres coming to Iraq, and Hassan Nasrallah, its leader, commenting on affairs in Yemen and elsewhere. Iran's growing influence encouraged Saudi Arabia and the UAE to look increasingly at Israel as an ally. It also changed the strategic thought of Jordan, Qatar, Turkey and Egypt. Qatar and Turkey grew closer, and Turkey reached out to repair relations with Iran. Jordan and Egypt became concerned about their internal stability.

Although the PDKI was a small party, and its role in Iranian Kurdistan was relatively limited, it took on greater symbolic importance because of Iran's role in the region. The PDKI wanted to work with other minorities in Iran, including the Azeris, Turkmen, Arabs, Baluchis, Lors and others. But there was chance of blowback for this. "From the beginning, Iran has tried to make the KRG unstable and weak and wants to put their influence on it," said Hijri in the summer of 2016.[93] "Iran plays a major role in creating conflict between Kurdish political parties, and now Iran has Hashd al-Sha'abi in Tuz Khurmato [south of Kirkuk]. Iran has worked through the Hashd to harm average people, so Iran is the main enemy against Kurds in the world, especially here in Kurdistan. In the recent times, as Barzani speaks about [an independence] referendum, so Iran is the main one against the referendum." Hijri hinted that Iran would work through its allies in the Kurdish region, primarily through influence in Sulaymaniyah and the PUK and Gorran parties, to prevent a referendum. If that didn't work, it would go through Baghdad and the Popular Mobilization Units.

Hijri bade us goodbye. He was pessimistic about the US role in the region. "Americans function like a road map; they look at today's route, but don't look at the future. For instance, they had a plan to defeat Saddam but not what to do after, and with Assad, and when Syria revolution began, America was watching it, and then when Iran came and built bases there and other terrorists all came there, and America watched." Now Iran was watching America's next move in Iraq and Syria, and it was watching the Kurds.

For Iran, the Kurdish threat was paramount; it was a hinge of the region. Too much Kurdish power in Iraq would be a stumbling block to Iranian power. But before the stumbling block could emerge, ISIS would have to be defeated. For Iran, this was still a priority, and it wanted to make sure its boots were on the ground when it happened.

Q-West's Refugee Problem

The refugees came in trucks out of the smoke rising from Qayarrah. ISIS had lit the oil wells on fire. It was scorching the earth, and the sky was full of ugly black soot and smoke. The refugees were stopped at a Peshmerga checkpoint, where several Kurds and members of the Hashd al-Watani helped them come off the trucks. Then the Kurds lined them up in two lines, men and women. Each man was searched for weapons. They were fearful of ISIS members hiding among the IDPs. The women, waiting with their children, sat down on rocks and looked into the distance. They were drained and tired. Many had spent days trying to escape Mosul and come south. They were Sunnis and wanted to get to the Kurdish region. They feared the Shi'ite militias.

On July 24, 2016, KRG prime minister Nechirvan Barzani warned that there might be 500,000 refugees fleeing Mosul as the battle approached.[94] "We are working with Baghdad and looking forward to assistance from the international community."[95] The US State Department said it had received pledges of $2 billion for Iraq to help with the humanitarian problem. As the refugees came by the truckload, several hundred in an hour, there were no NGOs to help them, no UN, no food. Some were so exhausted they slept outside, next to the one of the ubiquitious berms the Peshmerga had constructed as a defensive line. The Sunni Arabs from the Hashd al-Watani encouraged them to keep moving. There were new refugee camps being built.

The women who had fled ISIS told tales of living under the caliphate.

"We wanted to leave the first day ISIS arrived," said one woman, covering her face with her abaya. They were still afraid ISIS would see photos of them and abuse their families or confiscate their homes in Mosul. They said ISIS was withdrawing in the face of the Iraqi army's slow advance in Qayarrah. The women described living under the extremists. Even their daughters had been forced to cover their faces at a young age. "They're little girls – they're not even married," said one woman. Accusations and crimes were common. One woman said ISIS had imprisoned her son for smoking. He had been lashed for it. ISIS would go house to house and make sure the men went to mosque. Sometimes ISIS stole their food.

Several days after we saw the refugees arriving from the direction of Qayarrah, Ayub Nuri made his way toward the city. Nuri was one of the Kurdish media network Rudaw's senior journalists. He accompanied Iraqi soldiers in their efforts to take the village of Osaja on the eastern side of the Tigris. "The sound of intense gunfire was carried to us by the winds like the celebratory fire of a distant wedding," he recalled in late July 2016. He went up to the roof of a house and peered through binoculars. A row of tanks was advancing against ISIS.

The same soldiers now assaulting Osaja had been in the battle for the village of Nasr in February, when the Iraqi army had gotten stuck in the mud and fog in a largely failed operation. It had been slow going since then. ISIS was fighting to the death. "They only surrender when they run out of ammunition and have nothing left to fight or kill themselves with," a twenty-eight-year-old Iraqi soldier told Nuri.[96]

The Iraqi army had to take Qayarrah. It was the gateway to Mosul, just sixty-five kilometers from the city. A strategic crossroads, the Q-West air base, hospital and electric plant. But the army was riven with problems. "We have caught soldiers passing on information to ISIS from inside our camp. We caught a militant, and when his phone rang, it was one of our soldiers calling him," a commander told Nuri. The Iraqi soldiers also liked the show of victory. They brought along their own homemade ISIS flag to photograph at areas they had liberated. They didn't even bother to fully liberate some areas. In the village Nuri spent time in, a sniper fired at the Iraqis who were busy celebrating. It would take the Iraqis another month to liberate the whole of Qayarrah. The city was in ruins, oil fires belching from around it, purposely lit by ISIS. It would take until the spring of 2017 to put the oil fires out completely. By then the Americans had moved in to Q-West Air Base outside the city and were preparing for operations to liberate Mosul.

Operation Inherent Resolve moved into Qayarrah in July. Coalition engineers refurbished the base, and personnel from the 821st Contingency Response Group from Travis Air Force Base in California came to the site. In the austere conditions they found, the coalition set itself up to carry out command and control, airfield operations, security and maintenance. "We are designed to go where air infrastructure doesn't exist in order to bring to bear airpower where it needs to be," Colonel Rhett Champagne of the 821st said.[97] Their task was to bring the base up to standard so it could be relied on heavily as a staging base in the upcoming Mosul operations. ISIS didn't know it, but the coalition was about to greatly increase its air strikes and carry out what it would later describe as the most precise war in history.

Chapter 14
A Coup in Turkey

Ankara Transformed

"No compromise, no hesitation," a Turkish major texted his colleagues. "Hit them, crush them, burn them."[98] Just after midnight on July 16, 2016, he was with a group of Turkish soldiers in Acibadem, a neighborhood in Istanbul.[99]

A crowd was watching the soldiers who were trying to take over a building belonging to Türk Telecom. It was part of a coup taking place across Turkey. But locals were outraged. They came to shout at the soldiers. Eventually the Turkish major fired a single shot into the crowd. "Show no compassion," the major texted his coconspirators. "We are about to win...as someone who is in the field, I am firing, firing into the crowd and waiting."

The next day the coup was over. In striking pictures, the crowds of civilians were seen helping to overwhelm soldiers, and police commandos had done the rest. The coup attempt cost 240 lives and changed Turkey, perhaps irreversibly. There had been coups before, but this one was unsuccessful, and Turkey's ruling party used it as an excuse to launch a massive purge of tens of thousands of civil servants. "Every coup which does not kill us makes us stronger," Prime Minister Binali Yildirim told millions gathered in Istanbul at a "Democracy and Martyrs" rally on August 7.[100] Turkey's government blamed exiled Islamist cleric Fethullah Gulen for the coup.

Burak Bekdil, a Turkish columnist for *Hurriyet*, argued that the 2016 coup attempt came against a complex background. "You must note that Erdogan and Gulen were best allies for several decades, until they broke up over methodology to reach a common goal...the two camps [of Erdogan and Gulen] fell apart; it became evident that the Gulenists are a small elite group within the state bureaucracy. They do not have any massive popular support."

Turkey was already fighting a war with the PKK, and the coup sharpened the cleavages in society. For Kurdish activists such as Kani Xulam, the founder of the American Kurdish Information Network, the lead-up to the coup attempt and the results have a deeper meaning as well. "The words of Erdogan definitely herald a new beginning in Turkey. Today he has put the Gulenists in the crosshairs of his vengeance. Tomorrow or sooner he will add the Kemalist [secular] Turks and recalcitrant Kurds."

I watched the coup unfold from northern Iraq, sitting at a café with a giant narghile (water pipe). The Kurds at the table were glued to their phones and computers, reading the news. "*Son dakika*," red banners flashed on Turkish websites declaring "up to the minute" breaking news of what was unfolding. An F-16 buzzed Ankara. I tried to reach friends in Istanbul and Ankara. It was a chaotic time; we didn't know what would happen. An inkling of what was unfolding came later in the night, when Erdogan appeared on NTV, a Turkish network, speaking live from his smartphone using FaceTime. He called on supporters to oppose the coup, and in that moment probably turned the tide.

Syrian refugees in Turkey also found themselves at the forefront on the night of the coup. They supported Erdogan and wanted his patronage of the rebellion in Syria to continue.

In Ankara, Mohammed Ruzgar, a Syrian journalist, saw TRT, the public broadcaster, go black on the night of the coup and thought it was a "bad signal." Many Syrians in Turkey supported the government because it had welcomed them during the Syrian conflict and also supported them against Assad. They feared the coup and rising anti-Syrian sentiment in Turkey. Those connected to the secular opposition feared that the Syrian war had dragged Turkey into problems with its neighbors, in contrast to the Ataturk slogan of "Peace at home, peace in the world." As for former prime minister Ahmet Davotoglu's more succinct "Zero problems with neighbors" policy, the Syrian war was not benefiting

Turkey either. "It was horrible," recalled Ruzgar. "I was frightened that by toppling the government, our status here, which is relatively good, would be harmed, and it was awful to see democracy toppled by the coup in a Muslim country, and then dictatorship will rule in the Muslim world, because we in Turkey are an exception."

Muharrem Ince, a CHP opposition politician, wrote in an email to me in 2016 that the effects of the coup attempt were tremendous. "We are an important country to the region, surrounded by problems, fighting terrorism for 35 years." Although there is a spirit of unity after the coup, the state of emergency that was declared on July 20, 2016, resulted in fifteen thousand arrests initially. Eventually the number would balloon to more than 160,000, with fifty thousand charged and 152,000 civil servants dismissed.[101]

The opposition said there was an erosion of the rule of law and was critical of the state of emergency and the closure of institutions. But the opposition was also opposed to the coup, and the coup became a rallying cry across the political spectrum in Turkey. Whatever critiques of the AKP existed, military rule was seen as a worse option, and many had bad memories of the old days under military rule. "AKP leaders, especially the president, see the government as the target of the coup; we see this as an attack on the existence of the Republic of Turkey, particularly the bombing of parliament," said Ince. In order to defeat the coup, therefore, it was important to "strengthen democracy rather than suspend the rule of law, to protect our uniqueness in the country and solutions that include everyone to overcome this danger." Had the coup succeeded, he said, there would have been a civil war in Turkey.

Popular opposition to the coup brought unity to Turkey and strengthened the hand of the AKP. It would win 51 percent of the vote in the constitutional referendum in 2017 and 52 percent of the vote in the April 2018 elections. Although half of Turkey does not vote for the AKP, many people opposed the chaos and uncertainty that a successful coup would bring, as well as the likely erosion in the international status of the country.

The ruling party exploited the momentary unity to go after opponents. The parliament had already stripped its members of immunity, in May 2016. Soon police began rounding up left-wing Kurdish MPs, such as

Selahattin Demirtas, who was arrested in November 2016. They were accused of links to terrorism. Politicians, journalists, artists and others were also imprisoned. In April 2017, the narrow referendum win would give the presidency new powers, further solidifying Erdogan's rule. By then Turkey would already be involved in a wide-ranging new stage of war in Syria. The coup attempt would weaken opposition to Ankara's policies in Syria and Iraq, removing obstacles to further military involvement in support of the rebels and against the Kurdish PKK. The rise of ISIS and terrorism in Turkey had created the instability and fertile ground that may have set the coup plotters in motion. After the coup attempt, Ankara's muscular foreign policy would be well positioned to benefit from the vacuum left by ISIS in Syria and Iraq.

The rise of ISIS overshadowed Turkey. Many ISIS volunteers had come through Turkey, and Ankara's pro-Syrian rebel policy had, at first, not distinguished well between the more extreme jihadists and others. As ISIS was defeated, some of its members sought to return to their home countries via Turkey.

After the coup, Turkey reasserted its authority over the Syrian rebels, turning those it was working with into clients. It sought to use them against the Kurds in Afrin and also to create a buffer zone between Turkey and the Assad regime–controlled areas. The coup attempt helped to accelerate processes already taking place and would fuel Turkey's feelings that it could confront any challengers, including the US and other powers in Syria. McGurk and US officials were critical of Turkey's role in Syria, saying it was not a reliable partner. The tepid response of Western powers to the coup further pushed Turkey to work with Russia and Iran. By April 2018, Ankara was hosting the leaders of Moscow and Tehran to discuss Syria, and Turkey was growing closer to both Iran and Russia.

Last Stand at Haditha
As Turkey was recovering from the coup, a Sunni Arab tribe in Iraq was celebrating survival after almost two years under siege by ISIS. The Jughayfa tribe is located near Haditha and the strategic dam and the Ayn al-Asad Air Base nearby. Based in Anbar Province, it has members across the province's vast extent, some 148,000 square kilometers, and clans in Saudi Arabia and across the border in Albu-Kamal in Syria.

Because the Jughayfa had a complex history of difficult relations with Saddam Hussein, they had welcomed work with the Americans after 2003. They were one of the tribes that had been a key to the Sunni Awakening that helped defeat the Iraqi insurgency in 2006. The insurgency had been based among the Sunni population, and it was only by recruiting moderate Sunnis among the tribes that Baghdad and the US were able to roll back the extremists.

The Jughayfa were therefore inclined to oppose ISIS, like some other Sunni Arab tribes such as the Shammar in northern Iraq and Syria, who also resisted ISIS. When ISIS arrived in force, the extremists had offered money for the tribes to surrender. The local Haditha-based sheikh responded, "*Taksha wa-takeb,*" which means something like "Screw off." Instead of handing over its territory, the tribe settled in for a long siege. Only in May 2016 were they finally liberated by the Iraqi army. Brett McGurk, US special envoy to the anti-ISIS coalition, tweeted congratulations, noting that ISIS had thought it could wipe out the Jughayfa. "Not quite. ISIS terrorists impaled themselves," McGurk said.[102]

A member of the tribe I spoke to in 2016, named Ahmed al-Hadithi, said the Jughayfa fighters had opposed jihadists for years, including Ansar al-Sunnah, Jaish Muhammed and Al-Tawhid wa-Jihad. Along with the neighboring tribe called Albu Nimr, he said they had been part of the Sahwah or "Awakening." He was proud of the role his friends had played in stopping extremism.

Haditha is located two hundred kilometers northwest of Baghdad, and is the third-largest town in Anbar. It is around twenty kilometers from the Ayn al-Asad Air Base. Like Q-West, this had been a strategic US base until the Americans withdrew in 2011. When ISIS came in 2014, the Iraqi army ran away. "We took their weapons," said Hadithi. He said the ISIS fighters they faced had come from Syria, and some had been released from Bashar Assad's prisons in 2012. Others had been allowed to enter Syria by Turkey. Thousands of foreign fighters undermined the rebellion against Assad and spread into Iraq, where they captured masses of equipment from the Iraqi army. They were financed by the speed of of their conquest, in which they captured banks and other resources in Mosul. Some ISIS members carried pictures of Saddam Hussein, the Jughayfa recalled.

Like many Sunnis who initially welcomed ISIS as a liberator from the Maliki government in Baghdad, the tribesmen in Haditha soon saw how ISIS manipulated local people. It appeared to create local councils and employed Saddam-era officers. Then the killings and massacres began. ISIS slaughtered members of the Nimr tribe. The Jughayfa outfitted themselves for the long war ahead. They put up images of the Punisher comic book vigilante as a logo for their fighting units. "The Iraqi central government did not support us with one rifle," Hadithi told me. "We bought our ammunition and guns on the black market or seized them from ISIS failed attacks."

ISIS tried to take Haditha. They used human-wave attacks. Eventually the liberation came in May 2016. But the Haditha tribesmen were suspicious. They had resisted ISIS, but the Iraqi army was heavily made up of Shi'ite volunteers now, and the tribesmen feared discrimination. Like the Kurds, the Sunnis of Anbar feared the rise of the Shi'ite militias. "The other face of terrorism," Hadithi said. Like the members of Hashd al-Watani, the Haditha tribe was watching the US elections in 2016. They also did not fear Trump, arguing that his posturing would be respected in the region. "In Arab culture, if someone is killed, someone else should take revenge." The US had lost thousands of soldiers, so Trump would be seen as returning with a vengeance, they thought. They wanted a continued US presence to counterbalance Baghdad and Iran's influence over the Iraqi army.

Like Mosul, Haditha has a picturesque dam near it. After liberation, the tribesmen returned to their daily lives, picnicking near the dam and suffering through the long, hot summers in Anbar Province. For them the war was over, as the Iraqi army moved slowly and cautiously toward the Syrian border, reducing ISIS power in the province. In January 2019, the tribesmen were targeted again by kidnappings and murders at the hands of some ISIS members who had survived the war and melted into Anbar's vast desert.[103] All the Jughayfa and other Sunni tribes could do was hope for a future Iraq that would be secure and in which they would receive their fair share.

Chapter 15
Zero Hour

Iraq's Army Moves North

Since the spring of 2016, the Peshmerga had slowly pushed forward their areas of control, especially northwest of Erbil near Khazir.[104] On August 14, more than five thousand Peshmerga moved forward from the area near the Kakei villages around Wardak and liberated twelve other ISIS-held villages. Then Iraqi prime minister Haider al-Abadi told the Kurds to stop their offensive on August 17. He asked them not to expand their presence. The US State Department agreed. "I think it's absolutely important and we've emphasized this all along, that the Peshmerga and all the various fighting groups in Iraq need to be under the command and control of the Iraqi government," Mark Toner, deputy State Department spokesman, told Rudaw.[105] In Baghdad, Mohammed Saihoud from Abadi's State of Law Coalition said that if the Kurds moved forward into Nineveh, they would be seen as "occupiers."

The Kurdistan Regional Government responded by noting that the Iraqi army had only one way to get to Mosul, moving north from Qayarrah. By contrast the Kurds controlled numerous approaches from the northeast and southeast. Erbil was weighing its options. It knew there was pressure from the coalition and Baghdad to begin the Mosul offensive. The Kurds had agreed that the Peshmerga would not enter Mosul city during the operation. On September 8, President Barzani went to France and met with Defense Minister Jean-Yves Le Drian. They discussed the Mosul operation.

Three weeks later, Barzani flew to Baghdad and sat down with Prime

Minister Abadi. Barzani described the meeting as "brotherly" and said that the KRG had come to a "common understanding" with Bagdad. "Our visit to Baghdad is to show our full support for the Prime Minister as we have many challenges ahead of us and we have joint priorities, the top one is the fight against Daesh terrorists. There is good coordination between the Iraqi army and Peshmerga forces to have a plan for [the] Mosul operation."[106] The meeting was wide-ranging and also touched on oil issues. "The disaster in Iraq got many things unresolved since 2003, and we aspire to develop complete solutions and cooperation to resolve Kirkuk and the budget of the Kurdistan oil problem," Abadi said.

Under the new cooperation agreement, the Iraqi army would pass through Kurdish front lines and deploy near Kurdish forces. Several Iraqi units would move to areas near Telskuf. Another group would move to Khazir and another would move to the Gwer front line. Meanwhile, the Iraqi army near Qayarrah would begin to move north. This would mean the offensive on Mosul would be launched from four directions to the south and east of the city. ISIS could only flee westward, toward Syria.

Just before the offensive was supposed to commence, as convoys of Iraqi military vehicles, trucks loaded with supplies, and long lines of the black Humvees of the counterterror units clogged the roads north, Erdogan entered the fray. In a speech to Islamic religious leaders from the Balkans in Istanbul on September 14, he threatened that Turkey would play its own role in the liberation of Mosul. "Turkey's army hasn't lost enough of its quality to take orders from you," the Turkish president said, referring to Abadi.[107] "You are not my interlocutor, you are not at my level, you are not my equivalent, you are not of the same quality as me. Your screaming and shouting in Iraq is of no importance to us. You should know that we will go our own way." Turkey was concerned that the Mosul operation would involve Shi'ite militias and lead to demographic change. Turkish prime minister Binali Yildirim said that the operation should be "limited to removing Daesh."

In August, Falih al-Fayadh, a Popular Mobilization Units leader and national security adviser to Abadi, had said that the PMU would participate in the Mosul battle and even said the list of forces, totaling some fifteen thousand, had been drawn up. Mueen Hameed Kadhumi, a senior Badr commander, and Hadi Amiri, the leader of Badr, both expressed interest in playing a role in the battle. By October, Baghdad had been able to get the PMU to agree that it would play a role only around Mosul, but not directly in the battle for the city. The Iraqi army had lost Mosul. It would retake it.

As the Iraqi army units moved north, several of their vehicles were halted by Kurdish Peshmerga checkpoints near Makhmour. They were flying Shi'ite sectarian flags with images of Ali on them. The Kurds wanted the flags taken down. When the convoy took the flags down, the Peshmerga waved them on. In Kalak, an Iraqi army convoy rolling through town led to celebration among Shi'ite Shabaks, a minority group. Some of the Iraqi soldiers shot in the air. It illustrated that although the Iraqi army and Kurds were united in the war on ISIS, major unresolved issues would overshadow the rest of the war and its aftermath.

"Godspeed to the heroic Iraqi forces, Kurdish peshmerga and Ninewa volunteers. We are proud to stand with you in this historic operation," the US special presidential envoy for the Global Coalition to Defeat ISIS, Brett McGurk, tweeted just after midnight London time on October 17.[108] It was still several hours before daybreak in Iraq, but Prime Minister Abadi had decided to announce the operation overnight. By daybreak, long columns of Humvees, provided to the Iraqi and Peshmerga forces, were on the move. Artillery and coalition airpower pounded ISIS. Abadi appeared on TV before sunrise, flanked by his army chiefs.

By sunset over the front line in northern Iraq on the first day of the long-anticipated Mosul offensive, Kurdish Peshmerga and Iraqi army soldiers had already begun to celebrate the first victories over Islamic State. Videos of Kurdish men dancing next to their armored vehicles were posed on social media. Almost a dozen villages had been taken and more than 200 square kilometers liberated southeast of the ISIS stronghold on October 17.

Thousands of Iraqi army troops, their artillery and armored vehicles carried north on trailers in the last week, had been deployed alongside the Kurdish Peshmerga. This was a new kind of war on ISIS. Over the last two years the Iraq central government had largely fought its own war against ISIS in central Iraq, while the Kurds had been fighting ISIS in the north. Now the groups would serve side by side.

By noon, most of the objectives of the first day had been met. "Villages

the Peshmerga set out to liberate have been liberated," Sheikh Jaafar
Mustafa, a Peshmerga commander, told the Kurdish news station Rudaw.
A local news crew caught up with a Kurdish fighter and his comrades
who had just killed a half dozen ISIS men on a front line near Khazir.
One man, his face smudged from smoke and ash from the battle, waved
his machine gun in celebration. "This is the fate of ISIS; let Abu Bakr
al-Baghdadi know that this is the fate." Reports in Kurdish media said
six Peshmerga had been killed; it was unclear if Iraqi forces had suffered
losses. ISIS attempted to blow up an Iraqi tank with a suicide bomb, but
overall it seemed the enemy was unable to resist.

While the Iraqi forces advanced from Qayarrah to the north, the
Kurds and Iraqi forces attacked from Khazir and Gwer. On the Qayarrah
axis of advance, the Iraqis took a series of villages along the Tigris.

Nawaran: Mosul Offensive, Day 3

At four in the morning in Erbil on October 20, the Trump-Clinton debate
was being carried live on radio, with simultaneous Kurdish translation.
Both presidential candidates answered questions about the Mosul
offensive at the University of Nevada, Las Vegas. "I am encouraged that
there is an effort led by the Iraqi army, supported by Kurdish forces and
also given the help and advice from the number of special forces and
other Americans on the ground. But I will not support putting American
soldiers into Iraq as an occupying force," said Clinton. "The goal here is to
take back Mosul. It's going be a hard fight. I've got no illusions about that.
And then continue to press into Syria to begin to take back and move
on Raqqa, which is the ISIS headquarters."[109] She implied that if the US
stayed in Iraq, it would be a "red flag" for ISIS to reconstitute itself.

Trump argued that Clinton and the Obama administration had been
responsible for the city's fall in the first place. "We lost Mosul [and] now
we are fighting again to get Mosul," he said. "About three months ago, I
started reading that they want to get the [ISIS] leaders and they're going
to attack Mosul. What ever happened to the element of surprise?" Trump
also claimed that the real winners in the battle would be Tehran, and
that Iran should write the United States a thank-you letter for "[making]
it so easy for them" to take Iraq.

The Peshmerga's objective in the Mosul offensive was to liberate mostly Kurdish villages near Bashiqa. This was an area that the Peshmerga had been overlooking from the nearby mountains for years. To capture it, they decided not to advance head on, but to strike at it from the south and the north. One column would move north from Khazir, and another from the Nawaran front line. At Nawaran the Peshmerga had assembled hundreds of vehicles and dozens of units. When I arrived on October 20, it was a kind of chaos. The old frontline berm and trenches had been breached and the road opened. The loud, deep, soul-fracturing percussion of artillery sounded in the distance. The guns were down the road, a few kilometers behind the line.

A huge number of Peshmerga, some journalists and foreign medical volunteers crowded the berm overlooking the village of Nawaran, from which the front got its name. The village sat along a road that ascended to a pass that cuts through the long chain of hills that runs from the northwest to the southeast, toward the Khazir River and Erbil. All of these hills had been held by the Peshmerga during the war. From October 2014 to October 2016, the Peshmerga had overlooked Mosul from here, watching the lights twinkle in villages such as Nawaran, Bashiqa and Fazalia. This was the historic Nineveh Plains that was outside the borders of the Kurdish region and under federal Iraqi control before the war. They were diverse and historic areas.

At one end of this thirty-kilometer front line were Tel Keppe and Batnaya, Christian villages taken by ISIS in 2014. Bashiqa was a mostly Yazidi and Kurdish town. Toward the south were more Christian towns such as Bartella, Karamlesh and Qaraqosh. In 2014, there had been up to a hundred thousand Christians living in these historic towns. They had all fled ISIS in June and July 2014, to Erbil. The whole of this front was bracketed by two main roads that served Mosul, both named Route 2. One road went to Mosul toward the southeast, past the Khazir River, Kalak and then to Erbil. The other branch left Mosul heading northeast toward Dohuk. In the old days these were the main trade routes out of Mosul to the Kurdish region. In 2014, refugees had used them to flee the extremists. In October 2014, it was where the terrible swift sword of war would be unsheathed and the whole power of the Iraqi army, Kurdish Peshmerga and the seventy-nine-member coalition would be unleashed against ISIS.

Down the road from Nawaran, there was an ambulance waiting to take out wounded, and several trucks with machine guns mounted on their backs. Kurds stood around and smoked. Some were coming back from the ongoing battle, to visit wounded comrades or rest. Others were walking forward. There didn't seem to be any control of who was doing what. On a hill to the south, several tanks – hidden behind dusty trenches – and coalition special forces watched over the battle. The coalition had slung up a series of posts on the hills overlooking Nineveh Plains. From there they directed fire and also sent out their special forces to join, quietly and largely unseen, the battle. Every time I'd approach a coalition temporary base, they would warn us off and demand we take no photos.

I walked down the road for several hundred meters. The Peshmerga had bulldozed a mound of dirt onto the road at the entrance of Nawaran, and the men were looking through binoculars into the village. Suddenly there was a huge explosion in the village. Smoke began to billow up. The Kurds cheered. Then the slow pitch of an incoming artillery shell hit the same spot again. The Peshmerga cheered again. For another minute, shells kept up their clockwork pounding of the village. ISIS didn't return fire.

On the outskirts of the village was a series of large warehouses. Several had been pancaked by air strikes and artillery fire, ripped apart, their frames now sticking into the air like long-dead metal creatures. There was no movement in the villages, no civilians running for cover. This area had been on the front for years, and the ISIS members had tunneled into the houses. Most civilians had either fled earlier or were huddled indoors somewhere.

To the south of the village, Peshmerga were driving trucks and Humvees into a field toward their new front line. To carve out the new positions as they expanded and liberated areas around the villages, they brought bulldozers and armored construction equipment such as back-hoes. Every once in a while, one would lumber back or forward along the road. Some had their tires torn up by mines and were limping back for repairs. One Humvee that came back had its entire front shredded from an IED. But it still was able to be driven.

I started to walk with some of the fighters. What began as dozens of armed men soon became a long line of dusty Peshmerga strung out along the road. They were young and old in a variety of uniforms. Some wore bandanas on their heads. Some wore matching uniforms, others not. Most carried AK-47s, some sniper rifles, rarely one carried an M-16 or German G-3. In the distance was the sound of sporadic gunfire and explosions from mortar shells. Artillery and air strikes rounded out the din.

The road felt exposed to snipers and mortars, and I got tired of the walking and hitched a ride with one of the many Peshmerga vehicles speeding by. A man wearing a tactical vest festooned with grenades grabbed my hand and lifted me onto the back of a pickup truck. He kept smiling a crazy grin as the grenades bounced back and forth from every dip in the road. I thought one of them would come loose somehow, its pin pulled, and we'd all be killed there, not by the enemy, but by this grinning man too happy with his grenades. The truck was stuffed with bedding, food, jugs and cans of water and fuel. An army marches on its stomach, I thought.

Eventually the truck came to a small traffic jam. A mortar team had unloaded its tube and positioned it next to the road to fire at the village of Fasalia. A sniper's bullet hit one of the tripod legs of the mortar. The men scattered for a second. Then they came back. Our truck drove off the road a bit and then back on to get around. There were supposed to be a lot of IEDs that ISIS liked to leave behind, and mines. But the men seemed oblivious to the threat. There was excitement. These men had been waiting for this day for years. Many had come and gone to various front lines since 2014, ten days on, twenty days off. Now they had come to fight. Victory was at hand. ISIS was weak, no longer the fearsome beast of 2014. But the men were still careful. They didn't want to enter the ISIS-held villages on both sides of the road. It made the situation precarious, because we were strung out along a long line of road, back to Nawaran. It could easily be cut by an attack. But ISIS was in no position to attack. It was estimated to have only five thousand fighters in Mosul, facing fifty thousand members of the Iraqi and Peshmerga forces. There were rumors that the village of Fasalia, north of Basiqa, had hundreds of ISIS fighters holed up in it. Kurds crouched behind a berm and fired into the village. A truck with a small rocket launcher on the back also let off several rounds.

There were casualties. As I'd sat there, several trucks took wounded back toward Nawaran. The ambulance that had been waiting came forward and then left. Reith, the American volunteer I'd met in Bashiqa in June, was on hand to help. There were also IDPs to be helped. Sometimes a truck carrying civilians would pass, the Peshmerga caked in dust, and the people would be taken to the rear.

Eventually darkness began to fall. Like at Bashiqa, some of the Peshmerga prayed. As the dark crept up, the gunfire grew more and more frequent. The tracers could be seen in the distance. The cold came on quickly. A unit of PAK had commandeered one of the liberated homes near Nawaran. They were settling in for dinner and brought out Styrofoam containers with rice and red sauce and beans. It filled the stomach. I gulped down some water, realizing the long day had led to dehydration. Some of the PAK members were fixing their heavy machine guns, taking them apart, oiling them, looking for some problem. A tubby American man who had volunteered with them stood around. He was one of many volunteers from the West who were serving with the Kurds, like Alan Duncan in Bashiqa. There were other foreign medical volunteers with a group called the Free Burma Rangers, and hangers-on who had come to help in some way. It had been a hard day for them, with numerous wounded.

It was October. Peshmerga men lit fires from old tires to keep warm. Trucks and Humvees passed back and forth, kicking up dust. Cigarette smoke mixed with the dust. The Peshmerga felt the day had gone badly; there had been more than a dozen wounded and several killed. Two men from the PAK, whose unit had helped lead the attack, were wounded; one later died. Kurds complained that the coalition had not provided enough air cover, instead using it to help the Iraqis on other front lines. They blamed the casualties on lack of support. The road the men were using to supply their units was hit by mortars and sniper fire. At night some former Peshmerga came with rifles to watch the fighting. One man showed up in a suit, having come from a wedding.

By the morning, the onlookers were gone. ISIS had attacked Kirkuk, and Erbil was suddenly focused on sending reinforcements to help Sarhad Qadir's police kill the sixty or so raiders. ISIS wanted to create a distraction and show it could still penetrate what was considered a safe area. At Nawaran, the Peshmerga settled in for a slow siege of the ISIS-held villages, moving street by street until they could clear them. Casualties were light. It seemed most of the ISIS fighters had fled over-night back toward Mosul and Bashiqa. But it would take until November 8 to reach Bashiqa and clear the villages around it. From the north near Telskuf, they liberated Batnaya, Qapisi, Abu Jarbuah, Terbaza, Tisxerab, Baz Khartan, Sheikh Amir and Badarli. The Peshmerga avoided going into most of the towns, waiting for residents to come out or for local forces such as the Christian Nineveh Plains Forces, who knew their own towns, to go in. It was the turn of the Iraqi army to do its job. The Peshmerga had secured the approaches to Mosul, but their forces were grinding to a halt. Bulldozers went forward and put up thirty kilometers of berms, trenches, positions. Now their neighbors would no longer be ISIS but the Iraqis, with Nineveh Plains neatly divided between the Kurdish and Iraqi flags, the sun and the stars.

Bartella and Gwer

As the Kurds assaulted ISIS positions, the Iraqi army was carrying out its own offensive toward Mosul further south. This would involve liberating a string of Christian towns and villages on the way to the suburbs of eastern Mosul. To get to the Iraqi front line required a long drive from Nawaran back toward Erbil, and then through Khazir toward Bartella. The road was straight, as if someone had just plopped it down amid the flat Nineveh Plains. On the hills to the north, where the Kurds were watching, ancient monasteries also kept a watch. The objective of the Iraqi army was to liberate Bartella and then move toward eastern Mosul.

Along the way, the war was laid out in reverse. Large refugee camps had been built near the Khazir River. A burned car from 2014 sat near the road. A husk of a suicide truck was being towed away. Closer to the front were Iraqi soldiers, relaxing and fattening up in a field near Karemlesh. They had a giant TOS-1 multiple-barrel rocket launcher, mounted on a tank chassis. The beast was capable of shooting twenty-four missiles at a time. It looked like something out of a video game, less like the kind of weapon one could use in a war like this. Its imprecision would destroy civilian houses and kill people. But the men manning it, mostly from southern Iraq, said they looked forward to seeing it in action.

ISIS was dug in nearby in Qaraqosh. The fires burned and the smoke billowed into the air. Every once in a while a huge explosion rang out. The Iraqi soldiers said the explosions were ISIS suicide bombers. Bartella had been liberated in one day of tough fighting, the ISOF (Iraqi Special Operations Forces) said. They were pouring in Humvees; we counted dozens moving forward. Each Humvee had a city name on its turret. Fallujah. Kut. Ramadi. Names of previous battles against ISIS, cities liberated and other Iraqi cities that troops had come from.

Many of the Iraqi counterterrorism personnel of ISOF were veterans of previous difficult battles. One of the men directing Humvee traffic into Bartella said he had fought in Fallujah and had helped to liberate Bartella. Another, waiting in the back seat of his Humvee, said he had joined the Iraqi army in 2009. He was now twenty-seven years old and had fought at Hit, Falujah and Ramadi. Like many of the other ISOF members, he wore a T-shirt underneath his tactical uniform with an image of a skull. Others had black masks emblazoned with a white skull. It gave the ISOF a fearsome look, as if they had come to reap what ISIS had sowed. No quarter would be given. ISIS had let loose such death and slaughter; the Iraqi army, its counterterror forces, and its Shi'ite militias would avenge what had been done in 2014.

A Kurdish soldier serving with the ISOF named Ahmed al-Buhari said that the battles were difficult. "The resistance is strengthening. There are many suicide attacks. There are snipers, and we suffered eighty casualties yesterday." As we watched smoke billowing from Qaraqosh in the background, amid the crackle of gunfire and explosions, an Arab man dressed in a long white robe and kaffiyeh came up to watch as well. He was followed by a small coterie of journalists and hangers-on. He said he was Ahmed al-Jarba, a member of the Iraqi parliament who was living in Erbil but whose constituency was in Mosul. "I have many relatives from Mosul who are now living in Dohuk and Erbil," he said. He praised the efforts of the Hashd al-Watani, the mostly Sunni Arab force trained by the Turks. But the Sunni Hashd was nowhere to be seen here. Jarba thought that the Iraqi army would be inside the city limits of Mosul in four days, and he hoped that the battle would go quickly and not destroy civilian areas.

The Iraqi army was advancing on Qaraqosh from two sides. From Bartella and Khazir, it had moved through Karamlesh and then into the large Christian town, once home to fifty thousand people. From the other side, the Iraqi 9th Armored Division was moving from the south. On the first day of their attack on October 20, several MRAPs in a scouting unit of the 9th Armored Division had been captured by ISIS, and their men had fled. ISIS put up videos bragging of its accomplishment, showing a bearded ISIS member with a white kaffiyeh and an M-16 rifle looting the vehicles. It was not an auspicious start.

We drove down to Gwer, to the bridge on the Great Zab River that the Iraqis had to cross to move forward. Gwer was a dusty town that looked semi-abandoned. It still had graffiti from when it had been fought over between ISIS and the Peshmerga. On the river the Peshmerga manned a series of sandbagged positions. On a hill overlooking the river was a base with coalition troops monitoring the battle.

To slow the advance, on October 21, ISIS burned a sulfur plant that was south of Mosul on the road to Qayyarah. The fumes belched into the air and caused breathing problems for thousands in Qayarrah. When we arrived at Gwer, we could see the smoke from the chemical fire in the distance on the other side of the Tigris. With the help of a local driver, we poked our way forward. The bridge on the Great Zab River was partly destroyed, and we had to put rocks down to get the car through. Meanwhile, Iraqi army supply trucks, flying Shi'ite flags, drove past to supply the front. Every Iraqi army vehicle seemed festooned with the sectarian flags. Even the M1A1 Abrams tanks had them. Americans who had supplied the tanks probably never thought they would be adorned with slogans about the Imam Ali and Imam Hussein, or that the soldiers manning them might carry pictures of the Ayatollah Khamenei into battle.

In the fall of 2016, Iraq's army was increasingly sectarian, and the US advisers who often served at the command level of these units had no say over what flags they put on the vehicles. The Kurdish Peshmerga watching the Iraqi armored vehicles make their way forward were also suspicious. One Peshmerga said that if he were in charge, he wouldn't permit the vehicles to cross his line.

The unity displayed by the Peshmerga and Iraqi army for the first week of the Mosul offensive didn't seem like it would last past that. Years of fighting separately and recriminations about who was at fault for the fall of Mosul in 2014 had led to this point. From the Kurdish perspective, the policies of Nouri al-Maliki had inflamed the Sunni Arabs and the Iraqi army had abandoned Mosul and northern Iraq in 2014, leaving the Kurds to face the extremists alone. Kurds had been forced to retreat from Sinjar, and thousands had been killed. The Iraqi army had also abandoned thousands of vehicles in their retreat, and Kurds said these weapons had then been turned against the Peshmerga in August 2014. The fickle and weak Iraqi central government showed why the Kurds must seek independence and couldn't trust the nonfunctioning Baghdad government. Iraq is finished, they said. Let it divorce. Baghdad had confiscated the Kurdish region's budget, plunging civil servants into poverty and forcing the Peshmerga to go hat in hand to the coalition. Baghdad also kept essential equipment and weapons from the Peshmerga, hogging them for its own forces.

The Iraqi Shi'ite politicians and soldiers saw things differently. They accused the Kurds of watching with delight as ISIS attacked the Sunni areas. The Kurds had retreated to Kurdish areas and then defended their own land, leaving the rest of Iraq to suffer. They said Kurds had even abandoned Sinjar, leaving Yazidis to fend for themselves. It was Ayatollah Ali al-Sistani and his fatwa that helped stop ISIS at the gates of Baghdad. Since then the Iraqi army and PMU had lost thousands of men retaking Iraq. The Kurds had played little role, they said. The Kurds had just dug in and watched the war unfold and stayed on the defensive. Every major operation had been carried out by the Iraqi army, they bragged. Kurds had used the last two years to take over Kirkuk and export their own oil and enrich themselves, while the rest of Iraq fought. The Kurds wanted to secede from Iraq and used ISIS as an excuse to do so.

There was some truth to both sides and their narratives. The coalition, however, was not interested in squabbling. It wanted to defeat ISIS and devoted itself to this mission alone.

"The coalition continues to advance into Mosul from different axes, and we are talking about ten to twenty kilometers from the city and have retaken many villages," coalition spokesman John Dorrian told me on October 23.[110] I was sitting at a branch of the Barista coffee shop in Erbil. Music played in the background. Despite the massive offensive unfolding just an hour's drive away, the coffee shops were full. People were enjoying themselves. A man modeled for a photographer, with a well-cropped beard and lumberjack-style shirt. Erbil was the center of a new hipster trend, it seemed. Not far from the hipsters in Erbil, coalition aircraft were carrying out sorties. On October 23, aircraft struck five ISIS units, twelve staging areas, sixteen mortars, rocket launchers, three heavy machine guns, twenty-one fighting positions, eight vehicles, command and control centers, seven buildings, five bunkers, four anti-aircraft guns, artillery, tunnels, three vehicle-borne improvised explosive devices (VBIEDs) and a shop used to make VBIEDs.

Dorrian characterized ISIS resistance as "light to moderate" and said the coalition was "conducting a relentless air and artillery campaign to support the Iraqi advance." A total of fifteen hundred munitions had been dropped in the first week of battle and twenty-two VBIEDs destroyed, along with sixty-six other vehicles and fourteen tunnels, as well as fifty-two mortars and artillery pieces. "One immutable truth about air power supporting a ground campaign is that you want as much as you can possibly get, and we understand that dynamic because the Iraqi counterterrorism forces are our partners, and they are fighting for their lives and freedom against a determined enemy." The coalition had stepped up its operation to help the offensive move forward and was conducting more strikes and dropping more ordnance than at any time during the two-year campaign. "The Iraqis and Peshmerga are risking their lives against an enemy that threatens every corner of the world." As a comparison, he noted that the coalition had conducted ten thousand strikes in two years.

The coalition had sent advisers and coordinators to embed with the units closer to the front; the coalition said this was helping them coordinate and sequence their attacks. "Some of this depends on what the enemy does; as they get closer into dense urban terrain, we may need to make some adjustments," said Dorrian. The coalition was effusive in praising the role of the ISOF "Golden Division," which Dorrian called the "crown jewel" of Iraq's army. "The highest level of troops put them up there with some of the best light infantry in the world. We spent a lot of time training and working with them. It's impressive to see."

The coalition felt the advance on Mosul had gone well the first week. "People must understand that once you uncork an operation of this size, scope and magnitude, we knew we would see attacks like the sulfur attack, or spoiler attacks like in Kirkuk; what they are trying to do is deflect attention from Mosul." The coalition also tempered any high hopes for a quick battle. They expected it to be difficult.

Over the skies of Iraq and Syria in late October and early November, the warplanes of a dozen countries congregated. In Iraq, this included Australia, Belgium, Canada, Denmark, France, Jordan, the Netherlands, the UK and the United States. In Syria, several Gulf states – Bahrain, the UAE and Saudi Arabia – and Turkey were added to that list. The coalition made most of its strikes and data for the campaign public, listing them on its Inherent Resolve website. The coalition maintained active Twitter accounts and Facebook throughout the war. It was probably the first war conducted with such rigor online and with such an attempt to provide as much information as possible to the public about daily strikes on the enemy.

The Desert March

"Our mission is to liberate our country," Hadi al-Amiri, a leader of the Badr Organization, told reporters two weeks into the Mosul offensive. Like an embarrassing family member, he was relegated to sit out the massive offensive at a small outpost south of Mosul where the Shi'ite militias had concentrated thousands of men and a gaggle of military vehicles and trucks uparmored to serve their units. Like the Peshmerga, the Shi'ite militias gathered around Amiri brought a variety of uniforms and weapons to the front. Some were fat men in white shirts and with fatigues for pants, others had dark green uniforms, others desert tan. Some wore green bands on their heads with religious slogans, white and black kaffiyehs around their necks to wick away the sweat.

Amiri told reporters that his men had been told to stay out of the Mosul operation. They had come to a different agreement with the Peshmerga and Iraqi army. The militias would conquer the desert to the west of Mosul, cutting off any avenue for ISIS retreat. Eventually their area of operation would stretch a hundred kilometers to the west, to the Syrian border. This was the area ISIS had emerged from in 2014. It would be driven out the way it had come. "If we have to, we will go to Syria," Amiri told the Los Angeles Times. "Because we believe if Daesh is not finished in Syria, then they will be a real danger to Iraq."[111]

Flying the red and light green flags with images of Iraq and a fist clenched with a rifle over it, the militiamen set off on a long desert march to secure the left flank of Mosul. Eventually it would take them around sixty kilometers to the northwest, and they would liberate around two thousand square kilometers by the end of November. They took one after another of the major roads ISIS had used to transfer ordnance between Raqqa and Mosul. In 2014, thousands of Yazidi women had been taken on buses down these roads to be sold. On November 23, 2016, the PMU finally reached Peshmerga lines west of Tal Afar. Amiri came to the front and met with Peshmerga commander Sarbast Tiranshi at his base in Ain Hisan. "There is no way out – Mosul is surrounded," Ammar al-Musawi, PMU spokesman, told reporters in early December, when the militias had solidified their control. Dozens of villages had been liberated. ISIS had mostly surrendered the landscape, melting back into the desert from where it had come.[112]

There were fears of reprisals as the militias rolled into the desert. "We used to find dozens of bodies each morning in Baghdad: if they'd been decapitated that was usually Sunni jihadist death squads, if they'd been drilled with an electric power tool that was normally a Shia death squad," British Maj. Gen. Simon Mayall recalled in a speech about his time in Iraq just before the US-led surge in 2006.[113] Many of the militia leaders from that era of tit-for-tat killings in Baghdad were now in charge west of Mosul. Just as the al Qaeda members had become ISIS members, the Shi'ite militias that were just sorting themselves out after 2003 had now matured. On November 22, 2016, the Iraqi parliament legalized the militias and made them an official paramilitary force. Now they were fighting under their sectarian banners but also under the flag of Iraq. Abadi said they would defend all Iraqis. Iraqi Sunnis and Kurds were skeptical. But there was little they could do.

Life and Death in the Garden of Aden

"I will not abandon my position as long as I am alive," said graffiti written in Kurdish on a building held by Peshmerga near Bartella. The Peshmerga had stopped their advance. Their men scanned the horizon with binoculars and watched the Iraqi army vehicles lumbering in the fields. "If we spill blood, it is only for independence," said President Barzani in March 2016.[114] "What is important for us is Kurdistan's borders. We will decide the extent of our borders by what has been liberated with the blood of our Peshmerga," Nechirvan Barzani, the prime minister, was quoted by the television station Kurdistan 24 as saying in July. This was the sentiment in the Kurdish region.[115]

At a hospital in Erbil, I went to visit a Kurdish man wounded in October in Kirkuk, when ISIS had tried to enter the city in a diversion. After two days of battles and more than a hundred casualties, the Kurds had killed the dozens of ISIS fighters. One of the Kurds who was wounded was shot in the neck. I went with his family to see him. He couldn't speak but grasped the hands of his relatives. For the Kurds, these would be the last casualties of two years of war. For the Iraqi army, the bloodletting would go on.

On the outskirts of Mosul, the ISOF scanned the skyline. The battles against ISIS in Bartella and Qaraqosh had gone quickly. Armored vehicles had rolled over IEDs, and coalition air cover had devastated ISIS units that tried to move in the open. Now the Iraqis thought that they could walk into Mosul the way the Americans had into Baghdad in 2003. In April of that year, US forces approaching Baghdad feared that intense street fighting and urban war could result in a bloody end to the Iraq war. However, after a rapid approach to Baghdad, elements of the US Army's 3rd Infantry Division executed a "thunder run," driving their tanks and vehicles into the center of Baghdad, surprising the resistance and capturing the city. Now Mosul was set to witness the same thing.

On the flat plain east of Mosul, the Iraqi Counter Terrorism Service's Iraqi Special Operations Forces punched a hole in the Islamic State defense and attacked Bazwaya, Gogjali and Karama, interconnected neighborhoods and villages east of the city center. Using masses of black Humvees, the ISOF tried to charge into the city. Many of the neighborhoods being fought over were empty of civilians. Before the war, eastern Mosul was populated by Kurds, Shabaks, Assyrians and other minority groups that had fled the city when ISIS arrived. According to the undercover blogger tweeting under the name Mosul Eye, who lived in Mosul under ISIS occupation, the ISIS fighters were heavily present in this eastern area in mid-October, when the Mosul offensive was launched. They had abandoned their headquarters, likely due to threat of air strikes.

"Soldiers of the Counter Terrorism Service are advancing very fast," General Talib Shegati told Iraqiya TV. He thought they would be inside the city limits on October 31. The distance from where the Iraqis were to the city center is about five kilometers. "We will start cleansing the city of Mosul from terrorism," the Iraqi general thought.

There was a problem, though. The ISOF had no other forces on its flanks to help get them into the city. The 9th Armored Division moved slowly after taking Ali Rash, a village eight kilometers to the southeast. Iraqi units that were supposed to attack Hamam al-Alil did not reach their objective, amid UN reports that ISIS had brought sixty thousand human shields into the town. The Iraqi 16th Division had stalled near Tel Yabis, northeast of the city. Nevertheless, the ISOF decided to move into the wide, grid-like streets of eastern Mosul. This was the modern and wealthier part of the city, compared to the Old City on the west bank, with its warren of small streets. In eastern Mosul, drones could easily track enemy movements. ISIS had warned that the city was festooned with IEDs and that it would light up "rivers of oil." But this imagery that conjured up the Battle of Berlin in 1945 was not materializing.

There was some evidence of the threat ISIS still posed. As the Iraqi army moved into the suburbs, it found one tunnel that stretched for three kilometers under the city. Photos inside showed little in the way of creature comforts, except for lights attached to wooden planks fixed across the top of the tunnel every few meters. In Sheikh Amir, a crew from *Time* said they found documents that explained the rules for provisioning the tunnels. Solar panels would be placed near an entrance to charge smartphones and other "devices."[116] Food for a month should be kept in a storeroom. Men shouldn't gather at the entrance or in the open. Entrances were concealed inside houses. "Metal frames" reinforced the walls in some places, but like most other tunnels, it consisted of dirt walls.

Hamid Alkshali watched his CNN colleagues leave for the battle in Mosul on the morning of November 4. He was on the outskirts of the city and had watched CNN senior international correspondent Arwa Damon and photojournalist Brice Laine load their gear into an MRAP and join a column of thirty ISOF armored vehicles and drive into the city.[117] They were joined by another convoy of vehicles close behind. In all, two regiments were involved in the operation. They left as the sun rose. The objective was to liberate the neighborhood of Aden. Five hours later, news of disaster emerged.

ISIS had waited until the first thirty-five vehicles passed and then ambushed the column. The second group of vehicles, nicknamed Kirkuk, retreated. They told Alkshali that ISIS was firing from the houses just meters away. Many of the Humvees and MRAPs were damaged. Suicide bombs had targeted the trapped convoy, the Salahuddin Regiment. The ISOF commanders were not too concerned. Their men had fought like this, house to house, in other battles. They had enough equipment to survive if cut off. So the commanders hunkered down for the night and ISOF sent a third regiment, nicknamed Diyala, to try to extract them.

By the next morning, the ISOF had sent more of its limited resources into Aden to try to extract the lost regiment. With Kirkuk and Diyala regiments unable to break through, the Mosul regiment was sent in with its thirty-six humvees. Eventually they were able to break through the ISIS ambush and save the journalists, as well as their comrades. Many vehicles were abandoned in the battle. They were among the toughest twenty-four hours of his life, Alkshali recalled. "To see my colleagues walking toward me in one piece fills me with indescribable joy." For dozens of ISOF members and their vehicles, there was no joy. ISIS had showed it could ambush and destroy one after another of the elite unit's columns. Later ISIS published video and photos showing their fighters stripping the Iraqi vehicles and taking the weapons from them. ISIS had shown that it could withstand the might of the Iraqi army and its "crown jewel."

On December 2, the United Nations Assistance Mission for Iraq (UNAMI) released casualty figures for the month of November. A total of 1,959 members of the Iraqi Security Forces had been killed and 450 injured.[118] The figures included members of the Peshmerga and the police and were for the whole country. "Daesh has been employing the most vicious tactics" in the battle for Mosul, the UN secretary general's special representative for Iraq, Jan Kubis, said.

The casualty numbers were staggering. They were also likely incorrect. There were only around eighteen thousand Iraqi soldiers in the Counter Terrorism Service, the 9th Armored Division and the 16th Infantry Division, which were engaged in the Mosul fighting. If nineteen hundred soldiers had been killed, along with the 670 estimated to have died in October, the fighting force would be devastated. On December 3, UNAMI said it would discontinue publishing data on military personnel killed and that its previous count was "largely unverified." The Iraqi Joint Operation Command had criticized the figures.

With casualty figures hazy, there was other bad news for the Mosul operation. By December, around seventy-seven thousand civilians had fled the city, but 650,000 remained trapped under ISIS. With the city surrounded and electricity outages common, there was fear of a humanitarian disaster. UNICEF claimed that a burst pipeline would force residents to resort to "unsafe water sources." Even in liberated areas in the eastern part of the city, water supply was intermittent. Residents said they refused to leave. "It is safe here, better than other places."

Iraq's Ministry of Migration and Displacement had come north to distribute food. The truth of life in Mosul was more complex than presented. Most Moslawis, the people of Mosul, lived under ISIS in relative peace. I remembered my interviews in 2015 with people who had fled ISIS to Erbil and how some of their relatives remained behind.

As the Iraqi army slowed its advance, the coalition was also reducing its air strikes. On December 6, the Combined Joint Task Force–Operation Inherent Resolve report noted that the coalition had used three air strikes near Mosul to hit an "ISIL tactical unit, a VBIED and an excavator." The day before, they had done better, taking out four mortars, three vehicles, a heavy machine gun, a bridge and a front-end loader. Yet ISIS could still counterattack. When Iraqi forces took al-Salam Hospital on December 5, ISIS took part of it back during the night. It also released a video of British hostage John Cantlie speaking about air strikes that had destroyed four bridges across the Tigris in November. It showed Cantlie was still alive, the only Western hostage ISIS had not executed.

The US presidential election had also changed the Mosul timeline. During the campaign, there was an increased tempo in driving the Mosul offensive, and Clinton indicated she hoped that it would be winding up by 2017. But the election changed those calculations. The Obama administration was packing up and preparing for Donald Trump to take over. This could complicate the war in Iraq. Trump had vowed to move the US embassy in Israel from Tel Aviv to Jerusalem, and this had ramifications in Iraq. In January 2017, Shi'ite cleric, politician and militia leader Muqtada al-Sadr called for the formation of a special force to "liberate Jerusalem," in response to claims Trump would move the embassy to Israel's capital. Sadr called the potential embassy move a "declaration of war on Islam" and threatened the US embassy in Baghdad.

Trump also put forward a ban on refugees from Iraq entering the US. The US had spent $181 million to assist IDPs in Iraq in 2016. In response to Trump's policy, a Kurdish man in Erbil said the US consulate had told those holding Iraqi passports with a US visa to postpone trips to the United States until April, when the ninety-day moratorium expired: "Regrettably, the Trump ban includes citizens from Iraqi Kurdistan, the closest ally to the US in fighting terrorism." Other Kurds who had been fighting ISIS felt the same, wondering why they should be punished for having an Iraqi passport when it is others who are extremists. In 2015, there were twelve thousand refugees entering the United States from Iraq. According to the Pew Research Center, the US admitted 12,500 Syrian refugees in 2016 and ninety-eight hundred from Iraq.[119]

The sense of continuity in the coalition would be retained along with Brett McGurk. Trump also sought to appoint several generals to his team, including James Mattis for defense secretary, Michael Flynn as national security adviser and John Kelly at Homeland Security. Flynn would soon be out, replaced by H. R. McMaster as national security adviser in February. McMaster had been an expert on fighting the Iraqi insurgency and was familiar with Tal Afar and the area near Mosul.

Chapter 16
The Battle for Mosul

ISIS Survival 101

As the Iraqi army penetrated deeper into Mosul, it began to come upon evidence of how ISIS had survived and thrived for two years in the city.[120] The group was facing a growing seventy-member coalition, but it was still amply supplied with food and electricity up until the final months of the battle.

In early November, after the Iraqi special operations forces had cleared the village of Gogjali on the eastern edge of Mosul city, they came across a hundred bags of sorbitol manufactured by the French company Tereos. These were found alongside a bag of potassium nitrate made by the Turkish company Toros. Sorbitol is a sugar substitute that "IS forces use ... in the production of rocket propellant," noted a research paper released on December 4, 2017, by Conflict Armament Research, an organization devoted to identifying and tracking conventional weapons and ammunition in conflicts.[121]

The sorbitol had been produced in 2015, a year after ISIS's worst atrocities. Yet even as Turkey was securing its border with a concrete wall along the areas ISIS occupied in Syria, the group was apparently still able to acquire supplies and transport them through Syria to Iraq. "Such a large quantity of chemical precursor, originating from the same manufacturer, and produced at the same time, suggests large-scale diversion and a single supply source," the report noted.[122] ISIS operated a sophisticated centralized supply network, procuring chemicals for its IEDs and also manufacturing mortars and others weapons it needed.

The twenty-month investigation Conflict Armament Research published in February 2016 noted that "except for locally available material, such as steel, IS forces source most of the products used to manufacture explosive weapons from Turkey."[123] Furthermore, "these findings indicate that the group has, first, a major acquisition network operating in Turkey and, second, a clear supply route from Turkey, through Syria, to Iraq."

At its height ISIS had access to some fifty thousand fighters, many of them foreign volunteers who traveled through Turkey from points in Europe, Chechnya, Tunisia and elsewhere. Initially ISIS relied on more than two thousand vehicles it captured from the Iraqi army in June 2014 to make its gains in Iraq and to solidify control of a corridor along the Euphrates River in Syria. Air strikes by the coalition had destroyed most of these vehicles by 2015.

The extremists embarked on a major program of building small factories to manufacture standardized weapons. Conflict Armament Research found manuals for producing rockets, with specifications for 9.5-kilogram warheads and detailed specs for 120 mm mortars, among other calibers. To build tubes to fire the mortars, ISIS used steel pipes. Conflict Armament Research documented two foundries for producing weapons in Gogjali, east of Mosul, that were located near scrap metal dumps. They discovered that the group cut car engine blocks into pieces for use. ISIS not only built an extensive network of tunnels, but it also sought to increase the effectiveness of its IEDs, something the coalition eventually sought to train the Iraqi army, Peshmerga and Syrian Democratic Forces to confront.

To build the explosives and propellants, ISIS needed supplies. Although many supplies came from Turkey, one bag Conflict Armament Research found was made by the Lebanese Al Khaleej Sugar in January 2015 and sold to the Ministry of Trade in Baghdad. Somehow ISIS got ahold of it, either through smuggling or through capture. Aluminum found near Mosul and Fallujah was fabricated at Metkim Kimyevi Maddeler in Turkey. "The batch numbers of these items indicated transactions dated October 2014 to January 2015 respectively," noted the report. Lubricants used in ISIS factories were made as late as September 2015. Fertilizers bags discovered in Tikrit after its liberation from ISIS control were also found to have come from Turkey in 2015. Detonators left behind by ISIS near Makhmour were found to have originated in Austria.

Conflict Armament Research called the supply route through Turkey a key "choke point" involved in stopping the supplies. In June 2016, Turkey's agriculture minister stopped sales of nitrate fertilizer after a car bombing. By that time ISIS had stockpiled quantities throughout Syria and Iraq. As the group prepared for its last stand in Mosul and Raqqa, much of these materials would be used to deadly effect.

When I drove into Mosul in March 2016, the evidence of this ISIS supply network was on display. At a shop in the Jadida neighborhood in eastern Mosul, there was a WIDO brand saw blade, abandoned by its owners as the Iraqi Federal Police took over the neighborhood. It fit a circular saw and was sold by a company in Suzhou, China. How had ISIS been able to import saw blades and civilian items while under siege? This was one of many questions about how ISIS survived from 2014 into 2017. It was producing high-quality propaganda films, often just a day or so after an event. For instance, after the Aden battle, it put out videos of ISIS members looting the trucks. Why wasn't the coalition able to target the ISIS media and communications network? ISIS also traded female slaves online, and yet little to nothing was done to track the networks on the Telegram internet instant messaging service and other apps.

In another hardware store in Mosul, I found a box of SEGA Fix adhesives from Turkey. There were lawnmowers from a firm called FERM B.V. from the Netherlands. All this had been imported after 2014. In Qaraqosh, the large Christian town, I found bags of potassium nitrate made in the Russian Federation. Imported to Iraq, they had been hidden in a church, in an improvised lab for making IEDs.

A report by Conflict Armament Research in December 2016, titled "Standardization and Quality Control in Islamic State's Military Production," suggests that ISIS was able to acquire massive amounts of goods even as the noose tightened around it. "Production dates spanning a range of years suggest that ISIS forces have made repeated acquisitions of identical products from the same sources – almost exclusively from the Turkish domestic market."[124] It was evidence of a "robust supply chain extending from Turkey, through Syria, to Mosul." The researchers concluded that there was a "major acquisition network in Turkey" operated by Islamic State and that there was a "direct line of supply." Not all the ISIS material was new. But other quantities of sorbitol were made by French company Tereos in 2015, at the height of the war on Islamic State. Sugar from the Chekka refinery in Lebanon was made in November 2015. Conflict Armament Research found products such as grease packaging produced by the Turkish company Petrol Ofisi in September 2015.

The supplies came to ISIS the same way the estimated thirty to fifty thousand foreign volunteers came. According to a 2015 report by the Institute for Economics and Peace, seven thousand had come in the first six months of 2015.[125] The Soufan Group estimated that thirty-one thousand fighters came to Syria and Iraq and that up to five thousand were from Europe as well as six thousand Tunisians, thousands from Russia and thousands from Turkey.

Not only was ISIS able to bring in men and material, it was also receiving money directly from Baghdad. The Iraqi government continued to pay pensions and salaries of state employees within areas run by Islamic State. In July 2015, that stopped. "All such payments have been halted, depriving whole cities' pensioners, civil servants, doctors, teachers, nurses, police and workers...of both their income and some of their last official links to Baghdad," wrote Reuters.[126] The proportion of Iraq's population held by Islamic State at its high point was around 15 percent. So 150 billion dinars a year might have accounted for salaries in its area, which is around $150 million.

A similar thing took place in Syria, where Damascus only cut off salaries in 2015. In many ways, Islamic State replaced the existing financial institutions and even replicated them, handing out subsidies for agricultural yields, for instance. The Associated Press reported in February 2016, relying on expert reports by Middle East Forum fellow Aymenn Jawad al-Tamimi, that Islamic State was cutting salaries to its own fighters and had begun to rely on US dollars in its economy. But people in ISIS-land were still receiving remittances from abroad, even in 2016.[127]

Electricity also functioned in Islamic State areas, thanks to the central governments in Syria and Baghdad, which kept paying for it and not bombing the generators. Even more bizarre is that when the Iraqi army liberated eastern Mosul, Islamic State cut off the power lines leading to eastern Mosul from its western Mosul Lazakah power station. At the height of the Mosul siege, ISIS held the keys to electricity, and people under its control had better access than those in the liberated areas.

ISIS also sold oil. According to a report in the *Financial Times*, through October 2015, when the coalition began targeting Islamic State oil supplies, it was earning up to $1.5 million a day via "a highly organized system, [in which] Syrian and Iraqi buyers go directly to the oil fields with their trucks to buy crude."[128] As with the oil, the coalition air strikes didn't begin seriously concentrating on Islamic State boats and barges plying the Euphrates until the fall of 2016. In the modern history of warfare, there has rarely been an example of an enemy entity having such open borders to trade, even via the states at war with it. That is because the war with ISIS was something new and different.

The Road to Western Mosul

"Get ready to welcome the sons of your armed forces and to cooperate with them, as your brothers on the left side [of the Tigris River] have done, in order to reduce losses and speed up the conclusion," read thousands of leaflets dropped over western Mosul on February 18, 2017. Emblazoned with Iraqi flags, they informed residents that the last phase of the battle for ISIS's last major stronghold in Iraq was about to begin. "The Iraqi security forces are going to be able to liberate the city. Daesh is going to be crushed in west Mosul. It is going to be finished," US Colonel John Dorrian, the spokesman for the US-led Combined Joint Task Force – Operation Inherent Resolve, told reporters.[129]

After eastern Mosul had finally been cleared in January, the Iraqi army began preparing for the liberation of the western half. This was expected to be difficult because it would be punching into the dense warren of streets in Old Mosul. It would also mean conquering the Nuri Mosque, where Abu Bakr al-Baghdadi had declared the "caliphate" in 2014. ISIS was cut off and expected to fight to the last.

To advance on western Mosul, the Iraqi army would use its Federal Police and Emergency Response Division while ISOF rested. The Federal Police moved up from Qayarrah through Hamam al-Alil. Hamam al-Alil is named for a famous sulfur spring and traditional bathhouse where local men would gather and rest in tubs or lie on benches while smothered in restorative mud to take in the waters. Soldiers rested at the spa, bathed, and moved on, a bizarre respite in the midst of war.

The advance in western Mosul went smoothly in its opening days. Around eighty square kilometers were taken leading up to Mosul's airport. The BBC's Quentin Sommerville, who was embedded with the Federal Police, said he saw no civilians in the first two days of battle. UK Maj. Gen. Rupert Jones, a commander with the coalition, told the BBC that it could take months to take all of western Mosul.

Along the way, the Iraqi army made a horrendous discovery. At a sinkhole outside Mosul called Khasfa, thousands of bodies were found. According to locals, the killing began in June 2014, when ISIS rolled into the city and targeted anyone who had worked for Baghdad. "I saw it with my own eyes. They brought people from Mosul or Qayarrah," Yaser Ahmed told The National in 2018.[130] "I was herding sheep and I saw Daesh shoot them with pistols and machine guns." Mass executions went on for a year. "ISIS would bring in people every day after 10 p.m. We could hear the gunshots and the screaming," Saad Abdullah told Human Rights Watch.[131] The locals said blood dripped into the area's wells. The smell wafted into the air for more than a mile around. But the sinkhole was not done claiming victims. Rudaw reporter Shifa Gardi came to report on the mass grave and was killed by an IED that ISIS had left behind, on February 25, 2017.

I arrived a month after Gardi had been killed. Along with a local fixer named Majd Helobi, I drove out toward the new front line. Part of the road was well known. Out toward Khazir over the river, swollen from rain, and toward Bartella. Then, next to the berm where the liberation of Nineveh Plains had begun in October 2016, Majd steered our white Toyota Land Cruiser to the left. Trucks were waiting in a long line to drive toward Mosul. There was a new antenna for cell phone coverage, erected by the Kurdish firm Korek. The Kurdish flags fluttered in the rearview mirror, and the Iraqi flags flew in front of us. Here was where one political system ended and another began.

As we turned left, the road became empty. "All the villages here are dominated by the Hashd," Majd said. The PMU had set up a dozen checkpoints between the Kurdish front line and Mosul. Eventually the road ascended a slight curve and entered the town of Qaraqosh. The

Nineveh Plains Protection Units, a Christian militia affiliated with the PMU, guarded the town. As we made our way through the liberated ghost town, we passed churches that had been burned and partially demolished by ISIS. At one the bell tower lay at an angle, ripped from its foundation and wedged between a wall and the nave. A small, concrete shed serving as a checkpoint was emblazoned in English with "Jesus loves." Down the road were old trenches from before 2014, used to defend Qaraqosh and abandoned in the face of the ISIS onslaught. A burned Iraqi army vehicle lay next to the road. Eventually we passed several more villages. The Sunni Arab residents kept their eyes askance; they didn't want to look at the cars coming through. They seemed in fear and in defeat. At each turn, I wondered if the Shi'ite militias would stop our car, ask for passports and turn us around. But they smiled as they saw Majd and waved us through.

The road took a sharp left and headed parallel to the Tigris. It passed next to the ancient city of Nimrud, once an Assyrian city, bulldozed and demolished by ISIS. We could see the mounds of the archaeological site in the distance. Then the road took another sharp right, and we drove toward the river. The Iraqi army had erected a pontoon bridge over the Tigris. It seemed rickety and low in the water. But our SUV made it over. At the other side was a checkpoint with a Shi'ite flag fluttering. It showed the double-headed Zulfiqar – the sword of Imam Ali – with blood dripping from it. An auspicious sign, surely. From there the road came to a major highway that stretched south to Qayarrah and north toward Mosul. Our path was now joined by other Toyotas, the SUV of choice, it seemed. Federal Police units in various blue vehicles also clogged the way. Civilians and refugee camps near Hamam al-Alil stretched into the distance.

At a local media center run by the Federal Police and the Emergency Response Division, other journalists were waiting around, lacing up boots and sipping hot coffee. It was morning and a bit cold. Residents of the village, down a muddy road in their small, one-story homes, looked out at the Iraqi army that had come to sit in their neighborhood. An uparmored white ISIS car sat in the driveway, a spoil of war.

Across the road was the headquarters of the massive military operation. The Federal Police and the Emergency Response Division, as well as the coalition, were poring over maps and computer screens. Helicopters took off intermittently. A drone buzzed in the air. Unlike the ISOF with its black Humvees, the Federal Police had painted theirs dark blue with little white blotches. It wasn't exactly camoflouge.

From the media office in Hamam al-Alil, the Emergency Response Division took us into the city. We passed a large factory, silhouted against the cloudy sky. A herd of buffalos plodded by. The road passed by the Tigris River and then came up to the Mosul airport. More factories, these broken and ruined from the war, were on the left side of the road. On the left was a line of Iraqi artillery and rocket launchers. After circumnavigating the airport, we came to an old boulevard and a street sign reading, "Mosul Airport, Mosul Hospital, Al-Mansor, Baghdad." On the wide street was a burned bus and dozens of people crowded around a truck. A local NGO had brought eggs to give away to the civilians. One of them paused to talk. "It's a black city; it was once great before ISIS, but ISIS brought the black flag, and that symbolizes what has happened here. There is no work, everything is destroyed. There will not be peace or safety in the future," said the man, who gave his name as Said.

Gunfire rang out in the background. Tat, tat, tat. The refugees shuffled off in pairs and threes. One group of women, all in black abayas, escorted a little girl wearing a colorful dress. When the girl looked back at me, I saw half her face had been burned and was healing.

Majd and the Emergency Response Division escort drove deeper into the city. They said it was the Agadat neighborhood, and we got out to walk around. It had been liberated recently. On a small hill, next to an old house, was some trash. Among it was the half-burned body of a man, his spine sticking out of soggy, plastic-like flesh. Next to a wall that ran around the old house, a man came out. He beckoned us inside, where he showed us to mounds in the yard. These were his brothers, whom ISIS had executed. He had buried them himself. We left the yard, walked over the dead body and came to a street barricaded by burned cars. An elderly man sat in a plastic chair, his bandaged foot propped up on another chair. The sun had come out, and he was relaxing. Only five families had stayed in the neighborhood after liberation. There was no water and no electricity. Every family seemed to have lost someone in the war. The residents described life under ISIS as difficult but not impossible. They pointed to one house on the street used by ISIS as a jail for locals. Those caught smoking cigarettes or committing other minor infractions were kept there. We poked our heads in. The jail had been burned, but the bars ISIS put on the rooms were visible. It had once been a pretty house, confiscated from those who fled.

The Emergency Response Division was excited to show us an ISIS arms factory, so we drove up the hill next to a mosque. The Federal Police had taken over the mosque, partly ruined in the fighting, and put up Shi'ite flags on the minaret. In the ISIS factory were hundreds of mortars, perfectly formed but never completed. In one room in the houses there was a mural; it was another wealthy home confiscated from the owners. ISIS had blotted out the images of people and horses' heads. They feared idolatary.

When we were done seeing the mortar factory, we got back in the SUVs and made our way back. At one Federal Police local headquarters, Shi'ite flags and posters of Ayatollah Ali Khamanei and Ayatollah Ali al-Sistani were on the walls. Birds were chirping. In the background the percussions of artillery and gunfire could be heard.

On the way back to Erbil, we stopped at Qaraqosh and spoke to the Christians from the Nineveh Plain Protection Units. Esevan Diyaa, who had fled to Erbil in 2014, said he had joined the militia in 2016. He fought alongside the 9th Armored Division to liberate the town, and now he was posted at the entrance to a church. He hoped the civilians would return and that the government would invest in the town. Once fifty thousand Christians had lived here, he said. "Our demand is to rebuild these buildings and houses of prayer and protect us." The city had twelve churches, and most had been damaged by ISIS. Graffiti had been left behind and the statues of Jesus and the Virgin Mary obliterated. Since liberation, the Nineveh Plain Protection Units had brought some posters to replace the statues, and Jesus once again rose inside the churches. At the entrance to the city, a giant cross was being erected. It was a symbol of return and resurrection on Nineveh Plains, where Christians had lived for almost two thousand years.

The Battle for Mosul

The coalition's presence in Mosul was out of sight and out of mind. But its presence was clear from the remnants of air strikes. We drove into the smoldering city with the Emergency Response Division, passing the airport and into the Jadida neighborhood. Here the coalition had bombed a building, killing civilians in late March. Initial reports indicated 240 people might have died. The strike had targeted ISIS snipers but had triggered a massive explosion. We saw the aftermath, still raw. An entire city block had been damaged and numerous buildings gutted. In the middle was a massive crater, partly filled with water. It was the worst damage I saw in Mosul.

US CENTCOM had responded to allegations of civilian casualties, saying, "strike data from March 16–23 indicates that, at the request of the Iraqi security forces, the coalition struck ISIS fighters and equipment on March 17 in west Mosul at the location corresponding to allegations of civilian casualties."[132] The coalition had a "zero civilian casualties" goal in the battle but claimed ISIS was using human shields. General Joseph Votel, head of the US Central Command, said the incident would be investigated.

In the first years of battle, when the coalition concentrated on limited air strikes aimed almost exclusively at ISIS vehicles and communications and fighting positions that were carefully established by monitoring, civilian deaths were rare. The US Department of Defense Civilian Casualty Assessment unit said in November 2016 that "as many as 64 civilians" had been killed in Iraq and Syria. The battle for Mosul coincided with the battle for Aleppo in Syria, where Russia was supporting the Syrian regime. Supporters of the Syrian regime alleged media hypocrisy in focusing on civilian casualties in Aleppo and not Mosul. The resident of Mosul tweeting as @MosulEye wrote that the strike had harmed his family members. "The explosion didn't only occurred [sic] only because of the VBIED [parked nearby] but was a combined explosion of a strike, IFP mortars, and VBIED together."[133] A total of sixty-one bodies were eventually pulled from the rubble I drove by in late March. The coalition later apologized but still blamed ISIS for the death toll. When the Pentagon investigated, it found residue of explosives used by ISIS in addition to elements of the GBU-38 Joint Direct Attack Munition the coalition had dropped.

The air strike still haunted the landscape a year later. On March 28, 2018, the Combined Joint Task Force – Operation Inherent Resolve monthly civilian casualty report reported that 855 civilians had been unintentionally killed by coalition strikes since the beginning of the operation. By then there had been 29,225 strikes. The bombing in Jadida was still the largest single killing of civilians.[134]

Eventually we entered the narrow streets leading to Old Mosul. We exited the SUV and walked on foot. In an alley, a Federal Police mortar team fired over the rooftops at an unseen enemy. The streets were laid out on a grid, so each alley stretched down passing other alleys, in a network of streets and blocks. On most of the alleys facing north, blankets were strung across each bisecting street so one could hide from ISIS snipers. The Federal Police, eager to show off their firepower, wheeled a .50 caliber machine gun into the alley and fired at ISIS. They let off an RPG and some AK-47 fire. In the distance was a more serious gunbattle. To fight this street-by-street battle, like at Stalingrad, the Iraqis had to tunnel through homes, get up to the rooftops and move building by building. We climbed a rickety ladder into a window of a home, then from the window through a hole blown in a wall, and we came to a man's living room. Oddly, he had an air conditioner on and was relaxing on a couch as soldiers walked through. From there we made it to a staircase, then through another hole in a wall and another staircase, this one half constructed.

The Iraq Emergency Response Division officer held up his hand and motioned us to stop. Then he pointed through a window facing the stairs. "Sniper." He asked us to jump across one by one. We obliged. Then, up more stairs, more windows to watch for snipers. Crouching, ducking. Up the stairs to the roof. On the roof the Iraqis had carved holes in the walls to shoot through. They had also rigged an SPG-9 tripod-mounted, 73 mm recoilless gun to fire at ISIS. The men took turns shooting RPGs at more unseen targets. We could see the grenades impact in the distance. The commander thought he was just a kilometer from the Nuri Mosque.

The ringing in my ears from the gunfire came and went. We made our way back. Stairs, tunnels, windows, stairs, snipers, stairs. It was surreal, with some men sleeping inside the houses they had occupied, others sipping coffee, and some civilians still living in the middle of the battle. Back in the alley, the Iraqi Federal Police relaxed. Some of them had also fought in other tough battles. They didn't think Mosul was so difficult, and they had the patience to wait months to slowly constrict ISIS to death, one fighter at a time. They knew there were many foreign fighters in front of them. Some estimated up to a thousand ISIS members were left, the hard-core foreigners. They said they had encountered many Chechans and Russian-speakers. There were so many that ISIS literature was sometimes printed in Cyrillic.

The battle for Mosul was carried out without much air support. There were drones overhead. There were no coalition snipers that we saw. The Iraqis were doing all the heavy lifting. They chose the pace, they plotted the offensives, and for the most part they sat around. They were in no hurry.

After several days, I decided to pay a visit to the Hamam al-Alil IDP camp. The Popular Mobilization Unit ran the borders of the camp and had put up instruction signs. They prohibited carrying weapons in the camps. As we tried to make our way to the camp, the Shi'ite militiamen, their faces swathed in the familiar Punisher skull masks, got suspicious. No journalists. A tall man, his AK slung over this shoulder, was shouting at our driver, a Christian man from Qaraqosh. I told him to turn around. The blood drained from my face, and my stomach tightened. These were the wrong people to mess with in the wrong place, in the middle of nowhere near Mosul, where people can disappear. We knew the militias were accused of executing ISIS members. I wanted no part of any problems. If they didn't want us there, better to leave. But the driver was insistent on arguing, shouting that he wasn't a terrorist and should be allowed through. He said he was driving a journalist, but this only angered the young men manning the checkpoint, and soon more men gathered.

Cars piled up behind us. Everything about the situation seemed wrong. The village had been a Sunni village before the war, and the PMU men were on edge for ISIS sleeper cells. The civilians looked angry, and so did the militiamen. I could see the situation deteriorating before my eyes.

We would be pulled from the car, the driver would be dragged away. I'd be taken to the local headquarters of the militias, thrown in a room and told to wait. A commander would come, perhaps one connected to Iran's Islamic Revolutionary Guard Corps. They'd google my name. They'd see I'd reported from Israel. I'd be accused of being a spy. And then... I grabbed the driver by the shoulder. Firmly I told him, "Tell them we've made a mistake, you're sorry, we need to get back to Qayarrah, we need to turn around, we have an appointment with the coalition, you're sorry, tell them." The driver, momentarily distracted, finally abandoned his pride-filled argument. He said he was sorry, the guards waved us off, we turned around and plodded back through the city. Most of my tense fears relaxed. I hadn't been scared in the battles against ISIS; what always worried me was being detained, kidnapped. The uncertainty worried me. The front line against ISIS always seemed certain. The enemy was there, I'm here. But checkpoints are always uncertain, especially in a land filled with war, where young soldiers are jumpy.

When we'd left the area of the Hamam al-Alil IDP camp, we came to a second checkpoint and finally got out to the main road. We were heading to Qayarrah. The driver got lost and drove too far. We had to go back and find the route to the pontoon bridge over the Tigris. Then finally we were on the way back toward the Christian villages of Nineveh Plains, away from the war. I breathed again.

Can Qaraqosh Recover?

Like so many older Iraqis, the Christian driver named Matti Rafo had lived the story of Iraq. Although Qaraqosh had been safe before 2014, he said that Mosul was never safe after 2003. "They were beheading people in the street. Kidnapping. There are many hidden extremists." He pointed to a shepherd by the roadside. "He looks poor, but he might come to our farm and tell us to remove our plants." Rafo said that after 2003, he had seen many beheadings in Mosul and looked back more fondly on the era of Saddam. "I was in the army for five years. I saw many dead bodies during the Iran-Iraq War. When we fought 1986–1991 [during the Iran-Iraq War and the Gulf War], we'd put the casualties in a pickup and they'd fall out sometimes."

He recalled the government in the 1980s, when Iraq was wealthier.

But he said that even though the state was wealthy, his wife, a teacher, only made a dollar a month. "You could barely get a meal." The villages that now have concrete houses were made of mud in the 1980s. He said the economy had improved after 2003. But now with the Shi'ite militias, he felt unsafe again. They belong to Iran, Rafo said. He said the Islamists would likely return to Mosul. "They threw chocolates when ISIS came, they celebrated. Many of them are uneducated."

At the Mar Ephrem Seminary in Qaraqosh, the desks had been left as they were in 2014. Although the city had been liberated in October 2016, it was deserted. I picked my way through the seminary. The classrooms on the bottom floor of a big, square building, with a picturesque courtyard in the center, were empty. One classroom was full of desks with a layer of dust. The curtains were drawn, and light picked its way through. In another room, papers had been strewn everywhere. Student IDs and files littered the floor. One read: "Syrian Catholic: Parish of Bashiqa, Iraq." Someone had left his copy of *Aristotele L'anima* (On the Soul) in a classroom. The students had been scattered to the winds by the war.

Outside in the courtyard, a statue of the Virgin Mary had been smashed. Most churches in the town were like this. Jesus and the Virgin Mary beheaded. Crosses blown up. But most of them had not been totally destroyed, and when the Christian militias returned alongside the Popular Mobilitation Unit, they brought new posters of Jesus. But they had no resources to rebuild the town that once housed sixty thousand.

The destruction in Qaraqosh included at least twenty-five hundred homes damaged, according to the locals. ISIS had targeted it as it had targeted the ancient city of Nimrud a ten-minute drive away. I'd avoided going to Nimrud for lack of time, and I realized I missed a once-in-a-lifetime chance. I saw the mounds from afar, from the main road. It had once been capital of the Assyrian Empire. Austen Henry Layard, the nineteenth-century British traveler and archaeologist who explored Nimrud in the 1840s, wrote in April 1850 that the site was so large, "there is enough to fill twenty museums."[135] He shipped some artifacts back to Britain, and they ended up at the British Museum, the Fitzwilliam Museum in Cambridge and even at the Metropolitan Museum of Art in New York. After ISIS arrived, it destroyed the winged effigies, much as the Taliban had blown up the Bamyan Buddhas in Afghanistan in 2001.

The archaeology that ended up in far-flung museums around the world was like the Christians from Qaraqosh, living stones that had ended up in distant places. When I'd met some Christians at a narghile café in Erbil in December 2015, they all said they were heading to Europe and seeking asylum. Iraq was "finished" for many of them.

Others remained behind. They joined militias and sought to retake cities such as Qaraqosh. Like the Kurds and the Shi'ite militias, the Kakei and the Yazidis, they had suffered under ISIS and understood that the rifle was the only way forward. "Maybe 15 to 20 percent will come back; most are waiting for immigration – there is no water or electricity here," Anis Khader, a member of the Nineveh Plain Protection Units militia in Qaraqosh, told me.

Rafo, the local Christian who was also my driver, said that the destruction of 2015 was the worst the area had suffered since the Persian invasion of 1743. As we drove back to Erbil in early April 2017, he kept pointing out places from this ancient past. An old monastery on a mountain. At the church of St. George in Qaraqosh, he bent to enter an old mud and brick shrine. He picked through Bibles at another church and recalled the warmth of this community.

Eventually some of the 120,000 Christians who had fled Nineveh Plains in 2014 would begin to return. According to Mindy Belz in an article titled "Starting from Zero" in *World* magazine in March 2018, some thirty-seven thousand people had returned, while six thousand families had left Iraq.[136] A Nineveh Reconstruction Committee had been established, and men like Father Georges Jahola had gone from presiding over Mass to helping return the town to its previous state. Some twelve hundred homes had been reconstructed so that families could return. Other committees were established in Bartella, Telskuf and Batnaya to the north. The diverse Christian groups, including Syriacs, Chaldeans and Assyrian Orthodox, pitched in. According to Belz, there was no help from the UN and other larger groups that had been helping out in Mosul. In late March 2018, the Christians celebrated Palm Sunday and then Easter. Assyrians also celebrated the 6,768th New Year in their calendar. There was a sliver of hope in the celebrations after years of tragedy.

However, other NGOs had come to Nineveh, including Operation Blessing, Samaritan's Purse, the Netherlands' SALT Foundation, Aid to the Church in Need and L'Oeuvre d'Orient. The problem for the Christians had now moved from the threat of ISIS to rubbing shoulders with the Shi'ite militias. Although the Nineveh Plain Protection Units was part of the Popular Mobilization Units, the Christians feared Shi'ite hegemony. A man named Emanuel Youkhana told Belz that "the Shia presence in Nineveh Plain is alarming. In some areas it looks like we are losing the battle." He showed her a photo of Hezollah leader Hassan Nasrallah now adorning the entrance to Qaraqosh, a symbol of the wider war against ISIS and how it had reversed things in Nineveh. The plains had gone from the site of Sunni extremist crimes to one of Iranian influence and the "Shi'ite crescent" stretching from Tehran to Beirut.

The Coalition's Hamam al-Alil Base

Before saying goodbye to Mosul, I met with the Americans at their Hamam al-Alil command center. They had set up several M109 Paladin self-propelled howitzers in a field and were firing once an hour into the city. To get to the American compound required a long wait at the gate, which was controlled by the Federal Police and the Emergency Response Division. The base had previously been an Iraq government installation. A large parking lot had been transformed into a helipad. The main road into the base came to a T, with one part leading to the helipad and another to a series of large sheds where US soldiers were washing their MRAP Mine-Resistant Ambush Protected vehicles. They were getting ready for a patrol. It was just after noon. Along a berm near the sheds, a large stock of ammunition was kept ready for the Paladins, which were in a muddy field beyond.

The US strategy unfolding in Iraq was part of a much larger context of US anti-terror operations growing out of the Bush and Obama years. This "by, with and through" approach of working with local partners and moving at their tempo was developed by officers who had grown up fighting in Iraq. This included Secretary of Defense James Mattis, National Security Adviser H. R. McMaster and Chairman of the Joint Chiefs General Joseph Dunford. The younger officers had often served in Iraq during the surge and sometimes during the 2003–2004 conflict. They knew Iraq and had a long-term view of it and of the Iraqi military personnel they worked with.

All meetings with the US military during the war on ISIS involved several layers of facilitating bureaucracy. First there would be the email exchanges to get permission. Then they would hand you off to a lower-ranking member of the team, and then that person would hand you off to someone usually attached directly to the unit. At Hamam al-Alil, we met first with a liaison officer of the public affairs desk for the coalition's campaign, before she said her goodbyes. Then a large, cheerful first lieutenant from Task Force Falcon introduced himself. I knew him from previous emails, which he always signed "ATW," for the 82nd Airborne Division's motto "All the Way." Usually the press affairs people like the first lieutenant asked not to be named, so I obliged when I covered their operations.

From the parking lot, the lieutenant and I walked through a muddy field churned up by tank treads. The Paladin artillery was paired with other vehicles that brought them logistic support. We watched as one of the logistical vehicles lumbered like a turtle toward one of the dug-in M109s. "We have the capability to address all targets; the point of the Paladin is a mobile artillery system. The fight that we begin is the precision munitions capability; we are able to program and set those fuses and provide those rounds downrange in a rapid time in order to accomplish [our task]," said Lieutenant Micah Thompson, a commander of one of the units. He was one of the recent generation of US Army soldiers serving in Iraq and was enthusiastic about providing fire support to the Iraqi security forces clearing Mosul.

Lieutenant Thompson said his team received its target coordinates from the Iraqis and then decided whether to provide the support. The rounds could go up to thirty kilometers. Nearby in the military base, the Americans had set up a war room within the Iraqi area. There were maps and a team of men at computer screens. We had some American coffee. Wherever the US Army goes, it seems to bring a bit of home along. In Erbil, I remember the whiteboards with motivational sayings and quotes from the Bible. In the field, coffee would suffice. "ISIS absolutely uses human shields," said Thompson. "They are cruel and barbaric and desperate, so they use human shields to protect themselves. They want to create civilian casualties."

The Americans had seen ISIS murder civilians or force them to shield fighting positions. "We do everything we can to avoid civilian casualties, but we will target ISIS and destroy them." The American footprint at Hamam al-Alil was small. It was all about "advise and assist" and the slogan "by, with and through." The Iraqis chose the targets and planned the operations. Even the US military vehicles exiting the base didn't fly the American flag. It was like they were not there.

Hamam al-Alil was the tip of the coalition's spear in the battle of Mosul. It was a major contrast with how things had been done during the surge of 2007. American military men like to talk in their own world of terminology, using words like "tempo" to describe the slow-moving campaign to take Mosul. By April 2017, the battle was stretching into its sixth month. Lt. Col. Hawbaker had joined the army in 1998 and served in Iraq in 2005–2006. He said ISIS represents the "same barbarism, evil and cruelty" that the US faced back during the surge, but is "a much larger and conventional threat. We were doing counterinsurgency with US leadership; the difference now is the Iraqi security forces conduct a fight not as a counterinsurgency but against a conventional force."

In the war on ISIS, the degree to which the US had moved away from the once-celebrated "COIN" approach, the US field manual on *Counterinsurgency* and the role of David Petreaus, was clear. Under the old concept, the US was engaged in a "comprehensive civilian and military effort taken to simultaneously defeat and contain insurgency and address its root causes," as the FM 3-24 *Insurgencies and Countering Insurgencies* manual of May 2014 described it.[137] Earlier versions had used similar language. American commanders such as H. R. McMaster, Trump's national security adviser until the spring of 2018, had sought to build the Iraqi army as an institution of national unity, according to a profile by George Packer in 2006 in the *New Yorker*. Most of the semblance of that concept was gone by 2017.[138]

Washington gave up some of these grandiose pretentions for a much smaller footprint on the ground and a reduced visible presence. "We have multiple ways we assist," said Hawbaker. "You saw the artillery indirect fire, mortars, and we also help coordinate air strikes, and we also help coordinate intelligence sharing, so we give them a lot of info on disposition and what he [ISIS] is doing and what he [ISIS] is thinking and intelligence for them to better array their operations."

What had the US learned in all these years in Iraq? These commanders like Hawbaker had their lives shaped by their wars. The team around Trump had grown up in Iraq. The Tomahawk missiles lifting off the USS *Porter* destroyer to strike the Syrian regime on April 7, 2017, were a similar sight, as were those that flew in January 1991 to strike at Saddam's army. The impact of the Iraq war on US military thinking looms large. With decades of involvement, it has done to the US officer corps what the Vietnam War did to Colin Powell and Norman Schwarzkopf. Where war taught them that the US needed a goal and a purpose, the "Powell Doctrine," the decades in Iraq have taught the opposite. The global coalition founded on October 15, 2014, with a "commitment of the US and partner nations in the region and around the globe to eliminate the terrorist group ISIS and the threat they pose to Iraq, the region and the wider international community," had grown to sixty-eight countries by March 2017. Eventually it would reach seventy-nine countries and partners.

The coalition against ISIS sought to get right what previous US policy had gotten wrong, by concentrating entirely on the goal of ridding Iraq of ISIS. It would add to the $49 billion already spent between 2003 and 2010, by spending another $2.3 billion through ITEF to fight ISIS between 2015 and 2018, renaming it the Counter-ISIS Train and Equip Fund.[139]

By 2017, the US was partnered not only with the new Iraqi army, forged in battles with ISIS over three years, but also with Shi'ite militias. Since Grand Ayatollah Ali al-Sistani's June 13, 2014, fatwa calling on Iraqis to fight ISIS, almost a hundred thousand mostly Shi'ite Iraqis had flocked to the colors of groups such as Kataib Hezbollah, the Badr Organization and Asaib Ahl al-Haq. Through them they served in the Popular Mobilizations Units or Hashd al-Sha'abi. These groups were linked to Iran and to Hezbollah in Lebanon. But they were also, oddly, linked to the US-led coalition. Even as Trump was rolling out a policy that would seek to confront Iran in the region, on the ground Americans were ostensibly fighting ISIS alongside men whose lives were carved in the crucible of the 1980s and were hostile to the US. According to Hawbaker, the Popular Mobilizations Units was not operating in Mosul, and "the Americans don't work with Hashd," but only work directly with the Iraqi security forces. The Hashd agreed, with some units such as Harakat Hezbollah al-Nujaba saying they would target the US.

The US understood the need to recognize the sectarian divide. The Department of Defense 2017 budget included equipment for twenty thousand troops and 350 Humvees. It included a note that some would support "Sunni Popular Mobilization Forces."[140] In 2016, the Train and Equip Fund noted the need to not "further the Sunni/Shia divide" and that the support would "provide a counterweight to Iranian influence." But this was a Defense Department war. Democracy promotion and state building, including the CIA and Department of State, were taking a back seat.

The Iraqi army fighting for Mosul, including the Federal Police and the Emergency Response Division, who were doing most of the heavy lifting on the eastern side of the city, impressed their American advisers. But they were also only a small piece of the Iraqi puzzle. Everywhere around the city, outside the urban area, there were Shi'ite flags and militias. Beyond them, to the east in the mountains of the Kurdish region, were the Peshmerga. It was a land of multiple competing flags and identities. On the road from Mosul, driving back to Erbil, a burned M1117 armored vehicle rested on its side in a wet, green field. It had been destroyed in 2014, a remnant of the old Iraq. Beyond it were remnants of other Iraqs, forts from Saddam's time, monasteries and mosques from the Ottoman period. In the battle to liberate the country from ISIS, the area around Mosul had become home to sandbagged berms, trench lines like in the First World War, and buildings destroyed by twenty-first-century drones and air strikes. To get anywhere in the areas liberated from ISIS required constant crossing of checkpoints. For foreigners, this might go smoothly. But for locals, the Shi'ite militias were a constant influence. The flags and photos of Iran's supreme leader, and images of imams, pointed at who was in control.

They posted notices laying out their own rules. Near Hamam al-Alil, one large message board called on locals not to carry weapons inside the local IDP camps, which the Popular Mobilization Units was administering. It didn't seem too threatening, but it was ominous. "Informing the directorate of the PMU security or any office of the PMU about anything that our displaced household may be exposed to" had a kind of Orwellian sound to it. What it meant was informing on local ISIS members or former ISIS members. In the Hamam al-Alil camps, the PMU were searching and cordoning off areas. Sunni villages had checkpoints at each road entering or exiting, with men in black balaclavas, many with an image of a skull pulled down over the face, guarding them. The militia presence was supposed to be temporary, but even after the spring 2017 offensive came and went, they would remain, holding on to the countryside.

The militias not only threatened locals but also represented a challenge to the US and its allies. Qais al-Khazali was a follower of Moqtada al-Sadr, who had unleashed his militias against US troops after 2003. Khazali's Asa'ib Ahl al-Haq has threatened Israel and the US. He called the battle for Mosul "the revenge for the killing of [Imam] Hussein [by Sunnis at the Battle of Karbala in the year 680]."[141] Once groups like Khazali's were incorporated into the Iraqi security forces in the fall of 2016, their role became even more complex. During the war on ISIS, their presence was understandable, but the official incorporation showed that Iraq's góvernment wanted them to be a permanent fixture. In October 2017, when US secretary of state Rex Tillerson criticized the role of the militias and said they should "go home," Prime Minister Haider al-Abadi said that they were the "hope" of Iraq.[142]

The militias are not a monolith. The Christians guarding Qaraqosh are part of the PMU. On the road from the Tigris River to Erbil, I passed one checkpoint manned by a young, smiling man. He didn't seem quite eighteen. On his tactical vest were the logos of the PMU, the Badr Brigade and also a small patch that indicated he was part of the Hashd al-Shebeki, the Shabak unit of the PMU. There are many thousands of the Shabak minority who live in Mosul and Nineveh Plains, part of the patchwork of groups that once flourished before ISIS and other extremists came to attack them. The young man stopped our SUV. He didn't care who we were but wondered if I could take a photo of him. I stepped out and snapped a few. He had a broad smile. Behind him was a small caravan that other members of his unit were living in. The flags of the militias fluttered. The clouds gathered above. The war was still on. But he was happy. And members of his minority group, seeing their own militiamen at the checkpoint, felt secure now.

The ISIS Rehab Center

Seventeen-year-old Khalid was fidgety and inquisitive. He asked not to have his photo taken and didn't want to give a full name. "I am Sunni and very anti-Shi'ite. I am afraid of them, that when I am released they will do something to me." Wearing a heavy black sweater and dark sweatpants pulled up to the ankles, Khalid sat on the couch at a rehabilitation center run by the Labor and Social Affairs Ministry of the Kurdistan Regional Government.

Khalid was a teenager when ISIS conquered his hometown of Hamam al-Alil, south of Mosul. Born in 1999, he lived for two years under ISIS. When they first came to his village, they killed one of his relatives who had served the Iraqi government on the local council. This was likely one of the thousands dumped in the Khasfa sinkhole not far away. "I was beaten by ISIS before I joined. So far that I joined." He said he spent a year working for the extremists. But life was difficult under the new system. "When ISIS killed a homeowner, they would then make the wife and kids pay rent." Khalid took a job guarding a local ISIS court. "When ISIS first came, they did kill a lot of people, those who had been in the [Iraq] army or police and military." Khalid's cousin fled and joined the Turkish-backed Hashd al-Watani.

As the Iraqi army and its militias reconquered parts of northern Iraq, thousands of ISIS members were captured and imprisoned. Between 2013 and March 2018, Iraq had issued 3,130 death sentences for membership of ISIS and other groups. There were at least nineteen thousand detainees. Other ISIS members fled to Kurdish areas and ended up in KRG detention centers as well. Khalid was one of these. In April 2017, I drove to the local detention center in central Erbil that housed women and children who were formerly affiliated with ISIS. Kawyar Shahed Omar, a member of the Prime Minister's Office press office, welcomed me at the gate. We shared a pastry as we waited. The brown wrapper read, "100% Halal, freshly cooked, freshly prepared." It was a cold, dreary day in Erbil. A mural on the wall of the entrance to the walled compound showed a painting of a pistol with an X through it. No guns in here. From the outside, the compound looked like a derelict 1970s-era building. The fence of a recreation center for playing soccer or basketball could be made out.

We walked through a security checkpoint. On a TV, members of the

KDP were meeting with a leader of the Kurdistan Islamic Union, a group called Yekgirtu. They were seeking an agreement on an independence referendum.

Inside the compound, there were little, gray temporary buildings from UNICEF. These were grouped around two main buildings, one for administration and another a kind of prison for the women and children who were living at the place. We walked inside and down a hallway. On one side were colorful murals of flags and flowers. At the end of the hall were metal bars and a gate that could be closed to keep the people in their rooms that lined the hall. A photo of Mullah Mustafa Barzani, the Kurdish leader, hung on a wall. Another photo showed all the provinces of Kurdistan – in Iran, Turkey, Syria and Iraq. We were welcomed into one of the offices just outside the metal bars. A Kurdish woman and man in security uniform came in and sat behind a large desk. We took seats on a couch. Then Khalid shuffled in.

He was happy to talk. He mainly wanted to stress his hatred for the Shi'ite militias in Hamam al-Alil. "The Shi'ite[s] are our enemy, and I am afraid of them." Khalid then turned to the fall of Mosul of 2014, blaming Iraqi officials. Then he went back to discussing the Shi'ites. "They are the same as ISIS; the difference is in the organization and system. They treat us badly and torture us the same as ISIS. Even if we go back to our place, if there were no Shi'ite [militias], then we would start a normal life. As long as they are there … [we cannot]." Khalid said that Shi'ites in Iraq hate Sunnis and Kurds. He claimed there were no Sunni mosques in Iran and implied that the militias wanted to do the same to Iraq. "In the Quran it says there are no differences between Muslims, but the original difference is one Shi'ites have made between us."

Khalid said he had fled the militias and come to Erbil and was relatively happy to stay at the detention center. But he would be eighteen soon and said that eventually he would go back to fight the militias in Hamam al-Alil. "There used to be agriculture in our village, but the militias have put a military camp there."

Khalid's life is representative of many in rural Sunni areas of Iraq that fell to ISIS. Because of the interruption in life caused by ISIS occupation from 2014 to 2017, he was denied the ability to get an education after primary school. Instead he had worked as an assistant to the imam at the mosque. A whole generation had lost these years of schooling. As Khalid got up to leave, he said he wished the US would do something to get rid of the Shi'ite militias. Send them back to Iran, then everything would be possible in the future. "[Prime Minister] Abadi should be selling sheep. He's a good chef. [Former prime minister Nouri] Maliki should be a jewelry salesman."

Diman Mohammed wore a black headscarf that sagged down so that her hair was showing in front. She had on a black jacket and a white dress shirt. She wore two long silver earrings and clutched her hands together as we spoke. The director of the rehabilitation center housing teens like Khalid and women who had been affiliated with ISIS, Mohammed was in the job for two years by the spring of 2017. "A lot of people have been through here – I cannot say the exact number," she said. "Today we have 406. We have thirty-nine adult women who have been judged by a court and eighty-nine accused or under investigation. There are also forty-eight boys who have received a judgment and 230 under investigation." Another thirty-seven children were living in the compound with their mothers.

The Kurdish authorities said they rounded up these suspects from among those who had fled from Mosul and other areas in Iraq. Some had been in IDP camps. Adult men ended up in other facilities. But the concept behind Mohammed's department was more progressive. "We want to rehabilitate these people and prepare them to go back to society again. Our aim is to provide them the best service when they stay with us." Some of the detainees were under threat from people still within ISIS or from relatives.

According to Mohammed, the detainees received visits from psychologists and met with local NGOs that deal with social welfare. They took classes in English and computer science and met with Islamic religious personnel who helped to provide a moderate, non-ISIS view of religion. For the teens there were also sports for boys and girls. The men had handicrafts to work on, and there was a music teacher. "The whole idea is to treat them as human beings and humanely."

Somewhere in the compound was the sister of ISIS leader Abu Bakr al-Baghdadi. She enjoyed doing hair styling. A year later, in March 2018, she was sentenced to death by a court in Baghdad, accused of "offering logistic support and help to [ISIS fighters] in carrying out criminal acts."

In 2017 when I visited, the closest we could get to Baghdadi's sister was another woman who had served in one of ISIS's morality police. Unlike Khalid, who was young, energetic and talkative, the woman in a red tracksuit who shuffled in was heavyset and didn't want to speak. A Kurdish woman in uniform, who looked to be about six feet tall, prodded the detainee to tell a bit about her life. She had been found at an IDP camp after fleeing Mosul. Like many former ISIS members, she preferred to be picked up by the Kurdish security services, or Assish, because of fear of retaliation from the Shi'ite militias.

Born in 1991, the woman said she was from Mosul. "It was very bad under ISIS; we had no jobs. They used to beat people; it was very bad." But despite her claims of ISIS abuses, the Kurds running the camp said that the large woman in red had admitted to being a member of ISIS. Her husband was an ISIS member, and she took up the job of lashing women whom ISIS accused of committing crimes. "She made sure they wore veils, for instance," said one of the Kurdish women who worked at the detention center. Her unit would detain women in the streets for various violations. "She used to beat them. More than fifty a day." But the woman in red then interjected, "I didn't enjoy doing it. We had no money, so we chose to do this. We didn't celebrate doing this." Her whole family seemed to have joined ISIS. Her brother had been killed in an air strike in 2014. She claimed that her brother had been born in 1995 and didn't support al Qaeda or Ansar al-Islam before ISIS. But he was the right age at the right time to join ISIS and had joined when they arrived in Mosul.

The woman in red said she wanted to go back to a normal life, maybe to become a psychiatrist like the ones she met with at the rehab center.

Chapter 17
The Hot Summer of 2017

Washington and the Post-ISIS Vacuum

The Iraqi security forces carried out the battle for Mosul slowly and methodically. The optimism of early 2017 gave way to drudgery. The soldiers I saw in Mosul from the Federal Police and the Emergency Response Division were confident of victory, but they also felt no prodding to move faster.

As spring turned to summer, the war against ISIS lost priority in Washington. Donald Trump made an ostentatious visit to Saudi Arabia for an Arab Islamic American Summit on May 21. He mentioned ISIS six times in his speech. "Many are already making significant contributions to regional security: Jordanian pilots are crucial partners against ISIS in Syria and Iraq. Saudi Arabia and a regional coalition have taken strong action against Houthi militants in Yemen. The Lebanese army is hunting ISIS operatives who try to infiltrate their territory."[143] He argued for cutting off the financial support for ISIS, stopping it from selling oil and eradicating it in Syria. He also mentioned it in a list of other terror organizations: "the true toll of ISIS, al Qaeda, Hezbollah, Hamas, and so many others, must be counted not only in the number of dead. It must also be counted in generations of vanished dreams." He contrasted these groups with the Middle East's rich and natural beauty, vibrant cultures and "massive amounts of historic treasures." In a sense the speechwriters were seeking to draw a line after ISIS was defeated and shine a light on a post-ISIS Middle East.

But the war wasn't over. A week after Trump's speech, the PMU reached the Syrian border. It liberated ISIS-held former Yazidi villages such as Tal Qasab and Tal Banat, sites of ISIS crimes in 2014. KRG president Barzani warned the PMU not to approach Sinjar, but the militias kept moving anyway, sweeping ISIS before them. On May 29, militia leaders posted photos of themselves on the Syrian border, and Hadi al-Amiri appeared on Al-Sumaria television. IRGC Quds Force commander Qassem Soleimani also came to the Syrian border.

Abadi came to Mosul at the end of May to "oversee liberation operations." PMU leader Abu-Mahdi al-Muhandis met the prime minister, and they posted photos together. Kurds were watching the growing power of the central government and the Shi'ite militias and wondering if this was a portent of things to come. One Kurdish commander told Rudaw that if the Shi'ite militias commited any "transgressions," they would "beat their heads against the mountains of Kurdistan."[144]

After ISIS crossed into Iraq in 2014 and the US-led coalition began fighting the extremists in both Iraq and Syria, the conflict in the two countries became one large war. However, these wars were fought largely independently because of the way ISIS controlled most of the border. Each group fighting ISIS largely fought its own private war. In Iraq, that meant the Kurds and the Iraqi army and Shi'ite militias had fought separate campaigns up until the battle for Mosul. Once that battle began, the Kurdish role largely ceased, and the war on ISIS was led by the Iraqi security forces.

In Syria, the war on ISIS was fought on several fronts. The Syrian regime fought one war on ISIS, concentrated mostly in Deir ez-Zor, where ISIS laid siege to the city, and around Palmyra, where the regime fought over the ancient archaeological site with the extremists. Eventually, with the help of Russian air power, the regime would push ISIS back toward the Euphrates River Valley.

ISIS had initially captured Palmyra in May 2015. It blew up the two-thousand-year-old Temple of Bel and the Arch of Triumph and murdered the chief archaeologist, Khaled al-Asaad. In March 2016, the Syrian regime army retook the city, and in May, the Mariinsky Theater Orchestra was flown in from Moscow for a victory concert. Then in December 2016, ISIS stormed back into the ancient city, brushing aside Iranian-backed mercenaries who were supposed to be helping the regime to defend it. This time the extremists blew up the Tetrapylon and part of the Roman Theater. In March 2017, Damascus retook Palmyra again.

From May 2015, Deir ez-Zor city was under siege by ISIS. Its hundred thousand inhabitants held on, bolstered by Syrian Maj. Gen. Issam Zehreddine, who maintained control of a section of the western side of the city and the airport. The World Food Program air-dropped food for the people trapped in the city. Operating from Amman, Ilyushin IL-76 cargo planes made a hundred airdrops by August 2016 and three hundred by August 2017.[145] The situation became direr by January 2017. But a Russian-backed offensive moved across two hundred kilometers of desert from Palmyra to break the siege. In August, Russian defense minister Sergei Shoigu said that "everyone is focused, set up for the fight against ISIS. Today there are such key points, like Deir ez-Zor." In September, the Syrian army reached the city after 840 days of siege.

With the Syrian regime moving toward the Euphrates River, it became increasingly important for the coalition, whose aircraft were also operating in Syria, to not end up in another conflict. In December 2016, the US and Russia agreed to a "de-confliction" line in Syria. This was briefly suspended in April 2017 after Trump ordered air strikes on Syria's Shayrat Air Base.

The waltz between the US and Russia, sometimes experiencing tensions, sometimes seeming to agree on Syria, would overshadow operations throughout 2017. In mid-September, Russian forces struck a target east of the Euphrates and injured several members of the Syrian Democratic Forces, or SDF. "We put our full efforts into preventing unnecessary escalation among forces that share ISIS as our common enemy," coalition commander Lt. Gen. Paul E. Funk II of the US Army said on September 16. In November, Trump and Putin met briefly in Vietnam and released a statement about fighting ISIS. It praised the dramatic defeat of the extemists. "The Presidents agreed to maintain open military channels of communication between military professionals to help ensure the safety of both US and Russian forces and de-confliction of partnered forces engaged in the fight against ISIS." But the US and Russians had different priorities in Syria. "Russia got themselves involved back when it was a civil war. In some respects, the effort to defeat ISIS changed priorities for some," a State Department official said in early

November 2017.[146] "Certainly, for us, the priority was defeating ISIS. I think for Russia it's a question of how long do they want to continue to support conflict."

As ISIS lost more of its territory, the vacuum was being filled by competing forces. While the Euphrates became a line of tension between the US and Russia, the area around Manbij became an area of tension between the US and Turkey. This was a result of the rapid gains made by the Kurdish YPG and the SDF alliance. Within a year of being under desperate siege in Kobani, the YPG had proved itself the most effective force against ISIS.

The major Syrian front against ISIS was the YPG's battle. The YPG captured the Jazira canton in Syria and a hundred villages around Tel Hamis in February 2015. In March, the YPG had pushed ISIS out of Kobani with help from US and coalition air power. Then they took Tel Abyad on the border with Turkey. In October, they captured another 240 villages and more than a thousand square kilometers in al-Hawl subdistrict. In 2016, they took Al-Shadadi, another key town on the road to pushing ISIS toward the Euphrates River Valley. From May to August 2016, they also liberated Manbij, close to the Turkish border, almost coming into conflict with Turkey.

Turkey was wary of the US relationship with the YPG since 2015. In a June 2015 speech at the Ankara Chamber of Commerce, Erdogan said that "the West, which has shot Arabs and Turkmens, is unfortunately placing the PYD and the PKK in lieu of them."[147] When the YPG paused their advance at the Tishreen Dam on the Euphrates in December 2015, Turkey said the river was a "redline." Turkey was distracted by events near Kilis and also by the coup as the US-backed SDF took Manbij in May and June 2016. The US Defense Department celebrated the success, claiming that coalition forces were "operating in support of Arab counter-ISIL forces."[148] It didn't mention the YPG of SDF, but rather the "local forces" and an "indigenous Arab force," and Pentagon spokesman Adrian Rankine-Galloway claimed the offensive was made "in accordance with commitments between the US and Turkey."

On August 9, Erdogan met Putin amid the rising crisis with the US and its partners. This was the first time that an Erdogan-Putin meeting would presage major Turkish military activity in Syria. Ankara wanted assurances that the Syrian air force and its Russian backers would not interfere. They needed the Russian stamp of approval. A similar act would play out in January 2018, when a Turkish delegation would fly to Moscow on the eve of Afrin operations.

Turkey needed to move fast to remove ISIS from the border, fill the void and, in its view, prevent the YPG from creating a corridor to Kurdish-controlled areas in Afrin in northwest Syria. The SDF had set its eyes on Al-Bab and created a military council to rule it when they liberated it from ISIS after taking Manbij. It would put them just a few kilometers away from link-up with the YPG in Afrin. Turkey preempted them, rolling into Jarabulus in Syria and striking toward Al-Bab and Manbij, sweeping ISIS away from the Turkish border.

Turkey's Operation Euphrates Shield began with T-155 howitzers striking sixty-three targets before Turkish special forces under the command of Lt. Gen. Zekai Aksakalli poured across the border.[149] Turkish tanks were accompanied by Arab rebel fighters from Faylaq al-Sham, Nour al-Din al-Zinki, Sultan Murad, Division 13 and others. Presidential spokesman and Erdogan adviser Ibrahim Kalin said the goal was "cleansing of all terrorist elements," which meant both ISIS and the YPG.

The US was caught by surprise. Secretary of State John Kerry sought to walk back US support for the Kurdish YPG, which Turkey continually accused of being terrorists connected to the PKK. "We do not support an independent Kurd initiative."[150] He claimed US support was a "limited engagement with a component of Kurd fighters on a limited basis." When clashes between the anti-Assad Syrian rebels and the anti-ISIS SDF broke out near Manbij, the Pentagon was clearer. Pentagon press secretary Peter Cook said, "we are calling on all armed actors to stand down immediately and take appropriate measures to deconflict." The difference between Kerry and the Pentagon was one of strategy and symbolized the US disconnect. The State Department wanted to work with Ankara, the CIA preferred the rebels, and the Pentagon preferred the YPG. The tensions in Manbij would continue through to the spring of 2017, when the US sent military units to patrol, flying the flag high in March.

In May, General Dunford told the Department of Defense that the

US would expand its arming of the SDF to take Raqqa, the ISIS capital in Syria. To get there, the US carried out a bold amphibious assault near Tabqa, crossing a lake to capture the local dam. The SDF captured the airfield where ISIS had massacred 160 captured Syrian soldiers in August 2014. Dunford said the US was working to "take measures on the ground to mitigate their [Turkey's] concerns. For example, weapons getting into the hands of the PKK or moving into Turkey, and we've taken steps to make sure that the Turks have transparency on what we're doing and measures to take place that the equipment that we're providing to the SDF is appropriate only for operations in Raqqa."[151] The weapons mostly consisted of small arms, ammunition and machine guns. In June, Mattis said that the US would equip them with what was necessary, such as "light trucks."[152]

In the same month, the SDF announced an offensive to take Raqqa. With Mosul crumbling, ISIS would lose both its major capital cities. The YPG and then SDF war against ISIS took the coalition by surprise. The battle for Raqqa was expected to take several months when it began. It was announced by SDF members, including women and men in fatigues and flags fluttering from the various units involved. "We have launched this operation against ISIS in Raqqa from the north, west and east," said SDF spokesman Talal Silo in June 2017.

He said the US-led coalition was delivering weapons that would aid the operation. He urged civilians in Raqqa, of whom there were an estimated 200,000, to avoid ISIS positions. Turkey warned against the operation, saying it could "present a threat."[153] Prime Minister Binali Yildirim was clearly warning the US and its SDF allies to tread carefully in coming months.

With the region distracted by battles in Mosul and Raqqa, and a Gulf state feud erupting between Saudi Arabia and the UAE on the one side, and Qatar on the other, the KRG announced a date for its independence referendum. Since the 1990s, the region had enjoyed autonomy, and in 2005, an independence vote garnered 98 percent support out of the 1.9 million voters. Peter Galbraith wrote in the *New York Times* at the time that "the news will not be welcomed by American and British officials, who have studiously ignored the Kurdish independence movement, pretending that the unity of Iraq is not at issue in the country's transition to democracy."[154] Galbraith noted that the Kurds had collected 1.7 million signatures as part of their desire to show the Americans they were serious. L. Paul Bremer, George W. Bush's proconsul in Baghdad, wouldn't even take a look at the issue at the time.

In 2017, the Kurds thought it was different. The region was a bulwark against ISIS and a key ally of the coalition. Masoud Barzani tweeted: "I am pleased to announce that the date for the independence referendum has been set for Monday, September 25."[155] He received support across Kurdistan's political spectrum. A Kurdish Islamic Party statement read: "Referendum and independence are an inalienable and natural right." Kirkuk governor Najmaldin Karim, a member of the Patriotic Union of Kurdistan, who had been outspoken on independence for many years, said his city would support it. Kirkuk is one of the "disputed" areas between the official Kurdish region and Baghdad.

Kurds knew that Iran and the Shi'ite militias would oppose the vote, but they gambled on support from Turkey, Saudi Arabia and other countries. The Kurdish flag had been placed beside the Iraqi one at a meeting in Turkey in June 2017. Turkey and Iraq had engaged in a war of words over its presence in Bashiqa, and Turkey was concerned about the Shi'ite militias entering Tal Afar, a Turkmen city near Mosul.

Israel supported Kurdish rights. "With respect to the Kurds, they are a warrior nation that is politically moderate, [they have] proved they can be politically committed and [are] worthy of statehood," Prime Minister Netanyahu said in 2014.[156] Legislator Ksenia Svetlova, a member of the Knesset's Foreign Affairs and Defense Committee and head of the Knesset Caucus for Strengthening Relations with the Kurds, said that the referendum will be a "turning point for millions of Kurds in Iraq and around the globe. For the first time in modern history they will have a real chance for sovereignty and freedom."

The Battle for Raqqa, Mosul and the Iraqi-Syrian Border

Raqqa's famous ancient wall, al-Rafiqah, was built in the eighth century. It survived the Mongol invasion of the thirteenth century, when many of the inhabitants of the city were killed. The ghost town became a hamlet on the north bank of the Euphrates River, a gathering place for Bedouin tribes. In the early twentieth century, Armenians fleeing massacres in the Ottoman Empire came to the area as refugees. The previously unremarkable city that came to thrive under the modern Syrian regime never thought that it would be the capital of the ISIS caliphate.

In June 2018, the SDF laid siege to Raqqa. From his office in Iraq, US Army colonel Ryan Dillon, spokesman for Combined Joint Task Force – Operation Inherent Resolve, praised the SDF efforts. Every day they were moving forward. Raqqa was a much smaller city than Mosul, about two kilometers across and four kilometers long. Dillon had experience in Iraq as a company commander in 2003. In 2017, his job was to explain the success of the operation. He said the SDF was "clearing neighborhood after neighborhood at incredible pace and this last week hit stiff resistance." They had made it to the ancient city wall. SDF units moving from the west encountered tough resistance. Victories were measured by streets and buildings, such as a large sugar factory liberated toward the end of June. ISIS put up more resistance in the western part of the city, so the SDF decided to move along the city wall, slowly strangling the enemy like an anaconda would. Everywhere they tried to penetrate, they faced IEDs.

"To the south of Raqqa it is completely encircled and you have SDF completely around the Euphrates River and the bridges are impassable, and we as a coalition are striking every type of water craft we identify as ISIS fighters, so it is difficult for ISIS to escape," Dillon told me. The US estimated around twenty-five hundred ISIS fighters were still holding out, including some foreign fighters.

The US was carrying out daily air strikes. In the third week of June, it struck 125 targets, including fighting positions and VBIED car bombs, mortars and machine guns. In Raqqa, the coalition special forces were embedded below the company level, working on the ground in a way they were not doing in Mosul. In Mosul, as I'd seen at Hamam al-Alil, the United States was sitting at the division or brigade level to advise and assist. In Syria, because the SDF were a much smaller force than the Iraqi army and lacked equipment, the battle was more intimate, and the US was closely involved. But there were far fewer Americans in Syria. Dillon put the number at 503 soldiers in Syria and fifty-two hundred in Iraq.

The United States said it was entirely concentrated on defeating ISIS. "We have no beef with the [Assad] regime, Russians or Iranians," Dillon said. "Our mission is clear, and we will continue to de-conflict and do exactly what we are there to do and not be concerned with strategic mishaps working around one another in air and on the ground." The Americans were confident of victory. Dillon said that ISIS, which used to get fifteen hundred fighters joining its ranks a month, now got around a hundred.

It wasn't all good news for the United States in Syria. In 2016, the US had established a base at al-Tanf in Syria, near the Jordanian border. There it began to train two Syrian rebel groups, the Maghawir al-Thawra and Shohada al-Quartayn, drawn from local IDPs and tribesmen. For a year the Pentagon thought it could train them to fight ISIS and move toward the Euphrates River Valley, securing the Syrian side of the Iraqi border.

"ISIS exists in the middle Euphrates River Valley, [and these trained forces] would be intended to be partner forces if and when we take on ISIS in the Euphrates River Valley," said Dillon in an interview. Then the Syrian regime surprised the Americans and drove through the desert to the Iraqi border, cutting off the al-Tanf garrison from any access to the Euphrates. "We have this fifty-five-kilometer radius around al-Tanaf that has been established that keeps [us] from getting into mishaps with the regime and that is established, and while we have gone outside that fifty-five-kilometer area, the presence of the regime now [restricts that]. We are being good on our commitment to try to de-escalate things; we are not patrolling as we were in the past," said Dillon.

The successful program to train around a thousand fighters then began to wither on the vine. The Syrian regime had delivered a fait accompli. There would be no way to link up operations from Jordan with those in eastern Syria and Iraq.

Linking up along the Iraqi border to secure the corridor from ISIS, which used the Euphrates Valley, was even more important to the coalition after Abadi declared victory in Mosul on July 9. Iraqi soldiers celebrated in their tan desert camo uniforms. In Baghdad, people celebrated. It had been a difficult last month in the street fighting in the city. When Iraqi forces reached shouting distance of the famed Nuri Mosque, where Baghdadi had declared the caliphate in July 2014, ISIS blew up the mosque. The Old City had been destroyed in the battle, with ancient alleyways bulldozed and blown to pieces. Thousands of civilians were said to have died.

Even as Mosul was falling, ISIS attacked a village called Imam Gharbi near Qayarrah, to show that it wasn't finished. It still held a large area near Hawija south of Qayarrah, and areas out in Anbar Province as well as around Tal Afar.

ISIS had proved a difficult adversary in Mosul. It took the Iraqi army and the massive coalition eight months to take back the city, which ISIS had conquered in twenty-four hours in 2014. The smoke from battle was clearing, but the rebuilding, the tensions, the new accusations of government abuses of the locals, new extremism, appeared likely to come back in the usual cycle that has played itself out in Mosul twice since the 2003 US-led invasion of Iraq.

In Baghdad, where summer temperatures reached 118 degrees, Dillon was confident that the Iraqi government of Abadi was up to the task. They would make the decision as to where to go after Mosul, whether Hawija, Tal Afar or al-Qaim on the Syrian border. The coalition was proud of the progress. A Canadian sniper had recently killed an ISIS member from a record-breaking 3,460 meters. The bullet took ten seconds to get to its target. "We are all about defeating ISIS, and the fewer we have to fight, the better for the world," said Dillon.

No Nuremburg for ISIS

Nadia Murad, who was kidnapped and raped by ISIS in 2014, had a tired look on her face when I met her in the summer of 2017. Since her escape in 2015, she had become the face of her Yazidi community's quest for justice and recognition. She founded an organization called Nadia's Initiative and received support from the UN and others. She seemed to take on the burden of being the living embodiment of perseverance after genocide, like Elie Wiesel had after the Holocaust. But it meant reliving the same stories of rape and abuse again and again, retelling them constantly to journalists.

When I met Murad, I wanted to ask about stories she hadn't told. On June 16, 2014, members of Islamic State attacked Tal Afar in northern Iraq. They came into a city of 200,000 that was divided along sectarian lines of Shi'ite and Sunni Muslims, and many of its residents were from the Turkmen minority. It had seen fighting before between the sectarian groups. It had also been a counterinsurgency success story. But ISIS found it easy pickings. Sunnis welcomed ISIS with celebratory gunfire, while Shi'ites fled for their lives. Thousands of them walked on dusty roads, their belongings on pickup trucks, passing through nearby Yazidi villages and the town of Sinjar.

Murad, who grew up in the village of Kocho near Sinjar, recalled the sight of fleeing Shi'ites. They were frightened and running from ISIS. She had no idea that in two months, the same fate would befall her community. "We heard that Shia had been killed in Tal Afar." ISIS was broadcasting videos of its mass executions of seventeen hundred Shi'ite Iraqi cadets at Camp Speicher on June 12. UN human rights chief Navi Pillay said that the "systematic series of executions almost certainly amounted to war crimes." Yet little was done to protect the Yazidis. Murad became one of the more than five thousand women sold into slavery. She eventually escaped.

"So far we haven't thought about our life and future. We don't know what is happening – a lot of family members are still captive," she said in 2017. That summer she found out her niece was killed, and she wore black during our meeting. "My sister-in-law and nephew were abducted by ISIS. They might tell us any minute that your relative was killed or bombed," she said. On June 1, 2017, she returned to her former village after it was liberated by members of the PMU. "It was my dream the last three years to go back and see that village." But the village was still in ruins. Many of the houses were destroyed. "We knew that a lot of men were killed there and thrown in [mass graves]." Walking through the rubble, she had to be careful of explosives and mines that ISIS had left behind. It looked like Sinjar when I had been there in 2015.

With more than 400,000 Yazidis still living in displaced person's camps, she said that they face the decision whether to leave Iraq or try to return to their destroyed communities, haunted by scenes of genocide and disappeared loved ones. "We are hoping for justice for them and infrastructure. The main thing is not just being compensated; the main thing is trust. The government authority needs to gain their trust." One hurdle Yazidis faced in 2017 was the competing interests between PKK-aligned Kurds and Yazidis on Mount Sinjar and Kurdish Peshmerga close to the KDP, as well as the PMU that had come to control some Yazidi villages. In March, the PKK had clashed with the Rojava Peshmerga on the same road I had traveled on in 2015.

In April, Turkish air strikes targeted Kurds in Sinjar, because Turkey opposes the PKK and claimed the PKK was setting down roots in Sinjar. The air strikes wounded Peshmerga and showed that Turkey was serious about sending a message that the PKK must leave. For Yazidis it meant uncertainty. Some had joined the PMU in case Iraq demanded Sinjar back from the KRG.

"Starting with the mass graves, there are forty-four mass graves, and 100 percent [of the victims in them] are Yazidi victims, and we are trying to tell the world that these mass graves need to be documented with forensics before evidence is lost," Murad said. "In terms of the International Criminal Court, we talked to many countries about bringing ISIS to justice, but to be honest, more than six thousand Yazidis have been killed and [others] abducted and victimized, [and] we haven't seen even a single case brought to justice by those members of the ICC." It was a tragedy to see how slowly the wheels of justice moved. "Not one ISIS member brought to justice for committing crimes against Yazidis." In August 2016, Iraq executed thirty-six ISIS members for their role in the Camp Speicher massacre. But the Yazidis are still waiting.

The genocide was still going on. "Last estimate two months ago [April 2017] is that there are 2,500–3,200 people still captive by ISIS," she said. Murad said that up to a thousand Yazidis might be held by ISIS in Tal Afar, which had not been liberated. In Raqqa, there were Yazidi boys who were brainwashed and trained by ISIS to fight. She also told the story of Yazidi girls who fled during the battle of Mosul and were shot down by ISIS snipers. "One girl told me that ten girls were trying to run away and were instantly killed by ISIS."

Murad hoped the international courts would bring justice. "It is not just my dream to bring them to justice; it is the dream of all Yazidis." Thousands of ISIS members came from all over the world, and a trial showing them as the criminals they are would kill their ideology, she said. "They could tell of the crimes they have committed, and people who wanted to join would change their minds."

Planning for Independence

"The people of the Kurdistan region overwhelmingly or almost unanimously want independence," former US ambassador Peter Galbraith told a symposium in Washington on July 28.[157] His speech was one of many at the event highlighting Kurdistan as "a strategic US ally," intended to showcase why the region deserves the right to decide on a future that may involve separating from Iraq.

For years Kurds had sought independence in Iraq, but each attempt and each planned referendum was postponed. In mid-August, rumors and reports circulated that the Kurdistan Regional Government in Iraq might postpone its referendum on independence, which was set for September 25. KRG president Masoud Barzani decided it would really go ahead. That month he was joined by members of the other leading parties of the region, including his own Kurdistan Democratic Party, the Patriotic Union of Kurdistan, the Kurdistan Islamic Union, the Kurdistan Islamic Movement and other small parties, including those representing Assyrian and Turkmen minorities. New signs on billboards throughout the KRG capital of Erbil touted "Yes to Independence."

But there were many local hurdles to the referendum. The Gorran (Change) Movement, one of the largest parties in the region's parliament, demanded that elections in the KRG be held before the referendum and that the parliament then be reconvened. The KRG had held elections for its regional parliament in 2005, 2009 and 2013.

"The time has come for our own people to determine their future," said Falah Mustafa Bakir, the head of the Department of Foreign Relations for the KRG, in an interview.[158] Fourteen years after the US-led 2003 invasion, he said that the problems between Baghdad and the Kurds have not been resolved by decentralization, autonomy and federalism. "To have a democratic environment, we need democratic practice and democratic culture," argued Bakir. The Iraqi government has breached the constitution, not distributed the federal budget correctly, and a referendum will bring about "stability and security." It will also be a mandate for the Kurdish leadership to negotiate with Baghdad. "We can be good partners as two good neighbors. This is a turning point in our history."

The KRG leadership felt that having a referendum before the end of the war on ISIS would be best, because Baghdad would be distracted by the conflict. It also hoped the same would be true for its powerful Iranian and Turkish neighbors. Syria was in chaos, so it wouldn't do anything. The KRG felt that its island of relative stability could be maintained via the referendum and eventual independence. It argued that years under Iraqi rule had only meant genocide and terrorism.

"We assure our neighbors that this step will not go against the interest of these nations ... We are for building bridges, and we can assure them that the future independent Kurdistan would be a partner and ally," Bakir said. The KRG also said it was reaching out to the US, UN and EU. On August 12, US secretary of state Rex Tillerson called Barzani and asked the Kurds to reconsider. Barzani's office "state[d] that the people of Kurdistan Region would expect guarantees and alternatives for their future" if they postponed the vote.[159] Kurdistan 24 reported on August 20 that Mala Bakhtiar, the executive secretary of the Patriotic Union of Kurdistan, had said the Iraqi central government should "assist the Kurds in overcoming a financial crisis," among other issues, if they were to postpone.[160] According to other reports, the discussions in Baghdad centered on other guarantees relating to the Kurdish region's oil and who will rule over disputed areas in Kirkuk, Sinjar and Khanaquin.

In meetings with EU officials in Brussels on July 12, President Barzani reminded them of the price paid in Kurdish lives fighting against ISIS. A total of 1,745 Peshmerga had been killed in battle with the extremists and more than ten thousand wounded. Peshmerga liberated thirty thousand square kilometers, he said. The Kurdish region was also hosting 1.4 million Iraqi IDPs and 233,000 Syrian refugees, so the world should stand by the region.

KRG prime minister Nechirvan Barzani and deputy prime minister Qubad Talabani met with a delegation of representatives from the US, Germany and UK in May, in the lead-up to announcing the referendum. President Barzani flew to Brussels to press his cause. There was no going back, he said, asking EU officials to at least stay neutral, if they could not support the right of Kurds to vote. US State Department spokesperson Heather Nauert called the referendum an "internal matter," which implied the US might not interfere.

On July 24, Russian foreign minister Sergei Lavrov said in an interview with Kurdish TV channel Rudaw that the referendum represents the "legitimate aspirations of the Kurds," but they must work within the "framework of existing international legal norms."[161] Bayan Sami Abdul Rahman, KRG representative in Washington, laid out the region's rights to Canadian media on July 3. "We have done our best to be partners in Iraq; it has not worked.[162] We believe this is the right time to allow people of Kurdistan to exercise their democratic right, a right that people across the world have to express their right to self-determination." Canadian defense minister Harjit Sajjan replied that he supports a "unified Iraq" as the best "long-term solution. But ultimately these decisions have to be made by the Iraqi people and the Kurds themselves." Sweden's ambassador to the UN Olof Skoog was quoted in Rudaw as saying his country does not support the vote: "The country to our mind should stay together."

According to reports in August, Prime Minister Barzani told the UK's Ministry of Defense senior adviser for the Middle East that the government and the Ministry of Peshmerga Affairs were pushing further reforms for the Kurdish forces. With the Peshmerga role in the war over, Bakhtiyar Mohammed, an adviser at the Peshmerga Affairs Ministry, said that reforms would cover thirty-five articles relating to issues as disparate as arming, training, logistics, and upgrading barracks and living facilities for Kurdish soldiers. Reforms also sought standardization of salaries. But it wasn't clear whether these reform promises – like others in the past – would actually materialize. If the region was going to confront Baghdad, it would need a more professionalized army.

The KRG also sought to have the vote cover the entire area it had come to control during the war on ISIS. This included territories around Kirkuk, Khanaquin, Sinjar and Makhmur. The governor of Kirkuk, Najmaldin Karim, a major supporter of independence, pushed in March 2017 for a provincial council vote to raise the Kurdish flag at local Kirkuk government buildings. Baghdad opposed the decision, and Iran's foreign ministry spokesman Bahram Qassemi said the flag would "increase tensions."[163] Erbil didn't seem to acknowledge the controversy. Kirkuk had been a sticking point in the 1970s and 1990s with Baghdad and had led to disaster for the Kurds before. Erbil was misreading the tepid reactions. It felt that the lack of threats and saber rattling meant the referendum would go ahead without repercussions. But Baghdad didn't seem in a mood to offer concessions in order to postpone the vote; it felt it had the strongest hand and international support. The US didn't understand the Kurds were serious.

ISIS on the Run

After Mosul, ISIS began to melt back into the desert and rural communities it had come from. This was a response to the massive firepower deployed against it. With dozens of countries hunting the extremists in Iraq, there was little else they could do. The coalition was carrying out what it said was the most precise air war in history. With ordnance ranging from ten pounds to two thousand pounds, it had more firepower at its disposal than in previous wars.

"The challenge we faced is we were operating in a city of 1.8 million, the size of Philadelphia, and the enemy was embedded in the civilian population, and we did everything we could do to protect civilians," recalled US Air Force Brig. Gen. Andrew A. Croft, the deputy commander general of the air for the Combined Joint Forces Land Component Command of Operation Inherent Resolve. "I am the guy who helped run and coordinate the air campaign in Mosul as it came down to the final days," he said in a phone interview from Iraq in the summer of 2017. The general, who holds an MBA from Embry-Riddle Aeronautical University, was appointed to his position in April 2017 and would stay until May 2018.

As the battle for Mosul raged, "We did a lot of coordination with Iraqi Security Forces (ISF) on the ground, figuring out where Daesh is, who is Daesh and being able to attack them.... They did everything they could do to frustrate our efforts using civilian structures, so that was the challenge. What enabled us was [that] the precision weapons are more precise than ever in history." This was war at its highest tech, a revolution as important as the one that took place in the 1990s and was unveiled in the First Gulf War. This military revolution used to be called the Revolution in Military Affairs. It came of age in 2017.

"We have unmanned aircraft, cameras and infrared and all networked together, so everyone on ground or air has the same picture, and that allows instantaneous communication with Iraqis. [That] enabled us with high situational awareness. We know where ISIS is, and civilians and ISF, and how to minimize the damage if possible; that is how we overcame the challenge of Mosul." After Mosul the coalition reduced the number of air strikes it carried out. On August 10, for instance, it conducted only four strikes against ISIS units, warehouses, buildings and tunnel entrances.

Like other Americans waging the war on ISIS, Croft emphasized the Iraqi role. He described it as "letting the Iraqis do the fighting and the planning," a major contrast from the US-led surge in Iraq. "They are the A-team," said Croft. The Iraqi air force was also improving. Using F-16s, Czech L-159s, Russian SU-25s and a large force of attack helicopters, they were hunting down ISIS. "They identify ISIS all over Iraq, and they use their aircraft for ground attack and precision strikes, and that goes on every day," said the general. "Their F-16 squadron drops laser guided bombs, and our assessment is their pilots are as good as any US squadron dropping them."

Having an Iraqi air force and more Iraqi gunners on the ground allowed the coalition some leeway. "There may be a case where Iraq intel says there is Daesh in a mosque or school, and we can't corroborate the intel and won't strike it, so they can go ahead and do it," said Croft. "So their ability to do independent intel gathering and strike ops [is a] benefit if they can do it faster than we can."

There was one problem. In many parts of the Iraq, the Shi'ite militias were running things on the ground. According to Croft, the US didn't coordinate with them. "We de-conflict, so our effort is to know where they are so we don't end up in a bad situation; we coordinate with ISF, and obviously sometimes they are part of the ISF." He stressed, "We coordinate with ISF but not those separate organizations."

The presence of the militias led to the possibility of friendly-fire incidents. On August 7, a group affiliated with the PMU called the Sayyid al-Shuhada Brigade claimed coalition artillery struck them near the Iraqi border, killing dozens. Croft clarified that this PMU unit was hit in Syria, and "that attack was done by ISIS. They thought it was the coalition, [but] we weren't doing anything out there."

Tal Afar

On the morning of Tuesday, August 15, the Iraqi air force began bombing Tal Afar in the country's north. The city once held around 200,000 residents and is strategically located on the road from Mosul to Sinjar and the Syrian border. The city was one of the first to fall to ISIS and had zealously embraced the jihadists. Isolated after Mosul, its northern side was held by a Kurdish defensive line, and the Iraqi army and Shi'ite militias had deployed south of the city.

As the Iraqis prepared to go in, Lt. Col. James Downing of the 82nd Airborne, a commander in the 2nd Battalion of the 325th Airborne Infantry Regiment, was advising the Iraqi 15th Infantry Division. "I think they have learned and adapted and become better at this type of warfare since Mosul…certainly [in the] the ability to use maneuver [warfare] and have different options when attacking ISIS positions, what I have witnessed [is] a marked improvement," he said.

The Iraqi army was confident, and ISIS was collapsing. Leaders of the latter had fled to the desert area between Iraq and Syria. ISIS morale was low. As the Iraqis pushed into the city with minimal opposition, Downing said, "You run into attrition [because] a lot of their fighters have quit and have given up on the caliphate, and some have tried to make their way out mixed with civilians, and ISF did a phenomenal job trying to separate innocents from individuals from groups trying to leave."

Downing had arrived in Iraq in December 2016. It was his third tour: he'd first been in 2004, and then during the surge in 2006–2008. "The vast majority of the area [of Tal Afar] was cleared by the Iraqi army. They did phenomenal, outmaneuvered the enemy and took a number of places without firing a shot. How far they have come on the army side, just in their internal fighting jointly in our doctrine, their security forces and army all working together for the country. Impressive to watch, and our role is to help them see that, in cases where they don't have precision fire, then we do help them from intel standpoint, how we see the enemy, and inform their decisions as they conduct operations."

Downing said he was humbled by seeing the successful operation. "To be a small part of this victory and watch them fight on behalf of the international community [such an] important fight in our eyes, [to be] good friends with Iraqi partners … [this is] different than anything I've participated in. These leaders have been targeted here and at home. Over the past months, getting to know a lot of these leaders, a lot of them and their families [have been] targeted, [yet they] continue to persevere after nonstop conflict. [It's] humbling as a military professional; my heart goes out to them and all the losses for the Iraqis."

The battle for Tal Afar went so smoothly that it led to rumors and conspiracy theories about where the ISIS members had gone. There was supposed to be a hard core of ISIS members in the city among the Sunni Turkmen who lived there. In addition, some Yazidi women were supposed to be there. But few were found. Some ISIS members did surrender to the Peshmerga. But most seemed to have disappeared. Rumors claimed they had slipped away and headed to the Hamrin Mountains and other areas in Iraq. Other conspiracy theories claimed a secret deal had allowed them to leave for Syria or Turkey. As far-fetched as this appeared, a subsequent arrangement to evacuate ISIS members from Raqqa and Baghuz would show that it was at least plausible to ask whether it had occurred.

Lebanon's Shield, Iraq's Convoy Problem

While the Iraqi army was clearing Tal Afar, 308 ISIS members and their families boarded buses on the Lebanese-Syrian border on August 28. Their convoy of seventeen buses and eleven ambulances carrying the wounded and weary crossed from the mountainous border region of Qalamoun, near Arsal in Lebanon, into Syria and headed toward Palmyra and the desert. In exchange, ISIS told Lebanon the whereabouts of the bodies of nine Lebanese soldiers who had been missing for years. It was an important victory in Lebanon for Hezbollah, which had styled itself the defender of the country against Sunni Islamist extremism. The Lebanese army played second fiddle as Hezbollah had intervened in the Syrian conflict on Assad's side and then, when ISIS and other extremists targeted Lebanon, claimed to be fighting in Syria to defend Lebanon from the "takfiri" jihadists. Fighting ISIS helped to empower and provide legitimacy for Hezbollah, after years in which it was controversially linked to the 2005 assassination of former Lebanese prime minister Rafic Hariri. In October 2016, Michel Aoun, Christian Lebanese leader and ally of Hezbollah, had been elected president of Lebanon. With ISIS gone, Hezbollah could accept plaudits for its very real role in ridding Lebanon of the black flag.

Under the deal with Hezbollah and the Syrian regime, the ISIS members were to travel several hundred kilometers to the Euphrates River Valley, near the Iraqi border. Iraq was incensed. Mohammed al-Karbouli, a member of Iraq's Security and Defense Committee in parliament, was quoted by Al-Sumaria TV as condemning the decision. He said the Iraqi government should investigate the "mysteries" and "secrets" of the deal as to why ISIS fighters might then be able to cross into Iraq via Abu-Kamal city into the area of al-Qaim and terrorize Iraq, bolstering some three thousand ISIS fighters he claimed were in that area of Anbar Province. Another Iraqi politician was quoted as saying, "The blood of our youth and our people is not cheaper than the blood of the Lebanese." Iraq's anger showed that despite the alliance of Hezbollah, the Shi'ite militias in Iraq, Tehran and the Syrian regime, the dumping of ISIS members on the Iraqi border aroused nationalist passions.

Under pressure from Iraq, the coalition condemned the "agreement between Lebanese Hezbollah and ISIS." The coalition also said that Russian and pro-regime statements "ring hollow" when they allow terrorists to transit their territory in buses. "ISIS is a global threat. Relocating terrorists from one place to another for someone else to deal with is not a lasting solution."

The coalition began monitoring the convoy, even though it was over the river border of the "de-confliction" area. Colonel Dillon, spokesman for the coalition, said that "those would be absolutely lucrative targets," a thinly veiled threat that the ISIS fighters could be targeted by air strikes. That threat became reality on August 30, when the coalition targeted a road the convoy was using. A statement posted by Brett McGurk, the US special presidential envoy for the Global Coalition to Defeat ISIS, noted that "the coalition cratered the road heading east between Hamaymah and Abul Kamal to prevent the further transport of ISIS fighters to the border area of our Iraqi partners and struck individual vehicles and fighters that were clearly identified as ISIS."[164] Eventually the coalition would target vehicles trying to get to the convoy. It was never clear exactly what happened with the convoy in the end. The coalition moved on. The ISIS members vanished into the desert.

Chapter 18
Kurdistan's Referendum

Kurdish Spring

I wanted to get out of my dinner plans in Erbil on September 26, 2017.[165] Kurdistan's politics filter down into friendships, and that's especially true among Kurds who are connected to rival political networks. One group of friends wanted to eat outside, next to the airport. Another wanted to go to a fish restaurant near the Arabella Grand Hotel, next to the parliament. I tried to do both and ended up pleasing neither.

At the open-air restaurant, I gobbled down some fried food and two beers. Helicopters were circling. It was the day after the Kurdish referendum. Young people were celebrating. No one wanted to talk about the future.

At the fish restaurant, things were a bit different. An older crowd, some in suits but no ties, was crowded in quiet groups around tables. Alcohol was served and then wheeled away on a separate trolley. Kurdistan is a conservative country, and for the older generation, having bottles of booze on the table was not normal. But they enjoyed a taste. Turkey was threatening to close the border. Baghdad had ordered the two international airports servicing the region closed. Baghdad was also deploying the army to take Kirkuk, just south of Erbil. Iran had expelled a film crew from Kurdistan 24 and said sanctions would come. The Kurdish region was about to be under siege.

The older men had seen worse. In the 1970s and 1980s, they had no friends "but the mountains," as Kurds tend to say. With 72 percent turnout and 93 percent in favor of independence, the Kurds appeared united. The older men thought the region could weather the storm. They hoped Israel and Saudi Arabia would come to Erbil's aid. Kirkuk oil would continue flowing to Turkey, because Turkey would lose more if it closed the border. If all else failed, the Kurds in Iraq would work with the Kurds in Syria, despite political differences. They would find a way. They had suffered genocide in the past and seen hardship. "We can survive," said one of the men, a skinny academic who had been a member of the PKK in the 1980s.

I had arrived in the KRG from Amman, two days before the referendum. A large, glowing sign greeted arrivals driving from the airport into the city. It had a Kurdish flag on it. Throughout the city, large flags were draped on buildings, on cars and on houses and businesses. The signs were a blend of English and Kurdish written in Arabic script. Some showed a map of the Kurdish region, including Kirkuk and Sinjar, with a ballot box on them.

The KRG was trying to attract voters from the Christian minority, many of them residents of Nineveh who had fled ISIS to Erbil's Ainkawa neighborhood. In Ainkawa's narrow streets, ill lit due to the brownouts and bad street lighting, there were posters encouraging people to vote. One was printed in four languages – Arabic, Kurdish, Turkish and Assyrian. *"Ahdimiz Bir arada Yasamak Kardeslik ve Baristir,"* it read in Assyrian, above a group of people dancing with a Kurdish flag.

The first day back in Erbil, I decided to take a quick trip to the south to see the front line against Hawija. On September 21, two days before I arrived back in Iraq, Abadi announced an offensive to reconquer Hawija. The operation would cover a front line around a hundred kilometers long to conquer a pocket twenty kilometers wide. Hawija was a pocket southwest of Erbil, three hundred kilometers north of Baghdad.

Hawija had always been a hotbed of insurgency and jihadists. Just sixty kilometers west of Mosul, it was a Sunni Arab area beyond a line of hills that separated it from Kirkuk. ISIS had easily conquered it in 2014, turning the Iraqi army's 12th Division headquarters into its new HQ.

It was never clear why Hawija was not liberated before Mosul, but it had been allowed to wither on the vine. US envoy McGurk arrived on September 4 in Erbil, where he held a press conference saying that the Peshmerga and the Iraqi army were still working on "very strong" cooperation. Despite his reservations about the independence referendum, he said that it was "important that we remain united and focused on the effort to defeat Daesh."[166]

The problem with Hawija was that the Iraqi army and its Shi'ite militias were advancing from the west, while the Kurds were holding what was called the Kurdish Defensive Line (KDL) to the east of Hawija. Iraq lined up all the units it could find for the battle, including the Federal Police, the 9th Armored Division, the 16th Infantry Division, the Special Operations Forces (ISOF) and units of the Popular Mobilization Units. These were veterans of the battle for Mosul, and many of them had suffered high casualties. But they faced limited opposition from ISIS, as in Tel Afar.

The coalition also threw its weight behind the fight, doing what it called "shaping the battlefield." It began the operation with fifty-five air strikes against VBIEDs, ISIS command posts and fighting positions.

I was staying with my friend and fellow journalist Paul Iddon in Ainkawa. He lived near a road called Du-Saad (Two-Side), and there was an overpriced Starbucks-wannabee coffee shop called Barista at the end of the road. I arranged with Yazdanpanah to send someone from the PAK to pick me up. Eventually the man arrived in a pickup truck. He was wearing a dark olive uniform and had an old revolver on his hip. We drove south from Erbil, passing the PUK's headquarters outside the city with its giant poster of Talabani, and then along side roads toward the front line. Oil flares burned in the distance.

Yazdanpanah was at the same positions he had held in December 2015, when I'd gone to meet him the first time. Two female PAK members stood guard. Nearby, the mustachioed Kurdish general was holding court with a bunch of other journalists. He embraced me when I caught his eye. Then he took me to a small caravan and asked for tea and food for us. ISIS was not his concern now. It would be defeated soon, and his men were playing no role but defending the line. Whatever McGurk had said about good relations, the Kurdish fighters such as the PAK didn't see ISIS as the priority now, and the plan by Baghdad had left them out. Yazdanpanah and his men were more concerned about Iranian agents penetrating the Kurdish region. He said that the next time I saw him, he might be on another front line, fighting Iran, not ISIS, or fighting the Shi'ite militias.

On one part of the PAK front line, there was a group of foreign special forces operators. They asked that no photos be taken. They were relaxing outside, waiting for the battle to come to them, waiting for any ISIS members who might drift through to surrender or to attack the Kurds. The special forces men said they would be leaving the front line for the day of the referendum. It seemed that the referendum brought concerns of violence and that the coalition was worried that Kurds might clash with Shi'ite militias or the Iraqis somewhere. The coalition, which was allied with both the Peshmerga and the central government, didn't want to be in the middle.

I looked out over the hazy desert from the PAK positions. Guns sat at their stations, and sandbags were piled high. Soldiers milled about. There was no urgency. ISIS was defeated. That was how people felt. Now they wondered what the future after the referendum would hold. One war was ending, and another might be about to begin.

After the PAK, I stopped by Kirkuki's headquarters once more. It was like my 2015 trip again. Kirkuki was also holding court with journalists. He showed off a captured white drone. ISIS had become more proficient in using drones in 2017 and used them to effect against Iraqi forces. In Syria, the SDF had also found houses full of ISIS drones, usually purchased abroad and then cannibalized for parts. ISIS used them to film its attacks for propaganda and also to drop small bits of ordnance on the Iraqi army. In some ways, the group was pointing to the future. It was innovating with VBIED car bombs, IEDs and drones.

Kirkuki was deeply supportive of the referendum. He scoffed at any suggestion it would be postponed. "It is a democratic process, and it must be respected by every democracy and pupil of democracy, and they should respect the democracy and the referendum," he said. He said the United Nations allowed countries to seek self-determination, and all the Kurds were doing was seeking their rights. He listed UN General Assembly Resolution 1514 (The Declaration on the Granting of Independence to Colonial Countries and Peoples) from 1960 and other documents.

The Kurdish general, at his office in the town of Dibs, was unconcerned about the Shi'ite militias. "They cannot do anything without coalition support." He said that if they tried anything or made problems, the Kurds would show them what would happen. Kirkuki's men were busy deploying in areas outside Kirkuk to secure the city. He wasn't concerned about ISIS, boasting that his men had captured and arrested many of the extremists. He reminded me that his units had stood alone in 2014, when the Iraqi army retreated, and that ISIS drew its strength from nearby Sunni villages. He said his men had killed 2,007 ISIS members and suffered 236 killed and 978 wounded in three years of battle.

The US was concerned that the referendum would be a distraction from the war on ISIS and that any conflict in Iraq between the Kurds and Baghdad would lead to instability. ISIS might exploit this, creeping back into ungoverned spaces again. "This is not true," said Kirkuki. "We will continue to fight ISIS as before and after until we bring them to an end." Kirkuki said he wanted a federal government like in the United States, with various states for different groups – a Shi'ite state, a Sunni state, a Kurdish state and even areas for other groups such as Turkmen and Christians. He reminded me of Sykes-Picot and that the borders of Kurdistan stretched to the Hamrin Mountains and north of Tikrit. He predicted that ISIS members would fade away from Hawija, mix with civilians and go up into the Hamrin Mountains.

Sunset was coming, and I said farewell to Kirkuki and his men. He was reviewing some Kurdish soldiers who had shown up, shaking hands with officers and patting them on the back. He was full of confidence, as many Kurds were, feeling they were on the eve of independence. His forces were bolstered by extra Peshmerga to secure the area ahead of the vote. The old fighter, Kirkuki, who had suffered numerous wounds during the fight against Saddam, seemed ready for what would come next.

On the way back to Erbil, a local Kurdish translator gave me a ride. We passed through the high, grassy plains near Dibs, skirting the main highway from Kirkuk to Erbil. The man said he had grown up in one of the villages we passed. As a kid, he had suffered under Saddam Hussein's Anfal campaign, fleeing and becoming a refugee abroad. He had come back in the 1990s but still couldn't return to the village because of its proximity to Iraqi forces that still controlled Kirkuk. Only after 2003 he returned. But then the jihadists threatened it from Hawija and other areas. And then came ISIS.

His story seemed to represent so many people in the area, their whole lives consumed by war for decades. For Kurds, it meant displacement and then return. For Sunni Arabs, it had meant going from being the rulers of the country, proud officers in the Ba'athist army, to feelings of humiliation under Shi'ite power. The repercussions of the decline of ISIS meant that two major power structures in Iraq were on a collision course. In the north, the Kurds had built an impressive economy and extended economic and personal freedoms to residents of the region. The KRG had flourished as Iraq declined and ISIS sacked cities. It was a bubble of success, like Lebanon had been in the early 1970s, before the civil war. People were speaking of Erbil like it would trend toward being the next Dubai. Beauty salons run by Lebanese were opening. Iraqi women came north for treatments. Foreign workers came, Gulfies, Turks.

But the Kurdish region was burdened by its divided politics and the overbearing influence of two large political families, more like tribes really. For activists, this was the criticism. The KRG could be great, but it had to remove its last barrier, the "tribal" politics. The Gorran (Change) Movement party was supposed to be part of that. But it had only thrived in peacetime, and its leader, Nawshirwan Mustafa, had died in May 2017.

Once the ISIS war came, the Barzanis and the Talabanis rushed to organize the front line and the fight against ISIS. Qubad Talabani, son of Jalal, became KRG deputy prime minister. Lahur Talabani created his own intelligence and security force. Masrour Barzani did the same with the KRG's security council. Nechirvan Barzani, once known primarily for his economic prowess and erudite tastes, was KRG prime minister. Waiting in the wings were others, such as Ala Talabani, a member of the Iraqi parliament, and Bafel Talabani, son of Jalal and his wife Hero Ibrahim Ahmed.

Masoud Barzani had pushed the referendum forward on his strength of will. Most Kurds supported independence, but they didn't know how to get there. Their region anyway felt independent. It had two of its own airports, its own visa system, its own armed forces, its own budget, sold its own oil and ran its own borders. The Kurdish flag flew from offices of its ministries, and it was difficult to find an Iraqi flag. In schools, children learned Kurdish, not Arabic like under Saddam. And they celebrated Kurdish Flag Day. There was no sense of being in "Iraq" when in Kurdistan. The only thing that especially bothered middle- and upper-class Kurds is that they suffered under having Iraqi passports. "The worst passport in the world," one lawyer complained to me. A Kurdish passport with travel connections to Turkey, the US and Saudi Arabia would benefit them.

The referendum had seemed like a gamble in June, but by September 2017 the train had left the station. The only opposition seemed to come from a wealthy businessman named Shaswar Abdulwahid, who owned a media group called NRT TV and had other interests.[167] With a power base in Sulaymaniyah, near the Iranian border, he held rallies called "No for now," in which he supported independence but not the referendum. Kurdish media connected to the KDP, such as Kurdistan 24, attacked him and insinuated he was working with Baghdad and Shi'ite former prime minister Nouri al-Maliki.

Sulaymaniyah always had a different orientation than Erbil. It was close to Iran geographically and politically. In the old days, Iran had supported the Kurds against Iraq. The shah had worked with the US and Israel to funnel supplies and training to them. That had wrapped up in 1975 and for good in 1979 when the shah fled Iran. The Islamic Republic fought a war with its own Kurds and was colder to aspirations in Iraq. Nevertheless, Kurds always thrived on the differences between Iraq, Iran, Syria and Turkey. For instance, when the PKK was fighting Turkey in the 1980s, its leader Abdullah Ocalan was hosted in Syria.

To gather steam for the referendum, Barzani held a series of massive rallies. On September 13, one was held in Akre, where the Newroz torch procession festival is held every year. On September 14, he was in Zakho, and on the 16th, he went to Dohuk, a KDP stronghold. On September 20, Barzani took the unprecedented step of traveling to Sulaymaniyah, where he told twenty thousand people: "My dear brother president Mam Jalal, I will never forget your brotherhood," referring to Jalal Talabani, who had never recovered from his 2012 stroke.[168] Hero Ahmed sat next to Barzani as he wore his trademark red kaffiyeh and green fatigues. It was historic because Barzani and Talabani were historic rivals, and the KDP and PUK had fought a civil war in the 1990s. Many leading KDP figures recalled that bitterly and told of brothers or relatives killed in the period. But Barzani wanted the referendum to cross party lines and not be seen as just a KDP project.

The KRG's referendum plans were also successful in Kirkuk, where the governor, Najmadin Karim, was very pro-independence. But up until the last moment there was hesitation. "If we receive an alternative in the coming days by the international community that guarantees Kurdistan's independence, we will postpone the referendum," Barzani had said in Soran on September 19.[169] The average voter dismissed this, hoping the referendum would go forward. Surprisingly, Israel flags began to appear at Kurdish rallies in northern Iraq and in Europe. There was a feeling that this was the "1948 moment" that Kurds had been waiting for, when they would become independent as the Jewish state had done. It was no secret that many Kurds admired Israel's struggles and that they had looked to Israel in the 1980s, when Arab nationalist regimes were brutally suppressing them. Kurds would tell how their parents in 1967 suffered under the greatest restrictions in Syria but would secretly listen to stories of Israel defeating the Syrian army. The same was true in Iraq when Saddam threatened to "burn" Israel with chemical weapons. Many Kurds told me that if the Jews could carve out a state in the region, so could they.

Barzani's Vision

The day before the referendum, journalists were invited to a major announcement at Massif, the Barzani compound in the mountains above Erbil. We drove up there, along the winding, pretty roads and through villages. In summer, Kurds like to picnic in the mountains, and the beauty revealed why. Eventually we came to a checkpoint and were allowed into a parking lot built around a hexagonal building. Inside, each member of the press was registered, while bags were checked for weapons. Badges were issued, and we were put on buses to travel to Barzani's compound, where everyone waited in a large lecture-style hall. In what became an all-day event, Barzani finally emerged.

The KRG representatives distributed flyers to the four hundred journalists, and then Barzani spoke in Kurdish for the greater part of an hour.

English translation came next. He touched on familiar themes. The Kurds had suffered under colonial-imposed borders as part of Iraq for a hundred years. Iraq had subjected them to genocide. After 2003, the KRG tried to work with Baghdad. The 2005 constitution was supposed to provide rights for Kurds in disputed areas, but Baghdad violated the constitution. Baghdad today has the same mentality as under Saddam, Barzani alleged. "It is better to be a good neighbor and depend on each other," he said. "We have been saying for a long time that we want to hold a referendum. The relationship with Baghdad is not working, and we are heading to ask our people what they want." Barzani was adamant that Erbil would not return to Baghdad and negotiate a "failed partnership," as it had in the past. But he wanted to assure the Arabs in Iraq that they "are our brothers," and he tried to assure countries in the region that the referendum would not be a destabilizing factor.

The US tended to view the Kurds as allies who had no choice but to stick with Washington. They needed Washington's support more than Washington needed them, and therefore they were expected not to rock the boat. In the fall of 2017, the priority was the defeat of ISIS and Iraq's preparation for elections in 2018. The US feared that a Kurdish referendum could lead to chaos and empower ISIS and Iran, according to sources I spoke to.

This had always been Washington's strategy: support Baghdad for a strong, centralized Iraq, which would somehow be a buffer against Iran and chaos. The problem was that Iran had infiltrated Iraq using politically allied parties, as it had used Hezbollah in Lebanon. By the fall of 2017, the Shi'ite militias were an official Iraqi force, and Badr controlled the interior ministry. But Washington refused to see this: Trump's administration and Secretary of State Tillerson thought they could pry Baghdad away from Iran and facilitate closer connections with Saudi Arabia.

In September 2008, Barzani had met with US ambassador to Iraq Ryan Crocker. Barzani claimed that "Iran wants Iraq to be in a permanent state of chaos," according to a US diplomatic cable at the time. Nouri al-Maliki was also replacing Kurdish officers in the Iraqi army in disputed areas such as Khanaqin. Barzani was livid. "How long do you expect us not to fight back?" he asked. He told the Americans that Turkey could be a counterbalance to Iran. Crocker didn't seem to care much for the problems and warned Barzani that any confrontation with pro-Iran forces would lead to the Kurds "losing everything."

The US had the same message for Erbil on September 14, when McGurk came to the city. "The referendum is ill-timed and ill-advised. It is not something that we can support. That is not simply our position. That is the position of our entire international coalition."[170] Washington was worried that the referendum would distract from the war on ISIS. It could create conflict with Baghdad or Iran and set in motion a new round of instability and chaos at the very worst time. There were last-minute attempts by the Americans to head off the referendum. Secretary of State Tillerson, who had experience in the Kurdish region as an oil man, sought out Barzani by phone, but to no avail. So Barzani brought together the region's press corps at his residence and explained the decision.

What Barzani didn't tell the press was that he was leaving office as president of the KRG and that the referendum would be his last major initiative. He saw it as his legacy. He thought this was the last chance for a referendum. Once the war was over, Baghdad would have no reason to say yes to a vote, and there would be no ISIS distraction. Baghdad would focus all its wrath on Erbil. As it was, in September 2017 Baghdad was still recovering and in disarray. There was an economic crisis, a political crisis and a military struggle. Baghdad was thinking about elections in May 2018. While the Americans were worried the referendum would distract from the war effort, the Kurds thought that the war was the distraction that would shield them so they could hold the referendum in peace. ISIS had therefore helped to accelerate Kurdish desires for independence.

The day of the vote was warm and sunny. In Ainkawa, people got up early to stand in line as polls opened at 8 a.m. They were supposed to close by 6 p.m., and final results would be announced three days later. I stopped by a school while waiting for a taxi. One man named Rizgar said Kurds had waited a hundred years for this day. "We want a state, with God's help. Today is a celebration for all Kurds. God willing, we will say yes, yes to dear Kurdistan."

The KRG decided to have VIPs vote at the Rotana Hotel in Erbil. It was well stage-managed. Journalists came through a rear entrance, passing the giant security wall and a security checkpoint, then being being ushered into the rear of the hotel, where there were several large rooms that could be used for conferences. In one room, a stage had been set up and a lectern and rows of chairs. In the second large room, the press was cordoned along one wall, while a voting box sat on a table in the center of the room. Along the opposite wall were several voting booths. Over the course of an hour, dozens of Kurds, many of them in suits, some in traditional Kurdish clothes, filed in to vote. Many of them were members of the Kurdish parliament or political leaders from various parties. There were KDP members, PUK, Islamic Party members and voters from Gorran. Women showed up in flowing dresses. Kids flashed the victory sign and showed off fingers dipped in purple ink, a sign of voting, even though the kids had not voted. Journalists shouted from the scrum for a quote. "Kak Fazil, kak Fazil," one man shouted at a senior KDP member, using the Kurdish term of respect "*kak.*"

As the Kurds voted, a group of international observers, including Bernard-Henri Lévy, looked on. The KRG wanted the vote to have an imprimatur of being fair and internationally recognized. This was despite the fact the UN and other countries rejected it as "nonbinding."

Eventually after the voting, Prime Minister Nechirvan Barzani gave a speech. He stressed themes similar to what the KRG had been saying over the last days. "There are [*sic*] no need for threats; we have a common enemy in ISIS." He sought to assure Turkey and Iran that the vote was not a threat. Ankara had become more apoplectic in the days leading up to the vote, reaching out to Baghdad and Tehran to say that any threat to Turkey might result in some kind of intervention or border closure. "Putting an embargo on people will not weaken our people," Barzani said. "We did the referendum to enable people to express their will; the next stage is not war or violence – let's come and talk. When they are ready, we are ready to fly to Baghdad to talk."

After the prime minister's speech, I went out for lunch at a Turkish restaurant and then down to the Erbil Citadel to sip tea at the iconic Machko Chai Khana teahouse. Located at the base of the walls of the Citadel, the sprawling teahouse had lines of chairs roped together with little tables in front of them. Customers would be stuffed next to one another in the little chairs. A second floor had better ambience and looked out on the fountains that make up the park in front of the Citadel.

On the day of the vote, the area around the Citadel was crowded. Many had on Kurdistan flags worn as scarves, and they milled about or took photos. By nightfall, initial returns showed more than 70 percent voter turnout. Eventually 4.5 million votes would be counted, of which 93 percent voted yes. There would be some celebrating, but in general the vote ended quietly. No mass rallies, no violence. It almost seemed that all the buildup and threats and also the joy Kurds had shown in the lead-up to the vote ended with a sigh.

The capital was still festooned with flags the next day. But there were no calls for declaring independence. The world had not changed. It was just another day. I went to a brief meeting with Falah Mustafa Bakir, the KRG's foreign minister. Like the Barzanis over the last few days, he said that now was the time for dialogue and discussions. He was proud of this moment and sat upright in a hall usually reserved for foreign guests, with the requisite round of tea, little personal waters on a tray and a Kurdish flag in the background.

While Erbil was quiet, Baghdad was plotting. On September 14, the Iraqi parliament had voted to depose the governor of Kirkuk, Najmaldin Karim. No one had noticed in Kirkuk because Baghdad had no real say. Baghdad had been passing laws and saying things for years, such as asking for the oil to be exported via Baghdad.

Abadi had appeared to take a short vacation prior to the referendum. In Erbil some interpreted it as a sign of weakness. Quietly, the Iraqi prime minister was confident. The day after the referendum, the parliament called on Abadi to send the army to Kirkuk and secure the oil fields. Four percent of the world's oil was now in play.

Baghdad decided to first isolate the Kurds, before moving on Kirkuk. It ordered the two international airports closed. The $500 million Erbil Airport was a major conduit for visitors and goods. Now all that would have to go through Baghdad, and the liberal visa system in the Kurdish region would end, because travelers would have to get visas valid for the rest of Iraq.

At five in the afternoon on Friday, September 29, two commercial airliners pulled away from their gates at Erbil International Airport in the Kurdish region of northern Iraq. ZagrosJet's Airbus A321 holds up to two hundred passengers and Pegasus Airlines' Boeing 737 holds 189 passengers. They were the last to leave the Kurdish region of Iraq before the airport closed. Tillerson continued to condemn the Kurds for the referendum. Four days after the vote, he said the US did not recognize the "unilateral referendum." He said it lacked legitimacy and that the US "continues to support a united, federal, democratic and prosperous Iraq." But the Americans also cautioned the Iraqis against using any force against the Kurds.

Force would come, but the Iraqi army first had to take Hawija.

Hawija II

On September 29, the Iraqi army launched phase 2 of its Hawija offensive. It rolled into the city itself and then took Rashad south of it. Coalition air strikes ripped apart fifty-one ISIS vehicles during the campaign.

The US-led coalition was confident in the progress being made. Colonel Charles D. Costanza, on his fourth tour in Iraq, sat at a desk in the coalition's strike cell planning area in the old part of Erbil's airport. He was in charge of the "target engagement authority," as part of the coalition's war effort, and a member of the US 1st Armored Division. He watched as the Iraqi 9th Armored Division, Federal Police and ISOF took back Hawija. ISIS was on the run. "A bit of this is attrition of their leadership – a significant number were killed in Mosul," he said.

Costanza's job was to run the "strike cell" approving targets over Hawija. After studying aspects of the new airpower guidelines for six months and going into the details of the laws of armed conflict, he was issued a massive manual, as thick as an elephant's trunk, and sent to target people. "It's not just about the technology; the technology is precise. It is our desire to minimize collateral damage and civilian casualties."

When it was all over and Costanza's drones and missiles had helped the Iraqis to take Hawija, the Iraqi armored columns paused. Thousands of soldiers were now abutting the Kurdish defensive line that had been held against ISIS for years. Iraqi soldiers and Kurdish Peshmerga had seen eye to eye in Mosul over the last year, but now, with the referendum in the background, tensions were higher. Rumors were circulating in Kurdish ranks. To reduce the tensions, around October 5 the Kurds began packing up to leave several positions south of Kirkuk.

Chapter 19
The Struggle for Kirkuk

Abadi's Third Act Denouement

During the lead-up to the Kurdistan independence referendum, Iraqi prime minister Haider al-Abadi took a vacation.[171] He went down south and paddled among the reeds of the swamps of southern Iraq. This is where the Marsh Arabs live. Their way of life had been targeted for destruction by Saddam Hussein. There is now a large memorial to their suffering among the reeds. Abadi was confident. He was at the height of his power, having defeated ISIS in Mosul while enjoying the support of Turkey, Iran and the United States. Iraq was also patching up relations with Saudi Arabia. Abadi's diplomats were negotiating the first commercial flights to link Baghdad and Riyadh in twenty-seven years. Abadi had set his sights on rebuilding Iraq to the state it had been in 1990, before the First Gulf War.

The Kurds were a petulant gear in Abadi's policy. Instead of bellicose language, he settled on a quiet stratagem. He would get Iran to help him retake Kirkuk, a province held by the Peshmerga since 2014. He would close the KRG's airports and break its international support. The Kurdish leadership would buckle, because they were not prepared for a new all-out war with Baghdad.

The Peshmerga knew what was coming but didn't want to believe it. The Kurdistan Regional Security Council complained on October 12 that Iraqi forces were moving toward Kirkuk. "Intelligence shows intention to takeover nearby oil fields, airport and military base," the security council tweeted.[172] Peshmerga decided to pull back from areas south of Kirkuk city, abandoning posts to its southwest. Meanwhile, the Iraqi military machine roared forward. In dusty towns south of Tuz Khurmatu, young men smoked narghiles and watched dozens of tanks and Humvees drive through at midnight. Many of these, including Federal Police, Popular Mobilization Units and ISOF as well as Abrams tanks from the 9th Armored, were veterans of the Hawija operation that had ended on October 8. The battle for Hawija had been rushed so as to get the Iraqi forces close to Kirkuk in time to retake the province. Baghdad gave its forces orders on October 14 to secure bases and federal institutions in Kirkuk Province.

There was one last chance to avert war. Kurdish officials from the KDP traveled to Lake Dukan, a picturesque summer vacation spot.[173] There they met with fellow Kurds from the PUK. They couldn't agree on what to do about Kirkuk. The PUK technically controlled the government of Kirkuk, but the KDP was powerful in the city. Security forces from both groups controlled the area around the city.

Meanwhile, Hashd al-Sha'abi leaders Hadi al-Amiri and Abu Mahdi al-Muhandis drove to Kirkuk, in an effort to quietly broker a deal. Amiri called the Peshmerga his "brothers" and encouraged them to leave peacefully. Meanwhile, Shi'ite militias were parading near Tuz Khurmatu. They had been there since September 27. Elements of Badr, Asaib Ahl al-Haq and the Khorasani Brigades showed off their weapons and trucks. Qais al-Khazali, the leader of Asaib Ahl al-Haq, warned that war was coming with Erbil if the Kurds did not leave Kirkuk. Shi'ite militia leaders said that conflict with the Kurds would come after ISIS.

On Sunday, October 15, Maj. Gen. Qasem Suleimani, the leader of the Iranian Revolutionary Guards' Quds Force, went to Sulaymaniyah to meet with the heads of the PUK.[174] He brought them a message. The Talabanis were without Mam Jalal. He had been sick for years, but his symbol had survived until his death on October 3. Now the Kurdish future rested partly on the shoulders of his sons and wife. Bafel Talabani said that Suleimani brought them an offer to leave Kirkuk peacefully. It was "honorable," Bafel said. Instead the KRG quarreled between PUK and KDP, and "catastrophe befell Kirkuk."[175]

Najmaldin Karim, the governor of Kirkuk, vowed that the city would resist to the end. Men and women, including the elderly, flocked to the streets on the night of October 14 and then into October 15, holding up AK-47s, vowing to fight and die.[176] Then they went home. As they were settling in, the Iraqi army began to push forward through Tuz Khurmatu toward the city. Initially the Peshmerga resisted. KRG vice president Kosrat Rasul's Peshmerga forces destroyed several Iraqi Humvees.

At the K-1 military base, Sheikh Jaafar Mustafa relaxed with his PUK Peshmerga leaders until midnight. Then the Peshmerga leaders and politicians began to leave their posts. The Peshmerga who chose to fight had no heavy weapons to resist Abrams tanks. They got in their vehicles and fled back through Kirkuk. The withdrawal was mostly orderly. By mid-morning it was complete. Checkpoints were abandoned as far north as Dibs, where Kirkuki's headquarters folded up shop and headed north. The debris of years of war, including captured Mad Max–style VBIEDs, rusted and slumping to one side like collapsed elephants, were left behind.

In Kirkuk city, there were a few brief skirmishes in the morning. Several fighters from the PKK exchanged fire from a bridge with the ISOF before withdrawing. Residents came out to beg the Peshmerga to stay. Some of the Peshmerga wept. By noon, about nine hours after the Iraqi offensive began, the Iraqi flag was raised in the city, and the Kurdish flags began to be taken down. Posters of Masoud Barzani were destroyed and KDP offices looted. For the Iraqi forces, Barzani was a symbol of secession. PUK offices were left alone. Quietly the PUK had made a deal to withdraw. Amiri and Muhandes arrived to witness a flag-raising. Surrounded by their soldiers from the Popular Mobilization Units, they celebrated in the city.

Intermittent skirmishes still remained. Abrams tanks from the Iraqi 9th Armored skirted the city toward the industrial zone, where they fired at some Peshmerga. A local commander was killed. "Many departments have left their posts without fighting. It's total chaos," a fighter said as he straggled along the long road of retreat toward Erbil. "We have tried to keep the lines to the north, but after several repeated attempts, we have had to exfiltrate many of the dead and injured Peshmerga. With little ammunition, we went north under rocket and artillery fire." Many of the frontline soldiers had no notice of what their commanders had decided. Like the civilians, they were left to make their own choices.

As the afternoon came on, the giant Peshmerga statue in Kirkuk, which had been unveiled in July 2017, was redecorated with the Iraqi flag. Black Humvees from the US-trained ISOF parked at the base of the twenty-one-meter-tall statue. The Iraqi flag hanging from the Kurdish statue was a symbol of the hubris of the Kurdish leadership in the face of the Iraqi army and Iran's dealmaking.

Many Kurds had staked their hopes on Washington restraining Baghdad. But in the lead-up to the referendum and Baghdad's decision to send the army to Kirkuk, Washington stepped back. Abadi was winning the war on ISIS, and his army was to be the recipient of $1.3 billion in US Train and Equip funds for the fiscal year 2018. The United States wanted Abadi to work more closely with Saudi Arabia and hoped he would win the May 2018 elections. This was the strong horse to back.

Brett McGurk said the US was working "intensely to maintain stability," and claimed the military operations had been coordinated.[177] But the feeling in Washington was that the Kurds were uppity in their demands for a referendum and not working with Abadi. "Pleading and coddling" was not a policy going forward. Instead the Kurds would be told to toe the line, and Washington would make it clear that "bad behavior" would not be tolerated. Threats of terminating military and financial support for the KRG were in the cards. For the UK, other interests were at work. The British ambassador, Frank Baker, maintained contact with the Talabanis, and the UK hoped that a deal could be worked out in Kirkuk. In the days after Iraq reasserted federal control, British Petroleum signed new deals to work in Kirkuk.

With a hundred thousand Kurds from Kirkuk fleeing north, the roads to Sulaymaniyah became one long line of traffic.[178] The Iraqi army paused for a day, but its commanders had orders to keep going. For the Peshmerga, the irony of the debacle was that it had begun a year after they had been fighting against ISIS, alongside some of the same Iraqi units that had now attacked them. One of the foreign trainers who had worked in Kirkuk with a Kurdish anti-terror unit called it a day that would forever live in infamy. "They sold us."

Picking up the Pieces

On October 16, just after midnight, Peshmerga in Sinjar were called by the Popular Mobilization Units opposite them. They were told they had until two in the morning to withdraw. The Peshmerga near Sinjar occupied a line that looked like a giant half-circle around the city. It stretched several kilometers to the north and south. Behind it was the Mount Sinjar. For many of the Yazidis who had joined the Peshmerga, the choice was obvious. They would go into the mountain and join their families to wait for any conflict to blow over. For the Kurdish Peshmerga, the choice was to retreat or to fight the PMU. They chose to leave.

By the morning of the 17th, the Peshmerga had moved north of Sinjar, over the mountain, to Snune. They burned several of their bases and packed pickup trucks to roll out. It was a testimony to how little they had invested in the ruined city since liberation in 2015 that they could leave in a day. The Rojava Peshmerga turned their checkpoints over to the YBS, the Sinjar Resistance Units. Haydar Shesho, the Yazidi fighter, stayed on with his HPE, the Ezidkhan Protection Forces. It was his land; he had fought ISIS, and he would remain on it forever. Like in Kirkuk, some of the Yazidis had hoped the US would stand by them and not hand them over to Baghdad and the PMU militias. Qasim Shesho, a relative of Haydar, had flown a US and German flag at a meeting before the referendum, believing international support would come. Now he was left out to dry, to find an accommodation with the Iraqi forces. By the 18th, trucks with Shi'ite militia flags were driving through Sinjar, and Khal Ali, commander of the Yazidi Lalesh Brigade, was posing in the old KDP offices.[179]

As the KDP and the Rojava Peshmerga left Sinjar, they drove past the battlefields of 2014–2015. Then they came to Rabiah. They paused and resumed moving, eventually setting up a perimeter just outside the city near an area called Mahmudiyah. The line stretched to the reservoir formed by Mosul Dam and gave them a short front line to defend against the PMU. In the days that followed, the Shi'ite militias from the Badr Brigade, Kataib Jund al-Imam, Ta'ad al-Saree Division and members of the Emergency Response Division attacked the Peshmerga several times, and were beaten back each time. Several vehicles were destroyed. By October 24, the two sides had settled in for an uneasy truce. Abu

Mahdi al-Muhandis and Hadi al-Amiri both came to observe the fighting. Peshmerga General Hakar Muhsin Amedi said he was determined to hold the position.[180] The Shi'ite commanders were apparently satisfied. The Kurds had been taught a lesson, and Iran-linked groups had gained a larger and key foothold on the Syrian border by securing the old border crossing at Rabiah. Ankara was pleased to see the PKK in Sinjar more isolated than they had been as Baghdad asserted control.

The only concern for Baghdad was that the KRG still held the Faysh Khabur crossing to Syria, where coalition aid to the SDF was passing through. There was also an oil pipeline going into Turkey. But the powers that be in Erbil, Baghdad and Washington had decided enough was enough. Their allies couldn't engage in full-scale war.

The same happened southeast of Rabiah. At Mosul Dam, clashes resulted in the death of a Peshmerga, and the Kurds withdrew toward the Christian town of Al-Qosh, where they stopped retreating. In Bashiqa, the town that I had looked down upon from the heights in 2016, the Peshmerga also retreated, leaving the mostly Yazidi town to its own devices. Only a month earlier, the people had voted for independence; now they were watching the liberators leave. In Gwer and Makhmur, the Kurdish forces withdrew, but only a few kilometers, occupying the heights at Makhmur and the river at Gwer. On Mount Qara Chokh, the Peshmerga maintained their positions.

The fighting reached a crescendo at the Turkmen town of Altun Kupri, which is upstream from Dibs. The Iraqi army was able to take the town, and the ISOF attempted to move forward. It found itself crossing a small stream near the poor town and came to a field surrounded by hills on three sides. Here the Kurds decided to make a stand. Men from the PAK had come down from their defensive line near Hawija, and using anti-tank weapons and heavy machine guns, they dueled with the Iraqis all day on October 20. An Iraqi Abrams tank was knocked out.[181] Iraqi artillery attempted to push the Kurds off their hills. Then the Iraqi army stopped.

More than 166,000 Kurds had become IDPs in just a few days. The Kurdish region had been sheltering more than a million Arab and Yazidi IDPs over the last years, and now had to make room for more displaced persons. Now the Kurds were once again fleeing conflict, and the region faced the possibility of being cut off from the international community, its airports closed and its borders strangled. Iran and Turkey were talking sanctions.

Iran's Gain

For the supporters of Iran in Iraq, things were going swimmingly. Iran's influence had filled the vacuum left by ISIS. The Kurds had attempted to fill the vacuum, riding into Kirkuk in 2014, Sinjar in 2015 and Bashiqa in 2016. Now, like the US and Russia coming to blows after the victory over Nazism, the Kurds and Shi'ites had come to blows. Exploiting their influence in Baghdad and power over the interior ministry, Iran and Qasem Soleimani had been able to engineer a kind of coup in Kirkuk – a secret deal to get the Peshmerga out, without almost any bloodshed. The US was privy to some parts of this deal, but the State Department expressed concern over reports of violence and called for the restoration of calm. In a step of supreme irony, Hadi al-Amiri attended an International Conference for Dialogue on Counterterrorism in Baghdad on October 28.[182] He held court in his fatigues, his lectern festooned with microphones. While the Barzanis and Talibanis were worrying about their own future, he was the new king of Iraq.

There was still more to the victory. Abadi had positioned himself as indispensible to the Americans. The more he flirted with Iran and worked with his PMU allies, the more the Americans would beg him to come to Riyadh. On October 22, Tillerson was in Saudi Arabia and said that the Shi'ite militias should "go home." The reaction from Baghdad was immediate. Abadi was in the midst of the victory lap. He had come to Saudi Arabia on October 22, then on to Jordan and Turkey, and was supposed to go to Iran. He was offended by Tillerson's comments. Tillerson received an angry call telling him to go to Baghdad, and he met with Abadi on October 23 in the Iraqi capital. There Abadi berated him, saying that the PMU was an Iraqi institution and the "hope of the country and the region."[183] Tillerson got the message.

In the Kurdish region, the crisis settled down. Once it was clear the Iraqi army was not going to Erbil and that the pipeline and border access with Turkey would remain intact, the Barzanis began to rebuild their self-esteem. Abadi had made many demands of the regionial government, to reduce its corruption and the number of employees on its payroll. He even wrote an article in the *New York Times* trying to curry favor with the American public in his spat with the Kurds, knowing that many commentators in the US had sided with the Kurds, and some saw their struggle as similar to the US quest for independence in 1776.[184] Baghdad argued that there were hundreds of thousands of "ghost" employees in the Kurdish region. It would need to tighten the belt. The freewheeling days of 2014–2017 with oil revenues from Kirkuk would end. The region was already in a financial crisis, paying salaries months behind schedule.

Kurds in Erbil protested against the United States, and a US flag was torn down outside a hotel in Ainkawa. Locals encouraged the government to work more closely with Russia. The Rosneft energy giant had signed a deal in September and would pay the region $1.3 billion in November.[185] Overall investment would reach $3.5 billion, an important Russian stake in the KRG and also a way for Russia to help link its growing alliance with Turkey with a role in Iraq.

In the aftermath of the Kirkuk crisis, PUK and KDP politicians traded accusations of treason. Now the Kurdish region would look inward and deal with finances and other issues, while Iraq kept fighting ISIS, and Iran and Washington squared off for the region. In Syria, a new crisis was developing. Turkey saw America's partners in Syria as a threat. Kurdish groups, which had seemed on the verge of carving out such power in Iraq and Syria, would now face a new crisis in Syria as well, pitting them against a NATO ally. As in Iraq, they would feel betrayed.

Chapter 20
Liberating Raqqa

Saudi Arabia Rides the Tiger

Saudi Arabia's Gulf affairs minister, Thamer al-Sabhan, traveled to Syria on October 17, 2017.[186] He was expected to survey the damage to the outskirts of Raqqa, which had been liberated from ISIS, and also to discuss plans for the kingdom to invest in the rebuilding of Syria. The US-led coalition and McGurk were already considering what would come next, when ISIS was defeated.

Sabhan was an interesting choice to lead Saudi Arabia's efforts in Syria. In the early years of the civil war, Saudi Arabia had supported the rebels. But the kingdom had become dismayed over their increasing radicalization. It was part of a larger shift by Saudi Arabia away from its Wahhabi roots toward major reforms. Previously the kingdom had helped give birth to some of the ideologues behind al Qaeda, including its leader, Osama bin Laden. The blowback from Islamist extremism deeply affected the kingdom. In May 2003, al Qaeda had struck a compound in Riyadh, and there were attacks in Yanbu and Khobar in 2004. After dozens of clashes with al Qaeda cells, the country had finally gotten a hold on the terror problem, when ISIS appeared. In 2015, ISIS targeted a Shi'ite mosque in Qatif and a Sunni mosque in Abha.

A product of the generation that had to come to grips with this threat, Sabhan was born in 1967 and received a degree in military science from King Abdullaziz Military College in 1988.[187] He was in the army during the First Gulf War in 1991 and worked in the special police forces after that, confronting terror. In 2014, he was sent as military attaché to

Lebanon. There, he was supposed to be a representative to a country that Saudi Arabia had played a key role in aiding. The kingdom had hosted the talks in Taif that helped end the Lebanese Civil War in 1990. The agreement enhanced the power of the Sunni prime minister in Lebanon. For the kingdom, this was a welcome development. Under Lebanese law, the president of the country must be a Christian, while the prime minister is a Sunni and the speaker of parliament a Shi'ite.

By the time Sabhan arrived in Lebanon in 2014, things had changed from the 1990s. Rafic Hariri, the Sunni former prime minister whose son Saad had been born in Saudi Arabia, was murdered in a 2005 bombing in Lebanon. The bombing was blamed on Hezbollah. By 2014, Hezbollah had intervened in the Syrian civil war, claiming it was protecting Lebanon from groups such as ISIS. But Sabhan saw something else, a country increasingly run by Iran and Hezbollah. He left Lebanon to be ambassador to Iraq in 2015. In Iraq, he saw how the liberation of Ramadi and Fallujah resulted in the spread of Iranian influence. "Falluja proves that they want to burn the Arab Iraqis in the fire of sectarianism."[188] Soon afterwards, his office claimed it had uncovered an Iranian plot to assassinate him. The controversy ended with him being recalled from Iraq. But it didn't dent his views, which were representative of a larger Saudi foreign policy taking shape.

In June 2017, Mohammed bin Salman was appointed crown prince of the kingdom. Born in 1985, he was only thirty-one years old. Large, with an imposing manner, and wearing a bushy beard, the prince became the central figure in the kingdom. He had played a central role in the war in Yemen, led by Saudi Arabia since 2015 and aimed at confronting the Houthi rebels who were allied with Iran. He was also close to Egypt's President Abdel Fattah el-Sisi and to Saad Hariri in Lebanon. But his largest gamble was leading the kingdom during the Gulf Cooperation Council Crisis rift with Qatar. In June 2017, Saudi Arabia, Bahrain, the United Arab Emirates and Egypt broke relations with Qatar, accusing it of hosting terrorists and spreading instability. Specifically, it was accused of allying with Iran and hosting the Muslim Brotherhood.

The Gulf Crisis grew out of concern in Riyadh that the Brotherhood and Hezbollah were sources of instability in the region. Each country that joined Riyadh in its concerns had its own reasons.

Bahrain felt threatened by a Shi'ite majority population that had risen up during the Arab Spring. The GCC had intervened to defeat the uprising. The UAE under the influence of Abu Dhabi crown prince Mohammed bin Zayez, often called MBZ, had sought to carve out a leading role as a center of culture and moderation in a region threatened by instability and extremism. This was on display in Abu Dhabi's building of its own Louvre and Dubai's dynamic economy and cultural scene. The UAE was even called the "little Sparta" of the Middle East by the *Sunday Times* in 2018.[189] Like Qatar, though, this was a Gulf monarchy with a veneer of liberalism.

Qatar too wanted to be the dynamic Gulf power, but it chose to blend its embrace of world culture, such as the 2022 soccer World Cup, with flirtation with extremist groups and preachers such as Yusuf al-Qaradawi. It was more than that. Qatar became a key ally of Turkish president Erdogan, and both countries supported the Brotherhood in Egypt and Hamas in Gaza. Hamas leaders were hosted in Doha, and funding from Qatar helped keep Gaza stable. Al-Jazeera was used to promote criticism of regimes abroad, but support for the regime at home. This angered leaders like Sisi, who saw in Qatar's support for the opposition an existential threat. Qatar's narrative would pose its Al-Jazeera as merely a form of free speech and claim that leaders like Sisi were authoritarian dictators imprisoning journalists. But the reality was more complex. Turkey, an ally of Qatar, which received supportive press in Al-Jazeera, was also imprisoning and expelling critical journalists.

The Gulf Crisis was connected to the rise of ISIS, because both Qatar and Turkey, and to a larger extent the Muslim Brotherhood and Hamas, had flirted closely with the extremism that created an unstable vacuum exploited by ISIS. The reverberations of the instability fueled extremism rather than empowering more liberal, democratic voices. ISIS members found a foothold in Egypt's Sinai Desert. They also established a foothold on the doorstep to Egypt in Libya, where Sisi's ally Libyan general Khalifa Haftar was fighting them in 2016–2017.

The blowback was all part of a misreading of the Arab Spring by regional and global powers. Qatar and Turkey thought the Arab Spring would bring the toppling of Assad and that their Brotherhood allies would come to power through the ballot box, as the AKP had in Turkey.

Instead, chaos filled the void of power left by dictatorship in places such as Libya, Egypt and Syria. It quickly became clear that allowing Islamists to be part of governing coalitions or rebel groups led to a descent into a hell of slaughter and terror. ISIS emerged from that hell. To roll that back, authoritarianism came into vogue in Egypt. In Syria, Saudi Arabia and the UAE stepped back from any interest in the rebels. When it came to Hamas, Saudi Arabia and the UAE sought to sink support into the nominally secular Palestinian Authority, while Qatar spent millions in Hamas-run Gaza. In 2018, Qatar pledged $90 million to the Hamas-run Gaza Strip.

By breaking relations with Qatar, Riyadh and its allies hoped they could get Doha to cave in to their demands. Instead, Turkish troops flew to Qatar, and Iran provided support. Tillerson came out to try to broker an agreement. Qatar upped its lobbying efforts in Washington, bankrolling millions in ads and other efforts designed to encourage the American public to see it as a victim. In addition, firms flew in to Qatar influential pro-Israel figures, hoping that they would influence the Trump administration, which was the most pro-Israel administration in US history.

Qatar also encouraged the notion that Saudi Arabia's new leader was unstable and breaking with the status quo. Mohammed bin Salman (MBS) sought to counter that with assertions that he was a genuine reformer, opening the kingdom's first movie theaters in decades and letting women drive. He proposed an economic plan called Vision 2030. But Qatar was successful in weaving stories of Saudi hypocrisy, portraying the kingdom as running a fake crackdown on corruption and accusing MBS of lavish spending amid the austerity.

The contretemps between Riyadh and Doha had broader strategic implications. The United States maintained the massive Al Ubeid military base in Qatar, and Washington wanted Qatar to continue helping in the war on ISIS and as a strategic partner in the region. Washington also wanted Qatar's help brokering talks with the Taliban to help end the Afghan war, now entering its eighteenth year.

In Qatar, the US faced the same problem it faced in Lebanon, Turkey and Iraq. These were all US allies, but each of them was flirting with US opponents. Iraq's leader was a friend of Iran. Lebanon's government included Hezbollah, which the US views as a terrorist organization. Turkey was growing closer to Russia and Iran in 2017, with Erdogan meeting Putin numerous times and sitting with Putin and Rouhani in Sochi in November to discuss peace in Syria. Qatar was also now hedging its bets with Iran. Washington was concerned that any cold shoulder to these countries or tough talk would drive them further away. In each case, there were massive financial investments. Turkey had the Incirlik Air Base that the US Air Force used. Qatar had its base. Lebanon's army received $120 million 2017.[190] The US would extend Iraq a $3 billion credit line in early 2018.[191]

Trump ostensibly wanted to work more closely with traditional US allies in Cairo, Riyadh and Jerusalem. But he was hamstrung by policy holdovers from the Obama years. During those years, the United States had been focused on getting the Iran nuclear deal inked in 2015 and had outraged Riyadh. The US had also been harshly critical of the 2013 coup in Egypt and Sisi's crackdowns. Washington had ignored Hezbollah's infractions and the Iranian influence in Iraq, hoping that lack of criticism would bring Rouhani to the table. Trump's State Department under Tillerson largely continued that policy. Lebanon, Iraq, Turkey and Qatar were to be treated with kid gloves, not criticized for their failures, lest they go into the enemy camp.

While Tillerson tinkered, Trump had reached out to Saudi Arabia. The US president met with MBS in March 2017 and attended the May Riyadh summit in which Trump urged countries to "drive out" terror.[192] He also came up with a plan to get the Saudis to pay for reconstruction in Syria. The full scale of this concept wouldn't be unveiled until April 2018, when Trump would say that if Riyadh wanted the US to stay in Syria, it would have to pay. But the roots of the plan were in Sabhan's October visit. At the time, the US-led coalition had largely carved out the area it intended to stabilize in eastern Syria. The country east of the Euphrates would be America-land, including Manbij, which was taken from ISIS in August 2016. Around Manbij, US forces and their SDF allies looked cautiously at Turkish troops and the Syrian rebels. Along the Euphrates, the United States and SDF were squaring off with the Syrian regime, its Russian backers and its Iranian advisers. The last ISIS cells were being hunted down in Raqqa, the former capital of the caliphate, and ISIS was expected to be defeated in the last areas it held in the desert on the Syrian border with Iraq, and in a tiny finger of land along the Euphrates near Iraq.

While Sabhan toured areas around Raqqa, he drove close to where a British volunteer named Jac Holmes was hoping to savor the victory over ISIS along with his SDF colleagues.

Jac's War

Jac Holmes decided to host a two-hour Facebook Live discussion on October 4, 2017.[193] A British volunteer with the YPG, he was one of hundreds of foreigners who had volunteered to fight ISIS alongside the Kurds in 2015–2016. The anti-ISIS fighters were a phenomenon of this peculiar war. ISIS had recruited fifty thousand volunteers from all over the world, including some five thousand members from Europe, and men and women from as far away as Bangladesh, China and the Carribean. Because this was a global war, there were also those who felt that they had an obligation to stand up against ISIS crimes.

I ran across these anti-ISIS volunteers on social media. Jordan Matson, one of the first to arrive, came to fight alongside the YPG in Kobani in September 2014. From Sturtevant, Wisconsin, he spoke no Kurdish but felt something must be done. He had watched US foreign policy wander away from Iraq after 2011. As ISIS put down roots, he was shocked by the fall of Mosul. "I was just done with it, just done with watching these people die and nothing being done about it."[194] At twenty-eight-years old, Matson flew to Turkey, where he then crossed into Iraq and contacted the YPG. At night he crossed into Syria and headed for the front.[195]

They came by the handful in the beginning and then by the dozen. Many had similar stories of wanting to help the underdog in Syria and to defend minorities. They had a mix of ideology as well. "I'm here to fight for common decency and humanity – I didn't come here to fight for the Kurds or for Kurdistan," wrote Freeman Stevenson, an American.[196] "I came here to fight for people. Some people who happen to be Kurds, Arabs, Turks and Assyrians happen to espouse an ideology I am willing to die for." And they did die. Jordan MacTaggert, William Savage and Levi Jonathan Shirley, three American volunteers with the YPG, fell in the battle for Manbij in 2016.

By the time the battle of Raqqa rolled around, only the toughest of the foreigners were left. Many had seen enough killing at Tel Tamer, Tel Khamis, Manbij, Shadadi and other fronts. Their tours were up. Too many of their friends were dead. One of those who remained was the gaunt British volunteer Holmes. Dragging on a cigarette, he used Facebook Live to answer questions from those who followed his fight against ISIS. Sitting in the darkened room of a YPG headquarters near Raqqa, he took questions for two hours. With the rattle of a generator in the background, he sought to describe life on the front line. It remains one of the few testimonies in real time of the battle for the caliphate's capital.

It was "hard work," he said. "You can sit around for six months or be in the shit the whole time; it depends on what the Kurds let you do." He said he smoked a lot on the front line. He said volunteers had to join for six months. He carried an M-16 A4 rifle with a silencer. He opposed the Syrian regime. "Rojava will survive; there are a lot of American bases in Rojava." What was the most risky thing? Dying. Mines, snipers. He had found an ISIS tunnel. Day-to-day life was typically sitting in a building guarding and waiting for ISIS to attack, all day and night. If ISIS didn't choose to attack, then it was doing nothing. There would be air strikes, mortars. "You can't stand in windows and look around, because you'll be shot by a sniper probably." He said that it was hunger, boredom and being tired of sitting around, and said it was better to be under attack than being sedentary.

At night, there would be thirty people on guard. For fire support, the SDF relied on its own mortars and artillery. War was "eating, sleeping, cleaning weapons, self and clothes, talking shit and smoking." None of the fighters had a helmet. "Honestly not very many foreigners here now, foreign YPG on the east side was only five–six medics and then four foreigners with Jac," he said. "I don't know others."

Holmes had come without any training. "I do not have sleepless nights," he said, relating to PTSD, but said he had experienced it. "It's hard to identify." He described the Russians and the Syrian regime as a threat. There was a satellite phone that he used for internet. "Russian and Iranian influence is a big thing; without them the regime would have fallen a while ago." He said he missed being clean the most, and being safe. "Apart from freeing civilians and then they can come back and do what they want," he said he had no stories of helping civilians. He had two pairs of underpants. "The heat was really bad a few months ago; it's cooling down now."

The volunteer was concerned about being detained in the KRG when trying to return home. Many of the foreign volunteers had come through Erbil in northern Iraq; they had violated the law by crossing into Syria without documentation. When seeking to return home, they had to admit to the Erbil authorities why they had overstayed their visas for so long. Some of them were detained for weeks or months and then released and told not to come back. Erbil was on bad terms with the YPG in Syria, which it viewed as part of the PKK. In the 1990s, the KDP had fought with the PKK, and their relations were cold and hostile. But for Holmes this was only a distant fear; he wanted to first see the end of ISIS in Raqqa.

The city was already a shell, its buildings gutted by air strikes, with gray rubble and dust on its skyline. The YPG was proceeding methodically, with coalition air support and special forces. Snipers played a key role on both sides. ISIS was surrounded, so the Kurds and their allies could afford to move slowly. The enemy wasn't going to go anywhere, and it wasn't getting any more support.

Jac said there was a group of Syrian rebels who had joined the SDF nearby, part of the growing coalition that the Syrian Democratic Forces had become. Initially just a new brand name for the YPG, by 2017 it had grown to genuinely include a plethora of small groups. The coalition was pleased with this situation, because it could say that Washington was working with the SDF, not the YPG. The YPG was controversial because Turkey viewed it as part of the PKK. So Washington had to tread lightly. Publicly it succeeded, never mentioning the YPG in statements. For the foreign fighters, this distinction was less important. They were YPG.

During his nighttime discussion, Holmes said that it was easy to obtain resupply of ammunition. What did he carry? A knife, multi-tool, frag grenade, smoke grenade, bag with food and water, and a rifle. He said that suicide vests were not very dangerous, "if you know what to look for." Two of his men had gone for four hours, to get to the front, and would spend a day there. "Me and the other guy are chilling in the base because we went last night." He said the only thing he hadn't experienced was a mine blowing up; he'd been shot at and had VBIEDs blow up next to him. The nearest medical facility was several kilometers away. He thought there were five hundred ISIS fighters left in Raqqa. Eventually, after two hours, Holmes sat back and sipped a soda. It was time to go.

Ten days after Holmes made his video, the city fell, and the YPG and the fighters "did doughnuts," driving in Al-Naim Square with an armored vehicle. ISIS had done the same in 2014. Now the Kurds and their allies, who had once been besieged in Kobani, had retaken the city. It felt a bit like the Red Army replacing the Nazi flag on the Reichstag in 1945. The enemy was defeated in its capital. But the effusion of blood had not ended.

Holmes had been asked several times about returning to the UK. "My family will be happy that I'm not in Syria anymore." He was killed on October 23, 2017, trying to defuse a suicide bomb belt, becoming one of the last of the estimated two dozen foreign volunteers who died fighting alongside the Kurds against ISIS in Syria.[197] He was supposed to leave Syria for Iraq the day he was killed. Holmes was twenty-four years old.

How ISIS Escaped Raqqa

Amid the celebrations of the defeat of ISIS in Raqqa, a rumor persisted. The city had fallen when it did because the SDF had negotiated with the surrounded ISIS fighters, and they had been allowed to leave the city. This had saved lives, but had it allowed war criminals to escape?

"We had no choice," said a foreign volunteer sniper who served with the Syrian Democratic Forces. "I didn't come here to kill women and children," he recalled when describing how ISIS members were able to flee Raqqa using human shields. A secret deal had allowed thousands to leave. Worse, ISIS took human shields and civilians with them.

Officially, the last days of the battle witnessed what the US-led coalition described as a "civilian evacuation." A statement put out on October 14, 2017, by Combined Joint Task Force – Operation Inherent Resolve revealed that "a convoy of vehicles is staged to depart Raqqa October 14 under an arrangement brokered by the Raqqa Civil Council and local Arab tribal leaders on October 12." ISIS loaded buses and trucks with booty, guns, ammo and civilians. Two hundred fifty ISIS fighters and thirty-five hundred family members were bused out. Coalition drones "monitored the convoy from the air," according to an account.[198] Overall, thirteen buses, a hundred ISIS vehicles and fifty trucks took part, including ten trucks loaded with weapons and ammunition.

Operation Inherent Resolve spokesman Colonel Ryan Dillon tweeted on November 13 that the convoy was "never a 'secret.'"[199] It was designed to minimize civilian casualties, the coalition claimed, and purportedly excluded foreign ISIS terrorists. Claims that the ISIS members leaving were searched or screened were largely just stories. In fact, the negotiations took place quietly, with the coalition expressing plausible deniability about them. It was the SDF and ISIS negotiating. This is the heart of "by, with and through." Since the US isn't running Syria, it works "through" the SDF partners and didn't take direct part in the negotiations. This would haunt the SDF and coalition later in Baghuz, sending a message to ISIS members that they would always find a way to escape justice and move somewhere else.

The SDF fighters on the ground said they saw something different from the official story. "The deal was for the surrender of three hundred ISIS fighters, a hundred of them to surrender to us that day on October 12, but the two hundred changed the deal the next day," said one fighter. A local tribe helped to facilitate the convoy because ISIS was holding some tribal members captive. "Initially, ISIS members wanted to be transported toward the Turkish border, but they were told they could either go toward Deir ez-Zor or toward other areas ISIS held near the Iraqi border."

The ISIS members mixed with civilians so that they would not be hit by air strikes once the convoy got moving. "I was there and saw it with my own eyes," the sniper said. He watched the escape unfold through his scope. ISIS took with them human shields, including Yazidi women enslaved in 2014. "Nobody checked them; they all were wearing explosive belts." Foreign fighters escaped as well.

The SDF felt it had no choice. "ISIS kept civilians kidnapped for more than six months against air strikes in the center of the city. I saw them many times through my scope." When Raqqa was finally liberated and the convoy had left, around three hundred civilians were found left behind. isis hadn't been able to take them all as human shields. "So we saved a lot of lives there, and this is a good job at least."

The coalition said it disagreed with "letting armed isis terrorists leave Raqqa." The coalition did not engage the bus convoy, something it said "is estimated to have saved 3,500 civilian lives prior to the liberation of Raqqa." The coalition also sought to stress that by November 2017, a total of 7.5 million civilians had been liberated in Iraq and Syria since 2014, and 103,000 square kilometers.

Yet some of those who left Raqqa ended up trying to get to Turkey. Others made it to the desert near the Iraqi border, where they put down roots, and the coalition and the SDF would have to fight them again in Operation Roundup in the spring and fall of 2018.

*A Kurdish man near a refugee camp in Suruc across
the border from Kobani, February 2016*

*A concrete wall constructed by Turkey stretching
beneath the hills of Afrin, February 2016*

*Macedonian soldiers struggling to contain refugees from the
Middle East arriving at the border, September 2015*

The skull of a Yazidi victim of ISIS atop a mass grave near Sinjar, December 2015

The Yazidi shrine of Sharf-a-Din near the foot of Mount Sinjar, December 2015

A man covering over ISIS graffiti in a Kakei village near Khazir, June 2016

Blindfolds ISIS forced Yazidis to wear in August 2014 before massacring them and burying the bodies in a mass grave in Sinjar, photographed December 2015

Women from the Rojava Peshmerga, a paramilitary unit of Syrian Kurds based in northern Iraq, standing guard near Mosul Dam, June 2016

Kurdish Peshmerga, the armed forces of the Kurdistan Regional Government, marching into battle near Fazalia and Nawaran, October 2016

A Kurdish Peshmerga, a member of the Kurdistan Regional Government's armed forces, squatting next to his sandbagged position above Bashiqa, June 2016

Kurdish women celebrating voting in the independence referendum, September 2017

*A Kurdish flag on the historic Erbil Citadel during the lead-up
to the September 2017 independence referendum*

The skyline of Erbil, March 2017

A Kurdish Peshmerga of the Kurdistan Regional Governments armed forces looking at the water level in Mosul Dam, June 2016

Sarhad Qadir, head of Kirkuk's regional police, in his office, December 2015

Members of the PAK *keeping watch over the hills above Hawija, December 2015*

Humvees supplied by the US to the Kurdistan
Regional Government in Erbil, June 2016

*A Kurdish Peshmerga, a member of the Kurdistan
Regional Government's armed forces, warming himself
by the fire during the Mosul offensive, October 2016*

The author on a US-supplied Iraqi army tank near Gwer, October 2016

*A member of the Kurdistan Training Coordination Center
watching a military exercise in Bnaslawa, June 2016*

*A member of Iraq's Federal Police firing an SPG-9 at ISIS
positions in the battle for Mosul, March 2017*

A destroyed armored vehicle burned by ISIS during the 2014 offensive in Nineveh

*Iraqis fleeing Islamic State–controlled territory arrive
at a checkpoint near Mahmur, June 2016*

The burned inside of a church destroyed by ISIS in Qaraqosh, Iraq

The ruins of a church in Qaraqosh, Iraq, March 2017

The author in Mosul, March 2017

Children and women fleeing ISIS sit on a road near Qayarrah, June 2016

*A member of the Iraqi elite Special Operations Forces and a Kurdish Peshmerga
on a road near Bartella during the Mosul offensive, October 2016*

Part IV
The Rise of Iran, 2017–2019

> "The enduring hardships during the war led those with ideas and thoughts to change military reliance on outsiders, as a result of which the Islamic Republic of Iran is now better than and superior to all the regional countries in terms of military and defense capabilities."
>
> *– Ayatollah Khamenei, speaking at the Imam Reza shrine in Mashhad, March 21, 2019*

Chapter 21
The Southern Flank

"We Will Not Bathe in Our Own Blood"

The InterContinental Semiramis Hotel in Cairo overlooks the Nile.[200] It boasts twelve restaurants and bars. In the spring of 2017, the hotel was sleepy and quiet. Tourism in Egypt had taken a major hit during the Arab Spring. Rioters in 2012 targeted the US embassy, and after Sisi took power in 2013, a smoldering ISIS-affiliate insurgency in Sinai bubbled on. Egypt, land of the pharoahs, birthplace of Arab nationalism under Gamal Abdel Nasser in the 1950s, seemed to be losing its place as an anchor of security and power in the Arab world. Sitting astride the Nile, the country of eighty million was the most populated in the region, but it also had a complex identity. Arab and pre-Islamic grandeur intermixed, as did the contemporary connections to Africa and the greater Middle East.

When I arrived at Cairo International Airport in 2017, the country still had the trappings of its past, but its future appeared unsure. The Cairo International Book Fair was in its forty-eighth year and humming with youth and energy. But some of the booths were empty. Libya, Iraq, countries that were undergoing their own crises. Security was ever-present: lumbering, tired Egyptian police in body armor and holding AK-47s and black caps were on patrol in the city. Jeeps with more police trawled the streets. Tahrir Square, where the Arab Spring had really taken hold, where journalists from the West had found hope and inspiration in 2011, was empty. I looked across at the Egyptian Museum bathed in red from the dying sun.

Egypt Confronts Extremism and ISIS

At the InterContinental Semiramis, Dr. Ibrahim Negm was waiting. An adviser to the grand mufti of Al-Azhar, he had served as an imam of the Islamic Center of Long Island in New York and became an expert in Christian-Muslim relations. Slightly portly, Negm wore a striped tie in February 2017. A piano played in the background at the Ambassador Club, a bar that looked like it had crawled out of an Agatha Christie novel. Negm sat outside the bar in a common area. His job was to help explain the new trend at Al-Azhar, the Sunni Islamic world's foremost institution. For Egypt the main problem was countering radicalization.

The problem for Al-Azhar was that for years the Islamic world had been going through a major upheaval. Old regimes such as Hosni Mubarak's ossified. Meanwhile, underneath, a passionate extremist line was burbling up. Al Qaeda made the first leap in this respect. Al Qaeda's leader Ayman al-Zawahiri, born in 1951 in Maadi in Cairo, was an example of the threat to Egypt. He was arrested following the 1981 murder of Anwar Sadat by Islamists. Zawahiri supported the mujahideen against the Soviets in Afghanistan and led members of Egyptian Islamic Jihad to attack the Egyptian embassy in Pakistan in 1995. He was implicated in other operations in Pakistan, including, in 2007, both the Lal Masjid siege and the assassination of former Pakistani prime minister Benazir Bhutto.

Al Qaeda, like ISIS after it, used new media to transmit its message, and it exploited the new technology globalization to expand. As head of the army, Sisi had demanded from President Mohamed Morsi that the army retain its special status in Egyptian society. He also wanted more forces to fight the growing insurgency in Sinai, and he was concerned about security threats and instability in Libya, the increasing authoritarianism of Morsi, and social unrest at home from liberals and Salafists on either end of the political spectrum. Many Salafists were leaving Egypt to fight in Libya and Syria, but what would happen if they came back or influenced local youth? In the end, Sisi sent the army to support mass protests in July 2013, and Morsi was removed from power.

After Sisi overthrew the Muslim Brotherhood in 2013, a priority of the new regime was to rip out the Brotherhood by the roots. That involved mass arrests and the hunting down of its leaders. But it also involved a religious campaign designed to counter not only the Brotherhood's message, but other extremist messages that had led Egyptians to join jihadist organizations. Egyptians had gone to Syria to fight. For Al-Azhar and government-aligned clerics, the question was bigger than just countering messages in Egypt; Al-Azhar wanted to have an influence throughout the world through its fatwas.

At the gathering in the spring of 2017, it was clear the religious establishment wanted to win the struggle for the twenty-first century via influencing believers. "It is so important to advise Muslims in a good direction through fatwas that any religious violence is wrong, such [as countering] that which we hear from ISIS or al Qaeda or radical groups," a source explained. ISIS was counseling its followers to hate non-Muslims and spread enmity and hostility. Al-Azhar hoped that it could counter what it saw as the false messages spreading in the world through its own fatwas. The only problem was in volume; via its numerous institutions, it was issuing two thousand fatwas a day.

For the Egyptian government and the religious leadership at Al-Azhar, the question was how to spread stability after the instability of the Arab Spring. But those countering extremism and messages from groups such as ISIS had started a bit behind the curve due to technology. It's not abnormal that ancient religious institutions will struggle to catch up with modern causes. But for Egypt it seemed like a life and death struggle. In Libya after Gaddafi fell in 2011, he had been replaced by warring factions, and ISIS and others had crept in to fill the vacuum. The same was happening throughout the Sahel and into Sinai. Egypt was under siege and sought to portray itself as an anchor of stability. The recipient of billions in US military aid, it saw itself as a friend of the West. But it felt betrayed during Obama's era, accusing the US of supporting the Brotherhood because Washington had tacitly accepted the fall of Mubarak and supported a democratic process that led the Brotherhood to power.

Negm asserts that the young generation is glued to smartphones. They are savvy; they are not into long conversations. The challenge was to meet them in this electronic space and contradict what they were hearing. It was also important to deal with the issues that Muslims in secular Western societies were facing. They were struggling and found solace in populist preachers who told them about booty and power serving with ISIS in Syria. It seemed romantic to young men. ISIS posed as an authentic message, bringing statements from the Quran and justifying acts based on the eighth century. But it was the twenty-first century, and Egypt wanted to find and provide twenty-first-century answers for a hungry public. It was also a young public, throughout the region. This young public had come of age during the Arab Spring and had been dismayed by the horrors that often followed, but the next generation would need answers.

The pro-government press and activists in Egypt after 2011 said that foreigners wanted the country to become a "swamp of blood."[201] It was an easy narrative to blame the problems on the US and outsiders. Some locals felt democratization had come too fast. Andrea Zaki Stefanos, of the Protestant Coptic Ecumenical Association, argued that many Egyptians had not expected the 2011 revolution. The masses who poured into the streets in 2011 in Cairo sought to remove Mubarak, the "Pharoah." Soon thereafter, Christians found that security had deteriorated. Religious tensions were an unexpected outcome, argued Stefanos. The Brotherhood had sold itself as uncorrupted and had promised to bring prosperity and freedom. But Brotherhood leader Mohamed Morsi, who won the 2012 elections, was soon behaving in a more authoritarian vein than expected.

Sisi, then the commander of the armed forces, was worried about the chaos spreading in Sinai and elsewhere. Every week, Egyptian soldiers were coming back in body bags. In 2013, when protesters returned to the streets of Cairo, Sisi ordered his helicopters into the sky flying Egyptian flags. He would support the new revolution against the Brotherhood. Egypt would not become Syria. That was the point of reference for many Egyptians who supported Sisi. They saw Libya and Syria as the next step with Morsi, and they didn't want the "swamp of blood." They wanted stability.

Many Egyptians quietly blamed the United States for the chaos after 2011. Barack Obama had given a speech in Cairo in 2009 in which he sought to reach out to the Islamic world. But Obama was seen as supporting the Muslim Brotherhood and ditching Mubarak, a historic US ally. The US said it was concerned by the decision of the armed forces to remove Morsi and suspended military aid from 2013 to March 2015. When Trump was elected in 2016, many Egyptian government supporters expressed pleasure at the defeat of Hillary Clinton, who they thought would have continued Obama's legacy.

In 2017, increasingly Sisi was portraying the war in Sinai against the ISIS affiliate Wilayat Sinai or "Sinai Province" as a war similar to the 1973 fight against Israel. What he meant was that it was a key struggle. It wasn't just an insurgency but a national war effort. In November, gunmen attacked a mosque in Sinai, killing more than two hundred people. It was part of a larger campaign. In February 2016, ISIS began targeting Christians in Sinai, and in December 2016, it struck St. Marks Cathedral in Cairo. It also struck at Christians in Alexandria and Minya. In February 2018, Cairo announced a massive offensive in Sinai. Patriotic videos showed columns of MRAP tactical vehicles, Humvees, tanks and men heading to the front. With ISIS largely defeated in Iraq and Syria, groups like the extremists in Sinai were the remnants of the organization. Many of these kinds of groups did not take orders from the leadership in Syria, but had joined the "brand" and operated independently. Nevertheless, they continued to play an important role in ungoverned spaces, with the chance that at any time they could pose a greater regional threat.

The Kingdom's Watchful Eye

On June 1, 2018, protests erupted in Amman, Jordan. The young men and women were outraged at the rising costs and a stagnant economy. "Finally we broke our silence, this is our way to freedom," tweeted a student. The protests spread from the capital to Irbid and Jarash in the north and Maan in the south. These were an atypical sign of unrest in the Kingdom of Jordan. The country had avoided the Arab Spring and had mostly avoided infiltration by ISIS.

Not entirely. In March 2016, Jordanian anti-terror units raided an apartment in Irbid and killed eight ISIS members. In June 2016, ISIS members from Syria assaulted a Jordanian border post. In December 2016, gunmen with machine guns and hand grenades attacked a police post in Karak, the desert city that is home to a twelfth-century Crusader castle. Then the terrorists moved into the castle, searching to kill foreign tourists. When the gun battle was over, seven members of the Jordanian security forces were dead, as were two Jordanian civilians and a tourist from Canada. Four terrorists' bodies were eventually recovered.

In January 2018, the security services foiled a plan for an ISIS attack on shopping malls, arresting seventeen.[202] In February, another terror cell planning an attack on an Israeli businessman was broken up. In March, another fifteen men were detained for plotting an attack on Ruseifa, near Amman. There were also two suspicious incidents involving Jordanian security personel. In one, a Jordanian police officer killed two Americans and two South Africans involved in training in November 2015. In another incident in November 2016, a Jordanian soldier shot three American military trainers at the King Faisal Air Base. A court did not find jihadist ties.

Jordan's stability was a key part of the war on ISIS. After captive Jordanian pilot Muath al-Kasasbeh was burned alive by the terrorists, the king had appeared in fatigues, vowing to strike back at ISIS. The US supplied Foreign Military Financing to the tune of more than $300 million a year from 2014 to 2018.[203] There were also hundreds of millions from other funds, including the Counterterrorism Partnership Fund, the Jordan Border Security Program, and coalition support funds. In addition, there was US support for the almost one million Syrian refugees in Jordan. Total funding was up to $1.6 billion annually.

I arrived in Jordan in July 2015, with the intention of traveling to the Dead Sea area and seeing how the conflicts in the region were affecting tourism. An affable tour guide named Awad Hajjara picked me up at the quiet – and deathly hot – Sheikh Hussein border crossing with Israel. The crossing has a single arrivals hall. You arrive by bus from the border and are dumped off in front of the small, white building. Inside are large posters of the king and his father and great-grandfather. From there the border police look over passports; you pay for a visa at a second window, and proceed. Outside in the beating sun there are no tourists, as if no one has ever come to the border crossing before.

"Each Jordanian considers himself a policeman," Hajjara said. "If we see two people fighting, we will stop and make them stop; that is how we take responsibility for our country." Hajjara described a national ethos committed to keeping the kingdom safe, where everyone, including the tour guide, was an eye of the state. "In the US or Europe they teach people not to talk to strangers; here we encourage them to talk to strangers."

But tourism had dropped by 70 percent as the Arab Spring unrolled. The regional chaos was affecting the country. "The media has a big effect," observed Hajjara. We pulled off in his car heading south. The road followed the Jordan Valley through small villages populated by formerly nomadic Bedouins and by Palestinian Arab refugees. In one of them, called Karameh, Palestinian Arabs had fought Israel in 1968, and the local mosque had become a kind of museum. That was the last time Jordan saw major internal tensions and chaos. The king had cracked down on the Palestinian groups in 1970, and thousands had been killed. Now things were quiet. The towns were dusty, and men carried masses of fruits and vegetables to sell. "People think we are just across the street from Syria or Iran. But there is a great distance," Hajjara said.

ISIS and other terror groups were threatening tourists and Christian religious sites. By the Baptism site on the Jordan, festooned with churches amid the reeds and hills overlooking the river, soldiers in trucks with .50 caliber machine guns guarded the road. At the church itself on the narrow Jordan River, more soldiers sat around. At the Movenpick Resort and Spa on the Dead Sea, security checked the undercarriage of each car for bombs. But inside the grounds of the hotel, there was no talk of ISIS. As dusk came, a belly dancer performed for the locals who had come down from Amman to take in the view. There was beer and narghiles.

By April 2016, when I traveled to northern Jordan, the situation on the Jordan-Syrian border had stabilized. A cease-fire agreement between the Syrian rebels and the regime had brought quiet. At the border in the town of Ramatha, the Syrian side could be seen. Many Syrian refugees had passed through here into Jordan over the years. Now the border was closed, and refugees had been shunted away to camps like Zaatari in the desert.

A local policeman said that in the old days, there had been a lot of trade via Ramatha. Many of the tribes in the area had relatives on both sides. Ten thousand people from northern Jordan had married men and women in Syria's Dara'a. The two border towns were like sister cities. Sugar came south, and meat was sent north. But the war changed all that. The border was mostly closed, except for humanitarian aid. The ISIS threat was a major concern. But ISIS had been mostly pushed back from the border. Although there was a small ISIS pocket in the Yarmouk Basin between Israel and Jordan, it had been removed from other border areas.

At the sprawling and massive refugee camp at Zaatari, a hundred thousand people were gathered, waiting for a future return to Syria, or to move on to the West. Many wanted the Assad regime to fall. But by 2016, with the Russian air force operating in Syria, they knew that was unlikely. Down the highway, King Abdullah's image was common, often with him dressed in fatigues. He had big shoes to fill. The Arab Revolt had made Jordan a cradle of its war against the Ottoman Empire. Here the tribes had gathered to stand alongside the British Empire to fight the Turks. The house in Umm Qais where seventeen Arab leaders signed a 1920 treaty can still be seen. The Arab sheikhs had come to "assure their loyalty to King Faisal" and their allegiance to Bilad al-Sham, the Greater Arab State that was not to be. Instead that state had become Jordan. Faisal went on to rule Iraq, and his son was butchered in the 1958 Arab nationalist uprising. The bloody history had begun there, but the modern Hashemites were devoted to seeing it end. An IED attack that killed several Jordanian police on August 11, 2018, saw the king visibly shaken and angry, vowing once again to hunt down terrorists. "It is a fight against terrorists not only in Jordan, but in the whole of Islam."[204]

In 2018, the king and his son would release a video of him training with the army, carrying out sweeps of buildings with a bullpup rifle. It was a message. Jordan was ready. The terrorists should know not to come knocking.

Rise and Fall of ISIS in North Africa

ISIS found a foothold in Libya from its earliest days in 2014, as it had in Egypt. "None of this would have happened without the return of Libyan volunteers from the Syrian Jihad," wrote Frederic Wehrey.[205] According to his account, the Libyans who went to Syria returned with fighting experience and drifted toward ISIS as the organization set down roots in Derna, in Cyrenaica. "Hundreds of Derna youths had gone to Syria," he wrote. A group called Al-Battar Brigade swore allegiance to ISIS, much as Wilayat Sinai did in Egypt.

As it had elsewhere, ISIS grew in Libya using brutal methods and by setting up a functioning extremist statelet. It had institutions such as a morality police and filled the vacuum that was left behind by the Libyan state that had ceased to function after the 2011 overthrow of Gaddafi. It also attracted foreign volunteers. They came from all over, from Iraq, Yemen, Sudan and Tunisia. For a period in 2014–2015, it seemed that the ISIS model of Iraq and Syria would spread to Libya and begin to consume North Africa, using the chaos of the Arab Spring and civil conflict as it had in Syria. Critics were murdered. Sufi graves were destroyed. Women were ordered to wear black.

ISIS proceeded methodically with brutality. It kidnapped and murdered twenty-one Egyptian Coptic Christians in February 2015 and murdered Ethiopian immigrants. Only in the last days of 2018 would the bodies of the Ethiopians be found. In all, thirty-four bodies were found in a mass grave, reminiscent of what ISIS had done in Iraq and Syria. As it grew, it also took over more territory, threatening Benghazi and Tripoli and taking over Sirte. Only by December 2016 would ISIS be driven from Sirte.

General Khalifa Haftar, the eastern Libyan strongman supported by Egypt, who had come to Libya from exile in the US vowing to eject extremists, helped to extinguish ISIS. One of his commanders, Mahmoud al-Warfali, was accused of rounding up ISIS suspects and executing them in 2017. By 2018, Haftar's forces had retaken Derna.

The Obama administration was concerned about the growth of ISIS in Libya. "The Islamic State posed a threat not just to Libya's stability, but to Libya's neighbors on the African continent," Wehrey noted.[206] The United States, UK and France sent special forces, according to his account. ISIS was still able to carry out attacks in neighboring countries, targeting Sousse and Tunis in Tunisia in 2015, where it killed sixty people. This included the Bardo National Museum attack in Tunis in March 2015. It also claimed credit for a November 2018 attack on Coptic Christians in Egypt, near Minya.

ISIS was still active in Libya in late 2018. An attack at Tazirbu in the southern Libyan desert killed nine in late November 2018. The head of the UN Support Mission in Libya (UNSMIL), Ghassan Salame, said in January 2019 that ISIS was still a threat in southern Libya.[207]

There was some good news. In late January, Khalifa al-Barg, an alleged senior leader of ISIS in Libya, was grabbed at a house in Sirte.[208] Special units surrounded his house at 3 a.m., and he surrendered without a fight. He had taken up arms in February 2011, joined a local city council in 2014, and then helped to create Ansar al-Sharia in 2015. Like so many ISIS fighters, his history was one of a long trajectory toward more extreme groups.

On February 6, 2019, Libyan foreign minister Mohammed Sayala asked the coalition to include Libya in its anti-ISIS program and to focus reconstruction efforts there due to the suffering the country had faced in recovering from ISIS.[209] The rest of the coalition, focusing on the US withdrawal from Syria and preferring more words over action, didn't seem interested in doing much for Libya. Libya was on its own to fight ISIS, a fight that would continue against ISIS cells, even if ISIS had lost most of its territorial base in Libya.

Chapter 22
Searching for Justice

The Prisoners

The Iraqi Police's General Mahdi al-Gharrawi was controversial even before he became the symbolic face of the fall of Mosul to ISIS.[210] Attempts had been made to prosecute him in 2008 for running secret prisons when he led the Second National Police Division in Baghdad. He was accused of personally taking part in torture. He was called "the Monster" by the *Daily Beast*.[211] Prime Minister Nouri al-Maliki resisted calls to prosecute him from General David Patreaus, Ambassador Ryan Crocker and other Americans, and then sent him to clean up Mosul before 2014.

In Mosul, Gharrawi, commander of operations in Nineveh Plains around the city, was alleged to have been on vacation when ISIS arrived and was sought for desertion. Meanwhile, the Second Division collapsed around the city, and it fell in June 2014. In April 2018, Baghdad finally meted out a sentence to Gharrawi: death by firing squad.[212]

Baghdad was trying to rid itself of the stain of ISIS control and everything that had been done wrong before ISIS arrived. A Russian-born ISIS fighter was sentenced to death by hanging in September 2017. A German woman who joined ISIS got a death sentence in January.[213] Two hundred twelve ISIS suspects were sentenced to death in April 2018. The trials were short – ten minutes long. Then the suspects were taken away. No mercy. Many of the accused were foreigners. Djamila Boutoutao sat in the dock, a wooden cage, in May 2018, and begged for her life.[214] She asked for the French ambassador, for a phone call to her parents. She wanted to go back to Lille in France. It had been a mistake to join ISIS. She didn't mention the crimes that had been committed.

The defendants sometimes said they were innocent. Ismail Saleh from Mosul claimed that a family feud had resulted in accusations that he was an ISIS member.[215] Shi'ite militias had come looking for him in 2017 and detained him twice. He ended up on trial for his life, receiving one of some three thousand death sentences handed out from 2015 to 2018. Two hundred fifty were executed by July 2018. Others admitted their roles. Ahmed Nijm, also from Mosul, told the Associated Press that he joined ISIS in a search for justice.

ISIS brides attracted a lot of attention in the summer of 2018. There were around 560 women on trial in Baghdad's central criminal court, a drab-looking building with a curved arch over its entrance.[216] Many women came from abroad, hundreds from Turkey, Russia, Azerbaijan and Tajikistan, as well as from France, Germany and the UK. They all seemed to "not know" what their husbands were up to. Despite having crossed several international borders, they feigned ignorance. A woman named Dina from Dagestan thought her husband never handled weapons. She was nineteen. Another woman named Ursalan said her husband died in an air strike.[217] He had lured her to Turkey and then taken her to Iraq. A third woman claimed that she had moved to Tal Afar, taking over houses that Shi'ites had been driven from, and that she didn't even know where she was living. A woman from Tajikistan said she had merely "immigrated" to Iraq, while another woman from Russia who had come to Turkey to study claimed she was forced by ISIS into a marriage in Iraq. They didn't want to admit any role, and most foreign countries didn't want the women back. One woman from Uzbekistan claimed she preferred prison in Iraq, where she could wear hijab and read the Quran.

While Iraq was seeking justice, Nadia Murad was traveling to the United States to seek more support in finding the thousands of missing Yazidi women. Her face was familiar to the world now; Rukmini Callimachi of the *New York Times* had described her as "among the bravest women I know."[218] On International Women's Day in March 2018, Murad wrote that it "should not only be a day to celebrate women but also to take action and end violence against women in many parts of the world. Many Yazidi women and girls taken by ISIS in 2014 are still being held as sex slaves in Syria. We have failed to rescue them."[219]

In July, Murad went to the United States to keep up the push for justice for Yazidis. She went to the US Holocaust Memorial Museum and listened to a Holocaust survivor speak. "Many of the horrific images we saw [at the] Holocaust Museum looked similar to what Yazidis witnessed in 2014. We [are] only days away from [August 3], thousands of Yazidis remain in captivity, around 350,000 [are displaced]."[220] August 3 is the anniversary of the 2014 ISIS attack on Yazidi areas near Mount Sinjar, marking the beginning of the mass murder and kidnapping of thousands of them.

Murad met with US ambassador to the UN Nikki Haley on July 27, discussing the UN investigation into ISIS crimes. Haley was inspired to spend time with her. "Not only did she survive being kidnapped and held captive by ISIS, but by using the power of her voice and telling her story she's making a difference and fighting back against their brutality," tweeted Haley.[221]

Murad met with US vice president Mike Pence on the sidelines of the Ministerial to Advance Religious Freedom gathering, held at the State Department, and thanked the department's Office of International Religious Freedom for its support. Pence clutched a copy of Murad's book, *The Last Girl: My Story of Captivity, and My Fight against the Islamic State*, for a photo.

But Murad's appeals during her long journey fell largely on deaf ears. Many countries had signed up to invest in Iraq, but most did not want to concentrate on Sinjar. They saw Mosul as a key to security. The United States had sent soldiers through Sinjar to help with Operation Roundup in Syria, trying to secure the border with Iraq. When the Americans briefly strayed into Sinjar on June 1, the Yazidis thought the US was returning to build a base. Locals were enthusiastic. But the coalition soldiers were gone as quickly as they arrived. Sinjar returned to the control of various Shi'ite militias and the few remaining Yazidi militia members, such as Haydar Shesho's fighters.

To get to Sinjar required traversing dozens of checkpoints, and Yazidis complained they lacked even the most basic of medical and other services. Women still had to go to Mosul or Tal Afar for some treatments, reviving their trauma from the experience of being enslaved. And ISIS cells were still present in the desert.

There was some hope on August 9, when the UN special adviser and head of the investigative team for accounting of ISIS crimes Karim Asad Ahmad Khan met the president of the Supreme Judicial Council of Iraq, Judge Faik Zaidan. The investigative team, established under UN Security Council Resolution 2397, was supposed to hold ISIS accountable for genocide of Yazidis, Christians and other groups. McGurk praised the effort. "Responsibility of all states to support this vital mission and ensure justice for ISIS victims," he tweeted on August 10.[222] It was four years since ISIS had attacked Sinjar, dividing women and children from their families in the horrid videos of the Solagh Technical Institute at Kocho, where men and women were separated in August 2014.

Across the border in Syria, some of the foreign members of ISIS who had been detained were interviewed, treated more like local celebrities than as people to be punished for crimes against humanity. Western countries had mostly decided they didn't want them back, stripping some of them of citizenship, and the SDF didn't know what to do with them. Alexanda Kotey and El Shafee Elsheikh, two of the ISIS members alleged to be "the Beatles" and suspected of brutal crimes, were interviewed numerous times by foreign press in April 2018. The UK had stripped them of their citizenship, but they wanted their rights. The US State Department accused Kotey, who was from Ladbroke Grove in London, of having been "likely engaged in the group's executions and exceptionally cruel torture."[223] But viewers who saw them interviewed got a different feeling. As they relaxed in civilian clothes, they were asked, "What keeps you awake at night?" They smiled and seemed happy. Nicolas Henin, a former hostage from France, said he didn't want them to have the satisfaction of the death penalty.[224] In August, a Spanish photojournalist and former ISIS hostage held by Kotey, Ricardo Garcia Vilanova, even returned to meet his former tormentors. He too thought they deserved to spend their lives in prison. "The first thing I thought when I saw them was Gaddafi or Saddam, who were not able to face death."[225]

News crews also sought out Samantha Sally, an American woman from Indiana who had journeyed with her husband to join the "caliphate."

She claimed to have been duped. Once in ISIS-held territory, she found herself lonely. Her husband Moussa Elhassani, according to a CNN interview, suggested "some Yazidi slaves would help keep Sally company while he was away, and he took her to the slave market."[226] They bought a young woman named Soad for $10,000. Her husband raped Soad. They bought a boy as well. "No one will ever know what it is like to watch their husband rape a fourteen-year-old girl," she told interviewers. In November, a former British doctor gave an interview while being held by the SDF. It appeared these kinds of interviews had become a small industry. For the SDF, there may have been another motive, to bring the detainees to the attention of their home countries, so that hundreds of them would be repatriated and not be a burden on the overstretched SDF. It didn't work. Instead the detainees became celebrities for a few minutes and were forgotten until more Western ISIS members showed up in Baghuz in January 2019, and the cycle began again.

In July 2018, the SDF transferred two US citizens to the FBI. Ibraheem Izzy Musaibli, from Dearborn, Michigan, was to face charges in Detroit for providing material support to ISIS.[227] Sally was also transferred to the FBI, charged with making false statements. She was not charged with enslaving women and children. Another man had been captured in September 2017. A dual US-Saudi citizen, he was quietly released in October and allowed to travel to Bahrain.[228] His US passport was canceled. The ACLU had taken up his case, keeping his name confidential. "Our client fought long and hard for his rights," Jonathan Hafetz said.[229] Nothing was said about how he ended up in Syria or why he wasn't charged by the United States. Another former ISIS member who garnered sympathy was Jack Letts, a British-Canadian citizen whose parents asked the Canadian government for assistance in getting him released in the fall of 2018.[230]

The SDF was also seeking support from Europe in exchange for keeping the detainees, who now numbered in the thousands. The SDF said it had at least seven hundred foreign detainees from forty countries. In February and April, several dozen were allegedly traded to ISIS for captured SDF members. According to *Telegraph* correspondent Josie Ensor, one deal involved Arab, Chechen, French and German ISIS members, while another in April included fifteen fighters and forty women, from

Morocco, France, Belgium and the Netherlands. "The SDF regularly asked foreign governments for more money to hold the jihadists," a negotiator said.[231] There were voices in Europe arguing that the ISIS fighters should be able to return home and that their home countries must take responsibility. But governments were reluctant. In November, a second report claimed that two of those traded back to ISIS near Hajin had been executed. Human Rights Watch also claimed on October 31, 2018, that at least five ISIS members had been transported by the US to the Iraqi Counter Terrorism Service. It was concerned about how Iraq might treat its own citizens.[232]

Other ISIS members in Hajin decided they had had enough of the war and wanted to return to Europe via Turkey. In one case, a man who was holding a thirteen-year-old Yazidi girl named Layla captive sold her back to her family. She said in November 2018, after being freed, that she had been frequently tortured by the ISIS members.

Meanwhile, the UN was still finding mass graves throughout 2018. Two hundred two mass graves would eventually be found, with an estimated twelve thousand victims in them. Only 1,258 bodies had been identified by the Iraqi Mass Graves Directorate by the fall of 2018.[233] The UN used terms like "harrowing human loss" to describe what was often a targeted campaign of extermination. The generalizing of the crimes, to describe the victims as "women, children, elderly people," made it seem that many groups were equally targeted. But the reality was that the graves often contained specific groups, such as foreign workers or former Iraqi security forces members.

Mosul Comes Back to Life

The prosecution of Lt. Gen. Mahdi al-Gharrawi was a bookend to the fall of Mosul. The city he had abandoned was coming back to life. There was a book fair. Assyrian Christians celebrated holidays. An ancient Jewish synagogue was discovered. Christian churches were being cleaned.

Mosul's redemption came about due to a small group of people who wanted the city to never again fall into the hands of extremists. One of these was Ali Baroodi, a photographer and scholar. Riding his bike around the city, he narrated on videos the recovery of the urban area. During the lead-up to the May Iraqi parliamentary elections, he drove along highways festooned with campaign posters. There was a hunger in the city for democracy and freedom. That might have sounded clichéd after all the disasters the city had faced, the decades of violence. But it was clear that people wanted something new.

Covered in trash, an old synagogue also emerged from the ruins. Locals had been photographing some old inscriptions they found in the city, and when they shared them online, people realized the writing was Hebrew. People wrote to Omar Mohammed, the blogger known as Mosul Eye who had shared the photos, saying their parents and grandparents had prayed in the place. By the time the synagogue had been found, Mohammed was on his way to the United States as one of Yale University's Greenberg World Fellows. Like Nadia Murad, he would be one of those whose lives were transformed by the war, finding themselves on the global stage, speaking with a weighty conscience about the future of Iraq and the need to preserve its history and diversity.

In Mosul, new cultural hubs emerged. Al-Ghad radio station helped showcase Mosul's new face: book stores, local concerts. But amid all this, the bodies were still being pulled from the rubble, and there were haphazard reconstruction efforts. There was also fear that terror might return.

One group that didn't yet return to Mosul was Christians. Although some had come for the Assyrian New Year in April 2018, lighting a thousand lanterns, most didn't stay overnight. "This used to be their city," one old man said, referring to how Mosul had changed over the decades from a city of diversity to one of destruction and homogeneity.

The Coalition Goes to Morocco

A meeting of the coalition in Morocco in June 2018 showed the mission creep would continue. In July, Senator Lindsey Graham visited Turkey and then Manbij, in Aleppo Province, as the US road map was unfolding and Operation Roundup continued. It was clear that the coalition hoped it would run this war for several more years. There was no time frame to wrap up operations in Syria or to draw down the mission in Iraq. If anything, McGurk appeared to hope the coalition would continue to expand until it had seventy-nine countries and organizations in it. The heavy lifting was done by the United States, but France and the UK had forces in Syria. Other countries were signing on, but it wasn't always clear what they would contribute. The ISIS threat in Europe and North Africa also appeared to be fading.

Graham's visit to Syria was an important fact-finding trip. He toured Manbij and saw firsthand the successes of the liberation.[234] With ISIS gone, markets could function again, and peace could return. But the nagging question about Turkey's threats and concerns was always there. Graham, whom Trump appeared to listen to, sought to see for himself what was happening. He went to Iraq as well, where he got a sense of the progress there. No one would have thought in 2015 that just three years later, a US senator would be making the trip from Turkey to Syria and Iraq after ISIS had been vanquished. But it was happening. The United States appeared to be juggling the various concerns and missions in each country. It appeared to have successfully threaded the needle of an expanding mission in Syria and a stabilization mission in both Syria and Iraq.

The Shammar Martyrs: ISIS Returns to Iraq

The Shammar tribe is one of the largest in the Middle East, with members across Iraq, Syria and Saudi Arabia. Traditionally hostile to the rising forces of political Islam that became popular in the region in the 1990s, its members attempted to weather the storm of the al Qaeda-led insurgency in Iraq after 2003. Some worked with the Americans during the surge and the "Sunni Awakening." As Sunnis, they were pressured to join in the fight against the Shi'ite government of Nouri al-Maliki. When ISIS arrived in 2014, the Shammar looked on with suspicion at the extremists. ISIS had massacred Bedouin tribes who resisted and was laying siege to Haditha, northwest of Baghdad, where Sunni tribesmen were resisting.

Members of the Shammar helped save Yazidis during the August genocide, and some joined units affiliated with the SDF in Syria in 2016 and also formed amicable relations with the Kurdish Peshmerga in Iraq. But when ISIS was defeated, they found their areas dominated by Iranian-backed Shi'ite militia checkpoints. They were also being targeted by ISIS as "collaborators." On June 17, 2018, thirty members of the tribe, driving at night in Iraq's Salahadin Province, were kidnapped by ISIS. The ISIS members had slung up a fake checkpoint on the road and were lying in wait. It was becoming an increasingly common ISIS tactic in the summer of 2018, as ISIS cells operating in desert hideouts between Kirkuk, Diyala and the Hamrin Mountains began to strike at soft targets. They killed members of the PMU and used checkpoints to murder local police or those they thought were working for the government. They would walk into villages at night, and many of the locals said they felt ISIS still controlled a wide swath of area.

The head of Al-Dour District Council, Ali Nawfil al-Hasan, a Shammar leader, said that the thirty members of the Shammar tribe had been kidnapped, and he was waiting for word on their fate. ISIS showed no mercy.[235] They took seven of the men, handcuffed them and gunned them down, leaving the bodies and videotaping the killing.

Hasan demanded security for his area, saying that if the government armed his tribe, it would hunt down the perpetrators. Instead, Baghdad shrugged its shoulders. He said that eighty of his men had been killed by ISIS between 2016 and 2018. He pointed to an area of rolling hills called Mutaybija, where ISIS was still active. "It is their capital today; they have been there since 2006." All around Salahadin Province and on the border areas of Kirkuk and Diyala, ISIS was increasing its activity. The Shammar sheikh said ISIS had moved into Al-Ayn, Shirwat, Hawija and other areas. Many of these places had been retaken by Iraqi forces in September 2017, but never fully secured, because the Iraqi army was preparing to roll into Kirkuk.

Two weeks after the kidnappings, the Iraqi government finally moved. Lt. Gen. Mezhar Al-Azzawi sent helicopters, artillery and units from the army, PMU and Federal Police to search for and destroy ISIS targets. Iraq dubbed the operation Revenge of Martyrs, and it would continue for a month. They claimed to have cleared sixty villages in a few days, and 171 by the end of July. Dozens of ISIS members were killed and arms caches in the desert discovered. But the size of the operation appeared to only show how much ISIS infrastructure remained. The US Defense Department would claim in a Lead Inspector General Report released in November covering June to September operations that ISIS had been cleared from Iraq. Yet the coalition was still carrying out air strikes and using drones to search for ISIS in the provinces north of Baghdad and in Anbar and Nineveh.

Much of the fighting against ISIS consisted of raids into the country-side seeking to bring the enemy to battle. But no enemy could be found. Instead, rusted ordnance was located, old mortars and rockets. Some of these might have been from insurgent stockpiles going back a decade. But the soldiers held them up as evidence of success. Here and there, an ISIS member would be killed and his emaciated body, with speckled full beard, shown off as a trophy. Online, Iraqis said that this showed ISIS had been brought to the ground. These were the bitter-enders. The quality fighters were dead. However, video from the raids showed that some of it was just intended to show the flag. Iraqis fired off hundreds of rounds into underbrush near rivers and said this was an example of "fighting ISIS." The rounds started a fire. No ISIS members came running out.

On October 23, a car bomb exploded in Qayyara, the large town south of Mosul. Several were killed. Then ISIS attacked Baghdad on November 5, targeting Aden Square and the Al-Shaala, Al-Turath and Kadhimiya neighborhoods, showing that it was still a threat.

Crushing Jaysh Khalid bin-Walid

Tal Jamou was a Syrian army base carved into a small hill shaped like a volcano. It dominated the area around it, overlooking the towns of Nawa and Tasil. In June 2014, Syrian rebels had seized the base from the Assad regime. In February 2017, the local ISIS affiliate, known as Jaysh Khalid bin-Walid, swept into Tal Jamou and wrested control of the base from the rebels. Skirmishes followed over the next weeks as the rebels and ISIS fought for control of the hill. Dozens of rebels were killed.

ISIS dug in. As February turned to spring, the ISIS members holed up in Yarmouk camp in Damascus had come under heavy assault from the regime. Bashar al-Assad was trying to recapture all the areas lost since 2011. Little by little, he set his sights on first one rebel bastion and then another. ISIS's Yarmouk stronghold was the last area to be retaken in Damascus.

In mid-April, the regime launched a major offensive on the ruins of what was once a large Palestinian refugee camp. Palestinian Arabs had fled to Damascus after the 1948 war, and Yarmouk became a bustling camp and then a suburb. It had its own culture and economy and played a role in Palestinian politics. At least 160,000 Palestinians lived there in 2011, when the Syrian conflict broke out. By 2015, 140,000 had been displaced by fighting, but eighteen thousand remained in Yarmouk as 60 percent of the area came under ISIS control.

Damascus arrayed the 42nd Brigade of the 4th Mechanized Division around the camp, backed up by Palestinians from the Liwa al-Quds or Jerusalem Brigade of the PFLP, a left-wing Palestinian armed group that supported the regime.[236] By late April, ISIS was pressed so hard it decided to surrender. It left behind a sea of ruins that looked like a German city at the end of the Second World War. The ISIS fighters who survived were quietly allowed by the regime to leave in April. By June, they had ended up in a desolate Syrian desert area, dumped to be left to their own devices. They were expected to disappear, making their way to the Euphrates Valley and going away. This was the policy of the regime with ISIS fighters, just as it had done in Qalamoun in August 2017, when ISIS signed an agreement with Hezbollah and the regime allowing the ISIS men to be moved from the Lebanese-Syrian border near Arsal to the Euphrates Valley. The coalition had condemned these kinds of deals, seeing them as a method that the regime was using to dump its ISIS problem on someone else.

ISIS near the Golan Heights had been able to avoid conflict with the Syrian regime and its Russian Air Force ally, because it was behind a buffer of Syrian rebels on one side and up against the Israel border fence on the other. Since 2015, when Russia's air force had intervened dramatically in the war, Israel and Russia had come to an understanding about "de-confliction" that meant the Russians would stay away from the Golan. Israel was increasingly active against Iranian-backed forces in Syria, carrying out more than a hundred air strikes, and it didn't want to run into Russian airpower while doing so.

In July 2017, ISIS near the Golan got another reprieve from the conflict, when the United States, Russia and Jordan signed a cease-fire impacting southern Syria. ISIS also had not wanted a conflict with Israel. After brief clashes in November 2016, ISIS understood that any attempt to harass Israelis would result in massive retaliation.

At Tal Jamou, the ISIS members were able to survey the regime's military activity. In mid-June, Damascus opened a major offensive in southern Syria. The United States announced that it would not intervene to help the rebels. They were on their own. They agreed to reconciliation agreements and surrendered quickly. By July 6, the Syrian army was back on the Jordanian border, and a few days later, air strikes began to pound rebel positions near Nawa and Quneitra. As the rebels melted away, ISIS finally found itself facing the Syrian army.

Smoke covered Tal Jamou on Saturday, July 21. It was a warm day, with little wind. The Syrian soldiers first tried a frontal assault, then they tried to work their way around the flanks of the hill. A Syrian armored vehicle was destroyed by the ISIS fighters. The regime brought up artillery and laid siege to the mountain. They raked it with artillery and mortar strikes, one every two minutes. But despite the overwhelming power, ISIS held on.

In its quest to defeat ISIS on the Syrian-held side of the Golan, a Syrian Sukhoi Su-22 strayed briefly near Israeli forces and was shot down by two Patriot missiles. The downing of the Sukhoi Su-22 showed how the battle to defeat ISIS could lead to a major international conflict. With the Russians and Iranians backing the Syrian regime, and Israel warning that the Syrians must withdraw Iranian forces, a step too far next to the Golan could lead Israel to carry out more air strikes, potentially putting Israel and Russia on a collision course.

The few dozen ISIS fighters near the Golan, in an area called the Yarmouk Basin, didn't mention the international ramifications of their defeat on social media or on secret Telegram channels. Trump attended a NATO summit on July 12, and two days later spoke to Netanyahu about Syria. The US president had met with Putin on July 16. Syria was on everyone's mind. What would happen when ISIS was defeated in the south and the regime returned to the border? On July 26, as the last areas held by ISIS were retaken, Syrians flocked to Quneitra. SANA news, Iran's Press TV and local politicians came. Druze and Circassians dressed up in traditional dress. Syrian flags were hoisted on buildings and in the abandoned church. Quneitra had been a thriving town, with many Circassian residents, until 1967, when it was abandoned. It sat in the middle of the 1974 cease-fire lines and was a ghost town until 2011, when the civil war caused some Syrians (including rebels) and Lebanese Hezbollah members to make use of the town.

For ISIS, the celebrating in Quneitra was not to be a nail in the coffin. Jaysh Khalid bin-Walid might be almost destroyed, but its friends in eastern Syria were plotting a massacre. ISIS still had assets in the desert southeast of Damascus. On July 25, dozens of ISIS fighters assembled in the desert. With local Bedouin guides, they drove west toward the Druze town of Suwayda. Four suicide bombers set off for the large town. The Druze in Suwayda had carved out a kind of autonomy during the civil war. They timidly supported the regime and were suspicious of the rebels. But they also wanted more local independence. Many of them deserted from the army or didn't go at all. This caused tensions with Damascus. But Damascus was concentrating on destroying the rebels, and the Druze area could wait. Nevertheless, Suwayda was starved of resources and security. It had been relatively quiet throughout the conflict.

In the early hours of July 25, the Druze were awakened by news that ISIS members had attacked the town of Rami and other villages nearby, east of Suwayda. Then suicide bombers began detonating in the town.[237] Next to the vegetable market, a man blew himself up. Around thirty people were killed. Local men took up their AK-47s and rushed to see the destruction. When they heard that outlying villages were being attacked, they ran to help. According to a report by Kareem Shaheen, Karam Monther was one of the volunteers.[238] His mother helped to gather ammunition for his car before he set off to fight ISIS. He joined a squad of men trying to retake the dusty village of Rami from ISIS. What they found was slaughter. Men had been shot down and left in the street. Families had been butchered in their houses. A few were left alive to tell of the brutalities. Women had been rounded up and kidnapped, as ISIS had done in 2014 in Sinjar. Like the Kurds, Yazidis, Shi'ites, foreign volunteers and others who had taken up the gun to fight the black flag, the Druze were now on the front line.

Druze had lived in this area for hundreds of years. This was Jebel Druze, the Druze Mountain. They had suffered persecution in other areas in the eighteenth century, but on the mountain they found safety. The ISIS attack was the worst massacre anyone had experienced in generations.

The Suwayda attacks eventually left more than 250 dead. It left angry feelings among locals, who blamed the regime for leaving them defenseless. It also fed conspiracy theories that the regime had purposely dumped the ISIS fighters in the desert near Suwayda to intimidate the Druze and encourage them to return to the government for help and control. Pro-regime voices had different theories. They blamed the Americans at the coalition-run base at Tanf, down the road from Suwayda near the Jordanian border. The base had a sixty-kilometer radius around it where the Americans had demanded the regime not enter. Had ISIS used this area as a transit point? The regime conspiracy theorists had always blamed the US and Israel for "creating ISIS," much as regime critics had claimed Assad purposely released jihadists to radicalize the rebellion. For both sides, the other was at fault for helping ISIS. The reality was somewhere in between. The regime had allowed ISIS to fester in the volcanic desert areas. The Americans were in Tanf. But neither party was collaborating with ISIS. ISIS simply thrived in ungoverned spaces and was good at exploiting the differences between the various groups that were at war with it. This was because many groups hated each other more than they hated ISIS.

This had often allowed ISIS to survive and even thrive. In Iraq, the Kurds resented Baghdad and thought ISIS would rid them of the burden of Iraq. Iran thought ISIS extremism would undermine Sunnis and make the West rely on Iran as a moderate ally. The Syrian regime also saw ISIS having a positive effect, as it attacked the Syrian rebels and weakened the opposition. Ankara blamed Europe as ISIS supporters sought to transit through Turkey. Chechen ISIS members were a serious threat, and Chechnya likely allowed them to leave in the hope they would not come back.

In July, the killings at Suwayda were one more lesson that ISIS could not be allowed to keep exploiting ungoverned spaces, or it would seek to slaughter minority groups like the Druze. For its own part, ISIS was also trying to influence events further afield. At the same time as it struck at the Druze, another cell in Pakistan killed thirty at a voting station in Quetta. ISIS released a new religious devotionary tract the same day and was in the process of revising its governing structure, dividing Iraq and Syria into separate vilayets or provinces.

To remove ISIS from Suwayda, the Syrian regime sent forces from its newly completed offensive in the south that had brought it back to the Golan Heights' 1974 cease-fire line with Israel. In the first weeks of August, the regime, backed by locals and aided by former Syrian rebels, was able to slowly hammer the ISIS pocket into submission. Nineteen Druze hostages were eventually released in November 2018.

Chapter 23
Shifting Gears to Iran

Stabilization, Stabilization

"They are the exporter of instability across the region," US secretary of defense Mattis, his voice gruff and no-nonsense as usual, said in late July 2018.[239] He was talking about Iran. On Syria, he quoted Dr. Martin Luther King Jr. "Keep your eye on the ball."[240] There were some nations, such as Russia and Iran, keeping Assad in power. "Our job is to try to find a way in the midst of this chaos to help the innocent people." To do that the US wanted to "get stability in northeast Syria. This starts with destroying ISIS. They are not destroyed yet. It's not over yet. It's going to be a lot longer, tougher fight." In the midst of the last days of the war on ISIS, global and regional powers were jockeying to see who would win the peace. Trump, Putin, Rouhani, Erdogan, MBS and Netanyahu were all watching closely.

Since February 2018, the US had begun to concentrate on "stabilization" in Syria. But it was doing that at the same time that it hunted down the remnants of ISIS. "We are almost complete with liberation of the physical caliphate," Maj. Gen. James Jarrard, commander of special operations in Syria, said.[241] He praised the Syrian Democratic Forces as "great partners who have done a phenomenal job liberating terrain." The challenge was that these partner forces, made up of Kurds and Arabs from various units, including the YPG, had a slog ahead to defeat the ISIS remnants. In the Euphrates Valley near Iraq, "once you liberate terrain it's not over. ISIS and al Qaeda are experts at blending in to the population and remain in a cellular structure and commit activities that delegitimize governance." So the US was training local security forces in the "near term," to give the local government breathing space to stabilize the countryside.

There was also a lot of reconstruction to be done and clearing thousands of IEDs. Jarrard said in February 2018 that in Raqqa, Manbij and Tabqa, it could take up to ten years to clear all the mines left behind. "That is the biggest inhibitor to all the other stabilization efforts because of the dangers of working in areas not cleared of IEDs. It's a bit of a catch-22 because the US wants to help the local people have security to get their agriculture developed and start earning a living, while the coalition wants the US State Department donors to set down foundations under a program called START Forward. You can't have security if you can't clear IEDs, and you can't clear IEDs until the financial support is flowing to equip people to do it. Getting the financial support requires security and stabilization," the American officer said.

The coalition and its partners also faced a second major problem in northern Syria near Manbij, where tensions had caused local Turkish-backed Syrian rebels to clash with the SDF. Turkey continued to accuse the YPG of being the Syrian branch of the PKK.

In late January, Turkey launched a major military operation against the YPG in Afrin in northern Syria. The US was not operating in Afrin. However, on February 4, Turkish deputy prime minister Bekir Bozdag said that if the "PKK/YPG terror group" did not leave Manbij, 130 kilometers to the east of Afrin, Turkey would move again into Manbij as well, according to a report at TRT.[242] This could mean a clash between Turkish and US forces, or at least severe clashes between their partners. Mattis said that the US was balancing competing interests, and Turkey had indicated it could postpone its offensive.

The US-led coalition was outspoken on the Afrin issue. Maj. Gen. Felix Gedney, then deputy commander of the Combined Joint Task Force – Operation Inherent Resolve, tweeted on February 3 that "Military operations in #Afrin, #Syria are placing Coalition's #DefeatDaesh mission at risk."[243]

"The current situation in Manbij is fairly stable," Jarrard said. "There is sporadic interaction between some opposition [rebel] forces and Kurdish forces along that interim border in the Manbij enclave in the

Euphrates Shield area." Euphrates Shield was the 2016–2017 operation by Turkey and its rebel allies to intervene near Manbij and clear a corridor along the Turkish border in Syria. As for the "sporadic" clashes around Manbij, there were procedures in place to "de-escalate" them quickly, the general said. This involved liason between the coalition and Turkey. "We work to de-escalate that as quickly as we can. So the security situation has not changed much in Manbij."

Concern about the distraction, the once-stable part of northwest Syria, and the fact that the SDF was concerned about its YPG partners fighting there meant Jarrard had to focus on Afrin as well. But he hoped the conflict there would end, which it did in March with a Turkish victory. "We need to work with all partners and at all levels to restore stability and focus on ISIS."

Operation Roundup near the Iraq border progressed slowly. Mattis was proud of the US helping to push ISIS out of Dashisha, and he praised the SDF. "When it fell, we're now reoriented to their last bastions. As that falls, then we'll sort out a new situation. But what you don't do is simply walk away – and leave the place as devastated as it is. You don't just leave it, and then ISIS comes back."[244]

So the US was engaging in a long-term campaign to restore eastern Syria. Making drinking water available, clearing IEDs and providing financial support for rebuilding Syria. And that "most likely awaits Assad's leaving," Mattis said. USAID and the State Department were also coming in. "My job is to destroy ISIS and to make certain...ISIS can't get back in" by training local security forces to maintain the peace.

The US also faced a problem with Turkey. After sixteen joint patrols near Manbij, Trump had threatened sanctions due to Ankara's detention of a US evangelical pastor, Andrew Brunson, who had been held without charges since the aftermath of the 2016 coup attempt.[245] The joint patrols were a way to reassure Turkey that the United States took its concerns seriously and show that the US wanted to work with Ankara. Brunson, who had lived in Turkey for decades, was arrested in 2016 and accused of being linked to banned political groups. He was eventually released in October 2018. This had thrown cold water on US-Turkey relations after Trump expressed interest in the Brunson case. At the July 27 discussion, Mattis said that "we continue to work very closely together."

How that actually happened didn't sound like closely working together, however. "Well, it's already happening on opposite sides where the two of the patrols go along, and they get to certain points, they wait for the other one to get there. If somebody gets there first and then they do recognition signals back and forth and they move onto the next one. So those patrols are already going, but they're separate. In other words, they're on their side, we're on our side."

And then Mattis had to deal with Iran's presence in Syria. He felt Tehran was helping to keep Assad in power. On Iran, Mattis said nothing had changed. While Iran's influence grew, the US was working to defeat ISIS. Mattis repeated the key words "by, with and through," the US motto. "That process will hopefully remove not just the terrorists that we've removed physically or we've killed or incarcerated – they're under SDF incarceration – but also move foreign forces out of… Syria. That's part of a process, and that's not something that I can forecast… on a crystal ball."

One of the groups involved in stabilization work was the Syrian Recovery Trust Fund. Even Brett McGurk was still on the job in July, a year and a half after Trump succeeded Obama. The ambassador welcomed the work the Syrian Recovery Trust Fund was doing in supporting agriculture. The fund itself said this was about stabilization. "The activity aims to restore cereal and vegetable harvest to pre-conflict levels."[246]

But Paul Curtis Bradley and his humanitarian group team of Free Burma Rangers who visited Raqqa in the summer of 2018 found devastation.[247] The city was mostly in ruins, with few civilians around. After crossing two dozen checkpoints in Iraq to get to the city in northeastern Syria, his team brought colorful playgrounds to set up for the youth of Raqqa. Locals were still scared. Scared that ISIS might return. Scared of IEDs. Bradley and his convoy of SUVs stopped in the city. Several of their group had gone ahead earlier and put up the slides and playground. It was bursting with blue and white and yellow amid the drab, gray background of Raqqa, the bullet holes and the pancaked roofs. Children smiled for a photo. Bradley and his colleagues were devout Christians. They prayed and ate together. Then some of them would head back to Burma or the US. But Syria would stay on their minds.

Like so many others, the Free Burma Rangers had come to Iraq to help the Kurds against ISIS, and they had stayed – working with the Iraqis, watching the Iraqi army and its armored columns be devastated during the liberation of Mosul – and then moved on to help in Syria as ISIS was defeated.

Shifting Gears to Iran

On August 16, Secretary of State Pompeo announced the creation of the Iran Action Group to coordinate US pressure on the Islamic Republic. Brian Hook would head up the group. Congress was also making headway on shifting focus to Iran. "Tehran has been responsible for a torrent of violent and destabilizing behavior against the US, our allies, our partners and indeed the Iranian people themselves," said Pompeo.[248] The National Defense Authorization Act included new focus on Tehran's role in the region. Growing out of concerns about Iran's actions across Iraq, Syria, Lebanon and Yemen, the NDAA focused on encouraging the administration to develop a strategy.

In the House and Senate, bills seeking to sanction Asaib Ahl Al-Haq and Harakat Hezbollah al-Nujaba advanced in September and October. The Department of Defense was also examining Iran's role through its Inspector General Report covering operations from April to June 2018. Released in August, it said the US was already using "indirect" means to confront Iran. It claimed Tehran had ten bases in Syria and forty positions.[249]

In Syria, the State Department had secured $300 million to support "stabilization" and was growing its team on the ground.[250] At a briefing with acting assistant secretary for the Bureau of Near Eastern Affairs David Satterfield, McGurk and Satterfield were pleased as they announced Joel Rayburn as a new special envoy for Syria. Pompeo tapped Jim Jeffrey as Washington's representative for "Syria engagement." Ambassador William Roebuck visited eastern Syria from Bahrain. Altogether the picture was one of growing US involvement in eastern Syria. In Manbij, Turkey and the US were discussing more joint patrols and a "road map," even amid the tensions over the detained pastor.

Increasingly, the US began to move the goalposts in Syria as well. Trump's national security adviser John Bolton visited Jerusalem, where he emphasized that the United States was not interested in regime change in Iran, but was confronting Iran in the region. In early September, Jeffrey said the US was not in a hurry to leave and that ISIS must be dealt an "enduring defeat." A month later, he indicated the US might stay as long as Iran's presence remained.[251] With two thousand troops in Syria, the US was increasing its diplomatic presence, he said, but troops might be drawn down at some point.

US concerns about Iran's role in Syria appeared to come together on October 1, when the IRGC fired six ballistic missiles at ISIS positions near Albukamal, in Deir ez-Zor Province. The missiles were a response to an ISIS attack on September 22 in Ahvaz, in Iran's Khuzestan Province, that killed two dozen Iranians. It was only the second major attack on Iran by ISIS since the attack on parliament in 2017. Now Tehran used it as an excuse to use its missile arsenal. Lifting off in a blaze of fireballs near Kermanshah, western Iran, they lit up the mountains like a rising sun. Flying five hundred kilometers across Iraq, the missiles struck houses near the Euphrates, only five kilometers from US forces. A spokesman for the coalition said the United States had received "no notice."[252] The IRGC had painted "Death to America" and "Death to al-Saud" on the missiles it fired. But the US didn't initially condemn the Iranian barrage. General Joseph Votel, head of the US Central Command, eventually said on October 3 that it had endangered American lives but that the US was not "on the road" to war with Tehran.

Vice President Mike Pence had condemned Iran's use of missiles against Kurdish opposition in mid-September. The October strike went unmentioned. But it posed questions for Washington, which was still slogging along the Euphrates with the SDF to clean up the last ISIS pockets, in yet another phase of Operation Roundup.

The shift of focus to Iran was part of a larger regional strategy. Iran's militias had filled the vacuum left by ISIS, and Tehran was a major beneficiary of the chaos left behind by the Sunni extremists. In Iraq, the Iranian regime was seeking to form the new government after the May 2018 elections saw Hadi al-Amiri's Fatah list come in second. In Syria, it was annoyed to be left out of the Russia-Turkey Idlib deal in September, but Tehran was digging in around the country. It was also winning a war of words with Israel after Netanyahu accused Hezbollah of stocking an arsenal near the Beirut airport and showed images of a "nuclear" warehouse in Tehran. News crews followed the Lebanese and Iranians to both locations and found nothing. The Islamic Republic's foreign minister, Javad Zarif, flew to the United Nations General Assembly annual meeting in September, doing a round of interviews with media in which he accused the United States of being a rogue administration.

In Iraq, the US was concerned that the new government might be even more pro-Iran than the last one. Abadi had been Washington's great hope. He had been empowered by going into Kirkuk, and McGurk had helped Iraq patch up relations with Riyadh. But after Abadi punished the Kurdish region, he found himself coming in third place in the elections. With Washington's man in Baghdad sidelined, it was unclear who would come to power. A young mayor from Anbar named Mohammed Halbusi was elected speaker of the parliament. Pompeo called him on September 19 and told him that the United States would support him forming a "moderate, nationalist, Iraqi government." Nationalist was a euphemism for "less Iran, more Iraq in Iraq."[253]

Then Barham Salih of the PUK was elected president of Iraq on October 3. He chose Adel Abdul Mahdi to try to form a government as prime minister. Iraqis on social media celebrated the hope of the new government and expressed relief at the peaceful transition of power. They had waited five months and witnessed mass protests in the south as well as continued ISIS attacks in several provinces. The coalition was still carrying out air strikes against ISIS, approximately one a day. But the end of Abadi's term seemed like a bookend to the war on ISIS. Now Iraq could move on and deal with other issues, such as Iran's influence, Kurdish relations with Baghdad, and a spate of assassinations of prominent women activists.

In the Kurdish region, there were mixed reviews of Baghdad's choice. For the KDP, the rise of Salih was yet another defeat. Although the region had recovered its airport after the October 2017 disaster that followed the independence referendum, the KDP had been plotting revenge against Abadi. Maneuvering him out of a second term was a success. The KDP also took forty-five seats in the KRG's parliament in September 2018 elections. This was a success. But increasingly the region feared being sidelined now that the war was over. It also feared Iran's role and the US and Western powers seeking to play Kurds off against one another.

As Baghdad celebrated the new government, Yazidis were still fleeing. At Domiz camp near Dohuk, several children destroyed a small garden they had been working on. That night, their parents bundled them up and took them to the border, where they crossed into Turkey. The camp was desolate, without hope. The kids had lived there for four years. But there was no hope in Iraq. There was also no help forthcoming to help them immigrate to Western countries. So they decided to try their luck in crossing Turkey to make the dangerous water crossing to Europe. At least they were alive. On October 3, ISIS in Syria released a video of the murder of one of the Druze women kidnapped in Suwayda.

On October 5, the 2018 Nobel Prize was announced. Nadia Murad was one of two winners. She used it to keep raising awareness for missing Yazidis and the crimes of ISIS. She tweeted about the existence of an online account that had traded in Yazidi girls. One screenshot said "virgin sabiyya [slave]...12-year-old." Nadia was outraged. "This is how they sold Yazidi girls, when we say they raped 12 year old girls people think we are making up these stories. IT'S STILL HAPPENING with more than 3000 Yazidi women & children in captivity in Syria."[254]

Parents of fallen foreign volunteers who had fought alongside the YPG went with veterans to eastern Syria for a memorial service on October 6. Four days earlier, Jamal Khashoggi, the Saudi journalist and one-time political insider who had supported the Muslim Brotherhood, disappeared in Istanbul. He had visited the Saudi consulate. Turkey ordered an investigation. The blowback from the Arab Spring that began almost eight years earlier was still claiming lives.

Trump's Timeline
Trump had come into office wanting to end the war on ISIS. "I will knock the hell out of ISIS," he said in his campaign for the presidency. He had promised a quick decapitation strike during the campaign. But his staff had not expected to win the election of 2016. The surprising victory coincided with the beginning of the battle for Mosul. By the time Trump and his secretary of defense Mattis were sworn in, the battle was already inching to the west side of the river. Soon the battle for Raqqa would start as well. Trump was initially impressed with Mattis, hearing his nickname was "Mad Dog." Mattis was recommended by General Jack

Keane a week after Trump won the election. Trump wanted to "take the war to ISIS," and Mattis agreed, saying it shouldn't be a war of attrition but rather one of annihilation, according to the account told to Bob Woodward for *Fear: Trump in the White House.*[255]

Trump encouraged his generals to get the job done while he focused on other issues. In a February 2017 meeting with Mattis, Trump had been presented with a broader strategy for the Middle East. Trump wanted an ISIS-first strategy, as he'd promised in his campaign. Although he traveled to Saudi Arabia in May 2017, he didn't seem interested in visiting the conflict zones of the war on ISIS. Saudi Arabia and Israel would come first. That was the anchor of Trump's policy in the spring of 2017.

For minor problems, Trump expected others to deal with their files. Tillerson was sent to Iraq in October to deal with Abadi in an uncomfortable discussion about sending the PMU "home." But Trump's administration was presiding over a massive US mission creep in Syria. In Iraq, the coalition had done most of its work, and its advise and assist or "by, with and through" policy had worked. In Syria, there were no US casualties until March 2018, when an American and a British member of the coalition were killed by a roadside bomb near Manbij. Master Sergeant Jonathan Dunbar, from Texas, was the American casualty. It was March 29, 2018. Trump gave a speech the same day in Ohio. "We are knocking the hell out of ISIS. We'll be coming out of Syria, like very soon."[256] The next day he said he suspended $200 million in funding for Syrian recovery efforts.

Trump had seemed pleased with the victory over ISIS in Mosul and Raqqa, and his inclination was to leave Syria. He said in mid-March he hoped Saudi Arabia and others would pay for rebuilding, and the US could reduce its presence. It would cost $4 billion.[257] The US had wound up its role in southern Syria that way, ending support for the rebels and letting the cease-fire fall apart in June 2018.

But Trump's Defense Department and State Department told him to stay. Pompeo and Mattis saw work to be done. Once Pompeo and Bolton had gotten hold of the wheel in the spring of 2018, the new policy was clear. The US had tensions with Turkey and didn't want to abandon its allies to Ankara. It also didn't want to hand Iran a victory. The SDF had sent feelers to Damascus in July, but clashed with the regime in

September in Qamishli. Bolton decided: the US would pivot in eastern Syria to confront Iran. "We're not going to leave as long as Iranian troops are outside Iranian borders," he said in September.[258]

The US was moving slowly to defeat ISIS near the Euphrates. This wasn't just because the SDF was moving slowly. It appeared to be a deliberate policy. But leaving ISIS with an ungoverned space would allow it to plot attacks, like the ones in Suwayda and Ahvaz and also the attacks on Shammar tribesmen in Iraq in June, when thirty were kidnapped.

The Trump administration was buying in to the war in Syria. It was Trump's war. But Trump didn't talk much about Syria. He was stuck dealing with domestic problems, such as the nomination of a Supreme Court justice and continuing controversy over alleged Russian collusion in the US elections. So McGurk, the Obama holdover, was left dealing with Iraq and Syria, alongside Bolton, Pompeo and others. Everyone saw a positive to staying in Syria. "Russia's presence in the region cannot replace the long-standing, enduring and transparent US commitment to the Middle East," Mattis said.[259]

Trump also appeared to be buying in to the Kurds. At a press conference in late September, in response to questions from Majeed Gly and Rahim Rashidi, he called Rashidi "Mr. Kurd." Some thought the comment offensive, but Rashidi and Gly were proud. Trump said that Kurds had helped the US defeat ISIS. They were "great people." And the US would stand by them. But he was short on details. "We are trying to help them a lot ... we don't forget, I don't forget," the president said.[260]

The Killing of Khashoggi

On November 28, 2018, Crown Prince Mohammed bin Salman of Saudi Arabia touched down in Buenos Aires for the G20 meeting. He came in under a cloud. Rumors abounded that Argentinean prosecutors were seeking to open a case against him for the murder of a journalist. In the US Senate the same day, Lindsey Graham, a key foreign policy hawk who had visited eastern Syria in July 2018, was also peeved at Saudi Arabia. In a vote of 63–37, the Senate voted to end US support for Riyadh's war in Yemen.

Trump's agenda was in doubt now. He had staked a lot on Saudi Arabia, traveling there in the spring after his inauguration in January

2017 and hosting the crown prince in Washington. "They have been a great ally in our important fight against Iran," he said on November 20.[261] Saudi Arabia was supposed to help pay for stabilization in eastern Syria, and it might even bring other Gulf countries along to support US efforts there.

The real problems for the crown prince and Trump began in an unlikely place. The Saudi consulate in Istanbul. A modest building. On October 2, 2017, a portly and unassuming man walked into the consulate. He was seeking a document showing that he was divorced, so he could marry his Turkish fiancée. The man never came out. His fiancée, after waiting for hours, phoned Yasin Aktay, a Turkish AK Party member close to Erdogan. In the coming days it emerged that a team of Saudis had allegedly flown into Turkey the same day. The man who walked in was Jamal Khashoggi, and the kingdom wanted to talk to him. The Saudis who flew in did more than talk to the Khashoggi; they were accused of murdering him and disappearing his body.

Khashoggi was a Saudi Arabian legend, a journalist and insider who had run several powerful Saudi newspapers in the 1990s and 2000s. He was the go-to man for Western officials – particularly American and British – to learn about the latest in the kingdom. He had left Saudi Arabia in June 2017, though, after being told to stop writing.

He had become critical of Riyadh's war in Yemen and also of its apparent drift toward relations with Israel. He felt that Riyadh was wrong to support Sisi in Egypt and that it should be closer to Qatar and Turkey and the Muslim Brotherhood. He had supported the Arab Spring, but was concerned about the new totalitarianism in the region, and particularly the defeat for Brotherhood-supported parties. He was supportive of reform in Saudi Arabia but felt there was a need for political Islam, as he called it.[262] Yet the Muslim world was going through a major trauma. Saudi Arabia's Wahhabi clerics had ceased support for Salafist parties. ISIS was almost defeated. But the new crown prince wasn't listening to men like Khashoggi, the old guard, tainted perhaps by their connections to the previous king and their support for the Brotherhood.

Khashoggi went abroad, appearing on Al-Jazeera after the kingdom broke relations with Qatar, and he went to write for the *Washington Post*. The kingdom, which claimed to be reforming, was sensitive to dissent, especially in Washington, where Mohammed bin Salman was cultivating the Trump administration. When Khashoggi turned up in Istanbul, he became a target. After the killing, the Turkish authorities leaked details, bit by bit, about the crime. But after a month, the full details of what happened on October 2 had not became clear. Rumors swirled of a bone saw used to dismember Khashoggi, an attempt at kidnapping him to take him back to Saudi Arabia that went wrong. A struggle, drugging, strangling. A secret recording of the murder. Eventually the CIA director, Gina Haspel, flew to Turkey and returned to the US, but senior Trump officials said they didn't want to hear the recording. Congress was livid.

There were much larger implications to the Khashoggi affair. Khashoggi's fate was a symbol of an unpredictable Saudi Arabia. For years the kingdom had been a close US ally, but also one that was accused of being slow to counter extremism at home. Saudis who joined al Qaeda had played a key role in 9/11 and turned up in jihadist movements from al Qaeda to ISIS. But Saudi Arabia had changed over the years. Khashoggi was a key kingdom insider during that time. His murder was used by critics of the Saudi crown prince to highlight why the kingdom was a problematic US ally. Former Obama administration officials pounced to portray Trump as allying with a brutal dictator.

Trump had torn up the Iran nuclear deal and staked US policy on Saudi Arabia and Israel, but many in Washington felt the US should be engaging more with Qatar and Turkey, and talking to Iran to avoid a new conflict. Qatar's Al-Jazeera ran headlines almost every day for two months focusing on the Khashoggi affair. Some in Qatar saw the crown prince as the architect of the break between Riyadh and Doha. If he could be pushed aside, then things could go back to normal. There was also lasting respect for Khashoggi's views of the region, his support of the Arab Spring and embrace of what many Western career policy makers saw as moderate political Islamic forces. Khashoggi thus served multiple interests. For some he was a brave journalist, silenced by a brutal regime. For others he was a tool to embarrass Trump. For still others he was a quiet way to support the Brotherhood and Turkey. For Qatar he was a way to embarrass the Saudis.

His death hung over the post-ISIS Middle East. Turkey could use it to pressure the United States on Syria. It might even be used to reduce

US support for the YPG, to give Turkey a greater role in Manbij, as it had sought after Jarabulus in August 2016. It would weaken support for the Saudi war in Yemen and distract the US in Trump's drive to confront Iran. This would be good for Iran, Qatar, Turkey and others.

Khashoggi's death wasn't the only one hanging over the region. Raed Fares, another early supporter of the Arab Spring in Syria, and a brave local journalist from Kafr Nabl, was murdered in the last week of November 2018. He was likely killed by members of Hayat Tahrir al-Sham, another voice to be silenced. Hayat Tahrir al-Sham, previously known as al Qaeda in Syria, would go on to capture the last remaining rebel strongholds in Idlib in December and January 2019, driving even Ahrar al-Sham and Nur ed Din al-Zinki into Afrin.

ISIS had upended the worldview of those like Fares and Khashoggi who were disgusted by how the Arab Spring became a bloodbath. It also derailed the revolutionary spirit that sought to turn Sunni countries into democracies that would be led by groups similar to the AK Party. Instead, the brutalities of the Syrian civil war and ISIS led to Sisi's coup and Mohammed bin Salman's breaking relations with Qatar and the Brotherhood. The empowering of Iran fueled the Yemen war, which alienated Khashoggi from the kingdom. A day after MBS landed in Argentina, the Houthis in Yemen fired a ballistic missile at the kingdom. If the US thought withdrawing support for the war would end it, it was mistaken.

Jim Jeffrey's Struggle

James Jeffrey was a thirty-five-year veteran of the US Foreign Service when Mike Pompeo tapped him to return from retirement for a special mission. In August, he was asked to lead US efforts for Syrian engagement. A former ambassador to Iraq from 2010 to 2012 and to Turkey from 2008 to 2010, Jeffrey knew the region well. He had served as an infantry officer in Vietnam and obtained the State Department's highest rank as career ambassador.

He agreed to take on the role of Pompeo's Syria man, officially titled representative for Syria engagement.[263] His appointment was announced by State Department spokeswoman Heather Nauert on August 17, 2018, in a press conference with David Satterfield, assistant secretary for the

Bureau of Near Eastern Affairs, and Brett McGurk. Jeffrey's role was as a kind of proconsul for US affairs in Syria, which was especially important as the American diplomatic footprint was growing in 2018 and as the war on ISIS was winding down. With Operation Roundup in eastern Syria, the coalition was going to be pressuring ISIS in its last holdout in Hajin. At the same time, Washington faced a multisided problem in the rest of Syria. There was pressure to include more Sunni Arabs in the administration in places like Raqqa and Manbij. There was also pressure from Turkey, Russia and Iran. Jeffrey was supposed to help sort this out.

In a way, the appointment of Jeffrey also was sidelining McGurk a bit. McGurk would still handle the Global Coalition to Defeat ISIS, but Jeffrey would deal with Syria, and especially issues involving Turkey. McGurk had pioneered the US role in Syria along with the Pentagon, but his real wheelhouse was Iraq, where he had long experience. "Jeffrey will work closely with the under secretary of state for political affairs, once confirmed, as well as the Near Eastern and European bureaus on this issue. Given all the countries and the issues involved, from terrorism to refugees, these matters obviously cut across geographic bureaus, and therefore this requires a high level of coordination," said Nauert.[264]

Jeffrey would be joined by a sidekick, Joel Rayburn, who would join the State Department from the National Security Council. He had been involved in Iran, Iraq, Syria and Lebanon policy. Now he would be deputy assistant secretary of state for Levant Affairs and special envoy for Syria.

The American envoys thought Jeffrey would be focusing on "stabilization," the catch-all phrase the US was using for reconstruction efforts that were supposed to ensure a peaceful post-ISIS period. That would also mean keeping his hand on the pulse of the Geneva process, an ossified diplomatic track for the Syrian conflict that had largely been abandoned by the end of the Obama administration. Trump saw no real interest in it either, but the US was still talking about it. McGurk said in August 2018 that "we've made very clear that international reconstruction assistance for Syria will not be coming in until we have a – really an unalterable progress on the Geneva track, moving toward a political transition."[265]

Jeffrey's plate would be full from the start. He had to look at what the Russians were doing, the role of Iran and also Turkey's concerns. One of his first trips was to Israel on September 2, where he met with Netanyahu. Jeffrey discussed the importance of "maintaining Israel's security while countering Iran's destabilizing activity throughout the region."[266] Then he and Rayburn headed to Jordan and Turkey. The US State Department was trying to prevent a Syrian regime offensive that could create a wave of refugees flooding into Turkey. Turkey signed a deal in mid-September to prevent the offensive. Under the deal, extremists in Idlib would withdraw heavy weapons. Turkey would guarantee a buffer zone. It was another way for Turkey to become the master of northern Syria.

In Turkey, Jeffrey saw old friends. With Rayburn, he met with Turkish officials. A State Department readout said that Jeffrey discussed his new role and "underscored the importance of continued US-Turkish cooperation in resolving the Syrian conflict in a manner consistent with UNSCR 2254."[267] Jeffrey spelled out US opposition to the Syrian regime's threats against Idlib. "He commended the Turkish Government and people for their continued compassion for those affected by the Syrian conflict." But Jeffrey appears to have missed an opportunity to discuss eastern Syria.

On October 21, Jeffrey visited Manbij. He had just come from trips to Turkey and Saudi Arabia. Saudi Arabia had sent $100 million in October to support stabilization efforts. However, Riyadh was now in the midst of a crisis with Ankara over the murder of Jamal Khashoggi, and it was not clear how much more Saudi money would be forthcoming. Turkey might pressure Saudi Arabia to end its involvement, in exchange for Ankara not pressing charges over the Khashoggi issue. Jeffrey toured Manbij and met the head of the local military council. Local radio said that he also met with other SDF officials.[268] Jeffrey appeared concerned about Manbij. Turkey wanted to begin joint military patrols with the US on the outskirts of the city. Since the summer, the US and Turkey had carried out dozens of parallel military patrols, but Turkey wanted more contact. General Votel said it was only a matter of days before the next stage would come.

On November 14, Jeffrey held a briefing on Syria in Washington. "What we're looking for is the enduring defeat of ISIS, a reinvigorated and irreversible political process in Syria led by the Syrian people and facilitated by the UN, and de-escalation of the conflict that will include all Iranian-commanded forces departing from the entirety of Syria," he said.[269] He highlighted the presence of foreign forces in Syria, including Iranian, Turkish, Russian and even Israeli air strikes. There were also extremists. "There are many there, including very dangerous groups such as Hizballah, ISIS, and al-Qaida, al-Nusrah offshoots."

Jeffrey sought to spell out US goals. With seventy-nine coalition countries, the war on ISIS was going well. Defeating ISIS "affects other goals. It, in its work with our partners, indirectly helps affect Iran's malign activities, and by our presence and by our commitment to security in Syria and in the region, we demonstrate an interest in achieving a political solution by the various ways that we have, not just diplomatic but security and military, through economic tools and other assets that we have and that we're deploying in this conflict." He concentrated on the Iranian issue. "On getting Iran out, that is basically part of a process. It's not a military goal of the United States, it's not a mission of US military forces; rather, we see this as the outcome of [a] process that would end the internal conflict and provide guarantees to the Syrian people and the neighbors toward their security."[270] He sought to emphasize the legalities that underpinned US presence, the Authorization for the Use of Military Force against terrorists (Pub.L. 107–40), passed by Congress three days after 9/11. He also said the US was not involved in "regime change" against Assad. "We've made clear to everyone our three strategic goals in Syria. We don't see why it is in the interest of anyone to have Iranian forces, particularly power projection forces – long-range missiles and other systems that can threaten other countries – present in Syria if we have resolved the underlying conflict. And it's our job to convince everybody, including the Russians, that that's the best way to secure a peaceful result and stability and security, not just in Syria but in the region, and we'll keep on working until we achieve that."

By December, Jeffrey realized there was an addition problem that would consume his time in Syria. Turkish shelling in northern Syria had halted the SDF's Hajin offensive in early November. Jeffrey sought to go to Turkey and make nice with Ankara.[271] He had already given an interview to a Turkish television station in which he noted that the PYD was the Syrian offshoot of the PKK. In November, the US sent Deputy Assistant Secretary of State Matthew Palmer to Turkey, where he announced a

$5 million bounty for the head of the PKK, Murat Karayilan.[272] Other rewards were offered: $4 million for Cemil Batik and $3 million for Duran Kalkan. This was a signal to Turkey that the US cared about its concerns. But Ankara interpreted this as a bone or fig leaf. Turkish media said the United States couldn't use this to hide its relationship with the YPG, the main component of the SDF. Yet Jeffrey's comments in mid-November appeared to indicate that he felt the PYD was the PKK. Turkey wondered how the US would continue working with it.

Jeffrey traveled to Turkey with Rayburn in early December, for meetings from the 7th to the 9th.[273] There Jeffrey indicated that the US alliance with the SDF was temporary and tactical. "We want to have cooperation with Turkey across the board on all Syrian issues," he said. "We think that there will be no final conclusion of this [the Syria] conflict without very close Turkish-American cooperation, and as I said, Manbij is a good model for that cooperation."

Turkey was not impressed. Ankara wanted to focus on eastern Syria and a potential Turkish role. Ankara was threatening a major operation as it had done in Afrin. Foreign Minister Mevlut Cavusoglu said on December 2 that YPG-held areas east of the Euphrates "will top the agenda. During his visit to Turkey Jeffrey is expected to meet with Deputy Foreign Minister Sedat Önal along with other senior security officials and diplomats in Turkey."[274] Jeffrey had opposed Russia's Astana process, which excluded the United States. In December 2016, the foreign ministers of Russia, Turkey and Iran had met in Astana in Kazakhstan to discuss a ceasefire in Syria. Russia and Iran were backing the Syrian regime, while Turkey was backing the rebels. The Astana process resulted in a series of cease-fires, and under its auspices the Syrian regime was able to slowly take back large parts of Syria. "They tried and they failed, or at least up to this point they failed. And if they are still failing by the 14th, the US view...is let's pull the plug on Astana," Jeffrey said, and added, "and then we go back to the UN." Cavusoglu said Jeffrey's views were "very unfortunate."

After their meetings in Ankara, Jeffrey and Rayburn went to Gaziantep on December 8 to meet with US and Turkish military officials. They also met with Syrian refugees, civil society groups, and political groups from Syria. They discussed the joint patrols and "the importance of the unique military cooperation between the United States and Turkey in resolving the conflict in Syria," according to the US State Department. Clearly the meetings were Turkey's attempts to get Jeffrey on its side regarding the future of eastern Syria. Turkey brought civil society groups and NGOs to the meeting. Turkey wanted to showcase what it had in mind after its operation in eastern Syria. This was its version of stabilization. "Throughout, they discussed issues facing the Syrian diaspora and the necessity for a Syrian-led and -owned political process under UN Security Council resolution 2254," the State Department said.[275]

Four days later, Erdogan said that Turkey would launch an operation. He said ISIS was no longer a threat and that Turkey would make eastern Syria livable and return it to its "true owners."[276] Some fifteen thousand Syrian rebels were ready to enter the battle. Turkish television went to the border and began preparing for the operation. On December 14, Trump phoned Erdogan and sought to prevent the operation. The Pentagon said any intervention by Turkey would be unacceptable.

The US sent troops to observation posts along the border. US helicopters flew to Manbij. Trump and Erdogan discussed the two countries' "respective" policies. They also said they would seek more "effective" and "efficient" cooperation. Jeffrey's mission was potentially in tatters. The Russians had a firm hold in Syria. Iran was still there. Turkey, ostensibly a US ally, was about to upset the apple cart in eastern Syria. Only the anti-ISIS mission appeared to be going well. On December 14, the SDF took the hospital in Hajin, raising its yellow flag. Then YPG fighters, who had come to bolster the battle, went north to the Turkish border.

Turkey held off for the moment. It carried out air strikes in northern Iraq in mid-December, in Sinjar and at a PKK camp near Makhmour, killing four. Ankara said it would continue to operate in Sinjar. The message: if we can't operate in Manbij and Tel Abyad, we will strike in Iraq. Iraq summoned Turkey's ambassador and condemned the strikes. In Makhmour, the people picked through the rubble. A large funeral was attended by hundreds. Children sung songs of the revolution. Women wept. These Yazidi IDPs wanted to return to Sinjar and have a normal life. Once more war had come to them.

Chapter 24
The Great Withdrawal

Sudden Change in US Syria Policy

Between December 9 and 15, the US carried out 208 air strikes on ISIS in Syria. Warplanes targeted fighting positions, staging areas, oil facilities, supply routes, tunnels and mortars near Hajin. The fighting was tough. It had been for months. From October to December, ISIS had dug in and used fog and sandstorms to conduct counterattacks. The SDF was also distracted by Turkish shelling of the border area near Tel Abyad in northern Syria. It had to suspend offensive operations in late October.

The coalition was increasing its air campaign. UK special forces were on the ground. Two of their Thales Bushmaster wheeled armored personnel carriers, laden with supplies and the latest technology, sat in the early morning light, monitoring ISIS positions. The SDF forces in Hajin were Arab fighters recruited from tribes in the area. Some of these had been victimized by ISIS. The coalition also wanted to train more Arabs for the thirty-thousand-strong stabilization forces it wanted to build. According to General Dunford, only 20 percent of these had been trained. But it was essential to have Arabs in the SDF so that it couldn't be called just a "Kurdish" force or perceived as occupying Arab areas. This was the careful balance between Kurdish and Arab groups the United States wanted to achieve. Jeffrey, Rayburn and others who were trying to lay the foundations of years of US presence appeared convinced of this. They were trying to balance the varying competing agendas in northern Syria, and also the different ethnic groups, to make the US role appear less partisan in favor of one group and to put a different face on the SDF.

But there was a lack of clarity in the US mission in Syria. While Bolton and others were speaking about Iranians leaving, Jeffrey was among those who gave out mixed messages. The work with the SDF was tactical, temporary and transactional, he told the Atlantic Council think tank in Washington in mid-December. But he too wanted Iranian-commanded forces gone. At the same time, he wanted the Geneva political process to go forward. And the Pentagon wanted to crush ISIS.

Turkey was raising the rhetoric on the US role in Syria. It planned to meet with Iran and Russia in Geneva to discuss a Syrian constitution. Iran's Javad Zarif was a rockstar at the Doha Forum on December 15, meeting with Turkish officials and the emir. It was a visible show of Iran's ability to get around sanctions. At a speech on December 12, Recep Tayyip Erdogan said that "there is no longer any such threat as Daesh in Syria. We know this pretext is a stalling tactic."[277] He spoke with Trump two days later, asking the US president why he was still in Syria. ISIS was 99 percent defeated; why was the US there? Trump thought about it. Then he told Bolton it was time to leave. Bolton was told to coordinate with Ibrahim Kalin, Erdogan's adviser. Sort it out.

For several days, nothing happened. Bolton didn't appear to tell Mattis or McGurk. When Jeffrey spoke at the Atlantic Council on December 17, he was oblivious of the decision. He said the SDF should be a part of a future Syria. He discussed US efforts.

"We have defeated ISIS in Syria, my only reason for being there during the Trump Presidency," Trump tweeted on December 19.[278] His sudden decision shocked the administration. Mattis drafted a letter and resigned the next day. He didn't emphasize ISIS, but rather preserving US allies. He said the anti-ISIS coalition of seventy-nine partners and nations was proof of US global leadership. Trump hadn't warned US allies. France and the UK were dumfounded. Brett McGurk resigned as well.

But Trump felt that the United States had been subsidizing foreign militaries by doing the fighting. Slammed by Senator Lindsey Graham, who had visited Manbij earlier in the year, Trump said that Russia, Iran and others should deal with ISIS. "Bring our youth back home." He also said the US was initially supposed to be in Syria for three months, and had "never left." This was a reference to the US involvement supporting the Syrian rebels, not fighting ISIS. Trump reached out to Erdogan on

December 23 and said the US would withdraw "slowly," and it would be highly coordinated with Turkey. It was a 180-degree turn from what the US had been doing. In northern Syria, the joint patrols, Manbij road map and the observation points set up in November along the Turkish border had all been designed to warn Turkey against attacking the YPG. Now the US would work with Ankara, Trump indicated. "Erdogan of Turkey has very strongly informed me that he will eradicate whatever is left of ISIS in Syria."[279] Saudi Arabia had also told Trump on December 24 that it would be increasing financial support to help rebuild Syria.

The US president capped off his decision with a surprise visit to troops at Al Asad Air Base in Iraq. In the speech there, he said that his generals had originally asked him for six months to defeat ISIS. When that didn't happen, they asked for another six months, and another. Eventually Trump said enough was enough. He thanked the soldiers for liberating twenty thousand square miles and three million civilians. The US would remain in Iraq in case of an ISIS resurgence. They would be keeping an eye on Iran. "We aren't suckers," Trump said. Soldiers need "clear objectives," and Syria had become an open-ended mess.[280] The crowd cheered. Trump stopped for selfies. He even posed with secretive US special forces operators, their night goggles pulled up on their helmets. He told ISIS to watch out. "If they hit us on our homeland, they will suffer consequences over here like no one has suffered before."

In Syria, the SDF was thrown into confusion. They had been achieving victories against ISIS, pushing it out of Hajin. On November 30, they captured Osama Oweid Saleh, an assistant to Abu Bakr al-Baghdadi. They expected the United States to stay. But they had always wondered about the US commitment. In October, when new US diplomats came to Rojava, Kurdish politician Aldar Xelil said they felt the Americans were more committed. The SDF felt the US now had a political channel open to them. When Trump made his announcement, they immediately continued outreach to Damascus and sent emissaries to Paris. They also began discussions with Russia.

Amjad Othman, SDF spokesman, said that people were afraid and panicking at the possibility of a new round of conflict set off by the US withdrawal. "They are concerned about a war that will take their lives and their loved ones, and their self-esteem."[281] After four long years of privation in the war on ISIS alongside the US, they felt deserted. Many of these people had faced suppression under the Assad regime until 2011, lacking basic rights such as citizenship. Thrown into the Syrian civil war, they tried to navigate it, from opposing Assad to fighting ISIS as the Syrian rebellion gave way to extremism. Now they faced a new invasion by Turkey or the prospect of allying with the Assad regime and Russia and Iran against Turkey.

This was an impossible position the US had plunged them into, without warning or consultations or even preparation. Thousands had been killed and wounded fighting ISIS. Their cemeteries festooned the landscape; their makeshift memorials, such as the old tank in Kobani, had been built in memory of the slain. In Turkey and neighboring countries, there were also graves of the fallen, those who had come to help fight ISIS. Foreign volunteers such as Macer Gifford of the UK and the parents of those who volunteered, such as Chris Scurfield, also from Britain, were alarmed. "Where my son fell, twenty Arab families have returned, and houses and the single bridge [have been] rebuilt. This is their legacy, which doesn't make headline news," he told me.[282] He said that the media had failed to explain the real success on the ground of the war on ISIS and about those who stood up to defeat ISIS. Now the US decision had left the families of the fallen in shock. "But the legacy of international solidarity that they inspired is coming into place. The US Senate knows the Kurds. The case for betrayal is clear cut, but so is the case for other coalition members to come to the fore." He hoped the other members of the then seventy-four-nation coalition would step up in the vacuum the US was poised to leave behind.

The SDF was holding nine hundred Western ISIS members and some twenty-one hundred other ISIS detainees, including women and children. They captured more in late December and early January, including at least one man from Ireland. Now they didn't know what to do. The countries of origin of these ISIS members didn't want them back. The US didn't want to transfer them for trial elsewhere, and human rights organizations claimed that handing them over to the Syrian regime or Iraq was unacceptable. "Kurds are alone," said Othman. "Russia has a major role as a great power in Syria. Russia doesn't need to be like a bait for Iran or Turkey's trap," he said. Russia could step in and solve things in eastern Syria. This had been Mattis's fear, that Russia would gain.

In late December 2018, McGurk's pinned tweet (that is, pinned to the top of his Twitter profile for greater visibility) from August 15 still highlighted coalition-supported projects in Raqqa. "Reopened schools for thousands of children once traumatized by ISIS and now visibly eager to learn." McGurk was gone now, and the future of the schools was in question.

Near Hajin, Jonathan Reith was recovering.[283] A volunteer medic from Syracuse, New York, who had been at Bashiqa and Nawaran with the Peshmerga and then in Mosul with Iraq's Golden Division, he was helping out in Hajin, returning to war after sixteen months away. He had helped to save the life of a man who was wounded in battle. A young man had been wounded. Reith, in the middle of uploading photos, was called outside to help. He found a man on a stretcher. He had to cut through numerous layers with his Leatherman Raptor shears. "A winter jacket, a military uniform, five to six shirts." After cutting through, he found the gunshot wound in the upper chest. They took the man to the American base nearby. The Americans told him to take the man to Hasakah, more than two hundred kilometers away. "The instructions are easy. Breathe for the guy once every three to five seconds. Give 1 ml of Vecuronium every 15 minutes. 1 ml of Propofol/Ketamine blend every 15 minutes." In an ambulance ride to Hasakah, he had helped the man breathe for three hours. "It's never too late for anything; everything is salvageable." Reith was the kind of hero the war on ISIS had attracted. Now it was all in doubt in the last days of December 2018, as the US was withdrawing.

On the morning of December 28, the Syrian regime forces pressed past Arima, a village twenty kilometers from Manbij. Singing songs of praise of Assad, they were on the way to take back Syria as the American house of cards appeared to collapse. The US only had two thousand soldiers in eastern Syria and a handful of diplomats. The diplomats were already gone. The soldiers would leave soon. The SDF had told the regime it could come into Manbij. Syrian state TV said the regime was on the move. Turkey called it a "psychological operation." Syrian rebel units drove in circles with their pickup trucks, vowing to attack the city.

The Ahrar al-Sharqiya unit showed a video of a man brandishing a knife and saying he would kill Kurds. Russia said that the Syrian regime was right to press to take over US areas. But Moscow was also getting ready to host the Turkish foreign minister, defense minister, head of the MIT and Kalin, the adviser to Erdogan, on December 29.

Death in Manbij

Four Americans came to a meeting on January 16 in the town of Manbij. They knew that their mission was in the eye of the storm buffeting Syria. As the US was still debating how best to withdraw, and the first equipment was already leaving Syria, the mission continued in Manbij. But it was more complex now. John Bolton and Mike Pompeo were traveling to the Middle East. Bolton went to Israel and then Turkey. In Ankara, he was snubbed by Erdogan, angry over Pompeo's comments earlier in January that claimed Turkey would "slaughter" the Kurds.[284] Pompeo wasn't heading for Turkey, but rather to Iraq, Jordan, the Gulf and then Egypt, where he gave a major speech in Cairo arguing against Obama's policies in the region.

Pompeo wanted to hammer Iran. But with the US leaving Syria, it wasn't clear how that would happen. If Turkey's influence grew in Syria, the US would be leaving a major piece of the region to a country that was working more closely with Iran. US allies such as Riyadh, Cairo and Amman were farther away from eastern Syria. And US allies in the Gulf were already returning to Damascus, with the UAE, Bahrain and others reopening embassies. Syria's intelligence chief had visited Cairo as well. Senator Graham was coming to Ankara on January 18. McGurk had just penned an op-ed at the *Washington Post* urging Trump to stay in Syria and arguing that Turkey would break its word about confronting ISIS.[285]

The men and one woman meeting in Manbij likely knew that Trump had recently tweeted about a twenty-mile buffer zone or "safe zone," as Turkey called it. This would be a large swath of northern Syria including most Kurdish areas. A proposal had been prepared by the SDF to be presented to Damascus that would offer a deal. The SDF would become border guards, Rojava would get some form of autonomy and the regime would return to the area. At the center of all of it, like a linchpin and test case, was Manbij. Russian patrols were inching closer. The US and Turkish troops were continuing their joint patrols along the Shagur line. The Syrian regime was present down the road. The city was the great prize of this war as the US prepared to leave.

It was also a safe city. US officials, senators and soldiers had become used to visiting the city and its market. For two and a half years it had been safe. But January 16, 2019, saw the end of that safety. A suicide bomber, alleged to be affiliated with ISIS, targeted four Americans, killing two soldiers – a contractor and a naval cryptological technician. Shannon Kent was from the Navy's Cryptologic Warfare Group at Fort Meade in Maryland. This appeared to be an important intelligence meeting. An interpreter was present. How did ISIS know about the meeting and penetrate it? Was there a leak? Why did ISIS choose such an opportune time to strike at the US? This was the largest US death toll of the Syrian conflict. It was like a message to Trump: *You wanted to go home so as not to lose more Americans; here's a good reason.* But it could also be read another way. Trump had warned ISIS at Al-Asad that any attack would be met with massive force.

After the January 16 attack, there was silence in Washington. Trump was dealing with the US government "shutdown" and arguing about immigration and his border wall. But it came at a crucial time for the US effort in Syria. The coalition still said that there was fighting in Hajin. ISIS members were still being captured, including foreign female members. In Iraq, the coalition was training the Iraqis to continue the war effort and prevent an ISIS insurgence. And ISIS was attempting that insurgence. Creeping into areas around Khanaquin in late January, where villagers fled the renewed presence. In the Qara Chokh Mountains, ISIS members hid out in caves between Peshmerga and Iraqi army checkpoints. In the Hamrin Mountains, they haunted the landscape, coming into towns at night where locals put out food for them. Every once in a while, they carried out assassinations or roadside hijackings.

But mostly Iraq was doing well after ISIS. Western Mosul had recovered. Parts of eastern Mosul were being rehabilitated. A book forum celebrated its first anniversary at the end of 2018. Poetry readings, musical nights and cultural events were popping up.

For Yazidis, the path was harder. There was no real investment in their villages. Even though the road from Dohuk to Sinjar was reopened, many had still not returned. On January 19, 2019, an Iraqi human rights observatory group told the story of a Yazidi woman who had escaped ISIS, only to be trafficked and raped in Baghdad years later.

Snows blanketed Kurdistan in January 2019. Further south, Iran's foreign minister paid a visit to Iraqi tribes, cementing Tehran's influence in Iraq. Iraqi politicians increasingly called for US troops to leave, particularly former militia leaders like Qais al-Khazali. But Iraq had also celebrated Christmas with cheer. The Mar Behnam Monastery had been rebuilt. Christians flocked to Qaraqosh. Perhaps the worst of ISIS was over.

Iraq was also apprehending ISIS suspects. Jamal al-Mashadani, an ISIS member known as Abu Hamza al-Kurdi who had been active near Kirkuk and was known for procuring chemical weapons for ISIS and putting Kurdish prisoners in metal cages, was captured in the fall of 2018 while returning from Turkey.[286] Iraq's new president, Barham Salih, was trying to smooth Iraq's relations with its neighbors. Nechirvan Barzani and Masrour Barzani were taking the reins of the KRG, with Masrour moving to prime minister and Nechirvan seeking the presidency. Even Masoud Barzani had recovered from the difficulties of the post-referendum setback, going to Baghdad and the Gulf. He was trying to convince the Americans to let the Rojava Peshmerga into eastern Syria to help smooth Turkey's concerns.

The Kurds, on the cusp of such power in 2017, were greatly changed by the events of 2018. In 2019, they were trying to salvage what power they had in the KRG and Rojava. Incrementalism was their method now, not blandishments about independence. Pragmatism.

Preparing for the Post-ISIS Middle East

"He has defeated Daesh in Syria because he wasn't hesitant about deploying force," Saudi foreign minister Adel al-Jubeir told the Manama Dialogue confab in the fall of 2018. He was talking about Trump.[287] "He has defeated Daesh in Iraq, when it took years for the Obama administration to make any progress. He has put Iran on notice that business as usual cannot continue, and imposed sanctions against Iran." Jubeir, a former Saudi ambassador to the United States, was key to the Washington-Riyadh relationship.

In January 2019, he met Pompeo on the tarmac when the US secretary of state touched down. Jubeir was soft-spoken, but he was no-nonsense when it came to Iran. When the Obama administration had been on the verge of the nuclear deal, he had warned about its ramifications. He had been tough on Canada when it critiqued Saudi human rights issues. He appeared to share the worldview of Crown Prince Mohammed bin Salman. But after the Khashoggi affair, Jubeir was given a new title, and a more pliant foreign minister was appointed. Nevertheless, when Pompeo came to Riyadh, Jubeir was the familiar face to meet him. This was a show of respect. The Saudis had snubbed the Obama administration but placed their hopes in the Trump era.

The first two years of the Trump administration coincided with massive shifts in the region. As ISIS was defeated and the Syrian regime cemented its power, the appearance was of a return to a kind of previous regime, a return to 2010. But this appearance is deceptive.

The region had changed greatly over the war years. These changes had their roots decades before, as the rise of political Islam challenged the ossifying Arab nationalist regimes. But this Islamist challenge had various trajectories. On the one hand, it sowed chaos across a swath of countries from Senegal to the Philippines. This was a major challenge for Western policy makers who had sunk so much investment into the status quo in the region. The 1979 Islamic Revolution in Iran was one challenge. But the rise of extremists also had other effects. Anwar Sadat was murdered by Islamists in 1981. The blowback from the Afghan war and the mujahideen helped lead to the Taliban and 9/11. Jihadists were schooled in battles in Chechnya and the Balkans. They also went to Algeria in the 1990s. And they traveled elsewhere, to the West and eastern Asia.

The First Gulf War, a conventional war, helped to motivate Osama bin Laden. But his al Qaeda was like a grade school compared to the graduate school of ISIS. Western writers from Samuel Huntington's *The Clash of Civilizations* (1996) to Thomas Barnett's *The Pentagon's New Map* (2004) sought to diagnose this new world. Bernard Lewis in *What*

Went Wrong? (2002) and books like Benjamin Barber's *Jihad vs. McWorld* (1995) had provided some answers, but not enough.

In searching for answers, the United States went through different policies rooted in America's past. Law enforcement sought to confront terror as a criminal problem, before it was clear it was a war. Where Bush Sr. sought a New World Order and Bill Clinton supported humanitarian intervention, the US moved into democracy promotion after 9/11. This toppled the Taliban and Saddam Hussein. But the boomerang effect of that was more instability. Rafic Hariri was assassinated in 2005, Hamas won the Palestinian elections in 2006. Then came Obama and the decision to reduce America's footprint and get out of the endless counterinsurgency, the surge and COIN, in Iraq. The result was that people rose in rebellion in mass protests in Iran in 2009, and then in Egypt and Tunisia in 2010 and 2011.

The toppling of the regimes eventually led to a new totalitarianism in the region. But it also led to a crackdown on Islamist extremists. Even countries like Turkey that had supported the Muslim Brotherhood and Hamas came to understand that tolerating extremists crossing the border to Syria would have consequences. Eventually they sought to rein in the rebellion and create proxy forces. Ahrar Sham had to go. Nur ed Din al-Zinki had to go. A Turkish-backed Free Syrian Army resulted in 2018. By 2019, Hayat Tahrir al-Sham had defeated the other independent rebels in Idlib and chased them back into Afrin.

By January 2019, Turkey was looking at a problem all along its border. Ankara had said that ISIS was defeated in December 2018, but the sudden US planned withdrawal caught Turkey by surprise. Erdogan said he would return eastern Syria to its true owners, and there were hints that millions of Syrian refugees, mostly Arabs, would return to the Kurdish-controlled areas. But how to get rid of the YPG and HTS at the same time and end the Syrian conflict once and for all? This appeared to be the question haunting Turkish policy makers in the first months of 2019. The *Daily Sabah* reported that after Erdogan met with Putin in January, Putin gave "silent consent on the creation of a 30-kilometer 'safe zone' along the Syrian-Turkish border."

Turkey also discussed this "safe zone" with Trump, an initiative the US president had hinted at. But US policy makers were not sure what it meant. Pompeo and Bolton wanted to protect the Kurds. US Republican senator John Kennedy even introduced an amendment in the last days of January to support the Kurds. Turkey was watching closely and changed its rhetoric. In December, it had threatened that it wouldn't allow a "terror corridor" along the border. That changed to coordinating withdrawal with the US. Then it would change again to Ankara claiming it would take up the fight against ISIS in Syria and could wait several months for the US withdrawal and for Turkey to launch its operation.

In Washington, acting US secretary of defense Patrick Shanahan said on January 30 that ISIS was "99.5 percent" defeated. Trump tweeted that it would be 100 percent. "I inherited a total mess," he said on February 1. "Syria was loaded with ISIS until I came along. We will soon have destroyed 100% of the Caliphate, but will be watching them closely."[288] It's time to come home, he tweeted. From Syria and Afghanistan. Trump had indicated on December 26 in his Al-Asad speech that the US would be watching ISIS and Iran from Iraq. If there was an ISIS resurgence, the US would strike hard.

At the Office of the Director of National Intelligence, director Dan Coats seemed more pessimistic than Trump. The "worldwide assessment" that came out in January warned about ISIS threats across the globe. Across Africa and Asia, the extremists were still active. The Defense Department was also working on another quarterly report on Inherent Resolve that would show that ISIS could retake territory in Syria. And despite ISIS being defeated, the United States was still expending massive ordnance against the extremist organization: a total of 645 air strikes from January 13 to 26, a number unprecedented in the four-year war.

The coalition said, "In Syria, 645 strikes engaged 394 ISIS tactical units, and destroyed 244 fighting positions, 172 supply routes, 85 staging areas, 21 vehicles, 17 buildings, 15 vehicle borne improvised explosive devices, 14 mortar launching sites, 13 manufacturing facilities for improvised explosive devices, 12 command and control nodes, nine tunnels, eight weapons caches, seven pieces of engineering equipment, five launching sites for unmanned aircraft systems, two weapons storage facilities, two mortar tubes, two improvised explosive devices, one unmanned aircraft system, one machine gun, one logistic node and one checkpoint."[289]

The SDF and the Coalition Come to Washington

Washington was preparing for a spell of cold weather blasting the US in late January, when a Kurdish woman appeared in the American capital. Ilham Ahmad, the copresident of the Syrian Democratic Council, was on a mission to save eastern Syria from a new round of conflict. A representative of the political wing of the SDF, her message was clear. The US should slow its withdrawal. ISIS was still a threat. There would be sleeper cells to confront and an insurgency. Reconstruction needed to be supported.

She told *The National* that she expected the US to leave eventually.[290] She also hinted that the SDF would accept the Syrian regime returning to eastern Syria as long as the administration was "decentralized." The Syrian Democratic Council and the SDF were talking to Moscow and Damascus. She said in other speeches that she rejected the concept of a Turkish-controlled safe zone. They didn't want another Afrin. In fact, they wanted Turkey to withdraw from Syria. She had run into Donald Trump briefly and met members of Congress. She addressed the National Press Club on February 4.

But for the SDF it was an uphill struggle. Protected by the US Air Force, it had thrived and fought heroicly against ISIS. If not for the SDF, ISIS would still be a major threat. They had saved Yazidi lives. But in Turkey's view, they were the same as the PKK. And Washington also felt the relationship was temporary, tactical and transactional. Diplomatic speak for: we don't need you. And Trump wanted to withdraw troops. The short-lived fantasy Bolton and others had pushed of using eastern Syria to confront Iran was not going to happen. The experiment the SDF had created since 2014 would not come to fruition. It had been a unique time, but like all the independent groups that had emerged from the chaos of the Syrian conflict, their time was coming to an end. This was the fate of the hopes and dreams of 2011. Powerful states were coming back into the vacuum. Thousands had died, but now the SDF would have to pick the better of several bad choices.

Meanwhile, the now seventy-nine members of the coalition were coming to Washington for a ministerial meeting on February 6. The last ones had been held in Morocco and Brussels. Now the coalition would be meeting under much different circumstances. With ISIS largely defeated and the US leaving, the partners would be asked to pitch in more. Sources in the United States had indicated that Washington wanted the partners, such as France and the UK, to pick up the slack in Syria. Officially, the State Department was going to tell the ministers that they should focus on preventing a resurgence of ISIS through "stabilization and security assistance."[291] It was a key moment, the US said. Indeed, it was a crossroads and Washington knew it. But for many members of the coalition that had contributed only a paucity of support, the meeting was a mere formality.

On February 6, Washington's unusually warm winter weather turned to rain. I ducked into a restaurant near E Street. After two days of discussing US policy in the Middle East, it was clear that US fatigue for focusing on the details was winning the day. Kurdish issues were seen as a bother. Yes, they are our allies; yes, they fought ISIS; but there's no taste for standing by them. The Syrian Democratic Council had tried for two weeks to get meetings. They had been successful. But they had been ignored by some key players such as Lindsey Graham. After his trip to Turkey, it appeared he wasn't willing to deal with them. They were talking autonomy and also slowing the US withdrawal to a multistaged process.

The Turkish foreign minister was in town for the anti-ISIS coalition meeting and a US-Turkey working group. "Emphasized the need to avoid possible power vacuums in Iraq and Syria in post-Daesh period," Mevlut Cavusoglu tweeted. Turkey was ready to do whatever it took to help stabilize both Iraq and Syria. The Turkish delegation led by Sedat Onal met with David Hale, under secretary of state for political affairs. They discussed working groups for blilateral cooperation on Syria.

The Syrian Democratic Council delegation was across town, looking forward to meetings on December 7 with the State Department. But they were dismayed. The US wasn't pressuring them to make decisions. A bad sign that appeared to mean the US didn't care. The Kurdish copresident of the Syrian Democratic Council, Ilham Ahmad, had met with Congresswoman Tulsi Gabbard, the presidential candidate from Hawaii. Ahmad watched Trump's State of the Union address. But her delegation should have lobbied and forged close friendships in Washington years before. They had no ability to make real inroads among players and policy makers in DC, despite having laid down ten thousand lives fighting ISIS alongside the Americans. They were getting the cold shoulder. Although leading senators and officials said the Kurds in Syria should be protected, they had no seat at the table of either the anti-ISIS coalition of the UN-backed committees on Syria that included other opposition and pro-government groups.

The Pope Goes to the UAE

A more symbolic event was taking place in Abu Dhabi. Some 135,000 had gotten tickets to a historic papal mass. Pope Francis was coming during the UAE's "Year of Tolerance" to meet the grand imam of Al-Azhar, Ahmed el-Tayeb. He was also preaching a new era of interfaith dialogue and tolerance, part of the Egyptian government's decision to reduce extremism and to formalize the speeches and messages coming from that nation's mosques.

The partnership of Egypt and the UAE on pushing this message of tolerance was part of a wider program. The UAE had hosted India's Prime Minister Narendra Modi in 2018 and laid the groundwork for a Hindu temple. The UAE and Saudi emissaries had also joined the Jordanians at the Dead Sea with Egyptian, Bahraini and Kuwaiti counterparts to discuss the future. At the closed meeting, they discussed Syria and regional peace and security. They were weighing supporting Syria's return to the Arab League and finding a way to pull Syria away from Iran.

The pope's visit was symbolic, but it also bookended the ISIS war. In July 2014, ISIS had expelled Christians. Now the UAE was hosting the pope. It showed that interfaith narratives could flourish. However, they were thriving primarily among governments that were entrenching their regimes, cracking down on online dissent and more worried than ever about extremism and chaos. In short, religious tolerance could blossom, but only surrounded by the bayonets of the state. This was the Middle East emerging after ISIS. After so much trauma, security and tolerance would come, but at a price. Countries that experimented with instability in the form of too much democracy had paid that price, in the eyes of the monarchies and the strongmen.

The only challenge now was how to balance the emerging Turkey-Qatar alliance with Iran and the countries that looked to Riyadh and Abu Dhabi for leadership. Iran was about to make the next move.

A sunny day in Mosul on January 31 saw a group of Americans in tan camo walking on a street.[292] They were on patrol near the Ninewa International Hotel, the pyramid-shaped hotel that had once been one of Iraq's best. It was near an old Saddam-era palace, the university and an Iraqi military base where the US troops were stationed.

As the soldiers, kitted up with M-16s and backpacks, passed a gate, a black vehicle with an armored turret blocked their way. Members of the Hashd al-Sha'abi came out and looked at the Americans. A Black Hawk helicopter buzzed in the background. It was a tense standoff. Eventually the American patrol moved to the sidewalk and continued on their way. "Fighters stop US military patrol," Iran's Press TV boasted on February 2. Rezvan Al-Anzi, a deputy PMU commander, warned the Americans against further provocations.

Several hundred kilometers away, near Baghuz on the Euphrates, the last ISIS members were streaming out of two villages near the river. Thousands had fled since mid-January. Processed, fingerprinted and sent to refugee camps such as Roj camp in Hasaka, the people fleeing looked like ISIS members. But it was hard to sort the civilians from the fighters. The women were all clad in black, their faces covered. SDF members said they found many women from Turkey, Russia, and even Germany and France. One woman, who gave her name as Leonora to Agence France-Presse, claimed to have left Germany at age fifteen.[293] She was one of an estimated thirty-six thousand who fled the Hajin fighting. A "jihadi bride" also spoke with France 24, saying she faced a stark choice of fleeing the fighting and going to prison or remaining with the last ISIS fighters.

The ISIS male foreign fighters were also surrendering. Six men, from Turkey, Morocco, an unidentified South American nation, Germany and Russia, surrendered on February 1. They too seemed to expect that surrender was preferable to death. The mercy they denied victims of ISIS, they demanded now from the SDF. The FBI was in eastern Syria, to interrogate some of those fleeing Baghuz. It said on February 2 that it hoped to transfer the two "Beatles" members being held by the SDF to the US for trial.

Washington, February 2019

"Trenton Makes, The World Takes," said a white sign on a bridge over the river near the New Jersey capital's main train station. In February 2019, the Delaware River was choked with ice. The forests were dry and festooned with vines hanging off the leafless trees. I was on Amtrak's Northeast Regional train 185 from Newark's Liberty Airport, heading to Washington. The coalition was meeting the next day. Turkey's Erdogan had said he wouldn't wait any longer before launching an operation into northern Syria. The YPG must leave Manbij. And Turkey would demand to play a role in setting up a new administration in eastern Syria, along the border.

February was shaping up to be a crossroads in Middle Eastern history. In Iraq, the parliament was angry over Trump's comments about the United States using bases in Iraq to keep "watch" on Iran.[294] There were new calls for the US to leave. Coming on the heels of tensions in Anbar and Mosul between the PMU and local US patrols, it was clear that the US presence in Iraq was on shaky ground. The coalition emphasized that the US was in Iraq at the invitation of the Baghdad government. What happens if the government decides to withdraw the invitation? The US would have to leave Iraq, again. The consequences could be catastrophic. Presidential Barham Salih also condemned the US remarks about using Iraq to keep an eye on Iran. Within a year, the US administration's decision to pivot to confront Iran in Iraq and Syria was on thin ice.

Kurdish friends from Erbil texted me: "We want the Americans to stay." Do something to communicate that, they asked. In Washington, Ilham Ahmad was also trying to delay the US withdrawal. All of a sudden the KRG and the SDC were on the same page, despite their usual differences, which remained. Masoud Barzani had hosted members of the Syrian opposition, mostly parties close to Turkey that oppose the YPG. Meanwhile, protesters had briefly entered a Turkish military base in January in Shiladze, near Diraluk in the mountains of northern Iraq. They burned Turkish military vehicles, angry over Turkish air strikes that had killed beekeepers. The KDP sought to assuage Turkish concerns. After all, despite the difficult relations after the independence referendum, they needed the economic link to Turkey.

The train to DC rumbled through New Jersey. It passed old wooden houses, dismal highways, graffiti that read "soul," as in soul music. This was the America that was withdrawing. The US had had enough of foreign wars. Afghanistan would be next on the list for leaving. The dreams of the 1990s, of the "New World Order," were gone. A more insular America was emerging.

It felt foreign. I'd been away so long, confronted with so much misery and war. Transitioning to discuss large policies and strategies was a complex process. As the train pulled into Philadelphia, we left behind gray working-class towns and old monolithic schools for a picturesque scene along a river. A lone jogger made her way beneath towering trees. From Trenton to Philadelphia conjured up memories of American history. Where Washington had crossed the Delaware to where the Founding Fathers had met to imagine the Republic.

So much of the infrastructure in the US looked like it had not changed in decades, maybe for half a century. The school buses were the same as in my youth, thirty years ago.

Chapter 25
The Final Chapter

Scramble for Iraq and Syria

On February 22, 2019, Turkey's defense minister Hulusi Akar arrived in Washington. He came with chief of staff of the Turkish Armed Forces General Yasar Guler and Turkey's ambassador to the US, Serdar Kilic. Acting US defense secretary Pat Shanahan tweeted that he was honored to meet the Turkish delegation and confident that discussions would "strengthen US-Turkey relations for the future." The members of the delegation were hoping to discuss US plans for Syria amid the final defeat of ISIS near Baghuz on the Euphrates River. They also said they were there to express "concern" about US support for the YPG (People's Protection Units).[295] The visit capped weeks of high-level meetings by the US regarding its Syria policy. It also represented a further attempt by Turkey to play a role in eastern Syria, a goal it had set out years earlier when the US first partnered with the YPG against ISIS.

It had begun in early February, as the US prepared to host the seventy-nine-member coalition and as Trump was prepping for his State of the Union speech on February 5. The Syrian Democratic Coalition delegation was still in Washington, pushing for the US to slow down the withdrawal and put in place a no-fly zone.

"The good news for all of us, and thanks to all of you, we've made real and significant progress," Pompeo said on February 6, addressing the coalition. Some 110,000 square kilometers had been liberated, in which seven million people lived. Four million IDPs in Iraq had returned home.[296] Pompeo was flanked by Jeffrey, who had been handed McGurk's anti-ISIS

303

portfolio. Shanahan was also present. The meeting was important, but beyond the generalizations, not much was accomplished.

The United States had shifted to four main objectives. With ISIS now decentralized, the mission would change to intelligence gathering and sharing to ensure its defeat. "The drawdown of troops is essentially a tactical change; it is not a change in mission," Pompeo claimed. The drawdown would be coordinated, and the US would remain committed to a "political" solution in Syria in line with UN Security Council Resolution 2254. The US also stressed the need to support Iraq. "ISIS retains a real presence there." The usual statements about "stabilization" were made, but Pompeo went further, saying that the US would be using multimedia tools, such as its Middle East Broadcasting Networks (Alhurra Television and Radio Sawa), to support the post-ISIS period.[297] In addition, he called on the coalition to contribute financially and to take back foreign fighters who had joined ISIS. Lastly, Pompeo said ISIS had to be accountable for its crimes. Nadia Murad addressed the coalition members.

After the coalition meeting, a US delegation flew to Europe for a summit in Poland on February 13–14 that was supposed to concentrate on Iran. Although many European countries shunned the meeting, many US allies in the Middle East attended, including Egypt, Saudi Arabia, Yemen, Oman, the UAE, Bahrain, Jordan and Kuwait. These were the same countries that had met at the Dead Sea in Jordan in late January to discuss regional security. Along with Israel, they were key US allies willing to confront Iran. On the sidelines of the February 6 meeting in Washington, they had held another round of meetings.

Countering the Warsaw summit, Russia held its tenth round of Astana-format talks in Sochi on February 14. Erdogan, Rouhani and Putin arrived, smiling and seeking to discuss developments in Syria. This group of countries was growing ever closer, and they emphasized their agreement in a seventeen-point statement. It included generalizations about Syria's territorial integrity but also praised the US withdrawal: "the US decision on the withdrawal of its forces from Syria, if implemented, would be a step that would help strengthen stability and security in compliance with the above-mentioned principles."[298]

The next day, at the annual Munich Security Conference, dozens of US officials and politicians gathered alongside European leaders and others, including Iran's Javad Zarif, to speak on a variety of targets. Senator Graham, who had urged Trump to stay in Syria, said that the US would be asking European countries to contribute more forces. In his remarks, Vice President Mike Pence asserted that Iran was the leading state sponsor of terrorism and said it had fueled conflicts in Syria and Yemen, while supporting "terrorist proxies and militias."[299] He mentioned Iran nine times and ISIS only six times – a clear symbol of US priorities. Iran also spoke at the conference, slamming the US for leaving the Iran nuclear deal and threatening Israel.

The tensions with Iran were growing. Shi'ite militias had stopped a US patrol near Mosul on February 1. Rockets in Anbar were discovered pointed at a US base, and an Iranian drone monitored the crash landing of a US drone in a video released on February 22. Tensions rose more after a February 13 terror attack in southeastern Iran, blamed on Jaish al-Adl, a militant group. Tehran went further, blaming Saudi Arabia, the UAE, Israel and the US. It vowed revenge and Qasem Soleimani, at a speech on Babol in northern Iran on February 21, said that Saudi Arabia's Wahhabism was linked to ISIS and Judaism. Iran was celebrating the fortieth anniversary of its revolution in February and using the Munich platform to announce its success in the region. Foreign Ministry spokesman Bahram Qasemi said that Iran was working closely with neighboring states and "ironing out differences with certain regional countries." The IRGC boasted that Iran's friends were ruling Iraq.[300] Iran's Press TV ran conspiracy theories claiming the US was supporting ISIS and quoting an Iraqi lawmaker, Hassan Salem, who accused the US of sheltering ISIS at its bases in Iraq.

On Trump's mind was how to leave Syria. "United States is asking Britain, France, Germany and allies to take back over 800 ISIS fighters that we captured in Syria and put them on trial. The Caliphate is ready to fall," he tweeted on February 16.

The demand to take back the ISIS fighters was heightened by the sudden discovery among the people fleeing Baghuz that Western ISIS members were still alive. Although thirty-two hundred citizens of forty-one countries, many of them from ISIS families, were already being held by the Syrian Democratic Forces since mid-2018, the battle for Baghuz led to an exodus of foreigners. It appears many of them had been in Raqqa and fled as a result of the fall 2017 deal that led ISIS, which was under siege, to abandon the city. They had gone to areas around Mayadin and Hajin and then fled to tents near Baghuz as the SDF and coalition closed in. It had been a long slog for the SDF, but now the last village ISIS held turned out to be full of thousands of these ISIS families, as well as some Yazidi hostages. The SDF processed those who fled, fingerprinting them and sending the men to one detention center and women and children to Al-Hol (Hawl) camp. Some of the women said they had European citizenship. As she lifted her veil, it turned out that Shamima Begum was among them.

Begum had left the UK in 2015. Now nineteen, she told reporters, who came in droves, how she had survived. Her story painted a picture of life inside ISIS. For foreign women, life in ISIS was apparently relatively good at the beginning. Many were housed with other foreign women and then provided husbands based partly on their demand to have husbands who spoke their languages. Only later, in 2017, as ISIS suffered real reversals, did things become more difficult. Many of the men seem to have been killed in battle. Some of the Western women told reporters they wanted to go home, including an American named Hoda Muthana. It turned out that the Obama administration had revoked her passport in 2016. Now the Trump administration reiterated that she should not come back to the United States. The US had spent some time in eastern Syria interviewing suspects in the killings of Americans, such as those sought for murdering Foley and Sotloff.

The problem for the United States was that there was no interest in bringing back ISIS suspects. After the experience at Guantanamo, which Obama had sought unsuccessfully to close, no one wanted ISIS members brought to the US. And Trump wanted to leave Syria. In a phone call with Erdogan on Thursday, February 21, he discussed the US withdrawal again. Turkey appeared to be playing both sides. It continually stressed that it wanted close ties with the US, but at the same time it was promising Russia it would go through with the purchase of the S-400 antiaircraft missile system. The US had approved a $3.5 billion Patriot surface-to-air missiles sale to Turkey as Trump said the US was leaving Syria on December 19. How could Turkey get both defense systems and also acquire F-35 fighter planes? Ankara said it wanted to reach $75 billion in annual bilateral trade with the US, at a time when Turkey also had an exemption from American sanctions on Iran. Could Ankara get the best of all worlds, increasing relations with the US, buying the S-400 from Russia, and trading with Iran?

Trump and Erdogan spoke about the US withdrawal and also about support from international allies for what was termed a safe zone. It was unclear who would administer the safe zone in northern Syria. Ankara said that it wanted the YPG away from the border, a recurring demand. The next day, the White House put out a short statement saying that some US troops would remain in Syria. Reports indicated two hundred, but later over the weekend that grew to at least four hundred. Graham was pleased, putting out a statement applauding Trump and saying that "this will ensure ISIS does not return and Iran does not fill the vacuum that would have been left if we completely withdraw. This also ensures Turkey and SDF elements that helped us defeat ISIS will not go into conflict."[301] Instead, an international stabilization force would remain with the US as an anchor. European countries had been reticent to remain if the US left. Now they might feel more comfortable.

The SDF was also pleased. Polat Can, a senior commander in the SDF, told Voice of America that this was a positive step. "The international community should know that the presence of such a force can avoid this region a real humanitarian catastrophe."[302] The US forces would be split between northeast Syria and the Tanf border crossing to Iraq. They would consist of those with special forces-type expertise, such as intelligence gathering and surveillance. Air assets would be on hand as well. The Pentagon described it as a multinational observing and monitoring force that would include NATO allies. Dunford told reporters that it was part of the planned US transition to "stabilization" as the US continued to train local forces.[303]

On the ground, things were proceeding slowly. Dozens of trucks and small buses were brought up to SDF lines near Baghuz, where negotiations were taking place with ISIS. The coalition had slowed its air strikes, and a series of halts in operations allowed for discussions. The goal was to get the civilians and ISIS families out of the last pocket under ISIS control. Every day brought more and more civilians. At least five thousand got out in the week of February 19 to 26. In almost forty days, from January 21 to the end of February, up to ten thousand left, including men and families. Many were foreign fighters from Europe or Asia. Among them were hardened ISIS members, men with gnarled beards; one even had an eye patch. They showed no remorse. Lined up in rows by the SDF, they were searched and processed. They praised ISIS, claimed it would fight on, and pointed upward in a sign of devotion to God.

Several hundred were taken to the Iraqi border and handed over to authorities. At least a dozen French citizens were reportedly sent to Iraq on February 25. The overall way in which this was facilitated was shrouded in hushed tones and rumors. The SDF wasn't a state. It was a substate entity. It was excluded from coalition meetings. But European countries didn't want the ISIS members back, the SDF found it difficult to house them all, and human rights groups were pestering governments about leaving them in Syria.

Meanwhile, a macabre anniversary was taking place on the Khabur River, an hour away from the negotiations in Baghuz. It was there that dozens of Christian villages had been attacked on February 23, 2015, and more than two hundred people taken hostage. Some twelve hundred people had to flee. ISIS had blown up the churches. Initial reports had said 253 were kidnapped from thirty-five villages in the surprise attack. By December, one hundred people were still held by ISIS. Forty-three were released in February 2016, and another girl in March. But the refugees still described "torment" in 2017, and many refused to return to their villages by 2019, a last legacy of the crimes ISIS had committed.[304]

ISIS was still trying to terrify people. It carried out a terror attack against oil workers near Shaheel village on the road to Al-Omar oil field, in the eastern part of Syria's Deir ez-Zor Province, in mid-February, killing fifteen. It also kidnapped Iraqis out picking truffles in Anbar Province. And across Iraq, its cells continued to operate. Iraq bolstered its border security as the battle in Baghuz unfolded. US Central Command head General Joseph Votel, on a farewell tour of the region and Syria before leaving his post, said that ISIS might have tens of thousands of supporters and fighters left. They had melted into civilian areas. If there was a silver lining, in Mosul the Iraqi speaker of parliament Mohammed al-Halbusi accepted an invitation by youth to visit the city and celebrate youth projects. Former French president François Hollande also came to Mosul. On February 25, he toured the city, met local Christian officials and tweeted about the importance of helping the area recover. In Erbil, he took part in an award ceremony named in honor of Shifa Gardi, the Rudaw reporter killed in 2017.

The French visit to Mosul conjured up memories for me. I remembered Gardi's death. She had been one of so many who had been killed in this war. I felt like I had crossed her path in Mosul, traveling near where she had died. In the battle for Baghuz, another journalist felt the same sense of death come a whisper too close. Gabriel Chaim, a Brazilian whom I'd met in Bashiqa in 2016, described the day he saw life pass before his eyes. February 13, 2019, began with heavy fog. An ISIS counterattack had started. Shots hit nearby, he wrote in an account posted online. "A bomb fell within two meters of us."[305] A projectile fired at his position by ISIS threw him a meter and injured Italian journalist Gabriele Micalizzi. "I'll never forget it," Chaim wrote.

The end in Baghuz symbolized much of what had gone right and wrong in the war. ISIS was defeated. That went right. But everything around the war, the whole nature of what total war entails, did not go well. There were no services for the survivors and the victims. There weren't enough trucks to bring out the civilians. There wasn't a clear process to deal with investigating ISIS perpetrators. This is what happens when you have a seventy-nine-nation coalition but most don't want to take responsibility on the ground. The US and several allies such as the UK sent special forces operators, and the US sent air power. But the US didn't want to deal with detainees, and it didn't want a big footprint on the ground. With the decision to withdraw, the Pentagon was still putting a face of "continuity" and "transition" on the mission, arguing that it remained the same. But no matter how much Pompeo and Dunford and others said the mission was the same, it clearly wasn't. The US had wanted to stabilize eastern Syria. Even the SDF had talked about a three-phase process. Fighting ISIS was just the first phase. Training the local security forces, of which only 20 percent or so were trained, was another phase.

The US withdrawal meant that only a token force of the most sophisticated operators was scheduled to stay behind after April. The rest were leaving. This was war on a shoestring. In some ways, that was ideal for the mission. But it wasn't ideal for seeking justice for victims or for ensuring ISIS did not come back. With five to ten thousand suspected ISIS members leaving Baghuz and thousands of others already at the rapidly expanding camp at Al-Hawl, a potential disaster was in the making.

The SDF put its usual smiling face on the difficulty. Women danced with their rifles. Men gave warm hugs to each other. They treated the detainees with mercy. They spoke with the women. They searched for Yazidis among the families. Miraculously, they found eleven Yazidi children. The kids said they were from Sinjar. They asked what had happened to the city. The clearly traumatized children wanted to speak of something familiar. The SDF fighters told them not to worry, that Sinjar was waiting. But eventually the children did speak to reporters. One told of a father executed and a mother disappeared. "I want to return home," one told Kurdistan 24.[306] "I need to see my brothers and sisters." Worse was to come. The bodies of Yazidis were found, and Yazidis in Sinjar asked where the rest of their missing families were. A handful of children – mostly boys and two girls – and some men, were all that had been found alive.

Air strikes still pounded the enemy, 186 in the last two weeks of February. Trump, at a summit in Vietnam, claimed that the battle was 100 percent over. It wasn't.

It was truffle season in the Syrian desert, which extends into western Iraq. Amid the death and tragedy and refugees, the local people picked truffles in the desert. Tuffs of green poked out from the otherwise tan landscape. The winter had brought some grass. But even the truffle hunters were not safe. In Iraq's Anbar Province, they were being murdered by ISIS sleeper cells. In Syria, they enjoyed their snacks. And the eleven Yazidi kids saved from ISIS were promised they would be reunited with their families.

Zarif's Resignation Stunt and Iran's Gameplan

Iran's foreign minister, Javad Zarif, was flustered. Iran was celebrating the Islamic Revolution's fortieth anniversary. He should have been riding high. He had given yet another speech of a lifetime at the Munich Security Council. He mocked the United States and its "flip-flopping Trump officials," saying the US was isolated.[307] He praised the work

Iran had achieved at Sochi. Indeed, it had gotten Turkey to sign on to a statement praising the American withdrawal, even while Turkey was still telling the US that it wanted to cooperate on the safe zone. Iran felt it was getting what it wanted in Syria. It was also getting around sanctions, trading with Turkey, Russia and other countries. Its officials, including Rear Admiral Ali Shamkhani, secretary of the Supreme National Security Council of Iran, boasted that the US would leave Iraq by the end of 2019. Zarif had gone to Lebanon to show off ties with the country. Iran signed a deal with Syria to help rebuild the country. And Iran got Iraq to find a way around US sanctions on oil trade. It even got Iraq to warn Trump about his comments about "watching" Iran from US bases in Iraq.

Shamkhani and Soleimani gave speeches in February, both men hinting at the close Iraq-Iran alliance. Shamkhani said that Oman, Qatar, Kuwait and other states would likely break with the rest of the Gulf in seeking better relations with Iran. The Tehran regime seemed secure.

But Zarif was not secure. He went to China on February 20 and then disappeared from public view. Assad visited Tehran, but Zarif was not present. Soleimani, Rouhani and Khamenei met with Assad. Zarif posted on Instagram that he was resigning. He'd been in his position since 2013. Sixty-seven months, he wrote. He apologized for any failures and said the country should be proud. It was symbolic. He had been an architect of the Iran nuclear deal, and it was this deal that helped pivot US policy from opposing Assad to opposing ISIS and focusing less on the Iranian threat. It was this trend of US retreat from the region and perceived weakness by its allies that had changed the position of Saudi Arabia and likely led to Sisi's increased authoritarianism and other developments.

Iran was the major winner in all this. Iran and the US had been on the same side of the ISIS war. Groups that oppose the Assad regime had become increasingly extremist and then become proxies of Turkey under the banner of the Turkish-backed Free Syrian Army. What remained of the rebels was Hayat Tahrir al-Sham (HTS); the rest were under Turkish influence in Jarabulus and Afrin. The independent areas in Syria had been whittled down, and even the SDF had looked to work with the regime if the US left. Iran was seen as the more reliable country, alongside Russia, and its influence appeared to be spreading. Shamkhani boasted that Tehran had achieved 90 percent of its goals in Syria, in a mid-February interview in Iran. He said that Israel wouldn't dare attack it now, since Israel was in the midst of elections.

Amid this wave of what seemed like Iranian successes, the most successful face of Iran's attempt to cultivate a moderate image in the West was Javad Zarif. But for whatever reason, he decided to resign, and it appeared that more extreme elements in Tehran would benefit. This would mean more confrontation, not less. The Rouhani-Zarif team had accomplished a lot, including in the Astana process and elsewhere. But it appeared that with the war on ISIS ending, and the Syrian civil war reaching a denouement, Zarif was considering a stage exit, unless he secured more influence.

After Zarif's claimed resignation, Assad invited him to Syria. Rouhani's chief of staff denied he had resigned at all. But the rumors revealed some of the daylight inside the regime, the disputes and problems beneath the surface.

As Zarif was leaving, so were the American generals and policy makers who were the architects of the ISIS war. Mattis and McGurk had left in December. Votel was on his farewell tour. Dunford would be replaced in 2019 by US Army chief of staff General Mark Milley. This was a major transition in some ways. Votel was clearly an admirer of the work the SDF had done. Others, like McGurk, had been key architects of this policy. An Obama holdover, he was part of the Iran deal generation of US policy makers. He was also critical of Turkey.

Now Trump was trying to patch things up with Turkey. An uphill struggle, since Turkey wanted control of the safe zone or buffer zone in Syria, and Turkey demanded the mostly Sunni Arab refugees be able to return to mostly Kurdish-held areas in northeast Syria. The SDF was adamant that another Afrin would not take place, where Syrian Arab refugees came to live in a historically Kurdish area while hundreds of thousands of Kurds fled. Turkey's message to Trump was that trade could increase to $75 billion a year, and Turkey would buy the Patriot missiles for $3.5 billion. Trump seemed torn between his frequent conversations with Erdogan in the December–February period and the policies that Bolton and Pompeo wanted to put in place. Turkey was increasingly hostile to the US, vowing to receive the S-400, carrying out a naval drill with Russia. Trump decided in early March he was "100%"

in favor of staying in Syria with a limited footprint, and claimed ISIS was defeated. European countries had still not stepped up to support an international force in Syria.

In Washington, there was little stomach for another conflict, and there appeared to be support for bringing troops home. Although there was recognition of the sacrifices made by the Kurds, there was little interest in mission creep in Syria. And there were whispers about whether the Kurds in Syria were too close to the Assad regime or somehow harming the traditional US alliance with Turkey. Perhaps, somehow, Turkey might pivot to confront Iran. Or perhaps the United States should not be so harsh on Iran.

It was hard to remind people that Russia was closely involved now in Turkey and Iran, and in Syria. These countries shared an interest in ejecting the US from Syria. Only with the US gone might they fight over the spoils. And each resented the US presence. Iran wanted to humiliate the US in Iraq and Syria. It wanted to isolate US allies, such as the Kurds. Russia wanted the same, hinting in a February 24 statement that it supported Turkey's views on Arabs returning to eastern Syria and labeling some Kurdish groups "terrorists."[308] But Russia said that the Syrian regime had to agree to any Turkish military presence in northern Syria, and the Syrian government opposed such a presence.

On February 27, Netanyahu met with Putin in Moscow. The Israeli leader said that the September downing of a Russian IL-20 military aircraft during an Israeli air strike in Latakia was behind the two countries. Netanyahu still vowed to continue air strikes in Syria and hinted that Israel would work with Russia to remove foreign forces.

Meanwhile, Iran's president was preparing a visit to Iraq. Zarif saw it as a new chapter in relations. Parliamentarians in Baghad were preparing to demand the US withdraw from Iraq. The US Treasury Department had designated Harakat Hezbollah al-Nujaba, one of the Shi'ite militias in the PMU, as a terrorist organization, and the group was angry, threatening the US and Israel. Iran felt that with the war on ISIS over, it could now make a play for Iraq, grabbing another space on the chessboard of the Middle East.

No End to the War

Wars don't end the way we're told they do. There is no Appomattox courthouse, no Treaty of Westphalia, no simple victory. Instead, the enemy melts back into the towns and villages it came from. The allies look askance at those they thought they were fighting alongside. Nobody wins. Victims don't get justice. Perpetrators get sympathy. Mass graves return to nature, the secrets they hold forgotten. There is no catharsis.

I saw photos from Sinjar in mid-February. Khalid al-Mousily was credited as the photographer. He'd been to the same places I had gone to in December of 2015. The city was still in ruins. On Mount Sinjar, people still lived in tents and huts. It was dismal and dreary. Survivors were still picking through rubble. At a mass grave, overgrown with the winter grass that sprouts in the desert, a small sign reading "ICMP" had been placed. The International Commission on Missing Persons had received support from Canada to help to try to document the remains in the mass graves. But the mass grave was not cordoned off or protected from the elements.

It seemed that in most cases we would never know all the details. There were more than two hundred mass graves in Iraq. A handful had been found in Syria, and more would likely be found. One near Raqqa contained an estimated thirty-five hundred bodies. Another was found near Baghuz. ISIS was different from anything that had come before. Whatever crimes the Taliban or al Qaeda committed, they never attempted the kind of genocide and mass murder that ISIS carried out. They never attempted the total reorganization of society at such a level. And they never attracted so many foreign fighters. The detritus of ISIS in Baghuz, those foreign fighters left behind as the local ISIS members melted away, was just one part of the horrors that this organization was capable of. The landscape would never be the same.

That doesn't mean there weren't signs of hope. Who would have imagined in 2014 that the women kidnapped by ISIS would be liberated by women with AK-47s? Surely the women being liberated were shocked. In no other cases were extremist groups being confronted by the radical ideology of the SDF. There were other signs as well. Raqqa had a female co-mayor named Layla Moustafa. Could anyone have imagined such a reversal of fortune for ISIS? Paradise Square in Raqqa, where ISIS impaled heads on a fence, had a new fountain by the spring of 2019. The hopeful spirit of Iraqis. The cultural life in Mosul was revived by activists like Omar Mohammed, the man behind Mosul Eye, and Ali Y. al-Baroodi, an academic in the city. There were many signs of hope. But there was lot of pessimism and fear in the region as well.

On the night of February 28, a gray car pulled up outside the Masqa café near a gate to the University of Mosul. It exploded, killing one and wounding more than twenty. The wounded were taken to al-Salam Hospital. Flames leaped from the damaged car until emergency workers put them out. The pretty café was damaged, its windows blown in, narghile pipes still standing amid the rubble. Locals said that there were rumors of more attacks. Security forces demanded more metal detectors and ways to screen people. They were not forthcoming from Baghdad.

The next day, Yazidis protested in Sinjar, demanding investigations and justice for their lost loved ones. They were angry that ISIS members were allowed to leave Baghuz, and there didn't seem to be any answers or interrogations of the ISIS members to ask about the three thousand missing Yazidis.

On March 1, just after 6 p.m., the SDF began the final assault on Baghuz. Gunfire pounded the hundreds of ISIS members who had stayed behind. In the dark, SDF members pored over maps on tablet computers, identifying the enemy areas. The enemy had gone to ground, hiding in tunnels, and was waiting. Coalition helicopters and drones were on hand. Halfway around the world in Kashmir, the Indian and Pakistan armies were clashing. Suddenly the small battle in Baghuz seemed less important. Trump had declared the caliphate 100 percent defeated. Those on the ground were angered. There was still more slogging to do. Another kilometer of open ground to be cleared. But for all intents and purposes, it was over.

It was a poignant day on March 2, the fourth anniversary of the death of Konstandinos Erik Scurfield, a former British Royal Marine who had died fighting against ISIS with the YPG. One of many Western volunteers, he had gone to stand against the black flag when it was at the height of its power. Now it was almost defeated. In Iraq, another bittersweet day: Naser Basha Khalaf and other Yazidi leaders welcomed back twenty-one Yazidis rescued in Baghuz. The road to recovery for them would be long, but they were home. As the last battle raged, there would be no heroic flag to put on the Reichstag in the dreary tents of Baghuz. Instead, ISIS stragglers swam across the Euphrates and were shot down. Symbolically, ISIS had already been defeated in Raqqa and Mosul. This was the detritus, the bitter end.

Although defeated on the ground in late March 2019, ISIS would live on. Abu Bakr al-Baghdadi emerged briefly from hiding in late April, appearing in a video in which he praised ISIS attacks in Sri Lanka, Saudi Arabia and in Central Africa. US focus had already shifted to confronting Iran by that time. Washington designated the IRGC a terrorist group in early April, and by mid-May, US forces had been sent to the Gulf, prepared to confront any Iranian threats to the region.

Chapter 26
The Middle East at a Crossroads

The Return of the Middle East State System

A major theme of the conflict with ISIS and the instability it brought was that the states of the Middle East survived. ISIS had tried to erase a hundred years since the breakup of the Ottoman Empire. It had briefly succeeded. But Iraq, Syria and the rest had survived as states. Even Libya, Yemen and others, though weak, were still intact. The prophecies of a new map of the Middle East were mistaken. The states were back. But they were fundamentally changed.

The changes across the Middle East as a result of ISIS are what this book was about. It didn't explore every state, but it highlighted many of them with personal experiences and interviews with people on the ground during key junctures of the years 2014–2019. The changes in the period were immense in some places, more incremental and obscure in others. However, large trends are clear. Many of these countries had the same leaders throughout the period, such as Mahmoud Abbas in Ramallah, Benjamin Netanyahu in Jerusalem, Bashar al-Assad in Damascus and Tayyip Erdogan in Ankara. The ISIS period was a crucible for these countries. They went into it concerned about the instability, chaos and changes of the post-9/11 world of the Arab Spring, and they came out sure of themselves and with a more cynical and often more authoritarian outlook.

The region came out more skeptical of American power and whether the United States would remain a hegemonic player in the Middle East. Large, decades-long processes were accelerated in the period. The growing power of Iran, Russia and Turkey, and the changing policies of Saudi Arabia, are several examples. What follows is a look at some important outcomes of the war on ISIS and the after-ISIS years.

Three Alliances

Three alliance systems emerged from the decline and battlefield defeat of ISIS. The Iranian-backed system was the clearest. Consisting of Iran, Shi'ite militias in Iraq, the Syrian regime, Hezbollah and the Houthis, this was the Iranian nexus. Iran had grown confident and strong. It held naval drills and tested new missiles in 2018 and 2019. It was at the height of its power. Statements from leaders portrayed the United States as isolated and the Arab states as divided. Where the IRGC boasted of its weapons and threatened the Gulf, Pakistan and other adversaries, the foreign ministry was more reserved, cultivating relations and seeking closer engagement with Europe, Russia, Turkey and other countries. Iran closely followed its adversaries, encouraged by chaos in US policy and also by the weakness of Netanyahu going into Israel's 2019 elections.

Emboldened Iran shored up support among its allies. In Syria, it signed memorandums, and Iranian state media reduced criticism of Turkey. It also encouraged allies in Iraq to critique the US presence. It reached out to the Kurdish region in northern Iraq. In Lebanon, the government defended Hezbollah's role as the UK sought to label it a terrorist organization.

Turkey and Qatar formed another alliance. They had supported Hamas and Muslim Brotherhood affiliates over the years since 2000. Turkey was playing a role in Sudan, developing an island, and seeking a role in the Horn of Africa. It also had allies in Malaysia and wanted to work with Pakistan. When Iran-Pakistan relations soured in February 2019, Turkey's president reached out. In Libya, both countries supported allied factions. In Syria, they supported the rebel groups. Both were ostensibly US allies but had a complex relationship with Washington. Isolated in 2017 by the Saudi-led blockade, Qatar became closer to Turkey. Ankara sent troops. Qatar supported Turkey's economy. While Turkey hedged its bets between Russia and the United States, it also hosted Trump's son-in-law Jared Kushner in February 2019. Qatar hosted talks between the US and the Taliban.

Then there were the southern Middle East countries anchored by Saudi Arabia. These included close allies of Riyadh such as the UAE and Egypt and Bahrain. And then less-close allies such as Jordan, Kuwait, Yemen and Khalifa Haftar's fighters in Libya. These countries were allied to the US and critical of Iran. They also tended to see the region in much the same way as Israel does. Egypt and Jordan had official relations with Israel, and Israeli officials had visited Oman and the UAE in 2018. This group of allies met at the Dead Sea in Jordan in January 2019, and in Washington on the sidelines of the coalition meeting in February. Weakened by US anger over the Khashoggi killing and criticism of Sisi's policies, these countries were struggling to keep regional leadership. They also hedged their bets, considering welcoming Syria back to the Arab League. Supportive of the US role in Syria, the Saudis also reached out to Baghdad. They hosted Badr leader Falah al-Fayadh.

These three systems are in competition, whether in states such as Lebanon and Oman, or for hearts and minds among Palestinian Arabs. They compete to fill the vacuum of failed, weak states and ungoverned areas, including Libya, Iraq and Syria. They want to make sure a new ISIS does not rise. They are engaged in a three-sided cold war. Any false move can set off a conflict with Iran. But each system plays both sides. Nothing is completely black and white.

A Powerful Russia
Alongside the emerging alliance systems is an increasingly powerful Russia. Russia has leveraged the chaos in the region and the rise of ISIS to its benefit. It has also carried out a series of incremental but consistent policies that make it appear more reliable than the zig-zagging policies of the United States.

Russia's real ally is the Syrian regime, but it has also been seeking to sell weapons and the S-400 to countries such as Turkey. It also wanted to play power broker in the Syrian conflict and even to work closely with Egypt and Libya.

Russia had been able to capitalize on its consistent policy to end up with large numbers of friends, precisely as the US was reducing its influence under Obama and Trump. No clearer example of this emerges than in Turkey, where a NATO ally sought to buy the S-400. Turkey and

Russia began talks in November 2016, signing a $2.5 billion deal in 2017. Turkey vowed in March 2018 and February 2019 that it would buy the antiaircraft system.

Initially it seemed Turkey and Russia should fall out over the Syrian conflict. They were not only on opposite sides, but Turkey downed a Russian Sukhoi Su-24 in December 2015. A year later, the Russian ambassador, Andrei Karlov, was assassinated in Ankara by an off-duty police officer. But the countries grew closer during the Astana peace process that began in 2015. By November 2017, when Putin hosted Erdogan and Rouhani in Sochi, the countries had grown much closer. A year later, a section of the TurkStream natural gas pipeline from Russia was completed. They came together over joint support for US withdrawal in Syria. Russia also shifted its position on Syrian Kurdish issues, indicating that it would consider the Turkish position.

Russia, Iran and Turkey tended to get along because their leaders saw eye to eye regarding opposition to the United States. Each in its own way viewed the US role as spreading instability. For Russia, this meant the US support of Syrian rebels; for Turkey, it was the US relationship with the YPG; and for Iran, it was US bases in Iraq and Syria.

Russia has carved out an impressive space in the Middle East in a relatively short time, leveraging its success in Syria with minimum investment and maximum exposure. It was able to successfully outflank US support for the Geneva process on Syria by hosting talks in Astana and Sochi. It was also able to work with both the Syrian regime and Israel. It accomplished these tasks by appearing to agree to demands of both. It provided the Syrian regime with the S-300 surface-to-air missile system and indicated to Israel that it would not oppose Israeli air strikes on Iranian targets in Syria.

Russia's role in the defeat of ISIS included leveraging symbolic events to show it had achieved something. In March 2016, the Mariinsky Theater Orchestra played in Palmyra, showing that Russian help could defeat ISIS. Moscow also claimed to reduce ISIS oil exports through air strikes in November 2015, insinuating that the US-led coalition had not worked to stop ISIS trade in oil. Russian English-language media, such as RT and Sputnik, meanwhile, encouraged conspiracy theories that alleged the US had "evacuated" ISIS members in March and July 2018.[309] At each juncture, Russia seeks to portray itself as the responsible, strategic thinker, opposing terrorism and working for stability, while insisting that the United States has produced chaos through its policies.

Rising Authoritarianism

The region was transformed by the ISIS war in numerous ways. Most of all, it has become wary of change and sought shelter in authoritarianism. In my travels from 2013 to 2017, I'd watched as countries, one after another, became more difficult to report in and more complex to cover. Local activists became more and more reluctant to speak out. They sought to use encrypted messaging systems. The once-hopeful people of the Arab Spring had turned more insular. Social media was no longer connecting people. Social media giants were even fearful of all the extremist content that had flowed. Their response was to work with authoritarian governments and remove reasonable content. Cultural figures were imprisoned. Civil society was stifled.

Tyranny succeeds not through censorship but rather self-censorship. People simply are too concerned to speak out. And countries were finding a way to tap into new nationalism. They were also trying to crack down on independent religious extremists who might spread their views. They had learned that unfettered religious activism had led to a generation of extremists. Experimentation with Salafists and Wahhabism and Muslim Brothers and all these waves of religiosity had resulted in chaos and terror. People were searching. Angry at decades of postcolonial dictatorship and stagnating regimes, they sought shelter in religious extremes. ISIS was the end of that line of extremes. It shocked the region into a new awakening.

The authoritarian agenda doesn't completely succeed. Protests broke out in Sudan in January 2019, and there were protests in Algeria. Some countries continue to host dissidents from other countries. For instance, one of the narratives about Khashoggi was that he supported a more open society. This was certainly what he sought to say in the West and in interviews. But he also appeared on Al-Jazeera, where he argued in November 2017 that Saudi Arabia should return to proper religious roots. He was not a supporter of dissidents in Turkey or Qatar. This was part of the complex change in the Middle East. Al-Jazeera was accused of supporting change only in regimes it disagreed with, such as in Egypt, and of criticizing other Gulf countries. Similarly, adversaries of Qatar would support dissidents in Qatar, but not at home. Turkey routinely arrested journalists, accusing many of them of supporting terrorism for minor infractions such as tweets or cultural activities.

Although there is democracy in Iraq, and elections in Turkey, Lebanon, Iran and Tunisia, the general trend appears to be one of increasing clampdowns on freedom of expression. This means that even in Lebanon, where there is a freer press than in some other Middle Eastern countries, newspapers are wary of critiquing Hezbollah. Intellectuals who left Egypt said it was becoming more and more impossible to express dissent in the country. *Foreign Policy* called it "worse" than under Mubarak.[310] Yet Egypt sought closer relations with the EU in the spring of 2019, hosting France's Emmanuel Macron in January. This was at the same time that Sisi was seeking to stay in power until 2034.

The same criticism was made of Saudi Arabia and its Vision 2030 reforms. While it sought some reforms, it also was cracking down on other dissent. It faced the same hurdles that many states felt in the region: how to modernize and diversify the economy, while not giving space to critics and extremists. In almost every case, the result was that both liberals and Islamists were viewed as threats to the state.

In Iraq, where democracy now exists, the issue of a crackdown on freedoms was more complex. The complaint was that the system was too sectarian and ossifying. Candidates for office were the same faces, election after election. Independent parties did not perform well. Reformists were sidelined. Large families, clans and religious and tribal networks, and militias appeared to have more power. This was a result of the retreat into militia and clan politics that resulted from the war against ISIS. People had sought out old structures, such as the Shi'ite militias called up to fight ISIS, or the Peshmerga in the Kurdish region. Tribes held together through fighting together. The state had shown itself incapable of transcending this in the time of crisis in 2014.

This indicates that where authoritarianism did not succeed, other types of authority succeeded in keeping people within traditionally accepted degrees of dissent through threatening those who transgress. In times of chaos or rising militias, whether it is the Houthis in Yemen, or Hezbollah in Lebanon, or the Fatah party in the West Bank, these powerful organizations also suppress criticism not through state laws but via quiet threats. The same can be said of HTS in Idlib Province and the YPG in eastern Syria. Each became a one-party state.

Turkey

Turkey is a rising power. It has gone through various phases to get where it is. It wanted zero problems with its neighbors but got actively involved in Syria. This came about in fits and starts. First it had to contend with the HDP pro-minority political party winning more than 10 percent of the vote and reaching the parliament in Ankara in 2015. At the same time, the rise of the YPG in Syria helped embolden PKK activists to launch a war for the cities in Turkey. The result was a desperate conflict in which areas were destroyed, and Turkey's opening to Kurdish issues became narrower. Once the PKK was defeated, Turkey decided it wanted to end the YPG's rise. This was slowed by the coup attempt in 2016. Then Turkey intervened in Jarabulus, just over the border in northern Syria, to prevent the YPG linking up with Afrin, in the de facto autonomous area of northeastern Syria. Operation Euphrates Shield lasted from August 2016 to March 2017. Turkey launched the Afrin campaign in January 2018, dubbed Olive Branch, to provide some way for Syrian refugees to return, neutralize the YPG and show the United States that Ankara was serious. Turkey's threats against Manbij and Tel Abyad in the fall of 2018 were more of the same. It intervened in Syria to destroy the YPG, not really to help the rebels. It wanted to co-opt the rebels. Had it not stepped into Jarabulus, the YPG would have assaulted ISIS there, possibly with US backing. This was Turkey's fear. It was also motivated to move into Afrin for the same reason.

But Turkey's rise has complications for its policies that have seen Turkish soldiers deployed in Syria and Iraq for the long-term. It wants to work closely with Russia while maintaining an alliance with the United States. Toward that end, it wants to buy both the S-400 and the Patriot air defense systems, angering Washington. It also sees Iran as a country it can talk to and has sought ways around US sanctions. It thinks it has inspired the Arab world by hosting those like Khashoggi, dissidents from the region. And it has unique influence over Europe due to the refugees. All of this puts it in a key spot, forcing Ankara to juggle multiple agendas.

Turkey's rising rhetoric, challenging the US or European powers at times, harshly critical of any dissent at home and constantly flexing its military muscle, shows it wants to be a global player. Turkey criticized China for imprisoning Uighur Muslims and showed through its handling of the Khashoggi case that it wanted to get as much as possible out of the killing. Erdogan has positioned himself to stay in power through careful calculation. This means portraying the left-leaning domestic opposition as pro-PKK while co-opting the right's nationalism.

Many thousands of ISIS members used Turkey to travel to Syria. Ankara initially didn't see them as a threat. But later it sought to portray itself as fighting ISIS, even while it indicated it felt ISIS was not a threat in Syria, and that the US should leave the country. Many ISIS members who fled places like Raqqa sought to get back to Europe via Turkey. The reckoning for this policy is not clear. Turkey could face anger from former ISIS members or more extremist Syrian rebels if it is thought to have sold them out and if it leaves Syria. At the same time, networks of extremists could threaten Turkey if it cannot co-opt them and try to moderate them. Other countries have been successful at de-radicalizing people and channeling their energies elsewhere. Saudi Arabia is one example. But it remains unclear if Turkey will go that route.

Turkey sees the PKK as the main threat. This is its regional goal, to destroy the PKK in neighboring states. Ankara has now shown an interest in timidly confronting more extreme groups such as HTS, but it is worried about provoking a real conflict with them. It seeks to find a way around them and to mollify them into re-branding themselves, changing their flags and gradually accepting Turkey's role.

Iran

Iran has benefited the most from the rise and fall of ISIS. The Sunni extremists gave Tehran an excuse to put its role in Iraq on steroids and to increase its role in Syria and Lebanon. This was characterized as Iran searching for a road to the sea via a corridor through Iraq and Syria to Lebanon. This corridor now connects Iran's allies across a huge area of the Middle East. Precisely how Tehran views this road is not always clear. Some indication of this can be seen in threats from Iraqi militias to play a role in the next war with Israel, and in Hezbollah's major role in Syria. Hezbollah argues that it helped save Lebanon from the rise of ISIS, setting the Shi'ite group on course to be a regional actor. It is clear that these Iranian allies do not see the Syrian or Iraqi borders as real.

While policy makers tend to see each of these Iranian allies and proxies as acting on the local level, these groups see themselves as part of a nexus of Iranian-backed power, linked together by the IRGC. Some of these groups want to play a large role in the Euphrates Valley and to set down roots physically through bases and cultural-religious activities. The long-term plan appears to be to forge an arc of Iranian power that trends toward regional hegemony. ISIS helped hollow out the landscape, destroying infrastructure and spreading instability and terror that emboldened and accelerated this process.

Several state-within-a-state structures have emerged under Iran's agenda. Very few cultural or other achievements have been invested in. Although Iran says it wants to play a role in reconstruction in Syria, it doesn't appear that Iran has created better economic conditions. Insofar as there are major infrastructure projects in the region, it is the Gulf or Turkey or others that pay for them. Iran's role is primarily recruiting human capital and developing networks. It sees a long-term investment in this strategy, one it perfected since the 1980s. The pro-Iran groups in Iraq are led by men who served as allies of the IRGC in the 1980s.

Iran also sees its long-term strategy in reducing the US presence in the region. This means undermining the US in Afghanistan and working with Qatar to split up the Gulf countries. This means supporting the Houthis in Yemen, and Hamas and Palestinian Islamic Jihad in Gaza. At every turn Iran seeks a regional role and to challenge the US. It can't challenge the US militarily, so it works through politicians in Lebanon or Iraq. This has worked well. The US continues to train the Iraqi army and to give the Lebanese army matériel, while Iran reaps the benefit. Tehran doesn't have to invest financially. The US invests, and pro-Iranian groups benefit. For instance, in Iraq the US investment allows the government to fund the Federal Police and turn the Popular Mobilization Units into an official force. In Lebanon, Hezbollah controls the health ministry. The US modus operandi is the opposite of Iran's; it seeks to partner with government in a top-down approach. Thus the US does not plow resources into its allies, such as the KRG region; it focuses those resources in Baghdad. It actually reduces on-the-ground support for allies, at the precise time Iran is investing in political and religious networks. This inability of the US to see the forest for the trees has led Iran to benefit in one country after another.

Iran has also been successful in its relations with Russia and Turkey, gaining new partners that it hopes can be used to reconstruct Syria to Iran's benefit. For instance, Russia was critical of the US Warsaw summit in February 2019 and held its Sochi talks with Iran and Turkey the same day.

Iran is stronger than at any time in modern history, and the ISIS war helped make it what it is today. It has expanded production of new ballistic missiles and used them in 2018 to strike at ISIS in Syria and at Kurdish opposition groups in northern Iraq. It carried out a naval drill in the Strait of Hormuz in February 2019 designed to show off various indigenously developed weapons, such as drones. That does not mean that many Iranians do not oppose the regime's policy of slowly taking over the "near abroad" in Iraq and running foreign wars. There is anger at home as the economy collapses. But Iran has so far been able to keep a good face on its external policies.

Israel Alone?

The chaos of the Arab Spring and rise of ISIS brought challenges for Israel's national security. The rise of the Muslim Brotherhood was a threat to Israel, and this showed itself in the weapons transfers to Gaza via Sinai that extended the range of Hamas rockets in the 2012 and 2014 wars. Smuggling via Sinai and a brutal insurgency by extremist groups in Sinai led to chaos spreading along the Egyptian border. Israel had to erect a border fence and contend with Hamas rockets that had a range of up to 150 kilometers. The rise of Sisi brought more security to the border and also a welcome hand in negotiations with Hamas, because the Egyptian president opposed the Muslim Brotherhood's version of political Islam.

The Obama years, given the Iran deal of 2015, had taught Israel that it might need to face growing Iranian threats alone, especially regarding

Tehran's attempt to transfer missiles to Hezbollah. Israel found common cause with Saudi Arabia and several Gulf states in opposing Iran's role in the region. For instance, Riyadh led the intervention against Iranian-backed Houthis in Yemen in 2015. This was a sign that Riyadh and its allies had a willingness to go it alone. Israel understood it faced some of the same problems in the Syrian conflict.

Initially, the prospect of Hezbollah and Iranian IRGC members' involvement in the Syrian civil war posed only a marginal problem for Israel, because they were focused on fighting the rebels. But things began to change in 2015. Israel was providing medical aid to Syrian rebels and also carried out an air strike killing Hezbollah leader Jihad Mughniyeh in Quneitra, near the Golan cease-fire line with Israel. This was one of a hundred air strikes carried out in the first years of the war, according to then Israel Air Force commander Maj. Gen. Amir Eshel.[311] That number would rise to several hundred by 2018 and to thousands by January 2019. The increasingly frequent strikes came as Iran's entrenchment in Syria increased and the Assad regime consolidated power. The southern Syrian rebels were defeated in the summer of 2018 and ISIS cleared from the border. Israel watched with concern the prospect that Iran would now be close to the Golan border. Assurances from the US and Russia didn't result in Iran reducing its presence. Even when Netanyahu flew to Moscow in February, it was unclear whether Israel could find a way to reduce Iran's entrenchment. Ali Shamkhani, secretary of the Islamic Republic's National Security Council, said Tehran had achieved 90 percent of its objectives – a boast in response to Netanyahu's assertion that Israel wanted Iran to leave Syria.

For Israel, then, the rise and fall of ISIS brought chaos to the borders and left a new reality when the war was over. As for Israeli policy toward Egypt, that means an embrace of the status quo and what appears to be a close partnership with Cairo over anti-terror operations. As for Israeli policy toward Syria, that also means a return to the status quo, but with a larger Iranian presence. Hezbollah was able to season its fighters in battles in Syria, but the Lebanese group also suffered casualties. Israel launched an operation in the fall of 2018 to root out Hezbollah tunnels under the border from Lebanon. But Iran warned that Israeli air strikes would eventually meet with a response in Syria. Any war between Israel and Hezbollah could now involve Iranian troops in Syria and Shi'ite militias from Iraq.

High-level Israeli visits to Oman and the UAE, and rumors that Bahrain might be next, appear to be part of the post-ISIS configuration of the Middle East. With Trump seeking to roll out a "deal of the century" to solve the Israel-Arab conflict, several things are interconnected. The Iran threat brought Israel closer to some countries but also leaves Israel strategically threatened if the US leaves Syria and if a new US administration chooses to return to the Iran nuclear deal. The Trump administration has lacked clarity in its post-ISIS policy, seeking to leave Syria and also leaving questions about its role in Iraq. For Israel, the US drawdown in the Middle East is a problematic sign. Israel is thus paradoxically at both its most powerful and its most vulnerable time in the region. In military power, it has unparalleled technology, and its arms sales now make it one of the most important defense manufacturers in the world. But the zig-zagging US foreign policy could leave it alone amid a rising Iran and a more aggressive Turkey that is harshly critical of Israel and supportive of Hamas. Israel may be losing its freedom of action in Syria with the deployment of Russia's S-300 system, and that would enable Iran to do as it wills.

Syria's Return

Syria was the gaping wound of the Arab Spring, the country where the rising tide of protest was met with bullets and led to a reactionary counterrevolution and return of the ancien régime, with 500,000 killed, 6.5 million internally displaced and five million becoming refugees. It was the chaos in Syria that helped feed ISIS and enabled it to gather forces for the invasion of Iraq. Even though the strongest ISIS cadres were Iraqis and foreigners, Syria gave it the place to solidify and spread, secure from the regime and the rebels in 2012–2013.

ISIS was lucky to have this huge desert area to operate in. In a strange twist of fate, it ran up against the growing power of the YPG in 2014, at a time when the YPG was able to consolidate its control. It was a unique time; had ISIS appeared sooner – or later – it is not clear it would have confronted the same enemies. It fed off the divided nature of the Syrian rebellion and the thirst of a generation of extremists across the world searching for a "caliphate." It used Syria as an incubator, colonizing Syria and using it as a base.

ISIS also served as a bogeyman that many countries involved in the Syrian civil war could use as an excuse to increase their roles. Russia carried out air strikes in 2015, claiming to be fighting ISIS, when the majority of its efforts were against the anti-Assad rebels. Turkey also claimed to be intervening in Afrin against ISIS, when there was no ISIS presence there. Similarly, the US used the ISIS war to pivot from confronting the Assad regime to fighting ISIS, at a time when the Obama administration was working on the Iran deal. The Obama administration had avoided bombing the Syrian regime in 2013, and eventually the US would pull back from supporting the rebels. Other countries used the threat of ISIS as an excuse to crack down on dissent at home. Iran, particularly, used it as an excuse to extend its influence and power.

By 2016, the Syrian regime was able to turn the tables on the rebels, retake Aleppo and lay the groundwork to retake the rest of the country. The model was usually the same: massive bombardment and use of Russian airpower, and eventually getting the rebels to relocate to the north. Even ISIS was able to make the transfer in some cases, under agreements with the regime. By 2018, the war was largely over for Syria, and the major powers had stepped in. Turkey was in northern Syria, the US was in eastern Syria, and Russia and Iran were guaranteeing the Assad regime's survival. That reduced the level of conflict. By 2019, there was fatigue, and Syria was looking to reconstruction. Refugees were looking to return, and everyone involved wanted some accommodation. Syria was also willing to wait for the US to leave.

The weakened Syrian state has appeared to survive the war. In February 2019, Assad went to Tehran to show off his relationship with Iran and discuss the two countries' strategic cooperation. This would involve defense, economic and even religious issues. The question Syria's regime faces is how it will it return to eastern Syria. The US withdrawal enabled it to discuss a potential return with the Syrian Democratic Council, but the SDC's demands were too harsh. It wants autonomy, and Syria's regime wants total control. Damascus might agree to some changes in the education system or limited local control, but how will it incorporate the tens of thousands of SDF fighters, and how will it avoid a conflict with Turkey?

The longer eastern Syria remains outside government control, the harder it may be for the regime to return. But the regime has always maintained a presence in cities in eastern Syria, and it will leverage this. It appears the US thoughts of a ten-year involvement in the east is less practical, and the US refuses to pay any lip service to legitimizing the SDF as an autonomous force beyond a direct, temporary tactical and transactional relationship, as the State Department has termed it. That means the US has squandered a potential ally in eastern Syria and left questions about its own commitments. But the Pentagon and State Department prefer Turkey as an ally and view the SDF as problematic because of its links to the YPG and therefore to the PKK.

Eventually, Syria also wants Idlib, Afrin and the north back as well. How it can accomplish this is unclear. Tensions with HTS in Idlib mean weekly shelling by the regime, and the Idlib agreement between Moscow and Ankara is imperfect. But no one wants a new conflict. Kurds, angry about being forced out of Afrin and watching hundreds of thousands of Arab refugees be resettled there, fear a long-term Turkish military occupation and demographic change. But the regime appears willing to sacrifice their concerns. This is especially true if it means the regime can scare the SDF into thinking the same thing will happen in eastern Syria.

Syria is at a crossroads. The civil war brought chaos to the region and involved most of the countries in the Middle East. It was a regional war and a global war with importance similar to what the Thirty Years War meant for European history. It was in Syria that major ideologies and religious extremes clashed. It was there that the Sunni rebellion was defeated and that Iran and Hezbollah won. The civil war also changed the Saudi and Israeli view of the region and changed US-Turkish relations. It empowered Iraq as well, after momentarily threatening the existence of Iraq in 2014. Thus Syria turned out to be a key to the region, as important as it had been in 1920 to the fate of the Arab Revolt. It was then that the French role in Syria brought colonialism instead of a united Arab state.

The Ottoman Empire gave way to the Mandates, and the Kurds lost their chance at a state.

In 2019, the resolution of the war on ISIS and the arc of the Syrian conflict appear to have created a crossroads in history, denying the caliphate a chance to take over the region, breaking the Sunni rebellions and denying the Kurds their chance for increased autonomy in Syria and Iraq. Even if Syria returns to the Arab League, it will clearly be the country that is a key to regional stability, connecting the intersection between Iran's road to the sea, Turkey's ambitions and the Sunni Arab role in the region. It could also be a crossroads for a war between Israel and Iran.

The End of Islamist Extremism?

The defeat of ISIS in Baghuz in March 2019 posed a riddle: Where had so many ISIS supporters suddenly come from? After months of battle, there were up to ten thousand ISIS supporters, family members and fighters in a tiny enclave on the Euphrates River. Transported out from late January to the end of February, they clogged IDP camps. Experts in the US military and the US intelligence community warned that ISIS was still a threat.

The numbers were staggering. Tens of thousands of members, according to General Votel on his farewell tour in February. An Israeli intelligence assessment the same month estimated 150,000–200,000 worldwide.[312] A paper by Hassan Hassan at the Combating Terrorism Center at West Point also argued that it was possible "a significant number managed to slip into areas controlled by the [Assad] regime."[313] The US Worldwide Threat Assessment of the director of national intelligence argued that while ISIS had suffered territorial defeat, it was returning to its insurgent roots.[314]

A map of the continuing threat looks little different than the Thomas Barnett *The Pentagon's New Map* depiction of the "non-integrated gap" of countries where instability and terrorism are more common. That was in 2004. So is the post-ISIS era just a return to an earlier era? Five years before ISIS was defeated in Baghuz, its members had been fighting in Ramadi and Fallujah and across Anbar Province in Iraq in the spring of 2014. This was a time when it was losing territory in Idlib and consolidating control in Raqqa. Before the June offensive that year, Iraq had already been bogged down in battles. Reports said that Iraq risked turning "Sunni regions into a permanent battlefield."[315] There were many casualties and desertions in the Iraqi security forces. Some 380,000 had already fled their homes. We now know worse was to come and millions more would be displaced.

But there are clear changes after ISIS. The US Special Operations Command is currently deployed in around ninety countries, with an annual budget of $13.6 billion and seventy thousand personnel.[316] Time will tell if the defeat of ISIS began a long trend toward the defeat of extremist groups worldwide. It isn't clear whether ISIS can strengthen its foothold in parts of the Sahel, Sinai, the Philippines or Afghanistan. The battle against ISIS in Marawi, on the Philippines's Mindanao Island, for instance, lasted from May to October 2017. It was a long battle on par with the kind of urban battle that took place in Raqqa or Mosul. There is no doubt that there are challenges in Africa and other areas. The Taliban looks set to outflank the United States in negotiations in Afghanistan. But could that wind up similarly to the end of the US role in Vietnam, where instead of becoming a domino, the Taliban spends its time fighting ISIS? The US is also involved in multiple major air strikes against al-Shabaab and other groups in Somalia. Between October 2018 and February 2019, at least two hundred were killed in reported air strikes there. There are also ongoing wars in Yemen and Libya. But there are attempts to end them or at least reduce the worst violence.

The real question when it comes to extremism is its appeal. With hundreds of thousands of social media accounts linked to ISIS shut down, it appears that social media giants have learned the lessons of 2014, when an estimated forty-five thousand ISIS accounts helped not only to encourage crimes against humanity but also to get tens of thousands to join and journey to Syria and Iraq. The migration to join ISIS was unprecedented. It far outpaced the number of foreigners who had volunteered to fight against the Soviets in Afghanistan in the 1980s, the core group that helped lead to al Qaeda, and it is far more than those who went to fight in Chechnya and the Balkans in the 1980s. One of the major differences with ISIS is that while the 1980s and 1990s saw transnational jihadism, it often involved Arabs radicalized at home going to fight as foreign fighters. With ISIS, the process was the opposite: it was extremists from all over the world coming to the Middle East.

This illustrates that the process of radicalization has changed. Extremism is a problem in Europe and Asia and parts of Africa, but perhaps declining in the Middle East. This is likely a development that in the long term will reduce global extremism. The source of some of the inspiration were groups such as the Muslim Brotherhood or Salafists and others who believed in ideas like the "caliphate" or saw themselves as inspired by some version of Islamist fundamentalism. The exact nature of that phenomenon might be debated, but the source was seen as rooted in the region. If the region turns a page on exporting extremism via locals becoming foreign fighters, then the other sources of extremism may wither on the vine. A lot of the jihadist networks that began in the 1980s had their source in stagnation and dictatorship and failed rebellions closer to home.

It falls on the younger generation of leaders to chart a way forward. This will involve those like Syria's Bashar al-Assad, Egypt's Abdel Fattah al-Sisi, Saudi crown prince Mohammed bin Salman, Abu Dhabi crown prince Mohammed bin Zayed Al Nahyan, the kings of Morocco and Jordan, and emerging Kurdish leaders. It will also hinge on the length of Erdogan's tenure and on whoever is elected next to be supreme leader and president in Iran. This new generation came of age in the 1980s or 1990s, in an era of US hegemony, and they took over from leaders who had run the region since the colonial era. With the Saddam Husseins, Mubaraks, Gaddafis, and Salehs out of the way, there may be a new way forward.

Reduced US Influence

The post-ISIS period comes as the United States is reducing its role in the Middle East and being challenged globally. The period of the New World Order put forward by George H. W. Bush in the 1990s, the humanitarian intervention of the Clinton years, and the democracy promotion of the Bush Jr. decade are now in the past. The optimism of the post–Cold War era is no more. The US is becoming more insular in the transition from Obama to Trump and whoever comes next. US politics is becoming more domestically oriented and skeptical about long-term foreign policy commitments. It is also fatigued after decades of war.

The trend in the US is for a reduction of the American role globally. Insofar as there is still a major role, its nature will be to learn from experiences in Iraq and Afghanistan. This means having a small footprint and a long-arm strategy of using air power and new technology to confront adversaries. For instance, the war on ISIS was waged primarily "by, with and through" the coalition partners. That means supplying weapons and doing training, what is called "train and equip," while conducting an advise and assist strategy on the ground. The benefit is that very few Americans end up as casualties. The few who are deployed have special skills and operate as force multipliers for the locals.

No war is clean, and the United States does face some casualties, such as the four each in a Niger ambush in October 2017 and the Manbij bombing in January 2019. Compared to conflicts in the twentieth century, this is a major change (over 58,000 US military personnel lost their lives in Vietnam, and some 416,800 in World War II). And the US is transitioning toward more autonomous vehicles, UAVs and all the other weapons systems that make it less likely American personnel will be casualties.

However, the large picture of reduced US involvement means that other countries will step into the vacuum. That may mean Russia, Iran, Turkey and others in the Middle East. In other regions, it will mean more Chinese involvement. For instance, China's Belt and Road Initiative could one day move into the vacuum left by changing US posture in the Middle East. China's dream would be a more secure and stable region. With the ISIS war winding down and the US reducing forces, this could be a time for China to increase its role.

Does this change the calculations of the long war theory and small wars concept that has developed since the 1990s? Does it change counterinsurgency tactics if the US doesn't want as much of a global presence? What it likely means is that there are limited, tactical goals, but not larger regional or strategic goals. This means the US has fundamentally changed more than almost a century of foreign policy, in terms of looking at the big picture.

The precedent for this might be the isolationism of the post–US Civil War period and the post-WWI period. In a sense, then, the US is turning a corner in a one-hundred-year cycle, much as the Middle East is. ISIS was a bookend in that momentous change.

Chapter 27
A Way Forward

What Happens after ISIS?

After ISIS, the Middle East seeks a quiet period free from war. Many countries are searching for this new way forward. Economic development is a key issue that unites policy makers in each country. It has also brought together adversaries, such as Russia, Turkey and Iran. There are announcements of new initiatives almost every month. These include rail lines linking Iran and Syria as well as linking Jordan and the Gulf. New cities are being built.

But there are still millions of refugees and IDPs, and development and reconstruction aid is not forthcoming. Iraq has not received the billions it needs, for instance. At a conference on March 1, 2019, in Erbil, KRG prime minister Nechirvan Barzani noted that reconstruction and federalism were key to achieving peace and stability by eradicating the roots of terror. The Trump administration, in discussing its "deal of the century," has suggested major investment in Israel and the Palestinian areas.

This hinges on reconstructing areas ISIS ravaged and making sure that new conflicts do not break out. This will be difficult, because evidence shows that ISIS terrorists are still striking in Iraq and Syria. There is no long-term solution for Turkey's opposition to the Syrian Democratic Forces or for the Syrian regime accepting the US presence in eastern Syria. These intractable issues mean that it will be difficult to find a way forward that provides for the areas affected most by the war.

Lessons of the War

The war on ISIS and its importance often appear misunderstood. Some see it as exaggerated, arguing that the ISIS threat was never as large as it seemed and that the war should have been won more quickly. Others see exaggeration in the perception of ISIS as unique, preferring to see it as part of a spectrum of jihadist groups or as part of the milieu of religious extremism in the region.

There are also other questions about the war, such as insinuations that somehow the war on ISIS was actually fought to benefit Iran. For those who oppose Iran's role in the region, there is a theory that ISIS was actually a threat to Iran and that it could have been left in place somehow to let the Iranians fight it. Then there are those who see ISIS through the lens of disenfranchisement of Sunnis and argue that it was an insurgent reaction to poverty and marginalization. In this view, ISIS is merely one of many Sunni groups that emerged, linked to the Iraqi insurgency and the anti-Assad rebels. There are also those who look at ISIS through a religious or bureaucratic lens, seeking to explain its Islamic or non-Islamic characteristics and why it inspired so many. They want to look at the system ISIS put in place, its extensive documentation of how it was run, and even the records of its own crimes that it left behind. Like the Nazis, ISIS bureaucrats were zealous. Lastly, there are the sensationalistic accounts, the stories about ISIS cruelty and salacious details, as well as the stories of heroism in defeating ISIS. These usually focus on some improbable stories of special forces, whether phenomenal sniper kills or dogs ripping the throats of jihadists.

The problem with much of the focus is that it doesn't seem to take into account the overall picture of ISIS. It wasn't just another "insurgency," and it wasn't just an organic response to the brutality of the Iraqi and Syrian governments. If that was what it was, then it would have ended up like previous Iraqi insurgencies or like the rest of the Sunni rebels. The coalition against ISIS didn't make it into what it was; ISIS was a real existential threat to Baghdad and to parts of the Middle East. It wasn't the "JV team" that Obama dismissively called it in early 2014.

It's not always clear why one movement succeeds and others don't. In the chaos of the Russian Revolution, one zealous party came to power. In the chaos of Germany in the inter-war years, one party stood above the rest. The Khmer Rouge emerged quickly to the heights of its power between 1974 and 1979. All these movements can also be seen on a spectrum of other similar movements. But they achieved something more, and in capturing the apparatus of the state, they were able to carry out unspeakable and long-lasting crimes and changes in society.

A lesson of the ISIS war is that groups like ISIS must not be permitted to gain a foothold and expand. They should be taken seriously, and their pronouncements, such as threats of bringing back slavery and genocide, should be of global concern. A corollary to that is to take seriously growing radicalization at home and not to expect that foreign movements preaching extremism can be ignored in an era of globalized social media.

The Global Coalition to Defeat ISIS represented an unprecedented alliance, but it often didn't put its money where its mouth was. It talks about stabilization but doesn't appear to require much from its members. This leaves questions about its efficacy. It shows that many countries want to confront a group like ISIS, but also illustrates they don't want to commit a footprint to doing so. Where the coalition goes after 2019 is unclear. Because the members aren't burdened with much to join it, it may become a coalition in name only. Nevertheless, if it can translate some lessons into global campaigns against ISIS-linked groups, that will be an achievement.

There has been little justice for the victims of ISIS. The countries that signed on to fight should have been willing to establish war crimes trials. Instead, made wary by the aftermath of the Balkan wars, and not wanting endless responsibility, coalition members have made little attempt to keep track of all the alleged ISIS members and to punish them. This has been especially true in Syria. The first months of 2019 showed that the coalition was in such a hurry to end the conflict in line with the US schedule of withdrawal that little thought was given to housing, interrogating and detaining the tens of thousands who left Baghuz. That might mean that fifty thousand or more ISIS members were able to become IDPs and will eventually melt away. The Syrian Democratic Forces, saddled with caring for so many people, has sought compromises as well. ISIS members reportedly ended up in areas in northern Syria's Idlib Province and paid to be smuggled to Turkey in

February. The SDF even sought to hand over some suspects to local Sunni Arab tribes, accepting promises they would be de-radicalized. Similar promises might come from numerous countries and areas where these ISIS supporters came from.

The lack of justice for ISIS criminals is matched by the lack of investment in areas destroyed by ISIS. This is particularly true in Sinjar, where mass graves still exist without proper infrastructure to protect them, and where IDPs still live on Mount Sinjar in shacks.

There has been discussion of whether ISIS will have a next generation, an ISIS 2.0. This posits that the trajectory from groups like al Qaeda to ISIS is heading in one direction. But a lesson of the defeat of ISIS might be that the world has gotten better at fighting these groups. It is true that groups like al-Shabaab and Boko Haram appear to be undefeated and that there is no strategy to destroy them. They feed off weak states like parasites, creating Hobbesian areas of instability and killing. Many states around them are not getting stronger. Some are walling themselves off from these groups, as Somaliland has done in Somalia. Is a new kind of ISIS likely to emerge from these spaces, either in the Sahel or Afghanistan? Time will tell, but it appears that the power of ISIS was sui generis. A group like this will not appear again. This was the apogee of Islamist extremism and jihadist groups.

A lesson for the United States and Western militaries has been that "by, with and through" works. It is a model for fighting wars and can play a role in the kinds of small wars that make up the long war that has developed after 9/11. The US has decided that democracy promotion by reconstructing states or nation building is no longer a goal. It has also given up on humanitarian intervention of the type it did in Panama, Haiti, Somalia, Bosnia and Kosovo. The US has also become more cynical about concepts such as counterinsurgency (COIN) and has transitioned to filling only train and equip and advise and assist roles. Combined with technology, such as drones, this is a lesson that wars against groups like ISIS can be won by finding local partners.

However, the US has also decided not to stick by its closest allies in the wake of the war on ISIS. It has sought to walk away from eastern Syria and the SDF, a group it helped to form. It has also largely failed to stand by the KRG in northern Iraq. This presents a dilemma. While "by, with and through" may work to defeat enemies, it doesn't have a long-term goal, and this makes it less successful. The Powell doctrine of the Bush Sr. years taught the US to have a clear goal with public support and to end the conflict quickly through overwhelming force. But the war on ISIS was embodied by mission creep, fading public support, an open-ended conflict and the use of minimal force.

Wars fought primarily to win battles but not to win the war in the long term go against the Clausewitz concept of war being merely a form of politics. Generally, wars should be an outcome of policy and part of a larger strategy. Fighting small wars in the shadows all over the world has left the United States without clear objectives. A lesson of the ISIS war is that you can win the battle, but you might end up leaving the battlefield to adversaries – such as the Syrian regime or Iranian-backed militias in Iraq – when it is all over.

Possible Scenarios

In light of the trends unfolding in the period after the defeat of ISIS on the ground, there are several scenarios that could take place. It is worthwhile to consider them and their implications.

ISIS 2.0

ISIS reemerges in Iraq and Syria. Using existing networks in Iraq, it carries out a campaign of attacks across Sunni areas, challenging the Iraqi security forces. With pressure from Iranian-backed groups in Iraq, the United States is asked not to have a large presence on the ground, leaving the Iraqi security forces and Popular Mobilization Forces to conduct the counterinsurgency campaign. Parts of Iraq descend into the kind of instability they saw in 2004 and 2013.

In Syria, the inability of the SDF to deal with tens of thousands of ISIS supporters who fled Baghuz leads them to form new sleeper cells and launch an insurgency. The coalition, seeking to leave Syria, is left with yet another complex choice. Stay in Syria to fight while Russia, Iran and Turkey oppose the coalition's presence, or leave and let Russia, Iran and Turkey fight ISIS. Leaving behind instability leads to ISIS renewing its presence in formerly cleared areas and to fueling a cycle of instability in Iraq and Syria along their common border.

Meanwhile, ISIS grows in strength in the Sahel and Afghanistan and puts down roots in other countries in Asia. It continues to be a global threat, but the US tendency to reduce America's role in countries throughout the world leaves other countries attempting to fill the gap in American power with local policies that cannot defeat ISIS globally.

WAR WITH IRAN

Did the war on ISIS set the stage for a new war with Iran? Hezbollah and pro-Iranian groups in Iraq are empowered by the war on ISIS. Iran continues its entrenchment in Syria and its provocative behavior in the Gulf. This leads to greater tensions with Israel and a round of air strikes that lead to a larger war.

Iranian militias in Iraq attack American forces to try to get them to withdraw, leaving the US to choose between leaving and striking back. Encouraged by the Gulf states and Israel's existing conflict with Iran, the United States must decide whether to strike IRGC targets in Syria and/or carry out surgical strikes against pro-Iranian groups in Iraq, or to begin a larger war with Iran.

The Israeli war with Iran spills over into Lebanon and Syria, leading to calls by Israel to dismantle Hezbollah and finally disarm it. Saudi Arabia and other Gulf countries support this, but the US is concerned about weakening the Lebanese state, which would lead to new chaos in the region.

THE US LEAVES IRAQ

Encouraged by the US drawdown in Syria, the Iraqi parliament demands that the US leave Iraq. Having anchored its hopes in Baghdad rather than in the KRG, the US now finds itself with little choice but to leave Iraq, again. This sets the stage for an increased Iranian role in Iraq, stoking tensions with Saudi Arabia and other countries.

Departure from Iraq dovetails with Trump's desire to reduce US forces abroad, but means it will be difficult for the US to return to influence Iraq. The US also finds it more difficult to support the KRG, despite calls by Erbil for US forces to stay. This destabilizes the Kurdistan region and leads to Iran and Turkey increasing their presence in northern Iraq.

TURKEY LAUNCHES AN OPERATION IN EASTERN SYRIA

Turkey finally decides to carry out an operation in eastern Syria, as it has threatened to do for years. It seeks to destroy the SDF- and PKK-linked groups, such as the YPG. It gets Syrian rebel groups to aid its assault, promising that millions of Syrian Arab refugees in Turkey will return to a remade region in northern Syria.

The United States, forced to choose between its former partner the SDF and its NATO ally Turkey, chooses Ankara. The war in eastern Syria proves difficult and leads to a new PKK insurgency in eastern Turkey and to conflict in northern Iraq. Ankara's desire to destroy the PKK creates instability across a swath of Syria and Iraq. Iran and the Syrian regime look on, concerned about Turkey's actions but hoping they will force the SDF to beg the Syrian regime for help. Turkey agrees to allow the Syrian regime to retake most of Idlib Province, in exchange for permission to carry out what it says is its right under the Adana agreement. (The Adana agreement, made in 1998 between Turkey and Syria, ended Syrian support for the PKK and provided for security cooperation between Turkey and Syria against the PKK, ostensibly meaning that if it was violated and the PKK was on Syrian soil, then Turkey could intervene or pressure Damascus to end the PKK presence. Turkey sees the agreement as relevant in 2019 to pressuring Syria to remove the YPG from Syria.) Russia, desiring closer economic relation with Turkey, agrees to the operation. Iran, also needing Turkey to get around US sanctions, accepts the operation as well, wanting to see the former SDF partners of the United States humiliated.

Turkey comes out of the operation stronger and less willing to leave Syria. Having promised the Syrian Arab refugees support, it now feels it cannot abandon them. Russia sees this as a scenario similar to its role in the Donbas supporting rebels in Ukraine. It accepts this as a short-term solution to the Syrian conflict.

THE QATAR CRISIS ENDS

The Gulf states end the Qatar crisis, and Saudi Arabia and Qatar come to an agreement. At the same time, the Gulf states support Syria returning to the Arab League and agree to work on Israeli-Palestinian peace talks. The Trump administration, seeking to put forward its "deal of the century," is pleased, because it hopes that Qatar can influence Hamas in Gaza while Riyadh pressures Ramallah to accept the deal. Israel, under a new leader, also says it is willing to give a new round of talks a try after almost two decades of failed negotiations.

The end of the Qatar crisis leads to more stability in the Israeli-Palestinian peace process, and even warms relations between Turkey and Israel, paving the way for a variety of new engagements and a reduction in tensions between Iran and Israel. The Yemen war ends with investment in the country, and the Libyan conflict also finds some resolution, helping to shore up the defenses of the Sahel. This has a domino effect of leading to more cooperation against terrorist groups across Africa and the Middle East.

ANOTHER MIDDLE EASTERN SPRING

Protests in the Sudan and Algeria in the spring of 2019 illustrate that a generation of people in the Middle East feels its concerns have not been answered, and a new round of protests demands a reduction in authoritarianism. Using Tunisia as a model, the protesters seek to find a way to have more open societies without allowing extremist groups to benefit.

This leads to new tensions between the Muslim Brotherhood and governments in Cairo and Riyadh that are wary of political Islam. Qatar and Turkey support the new round of protests, so long as they do not result in protests in Doha or Ankara as well. The protests fuel instability in Iraq, which leads to pressure against pro-Iranian parties. This in turn fuels protests in Iran against the regime.

Epilogue
Coming Home

The first time I saw ISIS crimes, I thought they were fake, some kind of awful movie. The photos showed men being machine-gunned as they lay on the ground. Others showed men being marched from a truck, heads down, begging for their lives, fear of what would come next in their eyes. But people assured me these were real images, and soon the videos emerged. That was in June 2014.

Then we saw more images of mass murder in Tabqa, Syria, and of truckers being murdered for being Alawite. Social media was full of hundreds – it turned out later to be hundreds of thousands – of accounts supporting ISIS. People changed their photos to pictures of swords and the black flag and put as a background a photo of guns or flags. They gloried in discussing the killing of the *"kuffar"* (infidels) and stories of rape and selling of women. They boasted about the great times in Syria and Iraq. Some showed photos of themselves at the seaside, as if joining ISIS was a fun vacation. We would later learn just how many thousands of people born and raised in the West had joined. Even the education minister of ISIS was a German citizen.

Yet despite the obvious middle-class origins of this far-right religious hatred that appeared Nazi-like, people made excuses for it. Poverty, stories of "Islamophobia" and "discrimination." Even as ISIS was the one attacking the poor and putting forth its own phobia against minorities while discriminating against them, its members were still just "insurgent militants" with "grievances" who "felt humiliated." They sold slaves, but they were victims. They had villas they stole from locals, but they were "poor." It was Orwellian, and I saw it firsthand. I read the hatred on social media, and I saw the videos of murder and beheadings.

Other responses to ISIS were more interesting. Self-described "secular liberal feminist vegan Egyptian" Aliaa Magda Elmahdy defecated and smeared menstrual blood on an ISIS flag.

It became more gruesome with time, stories out of hell, so shocking they seemed impossible to believe. We saw images of people crucified, burned to death. There was no low to which ISIS did not sink. And even though more than seventy countries signed on to fight ISIS, it seemed to hold on against all odds. It grew roots as far as Asia and across the Mediterranean. And with its roots there was a reaction. It became the new al Qaeda terrorist brand; other groups joined it, and politicians talked about it. Its crimes probably fueled Brexit and helped Trump become president. It also helped to change views on the Arab Spring and the threat of instability in the region.

I lived through it, and when I learned others had taken up arms as volunteers, I wanted to go as well. I wanted to document the crimes. This was the Great War of my time, and I wanted to be there. I wanted to see Mosul liberated and ride on a tank like the US GIs who destroyed Hitler's Europe, like the Red Army with the flag atop the Reichstag. I believed ISIS to be the global threat of my time. A defining moment.

The first time I went to Iraq, I was happy to leave the country. But I thought of people who were in my field who had been murdered by ISIS, like Steven Sotloff. I wanted to go back. So I went back, again and again, until the war became an addiction.

I watched *Full Metal Jacket* recently. The scenes toward the end, when the Marines are battling for Hue city, felt more real than I'd remembered. As the men pick their way through the burning city, an explosion kills one of them, then another. Several are brought down by a sniper. This sense of walking through destruction, fighting an unseen enemy, reminded me of Mosul. I was back there, picking my way through an abandoned house, through holes in the wall, wary of snipers. In the film, when the men let loose all their firepower, pockmarking buildings, I was brought back to the Iraqi Federal Police shooting blindly down an alley. Stanley Kubrick had captured it. He had captured war.

The problem with having been in combat is that movies that are supposed to depict combat now seem rubbery, plastic, fake. Where is the background noise? Why is everything so clean in war movies? People can barely stay clean doing most outdoor jobs; how is it that in war films, men don't look like they've been in the field for days? Some movies get it right; most don't.

Post-traumatic stress disorder is something journalists who cover conflict rarely discuss. But there's no reason to suppose they are less likely to have it than soldiers. If you've walked through streets with burned bodies, gotten used to the deep, stomach-crunching percussion of artillery and wandered through mortar fire, you've experienced what soldiers do. The long-term effects of conflict are kept deep inside, but they emerge at different times. Maybe a noise brings back memories. Maybe it is just when the mind wanders on a bus or while walking. It can be in dreams or while standing in line.

There is also a confidence that comes with returning from war. It makes civilian life seem less real and the petty things in day-to-day life appear less important. The fear one has in war – even the fear a journalist might have of kidnapping or being discovered at a checkpoint to be something other than he says he is – is greater than most fears civilian life can conjure up.

I discovered an addiction to conflict after my first trip to Iraq in 2015. I'd already covered several Gaza wars in Israel and numerous Palestinian Arab protests. That had been a preparatory course. But the rush of driving to the front line, not knowing what will happen, expectation and fear, always drew me back. It went on for two years. A constant desire to plan the next trip, the next fix. Then one day it was enough. And I came home. Before that I'd come home physically, but mentally and in my hopes and desires I was always at the front. I was lacing up my shoes, putting on my body armor, slinging my helmet and camera. I was always there in the bunker, with the men. And then one day I was home. And I wanted to stay home with my family and my sons. And my mind and body were in the same place.

Notes

1. The information in this chapter comes from interviews during a trip to the Kurdistan region of Iraq in December 2015.

2. RAND news release, "Islamic State Control of People Down 83% in Iraq and 56% in Syria from Peak Levels," April 20, 2017, https://www.rand.org/news/press/2017/04/20.html.

3. "Islamic State and the Crises in Iraq and Syria in Maps," BBC, March 28, 2018, https://www.bbc.com/news/world-middle-east-27838034.

4. Barbara Starr, "Forensic Team Searches Syrian Mass Graves for American Hostage Remains," CNN, February 6, 2018, https://edition.cnn.com/2018/02/16/politics/us-forensic-team-syria-hostage-remains/index.html.

5. Barbara Starr, "Military: 50,000 ISIS Fighters Killed," CNN, December 9, 2016, https://edition.cnn.com/2016/12/09/politics/isis-dead-us-military/index.html.

6. Barack Obama, "Statement by the President," White House, Office of the Press Secretary, August 7, 2014, https://obamawhitehouse.archives.gov/the-press-office/2014/08/07/statement-president.

7. Orhan Coskun and Dasha Afanasieva, "Turkey Stages First Air Strikes on Islamic State in Syria," Reuters, July 24, 2014, https://www.reuters.com/article/us-mideast-crisis-turkey-islamicstate/turkey-stages-first-air-strikes-on-islamic-state-in-syria-idUSKCN0PY0AU20150724.

8. Tarek Osman, "Why Border Lines Drawn with a Ruler in WWI Still Rock the Middle East," BBC, December 14, 2013, https://www.bbc.com/news/world-middle-east-25299553.

9. "'Know Your Place': Turkish Leader Rebukes UAE Minister over Tweet," France 24, December 20, 2017, https://www.france24.com/en/20171220-know-place-turkish-leader-rebukes-uae-minister-over-tweet.

10. Euan McKirdy and Hamdi Alkhshali, "Syria Hits Back after Turkey's Erdogan Calls Assad a 'Terrorist,'" CNN, December 28, 2017, https://edition.cnn.com/2017/12/28/middleeast/assad-erdogan-terrorist-intl/index.html.

11. Robin Yassin-Kassab, "The Unravelling by Emma Sky Review – An Insider's

View of the Iraq Conflict," *The Guardian*, June 6, 2015, https://www.theguardian.com/books/2015/jun/06/the-unravelling-emma-sky-review-high-hopes-missed-opportunities-iraq.

12. Matthew Hilburn, "One-Time US Prisoner Now Key in Battling IS," VOA, March 15, 2015, https://www.voanews.com/a/qais-khazali-onetime-us-prisoner-now-key-in-battling-islamic-state/2679431.html.

13. The information in this chapter comes primarily from a trip to Turkey in December 2014, including numerous interviews in Istanbul and Ankara.

14. Seth J. Frantzman and Laura Kelly, "A Reckoning in Turkey," *Jerusalem Post*, January 8, 2015, https://www.jpost.com/Magazine/A-reckoning-in-Turkey-387096.

15. "The Davutoglu Effect," *The Economist*, October 21, 2010, https://www.economist.com/special-report/2010/10/21/the-davutoglu-effect.

16. Can Dundar, "I Revealed the Truth about President Erdogan and Syria. For That, He Had Me Jailed," *The Guardian*, December 28, 2015, https://www.theguardian.com/commentisfree/2015/dec/28/truth-president-erdogan-jailed-turkey-regime-state-security-crime.

17. "Qatar, Turkey Take Bold Step for Strategic Cooperation," *Hurriyet Daily News*, December 19, 2014, http://www.hurriyetdailynews.com/qatar-turkey-take-bold-step-for-strategic-cooperation-75852.

18. "Kirkuk, Kurdish Fields to Export 600,000 BPD as Iraq Announces Record Output," Rudaw, January 18, 2015, http://www.rudaw.net/NewsDetails.aspx?pageid=97933.

19. Coskun and Afanasieva, "Turkey Stages First Air Strikes."

20. The information in this chapter comes primarily from a trip to the United Arab Emirates in February 2015, including numerous interviews in Dubai.

21. "Jordan Carries Out New Air Strikes after Pilot's Murder," *The Guardian*, February 5, 2015, https://www.theguardian.com/world/2015/feb/05/jordan-air-strikes-isis-pilot-murder.

22. Seth J. Frantzman, "Region's Baptism Sites a Bridge Completing the Holy Land Pilgrimage," August 13, 2015, *Jerusalem Post*, http://www.jpost.com/Magazine/A-river-runs-through-it-411987.

23. Rob Garratt, "Nawal EL Saadawi on Beating George Orwell," March 9, 2015, *The National*, https://www.thenational.ae/arts-culture/nawal-el-saadawi-on-beating-george-orwell-and-being-banned-from-qatar-1.87323.

24. The information in this chapter comes primarily from a trip to northern Iraq's Kurdistan region and the frontline in Telskuf in June 2015. It is based on interviews with Peshmerga commanders, humanitarian aid workers and numerous locals.

25. "Official: IDPs Make Up 35 Percent of Kurdistan Region Population," Rudaw, October 20, 2015, http://www.rudaw.net/english/kurdistan/201020153.

26. "Erbil Airport Chief: Cargo down from 2,500 to Mere 10 Tonnes after Flight Ban," Rudaw, December 19, 2017, http://www.rudaw.net/english/kurdistan/19122017.

27. The information in this chapter comes primarily from a trip to Greece, Macedonia, Serbia and Hungary in September 2015.

28. Relief Web, "Mediterranean Migrant Arrivals," September 30, 2016, https://reliefweb.int/report/italy/mediterranean-migrant-arrivals-reach-302486-deaths-sea-3502.

29. NBC, transcript, "Hardball with Chris Matthews," November 17, 2015, http://www.nbcnews.com/id/58149347/ns/msnbc-hardball_with_chris_matthews/t/hardball-chris-matthews-tuesday-november-th/.

30. The information in this chapter comes primarily from a trip to Iraq in December 2015.

31. Luis Martinez, "6,000 Airstrikes in Iraq and Syria: A Look at the Numbers," ABC News, August 7, 2015, http://abcnews.go.com/Politics/6000-airstrikes-iraq-syria-numbers/story?id=32956745.

32. Sudarsan Raghavan, "Chart: How Much More the US Has Bombed Islamic State Than the Taliban," *Washington Post*, September 18, 2015, https://www.washingtonpost.com/news/worldviews/wp/2015/09/18/chart-how-much-more-the-u-s-has-bombed-the-islamic-state-than-the-taliban/?utm_term=.2c78449f8154.

33. Seth J. Frantzman, "Where ISIS Ends and Kurdistan Begins," *National Interest*, January 4, 2016, https://nationalinterest.org/feature/where-isis-ends-kurdistan-begins-14791.

34. The information in this chapter comes primarily from a trip to Iraq in December 2015.

35. Seth J. Frantzman, "Life after Islamic State," *National Interest*, December 30, 2015, https://nationalinterest.org/feature/life-after-islamic-state-14763.

36. Cathy Otten, "Slaves of ISIS: The Long Walk of the Yazidi Women," *The Guardian*, July 25, 2017, https://www.theguardian.com/world/2017/jul/25/slaves-of-isis-the-long-walk-of-the-yazidi-women.

37. Nick Squires, "Yazidi Girl Tells of Horrific Ordeal as ISIS Sex Slave," *The Telegraph*, September 7, 2014, https://www.telegraph.co.uk/news/worldnews/middleeast/iraq/11080165/Yazidi-girl-tells-of-horrific-ordeal-as-Isil-sex-slave.html; Rose Troup Buchanan, "Life under ISIS," *The Independent*, September 9, 2014, https://www.independent.co.uk/news/world/middle-east/life-under-isis-captured-teenage-girl-tells-story-of-horrendous-abuse-at-the-hands-of-islamic-state-9721746.html.

38. Rania Khalek, "How ISIS Wives Helped Their Husbands Rape Yazidi Sex Slaves," Alternet, September 22, 2017. https://www.alternet.org/2017/09/how-isis-wives-helped-their-husbands-rape-yazidi-sex-slaves/.

39. Alissa J. Rubin, "In Iraq, I Found Checkpoints as Endless as the Whims of Armed Men," *New York Times*, April 2, 2018, https://www.nytimes.com/2018/04/02/magazine/iraq-sinjar-checkpoints-militias.html.

40. Seth J. Frantzman, "The More Things Change, the More Iraq Stays The Same,"

National Interest, April 18, 2017, https://nationalinterest.org/feature/the-more-things-change-the-more-iraq-stays-the-same-20248?nopaging=1.

41. The information in this chapter comes from multiple interviews with members of the US-led coalition between 2015 and 2017.

42. PBS, "Interview Col. H.R. McMaster," *Frontline Endgame*, June 19, 2007, https://www.pbs.org/wgbh/pages/frontline/endgame/interviews/mcmaster.html.

43. Thomas E. Ricks, "Maj. Gen. H.R. McMaster on the Big Hole in the COIN and Armed Forces Manuals," *Foreign Policy*, April 29, 2013, https://foreignpolicy.com/2013/04/29/maj-gen-h-r-mcmaster-on-the-big-hole-in-the-coin-and-security-forces-manuals/.

44. Emma Sky, "Mission Still Not Accomplished in Iraq," *Foreign Affairs*, November/December 2017, https://www.foreignaffairs.com/articles/middle-east/2017-10-16/mission-still-not-accomplished-iraq.

45. Seth J. Frantzman, "Advise and Assist: The Iraqi Army through the Eyes of an American Advisor," *Jerusalem Post*, September 14, 2017, https://www.jpost.com/Middle-East/Advise-and-assist-The-Iraqi-army-through-the-eyes-of-an-American-advisor-505098.

46. Frantzman, "The More Things Change."

47. US Department of State, "US Security Cooperation with Iraq," March 22, 2017, https://www.state.gov/r/pa/prs/ps/2017/03/269040.htm.

48. US Department of State, "US Security Cooperation with Iraq."

49. "Combined Joint Task Force Operation Inherent Resolve Fact Sheet," http://www.inherentresolve.mil/Portals/14/D
ocuments/Mission/History.pdf?ver=2016-03-23-065243-743.

50. US Department of State, "US Security Cooperation with Iraq."

51. Brookings, "The Iraqi Counter Terrorism Service," March 16, 2015, https://www.brookings.edu/research/the-iraqi-counter-terrorism-service/.

52. Ned Parker, Isabel Coles, Raheem Salman, "Special Report: How Mosul Fell – An Iraqi General Disputes Baghdad's Story," Reuters, October 14, 2014, https://www.reuters.com/article/us-mideast-crisis-gharawi-special-report-idUSKCN0I30Z820141014.

53. "From the Horse's Mouth: The Day the ISIS Leader Declared His Caliphate," Rudaw, July 7, 2017, http://www.rudaw.net/english/interview/07072017.

54. Obama, "Statement by the President."

55. Mark Thompson, "What Are Those 1,600 (So Far) U.S. Military Advisors Doing in Iraq (So Far)," *Time*, September 14, 2014, http://time.com/3380424/what-are-those-1600-so-far-u-s-military-advisers-doing-in-iraq-so-far/.

56. Luis Martinez, "US Airstrikes in Iraq and Syria Have Cost $1 Billion," ABC News, December 19, 2014, https://abcnews.go.com/Politics/us-airstrikes-iraq-syria-cost-billion/story?id=27728260.

57. Phil Stewart and Yeganeh Torbati, "U.S. Deploying New Force to Iraq to Boost

Fight against Islamic State," Reuters, December 1, 2015, https://www.reuters.com/article/us-mideast-crisis-usa-military/u-s-deploying-new-force-to-iraq-to-boost-fight-against-islamic-state-idUSKBN0TK50G20151201.

58. Corey Dickstein and Tara Copp, "A Look at Newly Established Fire Base Bell Where Marine Was Killed in Iraq," *Stars and Stripes*, March 21, 2016, https://www.stripes.com/news/a-look-at-newly-established-fire-base-bell-where-marine-was-killed-in-iraq-1.400352.

59. "Marine Artillery Unit Fired 2,000 Rounds at ISIS in Iraq," Military.com, July 1, 2016, https://www.military.com/dodbuzz/2016/07/01/marine-artillery-unit-fired-2000-rounds-at-isis-in-iraq.

60. Raymond Thomas, "Statement of General Raymond Thomas III, US Special Operations Command," House Armed Services Subcommittee on Emerging Threats and Capabilities, May 2, 2017, https://docs.house.gov/meetings/AS/AS26/20170502/105926/HHRG-115-AS26-Wstate-ThomasR-20170502.pdf.

61. "Transcript of the Second Debate," *New York Times*, October 10, 2016, https://www.nytimes.com/2016/10/10/us/politics/transcript-second-debate.html.

62. Ash Carter, "Behind the Plan to Defeat ISIS," *The Atlantic*, October 31, 2017, https://www.theatlantic.com/international/archive/2017/10/isis-plan-defeat/544418/.

63. The information in this chapter comes primarily from a trip to Turkey in February 2016.

64. The information in this chapter comes primarily from a trip to Senegal in March 2016.

65. "Who are the Senegalese Joining Islamic State Group?" France 24, January 2, 2016, https://observers.france24.com/en/20160201-senegal-jihadist-islamic-state.

66. Jean Herskovits, "In Nigeria, Boko Haram Is Not the Problem," *New York Times*, January 2, 2012, https://www.nytimes.com/2012/01/02/opinion/in-nigeria-boko-haram-is-not-the-problem.html.

67. Alexis Okeowo, "The Enduring American Military Mission in Africa," *New Yorker*, May 3, 2017, https://www.newyorker.com/news/daily-comment/the-enduring-american-military-mission-in-africa.

68. The information in this chapter comes primarily from a trip to Israel in September 2017 and several trips to Europe the same year.

69. Seth J. Frantzman, "Takeaways from International Confab on Counterterrorism: The Threats Are Nowhere Near Over," *Jerusalem Post*, September 14, 2017, https://www.jpost.com/Middle-East/Takeaways-from-intl-confab-on-counterterrorism-The-threats-are-nowhere-near-over-505057.

70. Christina Captides, "Which European Countries Have Produced the Most ISIS Fighters," CBS News, January 25, 2016, https://www.cbsnews.com/news/isis-terror-recruiting-europe-belgium-france-denmark-sweden-germany/.

71. "So-Called IS Beatles El Shafee Elsheikh and Alexanda Kotey Dispute Extradition," BBC, August 6, 2018, https://www.bbc.com/news/world-middle-east-45087824.

72. Camila Domonoske, "Turkey Says It Deported Ibrahim El Bakraoui and Warned Belgium In 2015," NPR, March 23, 2016, https://www.npr.org/sections/thetwo-way/2016/03/23/471599731/turkey-says-it-deported-ibrahim-el-bakraoui-and-warned-belgium-in-2015.

73. Frantzman, "Takeaways from International Confab."

74. Frantzman, "Takeaways from International Confab."

75. Jacob Poushter, "European Opinions of the Refugee Crisis in 5 Charts," Pew Research Center, September 16, 2016, http://www.pewresearch.org/fact-tank/2016/09/16/european-opinions-of-the-refugee-crisis-in-5-charts/.

76. US Department of State, "Remarks at the Small Group Session of the Global Coalition to Defeat ISIS by Special Presidential Envoy McGurk in Washington, DC," July 13, 2017, https://www.state.gov/remarks-at-the-small-group-session-of-the-global-coalition-to-defeat-isis-by-special-presidential-envoy-mcgurk-in-washington-dc/.

77. The information in this chapter comes primarily from a trip to Iraq in June 2016.

78. "Iraqi Military Assessing ISIS Tactics in Makhmour Says Iraqi Defense Minister," Rudaw, March 30, 2016, http://www.rudaw.net/english/middleeast/iraq/300320161.

79. Carl Von Clausewitz, On War, ed. Michael Howard and Peter Paret (Princeton, NJ: Princeton University Press, 1976).

80. Seth J. Frantzman, "After ISIS, Then What? The Scramble for Mosul," The Spectator, August 27, 2016, https://www.spectator.co.uk/2016/08/isis-will-fall-in-mosul-but-what-happens-then/.

81. Ali Sangar, "1,466 Peshmerga Died, 8,610 Wounded in IS War," Kurdistan 24, June 13, 2016, http://www.kurdistan24.net/en/news/20892763-2b66-4432-9d0f-70f76735b7a2/1-466-Peshmerga-died--8-610-wounded-in-IS-war.

82. Dr. Khalid Al-Obeidi (@khalid_alobeidi), "Khalid Al-Obeidi arrives in #Sinjar & then visits national PMF training base in Zilikan, Duhok," Twitter, November 27, 2015, 7:56 a.m., https://twitter.com/khalid_alobeidi/status/670269970178265088.

83. Seth J. Frantzman, "Iraq's Silver Bullet in the ISIS Fight," National Interest, July 20, 2016, https://nationalinterest.org/feature/iraqs-silver-bullet-the-isis-fight-17053?nopaging=1.

84. Elizabeth Mclaughlin and Luis Martinez, "US to Deploy 560 More Troops to Iraq in Preparation for Mosul Offensive," ABC News, July 11, 2016, https://abcnews.go.com/International/us-deploy-560-troops-iraq-preparation-mosul-offensive/story?id=40489879.

85. Mario Fumerton and Wladimir Van Wilgenburg, "Kurdistan's Political Armies: The Challenge of Unifying the Peshmerga Forces," Carnegie Endowment for International Peace, December 16, 2015, http://carnegieendowment.org/2015/12/16/kurdistan-s-political-armies-challenge-of-unifying-peshmerga-forces-pub-61917.

86. Fazel Hawramy, "Kurdish Peshmerga Divisions Hamper War Effort," Al-Monitor, January 13, 2015, http://www.al-monitor.com/pulse/originals/2015/01/iraq-kurdish -peshmerga-division-islamic-state.html.

87. Gorran Movement (@Gorran_Change), "Imagine a Kurdistan, with a unified Peshmerga forces, professional and unbiased following orders from 1 Gov, not 2 families. #twitterkurds," Twitter, October 23, 2017, 3:13 a.m., https://twitter.com /Gorran_Change/status/922405495494889472.

88. us State Department press release, "The Global Coalition: Working to Defeat ISIS," March 22, 2017, https://www.state.gov/r/pa/prs/ps/2017/03/268609.htm.

89. Seth J. Frantzman, "Exclusive: Inside Kurdistan's anti-ISIS Training Camps," National Interest, July 27, 2016, https://nationalinterest.org/feature/exclusive-inside -kurdistans-anti-isis-training-camps-17155.

90. Coalition email to author, July 19, 2016.

91. Kurdistan Regional Government, "Kurdistan Region and the us Sign a Military Agreement," July 13, 2016, http://cabinet.gov.krd/a/d.aspx?s=040000&l=12&a=54717.

92. Tara Fatehi, "Dr. Abdul Rahman Ghassemlou," Medya, accessed March 1, 2019. https://medyamagazine.com/28/

93. "Mustafa Hijri: 'Iran Attempts to Create Instability and Conflict All around the Region,'" PDKI, July 1, 2015, http://pdki.org/english/mustafa-hijri-iran-attempts-to -create-instability-and-conflict-all-around-the-region/.

94. "President Barzani Warns Hashd al-Shaabi of Nearing Yezidi Areas in Shingal," Rudaw, May 12, 2017, http://www.rudaw.net/english/kurdistan/15052017.

95. "Kurdish PM Says Mosul Operation Still in 'Planning Stage,'" VOA News, July 24, 2016, https://www.voanews.com/a/exclusive-kurdish-prime-minister-mosul -operation-planning-stage/3432751.html.

96. Ayub Nuri, "Betrayals, Fake ISIS Flags, Unburied Militants: : A day with the Iraqi Army," Rudaw, July 22, 2016, http://www.rudaw.net/english/middleeast/iraq /220720161.

97. Charles Rivezzo, "621st CRW Enables Strategic Air Operations at Qayyarah West," us Air Force Expeditionary Center, November 16, 2016, https://www .expeditionarycenter.af.mil/News/Article-Display/Article/1007474/621st-crw -enables-strategic-air-operations-at-qayyarah-west/.

98. The information in this chapter comes primarily from speaking to officials and locals on background in July 2016.

99. Seth J. Frantzman, "Turkey at a Crossroads: A Look inside the Night of the Coup and Its Aftermath," Jerusalem Post, August 12, 2016, https://www.jpost.com /Magazine/Turkey-at-a-crossroads-A-look-inside-the-night-of-the-coup-and-its -aftermath-463845.

100. Frantzman, "Turkey at a Crossroads."

101. "Turkey Orders Arrest of 124 in Gulen Probe Targeting Military: Anadolu," Reuters, June 19, 2018, https://www.reuters.com/article/us-turkey-security

-gulen/turkey-orders-arrest-of-124-in-gulen-probe-targeting-military-anadolu
-idUSKBN1JF0T0.

102. Brett McGurk (@brett_mcgurk), "#ISIL spokesman Adnani one year ago said the Jughayfa tribe would be wiped out in #Haditha. Not quite. ISIL terrorists impaled themselves," Twitter, May 2, 2016, 1:32 p.m., https://twitter.com/brett_mcgurk/status/727234336878137344.

103. Shelly Kittleson, "In Iraq, Daesh Targets Siege-Surviving Tribal Fighters and Local Police," TRT World, March 5, 2019, https://www.trtworld.com/magazine/in-iraq-daesh-targets-siege-surviving-tribal-fighters-and-local-police-24675.

104. The information in this chapter comes primarily from a trip to Iraq in October 2016.

105. "US State Dept: Peshmerga Need to Be under Iraqi Government Command," Rudaw, August 19, 2016, http://www.rudaw.net/english/kurdistan/19082016.

106. Baxtiyar Goran, "President Barzani: Agreement Reached with Baghdad to Resolve All Issues," Kurdistan 24, September 29, 2016, http://www.kurdistan24.net/en/news/110c5403-6263-4580-8a59-30ca6c0ef10a/President-Barzani--Agreement-reached-with-Baghdad-to-resolve-all-issues-.

107. AP, "Turkey's President Tells Iraqi Leader to 'Know His Place,'" October 11, 2016, https://www.voanews.com/a/turkey-iraq-tensions/3545478.html.

108. Brett McGurk (@brett_mcgurk), "Godspeed to the heroic Iraqi forces, Kurdish #Peshmerga, and #Ninewa volunteers. We are proud to stand with you in this historic operation," Twitter, October 16, 2016, 3:44 p.m., https://twitter.com/brett_mcgurk/status/787786384094277632?lang=en.

109. Daniel White, "Read a Transcript of the Final Presidential Debate," Time, October 20, 2016, http://time.com/4535247/presidential-debate-final-transcript/.

110. Seth J. Frantman, "JPost on the Frontline: Inside the US-Led Coalition Helping Destroy ISIS in Mosul," Jerusalem Post, October 24, 2016, http://www.jpost.com/Middle-East/Jpost-on-the-frontline-Inside-the-US-led-coalition-helping-destroy-ISIS-in-Mosul-470775.

111. Molly Hennessy-Fiske, "Shiite Militias Have Joined the Battle to Push Islamic State from Mosul," Los Angeles Times, November 2, 2016, http://www.latimes.com/world/middleeast/la-fg-iraq-shiite-militias-20161031-story.html.

112. Orla Guerin, "Iraqi Shia Militias' Show of Force in Battle for Mosul," BBC, December 3, 2016, https://www.bbc.com/news/world-middle-east-38194653.

113. Simon Mayall, Royal Society Edinburgh, "Jihad and Surge in Iraq," Youtube, June 15, 2011, https://www.youtube.com/watch?v=ZxiXoY2yFp0.

114. "Barzani Promises This Time Kurds Will Only Spill Blood for Independence," Rudaw, October 3, 2016, http://www.rudaw.net/english/kurdistan/100320163.

115. Sangar Ali, "After IS, Kurdistan to Honor Border Drawn by Peshmergas' Blood," Kurdistan 24, June 25, 2015, http://www.kurdistan24.net/en/news/6950237e-7633

-4ced-9327-c8f412db4f9b/%E2%80%98After-IS--Kurdistan-to-honor-border-drawn -by-Peshmergas--blood%E2%80%99/.

116. Jared Malsin, "Qurans and Solar Cells — Inside the ISIS Tunnels around Mosul," *Time*, October 21, 2016, http://time.com/4541647/isis-defensive-tunnels-mosul-iraq/.

117. Hamdi Alkhshali, "Rescuing Arwa and Brice: The Toughest 24 Hours of My Life," CNN, November 14, 2016, https://edition.cnn.com/2016/11/14/middleeast/rescuing -arwa-damon-producers-notebook/index.html.

118. United Nations Iraq, "UN Casualty Figures for Iraq for the Month of November 2016," December 2, 2016, http://www.uniraq.org/index.php?option=com_k2&view =item&id=6455:un-casualty-figures-for-iraq-for-the-month-of-november-2016& Itemid=633&lang=en.

119. Phillip Connor, "U.S. Admits Record Number of Muslim Refugees in 2016," Pew Research Center, October 5, 2016, http://www.pewresearch.org/fact-tank/2016/10 /05/u-s-admits-record-number-of-muslim-refugees-in-2016/.

120. The information in this chapter comes primarily from a trip to Iraq in March 2017.

121. Conflict Armament Research, "Weapons of the Islamic State: A Three-Year Investigation in Iraq and Syria," December 4, 2017, http://www.conflictarm.com /reports/weapons-of-the-islamic-state/.

122. Conflict Armament Research, "Standardization and Quality Control in Islamic State's Military Production," December 2016, http://www.conflictarm.com/download -file/?report_id=2454&file_id=2955.

123. Conflict Armament Research, "Standardization and Quality Control."

124. Conflict Armament Research, "Standardization and Quality Control."

125. Richard Norton-Taylor, "Up to 30,000 Foreign Fighters Have Gone to Syria and Iraq since 2011 – Report," *The Guardian*, November 17, 2015, https://www.theguardian .com/world/2015/nov/17/30000-foreign-fighters-syria--iraq-2014-terrorism-report.

126. Isabel Coles, "Despair, Hardship as Iraq Cuts Off Wages in Islamic State Cities," Reuters, October 2, 2015, https://www.reuters.com/article/us-mideast -crisis-iraq-salaries/despair-hardship-as-iraq-cuts-off-wages-in-islamic-state-cities -idUSKCN0RW0V620151002.

127. Lizzie Dearden, "Isis Cuts Salaries, Brings in Fines…," *The Independent*, February 16, 2016, https://www.independent.co.uk/news/world/middle-east/isis-budget-cuts -iraq-syria-pay-bonuses-air-strikes-oil-militants-food-snickers-a6877226.html.

128. Seth J. Frantzman, "ISIS's Dirty Secret," *Jerusalem Post*, May 12, 2017, https:// www.jpost.com/Middle-East/ISISs-dirty-secret-490505.

129. "Coalition Spokesman: ISIS Threats to West Mosul Civilians to End in 'Coming Weeks,'" Rudaw, February 17, 2017, http://www.rudaw.net/english/middleeast/iraq /17022017.

130. Florian Neuhof, "Families of ISIL Terrorism Victims in Iraq Still Need Closure," *The National*, March 24, 2018, https://www.thenational.ae/world/mena/families-of -isil-terrorism-victims-in-iraq-still-need-closure-1.715762.

131. "Witnesses Recount Horrors of ISIS Mass Grave in New Report," Rudaw, March 23, 2017, http://www.rudaw.net/NewsDetails.aspx?PageID=291611.

132. US Central Command press release, "Allegation of Civilian Casualties in West Mosul," March 25, 2017, http://www.centcom.mil/MEDIA/PRESS-RELEASES /Press-Release-View/Article/1130282/allegation-of-civilian-casualties-in-west -mosul/.

133. @MosulEye, "The explosion didn't only occurred only because of the VBIED, but was a combined explosion of a strike, IFP mortars, & VBIED together," Twitter, March 25, 2017, 2:55 p.m., https://twitter.com/MosulEye/status/845756065773998081.

134. "CJTF-OIR Monthly Civilian Casualty Report," Relief Web, March 28, 2018, https://reliefweb.int/report/syrian-arab-republic/cjtf-oir-monthly-civilian-casualty -report-28-march-2018.

135. ORACC: The Open Richly Annotated Cuneiform Corpus, "Imperial Splendour: Views from Kalhu in 1850," University of Pennsylvania, http://oracc.museum.upenn .edu/nimrud/modernnimrud/onthemound/1850/index.html.

136. Mindy Belz, "Starting from Zero," World Magazine, March 29, 2018, https:// world.wng.org/2018/03/starting_from_zero.

137. David Kilcullen, Matt Porter, and Carlos Burgos, "U.S. Government Counterinsurgency Guide," January 2009, https://apps.dtic.mil/dtic/tr/fulltext/u2/a494660 .pdf.

138. George Packer, "The Lesson of Tal Afar," New Yorker, April 3, 2006, https://www .newyorker.com/magazine/2006/04/10/the-lesson-of-tal-afar.

139. US Department of State, "U.S. Security Cooperation with Iraq," March 22, 2017, https://www.state.gov/u-s-security-cooperation-with-iraq/.

140. Office of the Secretary of Defense, Department of Defense Budget Fiscal Year 2017, February 2016, page 4, https://comptroller.defense.gov/Portals/45/Documents /defbudget/fy2017/FY17_ITEF_J_Book.pdf.

141. MEMRI, "Iraqi Shi'ite Militia Leader Qais Khazali: 'Liberation of Mosul Will Be in Vengeance against the Slayers of Hussein,'" Clip 5713,, https://www.memri .org/tv/iraqi-shiite-militia-leader-qais-khazali-liberation-mosul-will-be-vengeance -against-slayers.

142. Maher Chmaytelli, "Abadi Defends Role of Iranian-Backed Paramiltaries at Meeting with Tillerson," Reuters, October 23, 2017, https://www.reuters.com /article/us-mideast-crisis-iraq/abadi-defends-role-of-iranian-backed-paramiltaries -at-meeting-with-tillerson-idUSKBN1CS26X.

143. "Transcript of President Trump's speech in Riyadh," VOA, May 21, 2017, https:// www.voanews.com/a/trump-speech-in-riyadh/3864144.html.

144. Rudaw (@RudawEnglish), "#Peshmerga: Those who try to enter Kurdish Teritory will 'beat their heads against the mountains of #Kurdistan,'" Twitter, May 30, 2017, 9:37 a.m., https://twitter.com/RudawEnglish/status/869593672538607617.

145. World Food Programme, "Air Drops Provide Lifeline in Syria's Deir Ezzor,"

August 22, 2016, https://panorama.wfp.org/air-drops-provide-lifeline-in-syrias
-deir-ezzor.

146. CNN Wire, "Trump, Putin Issue Joint Statement on Fighting ISIS in Syria," WGN9,
November 11, 2017, https://wgntv.com/2017/11/11/trump-putin-issue-joint-statement
-on-fighting-isis-in-syria/.

147. Tulay Karadeniz and Tuvan Gumrukcu, "Turkey's Erdogan Says West Backing
Kurdish 'Terrorists' in Syria," Reuters, June 11, 2015, https://www.reuters.com/article
/us-syria-crisis-turkey-erdogan-idUSKBN0OR11620150611.

148. Seth J. Frantzman, "How US Policy Almost Ended Up Fighting Itself in Syria,"
National Interest, September 2, 2016, https://nationalinterest.org/feature/how-us
-policy-almost-ended-fighting-itself-syria-17584.

149. "Turkish Special Forces Commander Zekai Aksakallı in Syria's Jarablus," *Hurriyet
Daily News*, August 25, 2016, http://www.hurriyetdailynews.com/turkish-special
-forces-commander-zekai-aksakalli-in-syrias-jarablus-103214.

150. "'We Want a United Syria, Not an Independent Kurdish Initiative,' Says Kerry,"
Daily Sabah, August 27, 2016, https://www.dailysabah.com/syrian-crisis/2016/08/27
/we-want-a-united-syria-not-an-independent-kurdish-initiative-says-kerry.

151. US Department of Defense, "Department of Defense Press Briefing by Secretary
Mattis, General Dunford and Special Envoy McGurk on the Campaign to Defeat ISIS
in the Pentagon Press Briefing Room," May 19, 2017, https://dod.defense.gov/News
/Transcripts/Transcript-View/Article/1188225/department-of-defense-press-briefing
-by-secretary-mattis-general-dunford-and-sp/.

152. Andrew V. Pestano, "Pentagon: U.S. Will Support Kurdish Militia after Raqqa
Fighting," UPI, June 28, 2017, https://www.upi.com/Pentagon-US-will-support
-Kurdish-militia-after-Raqqa-fighting/2591498661670/.

153. Jean-Marc Rickli, "US-Backed Forces Face Fierce Battle for Raqqa," June 8, 2017,
https://www.bbc.com/news/world-middle-east-40191718.

154. Peter Galbraith "As Iraqis Celebrate, the Kurds Hesitate," *New York Times*,
February 1, 2005, https://www.nytimes.com/2005/02/01/opinion/as-iraqis-celebrate
-the-kurds-hesitate.html.

155. Masoud Barzani (@masoud_barzani), "I am pleased to announce that the
date for the independence referendum has been set for Monday, September 25,
2017," Twitter, June 7, 2017, 9:52 a.m., https://twitter.com/masoud_barzani/status
/872496589868290049?lang=en.

156. Seth J. Frantzman, "Kurdistan Region Sets Referendum," *Jerusalem Post*, June
9, 2017, https://www.jpost.com/Middle-East/Kurdistan-region-sets-independence
-referendum-496343.

157. Sangar Ali, "It Is Riskier for Kurds to Remain Part of Iraq Than to Secede:
Ex-Ambassador," Kurdistan 24, July 29, 2017, http://www.kurdistan24.net/en/news
/e46f5135-0728-4302-8d2e-84abb8134435.

158. Seth J. Frantzman, "Will the Kurds Get Their Independence Referendum?"

National Interest, July 27, 2017, https://nationalinterest.org/feature/will-the-kurds-get-their-independence-referendum-21693.

159. "U.S. Asks Iraq Kurds to Postpone Referendum – Kurdistan Presidency," August 12, 2017, https://www.reuters.com/article/mideast-crisis-iraq-kurds/corrected-us-asks-iraq-kurds-to-postpone-referendum-kurdistan-presidency-idUSL5N1KY053.

160. Karzan Sulaivany, "Kurdistan May Postpone Referendum if Baghdad Provides Guarantees: Kurdish Official," Kurdistan 24, August 20, 2017, http://www.kurdistan24.net/en/news/6fb0e082-d842-4418-8473-9a815e2d0201.

161. Ministry of Foreign Affairs of the Russian Federation, "Foreign Minister Sergey Lavrov's Interview with Kurdish Television Channel Rudaw, Moscow, July 24, 2017," July 24, 2017, http://www.mid.ru/en/press_service/minister_speeches/-/asset_publisher/7OvQR5KJWVmR/content/id/2822361.

162. "Iraqi Kurds Want Same Right to Self-Determination as Quebecers, Diplomat Says," *National Post*, July 2, 2017, https://nationalpost.com/news/world/iraqi-kurds-want-same-right-to-self-determination-as-quebecers-diplomat.

163. "Iran Wades into Kirkuk Flag Controversy," Rudaw, April 3, 2017, http://www.rudaw.net/english/kurdistan/030420172.

164. US Central Command, "Coalition Statement on ISIS Convoy," August 20, 2017, http://www.centcom.mil/MEDIA/PRESS-RELEASES/Press-Release-View/Article/1294873/coalition-statement-on-isis-convoy/.

165. The information in this chapter comes primarily from a trip to the Kurdistan region of Iraq and Kirkuk in September 2017.

166. US Department of State, "Press Conference by Special Presidential Envoy McGurk in Erbil, Iraq," September 4, 2017, https://www.state.gov/press-conference-by-special-presidential-envoy-mcgurk-in-erbil-iraq/.

167. "Meet the Campaigners behind the Anti-Kurdistan Referendum 'No for Now' Movement," Kurdistan 24, August 8, 2017, http://www.kurdistan24.net/en/news/9bab7b44-edac-4bd4-b7ec-fc7efec6a5ee.

168. "Jalal Talabani, Former Iraqi President and PUK Leader, Has Died," Rudaw, October 3, 2017, http://www.rudaw.net/english/kurdistan/031020173.

169. Baxtiyar Goran, "Barzani: If We Receive Independence Guarantee as 'Alternative,' We Celebrate on Sep. 25," Kurdistan 24, September 19, 2017, http://www.kurdistan24.net/en/news/7492e97f-9ef3-4203-86ba-04cfe07434af.

170. Brett McGurk, "Press Conference by Special Presidential Envoy."

171. The information in this chapter comes primarily from a trip to the Kurdistan region of Iraq and Kirkuk in September 2017 and interviews with participants in the battle.

172. KR Security Council (@KRSCPress), "These forces are approx 3km from Peshmerga forces. Intelligence shows intention to takeover nearby oil fields, airport and military base," Twitter, October 12, 2017, 3:57 p.m., https://twitter.com/krscpress/status/918611576634126337?lang=en.

173. Lahur Talabany, "There Was No Agreement to Allow Baghdad to Control Disputed Territories," PUK Media, October 23, 2017, https://www.pukmedia.com/EN/EN_Direje.aspx?Jimare=42132.

174. Michael Georgy and Ahmed Rasheed, "Iranian Commander Issued Stark Warning to Iraqi Kurds over Kirkuk," Reuters, October 20, 2017, https://www.reuters.com/article/us-mideast-crisis-iraq-kirkuk-fall/iranian-commander-issued-stark-warning-to-iraqi-kurds-over-kirkuk-idUSKBN1CP2CW.

175. "Bafel Talabani: PUK Chose Tactical Withdrawal from Kirkuk after Casualties," Rudaw, October 21, 2017, http://www.rudaw.net/english/kurdistan/211020179.

176. "'Treasonous Elements Colluded to Surrender Kirkuk,' Says Deposed Kurdish Governor," The New Arab, November 13, 2017, https://www.alaraby.co.uk/english/indepth/2017/11/13/treasonous-elements-colluded-over-kirkuk-says-deposed-kurdish-governor.

177. Brett McGurk (@brett_mcgurk), "US working intensely to maintain stability in these areas, ensure all military maneuvers are fully coordinated," Twitter, October 17, 2017, 3:39 p.m., https://twitter.com/brett_mcgurk/status/920418908129103872.

178. "100,000 Kurds Flee Kirkuk since Iraqi Army Takeover -Kurdish Officials," Reuters, October 19, 2017, https://www.reuters.com/article/mideast-crisis-iraq-kurds/100000-kurds-flee-kirkuk-since-iraqi-army-takeover-kurdish-officials-idUSL8N1MU2NJ.

179. Matthew Barber (@Matthew__Barber), "1) New updates on #Sinjar – this thread provides details following KDP pullout. Photo: Haider Shesho greets #Yazidi Hashd commander Khal Ali," Twitter, October 22, 2017, 10:24 a.m., https://twitter.com/Matthew__Barber/status/922151742233509889.

180. Wladimir Van Wilgenburg (@vvanwilgenburg), "Video uploaded by Peshmerga fighter on Zummar front shows burning Iraqi vehicle. Peshmerga say they have repelled PMU attack," Twitter, October 26, 2017, 1:47 a.m., https://twitter.com/vvanwilgenburg/status/923471094610309120.

181. "Iraqi Army Retrieves Destroyed Abrams Tank to 'Hide Evidence' of Its Use," Rudaw, October 25, 2017, http://www.rudaw.net/english/kurdistan/251020173.

182. "Iran Helped us against ISIS, Not International Coalition: Iraq Militia Leader," October 29, 2017, http://www.rudaw.net/english/middleeast/iraq/29102017.

183. Maher Chmaytelli, "Abadi Defends Role of Iranian-Backed Paramilitaries at Meeting with Tillerson," October 23, 2017, https://www.reuters.com/article/us-mideast-crisis-iraq/abadi-defends-role-of-iranian-backed-paramiltaries-at-meeting-with-tillerson-idUSKBN1CS26X.

184. Haider al-Abadi, "Will Iraq Remain United," New York Times, October 18, 2017, https://www.nytimes.com/2017/10/18/opinion/iraq-will-remain-united.html.

185. Dmity Zhdannikov and Vladimir Soldatkin, "Russia's Rosneft to Take Control of Iraqi Kurdish Pipeline amid Crisis," Reuters, October 20, 2017, https://www.reuters

.com/article/us-mideast-crisis-iraq-kurds-rosneft/russias-rosneft-to-take-control-of
-iraqi-kurdish-pipeline-amid-crisis-idUSKBN1CP16L.

186. "Saudi Minister Visits North Syria for Raqqa Talks," Reuters, October 19, 2017,
https://www.reuters.com/article/us-mideast-crisis-syria-coalition/saudi-minister
-visits-north-syria-for-raqqa-talks-idUSKBN1CO2HG.

187. Seth J. Frantzman, "An Outspoken Critic: Riyadh's 'Anti-Hezbollah Minister,'"
November 8, 2017, https://www.jpost.com/Middle-East/Riyadhs-anti-Hezbollah
-minister-513660.

188. E. Ezrahi, "Saudi-Iraqi Tensions Rise after Saudi Ambassador Criticizes Iranian
Involvement in Iraq," MEMRI, October 2, 2016, https://www.memri.org/reports
/saudi-iraqi-tensions-rise-after-saudi-ambassador-criticizes-iranian-involvement-iraq.

189. Louise Callaghan, "UAE Becomes Little Sparta of Middle East," The Times,
November 4, 2018, https://www.thetimes.co.uk/article/uae-becomes-little-sparta
-of-middle-east-5rjkls89b.

190. "Lebanese Army to Get $120 Million in U.S. Aid," Reuters, December 13, 2017,
https://www.reuters.com/article/us-lebanon-military-usa/lebanese-army-to-get
-120-million-in-u-s-aid-idUSKBN1E72J6.

191. Yara Bayoumy and Maher Chmaytelli, "US Urges Help for Iraq, Extends $3
Billion Credit Line," Reuters, February 13, 2018, https://www.reuters.com/article
/us-usa-tillerson-mideast/u-s-urges-help-for-iraq-extends-3-billion-credit-line
-idUSKBN1FX0RK.

192. "Transcript of President Trump's Speech in Riyadh," VOA, May 21, 2017, https://
www.voanews.com/a/trump-speech-in-riyadh/3864144.html.

193. Jac Holmes Facebook page, October 4, 2017, https://www.facebook.com/jac
.holmes.3.

194. Ben Hendelman, "Back from the Battlefield: Sturtevant Man Returns Home
from Fighting ISIS in Syria," Fox6, February 16, 2016, https://fox6now.com/2016
/02/16/back-from-the-battlefield-sturtevant-man-returns-home-from-fighting-isis
-in-syria/.

195. Sophie Cousins, "American Explains Why He's Fighting ISIL," USA Today,
October 6, 2014, https://www.usatoday.com/story/news/world/2014/10/06/jordan
-matson-joins-kurds-against-islamic-state/16796487/.

196. Seth J. Frantzman, "What Kurdistan's Anti-ISIS Foreign Fighters Think of All
the Attention," National Interest, August 23, 2016, https://nationalinterest.org/feature
/what-kurdistans-anti-isis-foreign-fighters-think-all-the-17446.

197. "Jac Holmes: Killed Fighter, 'Due to Leave Raqqa,'" BBC, April 26, 2018, https://
www.bbc.com/news/uk-england-dorset-43906946.

198. Quentin Sommerville and Riam Dalati, "Raqqa's Dirty Secret," BBC, November
13, 2017, https://www.bbc.co.uk/news/resources/idt-sh/raqqas_dirty_secret.

199. OIR Spokesperson (@OIRSpox), "Was never a 'secret.' The Coalition issued
press releases 10 and 14 Oct, spoke with several outlets, to include BBC Radio on 14

Oct. This was a local solution to local issue...," Twitter, November 13, 2017, 12:11 p.m., https://twitter.com/0irspox/status/930166228727066626?lang=en.

200. The information in this chapter comes from interviews with participants as well as a trip to Egypt in 2017 and two trips to Jordan in 2015–2016.

201. Seth J. Frantzman, "Egypt Looks for Expanded Role in America's Foreign Policy," *National Review*, February 22, 2017, https://www.nationalreview.com/2017/02/egypt -abdel-fattah-al-sisi-united-states-foreign-policy-muslim-brotherhood-obama-trump/.

202. "Jordan Foils Major Terror Plot," *Jordan Times*, January 8, 2018, http:// jordantimes.com/news/local/jordan-foils-major-terror-plot.

203. US Department of State, "US Security Cooperation with Jordan," May 21, 2019, https://www.state.gov/u-s-security-cooperation-with-jordan/.

204. "Jordan's King Stresses True Islam in Templeton Prize Ceremony," Albawaba. com, November 14, 2018, https://www.albawaba.com/news/jordans-king-abdullah -stresses-true-islam-templeton-prize-ceremony-1213218.

205. Frederic Wehrey, *The Burning Shores: Inside the Battle for the New Libya* (New York: Farrar, Straus and Giroux, 2018), 305.

206. Wehrey, *The Burning Shores*, 306.

207. United Nations Support Mission in Libya, "Remarks of SRSG Ghassan Salame to the United Nations Security Council on the Situation in Libya," January 18, 2019, https://unsmil.unmissions.org/remarks-srsg-ghassan-salam%C3%A9-united-nations -security-council-situation-libya-0.

208. "Libyan Authorities Detain an ISIS Senior Leader in Sirte," *Libya Observer*, January 31, 2019, https://www.libyaobserver.ly/news/libyan-authorities-detain-isis -senior-leader-sirte.

209. "Foreign Minister Urges Global Coalition to Defeat ISIS to Include Libya in Rebuilding Program," *Libya Observer*, February 7, 2019, https://www.libyaobserver .ly/news/foreign-minister-urges-global-coalition-defeat-isis-include-libya-rebuilding -program.

210. The information in this chapter comes from interviews with participants as well as a trip to the Golan Heights during the battle against ISIS in Syria near Tel Jamou in July 2018.

211. Andrew Slater, "The Monster of Mosul: How a Sadistic General Helped ISIS Win," *Daily Beast*, June 19, 2014, https://www.thedailybeast.com/the-monster-of -mosul-how-a-sadistic-general-helped-isis-win.

212. David M. Witty (@DavidMWitty1), "Iraqi Military Court sentences former Mosul Commander, Staff LTG Mahdi al-Gharawi, to death by firing squad for withdrawing from Mosul without orders in 2014," Twitter, April 28, 2018, 12:56 a.m., https://twitter.com/davidmwitty1/status/990137686299152385?lang=en.

213. "Iraq Sentences German Woman to Death over IS Involvement," BBC, January 21, 2018, https://www.bbc.com/news/world-middle-east-42765106.

214. Martin Chulov and Nadia al-Faour, "'They Deserve No Mercy': Iraq Deals

Briskly with Accused 'Women of Isis,'" May 22, 2018, https://www.theguardian
.com/world/2018/may/22/they-deserve-no-mercy-iraq-deals-briskly-with-accused
-women-of-isis.

215. Hamza Hendawi, Qassim Abdul-Zahra and Maya Alleruzzo, "A Neighbor's Word
Can Bring Death Sentence in Iraq IS Trials," AP, July 9, 2018, https://www.apnews
.com/bc113d09dc2e46a68adf45de6b956a6e.

216. "Iraqi Court Sentences 19 Russian Women to Life for Joining IS Group," France
24, April 29, 2018, https://www.france24.com/en/20180429-iraq-19-russian-women
-sentenced-life-prison-joining-islamic-state-group.

217. Jane Arraf, "ISIS Wives, with Children in Tow, Are Handed Long Jail Sentences
or Death Penalty," NPR, June 9, 2018, https://www.npr.org/2018/06/09/613067263
/isis-wives-with-children-in-tow-are-handed-long-jail-sentences-or-death-penalty.

218. Rukmini Callimachi (@rcallimachi), "Read @NadiaMuradBasee's testimony. Among the bravest women I know. Few rape victims allow their faces to be
shown," Twitter, June 21, 2016, 11:08 a.m., https://twitter.com/rcallimachi/status
/745317532177960960.

219. Nadia Murad (@NadiaMuradBasee), "International Women's Day should not
only be a day to celebrate women but also to take action & end violence against women
in many parts of the world...," Twitter, March 8, 2018, 2:39 a.m., https://twitter.com
/NadiaMuradBasee/status/971697021185941504.

220. Nadia Murad (@NadiaMuradBasee), "Listening to a Holocaust survivor
speak at the [first] day of #IRFMinisterial. Many of the horrific images we saw @
HolocaustMuseum looked similar...," Twitter, July 23, 2018, 10:15 a.m., https://twitter
.com/NadiaMuradBasee/status/1021443811757707266.

221. Nikki Haley (@USUN), "Always inspiring to spend time w Nadia Murad...,"
Twitter, July 27, 2018, 2:21 p.m., https://twitter.com/usun/status/1022955168973893632.

222. Brett McGurk (@brett_mcgurk), "Important visit by Karim Kahn...,"
Twitter, August 10, 2018, 10:35 a.m., https://twitter.com/brett_mcgurk/status
/1027971645221335040.

223. US Department of State, "State Department Terrorist Designation of Alexanda
Amon Kotey," January 10, 2017, https://2009-2017.state.gov/r/pa/prs/ps/2017/01
/266762.htm.

224. Lizzie Dearden, "Former Isis Hostage of 'The Beatles' Doesn't Want Them to
Have 'Satisfaction' of Death Penalty," The Independent, February 9, 2018, https://www
.independent.co.uk/news/uk/crime/isis-beatles-jihadi-john-death-penalty-alexander
-kotey-shafee-elsheikh-hostage-islamic-state-capture-a8202666.html.

225. Quentin Sommerville (@sommervilletv), "'The first thing I thought when I saw
them was Gaddafi, or Saddam...Who were not able to face death...,'" Twitter, August
7, 2018, 1:47 p.m., https://twitter.com/sommervilletv/status/1026932926741716992.

226. Nick Paton Walsh and Salma Abdelazziz, "Beaten, Tortured and Sexually

Abused: An American ISIS Widow Looks for a Way Home," CNN, April 20, 2018, https://edition.cnn.com/2018/04/19/middleeast/syria-us-isis-bride-intl/index.html.

227. US Department of Justice, "Michigan Man Charged with Providing Material Support to ISIS," July 24, 2018, https://www.justice.gov/opa/pr/michigan-man-charged-providing-material-support-isis.

228. Charlie Savage, Rukimini Callimachi and Eric Schmitt "American ISIS Suspect Is Freed after Being Held More Than a Year," *New York Times*, October 29, 2018, https://www.nytimes.com/2018/10/29/us/politics/isis-john-doe-released-abdulrahman-alsheikh.html.

229. ACLU, "ACLU Secures Release of American Citizen Unlawfully Detained by Trump Administration," October 29, 2018, https://www.aclu.org/news/aclu-secures-release-american-citizen-unlawfully-detained-trump-administration-0.

230. "Father of Jihadi Jack Asks Canada to Help Bring Son Home," BBC, October 30, 2018, https://www.bbc.com/news/world-us-canada-46039145.

231. Josie Ensor and Brenda Stoter Boscolo, "European Isil Jihadists Released under Secret Deals Agreed by UK's Allies in Syria," *The Telegraph*, June 15, 2018, https://www.telegraph.co.uk/news/2018/06/15/european-isil-jihadists-released-secret-deals-agreed-uks-allies/.

232. Belkis Wille, "Families of Iraqi ISIS Suspects Transferred from Syria," February 24, 2019, https://www.hrw.org/news/2019/02/24/families-iraqi-isis-suspects-transferred-syria.

233. Ewelina Ochab, "Counting Bodies - How the UN Report Documents Mass Graves and Victims of Daesh Atrocities," Forbes, November 7, 2018, https://www.forbes.com/sites/ewelinaochab/2018/11/07/counting-bodies-how-the-un-report-documents-mass-graves-and-victims-of-daesh-atrocities/#6757c9f6ad41.

234. Ben Hubbard and Eric Schmitt, "A Favourite Restaurant in Syria Led Islamic State to Americans," *Irish Times*, January 21, 2019, https://www.irishtimes.com/news/world/middle-east/a-favourite-restaurant-in-syria-led-islamic-state-to-americans-1.3765102.

235. Kareem Botane, "Shammar Tribe in Iraq Confronts ISIS Attempts at New Insurgency," Middle East Center for Reporting and Analysis, June 27, 2018, https://www.mideastcenter.org/research-blog/shammar-tribe-in-iraq-confronts-isis-attempts-at-new-insurgency.

236. Seth J. Frantzman, "Syria Prepares for Offensive against ISIS in Palestinian Camp of Yarmouk," *Jerusalem Post*, April 16, 2018, https://www.jpost.com/Middle-East/Syria-prepares-for-offensive-against-ISIS-in-Palestinian-camp-of-Yarmouk-550009.

237. Kareem Shaheen, "Swedia Province: Isis Knocked on Doors Then Slaughtered Families," *The Guardian*, July 27, 2018, https://www.theguardian.com/world/2018/jul/27/isis-knocked-on-doors-calling-out-locals-by-name-and-slaughtered-families.

238. Shaheen, "Swedia Province."

239. US Department of Defense, "Press Gaggle at the Pentagon with Secretary of

Defense Mattis," July 27, 2018, https://dod.defense.gov/News/Transcripts/Transcript-View/Article/1586807/press-gaggle-at-the-pentagon-with-secretary-of-defense-mattis/.

240. The information in this chapter comes from interviews with participants in the war against ISIS.

241. James Jarrard interview with the author, February 2018.

242. "Turkey to Move into Manbij if YPG Refuses to Clear the Area," TRT World, February 4, 2018, https://www.trtworld.com/turkey/turkey-to-move-into-manbij-if-ypg-refuses-to-clear-the-area-14860.

243. Felix Gedney (@oirdcom), "Military operations in #Afrin, #Syria are placing @ Coalition's #DefeatDaesh mission at risk," Twitter, February 3, 2018, 8:42 a.m., https://twitter.com/oirdcom/status/959829524883165188.

244. US Department of Defense, "Press Gaggle at the Pentagon with Secretary of Defense Mattis."

245. On October 12, 2018, a Turkish court found Brunson guilty of "aiding terrorism," but sentenced him to time already served and returned him to the United States after two years of imprisonment.

246. Syria Recovery Trust Fund, "The SRTF Launches Phase 1 of its 'Agriculture Support to Farmers – Phase 1' Project as Part of Its Stabilization Efforts in Raqqa Governorate," July 25, 2018, http://www.srtfund.org/articles/258_the-srtf-launches-phase-1-of-its-agricultural-support-to-farmers-project-as-part-of-its-stabilization-efforts-in-raqqa-governorate.

247. Seth J. Frantzman, "The Free Burma Rangers Bring Hope to Raqqa in May 2018," Middle East Center for Reporting and Analysis May 31, 2018, https://www.mideastcenter.org/research-blog/interview-the-free-burma-rangers-bring-hope-to-raqqa-in-may-2018.

248. Mike Pompeo, "Remarks on the Creation of the Iran Action Group," US Department of State, August 16, 2018, https://www.state.gov/remarks-on-the-creation-of-the-iran-action-group/.

249. Department of Defense Office of Inspector General, "Lead Inspector General for Operation Inherent Resolve and Operation Pacific Eagle – Philippines 1 Quarterly Report to the United States Congress 1 April 1, 2018 – June 30, 2018," August 6, 2018, https://www.dodig.mil/In-the-Spotlight/Article/1594208/lead-inspector-general-for-operation-inherent-resolve-and-operation-pacific-eag/.

250. US Department of State, "The Global Coalition – Working to Defeat ISIS," February 6, 2019, https://www.state.gov/the-global-coalition-working-to-defeat-isis-2/.

251. Joe Gould and Tara Copp, "Bolton: US Troops Staying in Syria until Iran Leaves," Defense News, September 24, 2018, https://www.defensenews.com/global/the-americas/2018/09/24/bolton-us-troops-staying-in-syria-until-iran-leaves/.

252. Nasser Karimi and Jon Gambrell, "Iran Fires Ballistic Missiles at Syria Militants

over Attack," AP, October 1, 2018, https://www.apnews.com/b51c59aea52f4f788e50
6f0232122a64.

253. US Department of State, "Secretary Pompeo's Call with Speaker Mohammed al-Halbusi," September 19, 2018, https://www.state.gov/secretary-pompeos-call-with -speaker-mohammed-al-halbusi/.

254. Nadia Murad (@NadiaMuradBasee), "A virgin Sabiyya, 12 year old was up for sale. This is how they sold Yazidi girls...," Twitter, October 26, 2018, 4:12 a.m., https:// twitter.com/nadiamuradbasee/status/1055779196335726593?lang=en.

255. Bob Woodward, *Fear: Trump in the White House* (New York: Simon and Schuster, 2018).

256. "Trump Wants 'out' of Syria 'Very Soon,' Contradicting Top Officials," Politico, March 3, 2018, https://www.politico.com/story/2018/03/29/trump-syria-military -isis-491856.

257. "Trump Asked for $4 Billion from Saudis for Syria," *Washington Post*, March 16, 2018, https://www.denverpost.com/2018/03/16/donald-trump-asked-saudi-arabia -for-money-for-syria/.

258. Gould and Copp, "Bolton: US Troops Staying in Syria."

259. "Mattis Says Russia Cannot Replace U.S. Commitment in Middle East," Radio Free Europe/Radio Liberty, October 27, 2018, https://www.rferl.org/a/mattis-says -russia-cannot-replace-u-s-commitment-in-middle-east/29566838.html.

260. Emmanuella Saliba, "Trump Addresses Reporter as 'Mr. Kurd,' and Kurds Are Delighted" EuroNews, September 287, 2018, https://www.euronews.com/2018/09 /27/trump-addresses-reporter-as-mr-kurd-and-some-kurds-are-delighted.

261. "Text of Trump's Statement on Standing with Saudi Arabia," AP, November 20, 2018, https://www.apnews.com/378ed64a5ae0469f88e0cd9b333652ba.

262. Ali Younes, "Saudi Arabia 'Must Go Back to Proper Religious Roots,'" Al-Jazeera, November 24, 2017, https://www.aljazeera.com/news/2017/11/jamal-khashoggi -saudis-religious-roots-171123161746247.html.

263. "Briefing on the Status of Syria Stabilization," US Department of State, August 17, 2018, https://www.state.gov/r/pa/prs/ps/2018/08/285202.htm.

264. David M. Satterfield, Acting Assistant Secretary, Bureau of Near Eastern Affairs, "Briefing on the Status of Syria Stabilization Assistance and Ongoing Efforts to Achieve an Enduring Defeat of ISIS," US Department of State, August 17, 2018, https://www .state.gov/briefing-on-the-status-of-syria-stabilization-assistance-and-ongoing-efforts -to-achieve-an-enduring-defeat-of-isis/.

265. Satterfield, "Briefing on the Status of Syria Stabilization Assistance."

266. Tovah Lazaroff, "Netanyahu Met US Envoy to Syria to Talk Iran," *Jerusalem Post*, September 2, 2018, https://www.jpost.com/Middle-East/Netanyahu-met-US-envoy -to-Syria-to-talk-Iran-566357.

267. US Embassy and Consulates in Turkey, "Visit by Ambassador James F. Jeffrey, Special Representative for Syria Engagement, to Turkey," September 4, 2018, https://

tr.usembassy.gov/visit-by-ambassador-james-f-jeffrey-special-representative-for-syria
-engagement-to-turkey/.

268. "US Envoy to Syria Visits Northern Town of Manbij," Associated Press, October
22, 2018, https://www.militarytimes.com/flashpoints/2018/10/22/us-envoy-to-syria
-visits-northern-town-of-manbij/.

269. US Department of State, "Briefing on Syria," November 14, 2018, https://www
.state.gov/briefing-on-syria-3/.

270. Ibid.

271. Seth J. Frantzman, "How the US Saw Its Syria Policy Reversed," *National Interest*,
December 26, 2018, https://nationalinterest.org/feature/how-us-saw-its-syria-policy
-reversed-39872?page=0%2C1.

272. Hilal Kaplan (@HilalKaplanEng), "#Jeffrey before becoming special representative for #Syria: 'There's no doubt that the #PYD is the Syrian branch of the #PKK…,'"
Twitter, November 15, 2018, 1:04 a.m., https://twitter.com/HilalKaplanEng/status
/1062994856094695424.

273. Frantzman, "How the US Saw Its Syria Policy Reversed."

274. "US Syria Envoy Jeffrey to Visit Turkey amid Ongoing Disagreements," *Daily
Sabah*, December 5, 2018, https://www.dailysabah.com/diplomacy/2018/12/05/us
-syria-envoy-jeffrey-to-visit-turkey-amid-ongoing-disagreements.

275. Frantzman, "How the US Saw Its Syria Policy Reversed."

276. Turkish Presidency (@Trpresidency), "President Erdoğan: 'We are determined
to turn the east of the Euphrates into a peaceful and livable place for its true owners
just like the other areas we have made secure in Syria,'" Twitter, December 12, 2018,
3:14 a.m., https://twitter.com/trpresidency/status/1072811910863745024.

277. Turkish Presidency (@Trpresidency), "President Erdoğan: 'There is no longer
any such threat as DAESH in Syria. We know this pretext is a stalling tactic…,'"
Twitter, December 12, 2018, 3:13 a.m., https://twitter.com/trpresidency/status
/1072811800314417152.

278. Donald Trump (@realDonaldTrump), "We have defeated ISIS in Syria, my
only reason for being there during the Trump Presidency," Twitter, December 19,
2018, 6:29 a.m., https://twitter.com/realdonaldtrump/status/1075397797929775105.

279. Donald Trump (@realDonaldTrump), "President @RT_Erdogan of Turkey has
very strongly informed me that he will eradicate whatever is left of ISIS in Syria…,"
Twitter, December 23, 2018, 8:54 p.m., https://twitter.com/realDonaldTrump/status
/1077064829825966081.

280. Donald Trump, "Remarks by President Trump to Troops at Al Asad Air Base,
Al Anbar Province, Iraq," December 26, 2018, https://www.whitehouse.gov/briefings
-statements/remarks-president-trump-troops-al-asad-air-base-al-anbar-province
-iraq/.

281. "Syrian Democratic Council: Eastern Syria Fears Turkish Invasion," Middle East

Center for Reporting and Analysis, December 22, 2018, https://www.mideastcenter
.org/research-blog/syrian-democratic-council-eastern-syria-fears-turkish-invasion.

282. Seth J. Frantzman, "US Syria Withdrawal 'Betrays' Legacy of Volunteers Who
Died Fighting ISIS," *Jerusalem Post*, December 23, 2018, https://www.jpost.com
/Middle-East/US-Syria-withdrawal-betrays-legacy-of-volunteers-who-died-fighting
-ISIS-575169.

283. Jonathan Reith's story reposted from his Facebook on Afterisis.com with
his permission, https://afterisis.com/2018/12/28/its-never-too-late-for-anything
-everything-is-salvageable-a-medic-tells-a-story-of-2820-breaths-and-a-man-injured
-in-the-battle-against-daesh/.

284. "Turkish President Snubs Bolton over Comments That Turkey Must Protect
Kurds," *New York Times*, January 8, 2019, https://www.nytimes.com/2019/01/08
/world/middleeast/erdogan-bolton-turkey-syria-kurds.html.

285. Brett McGurk, "Trump Said He Beat ISIS. Instead, He's Giving It New Life,"
Washington Post, January 18, 2019, https://www.washingtonpost.com/outlook
/trump-said-hed-stay-in-syria-to-beat-isis-instead-hes-giving-it-new-life/2019/01
/17/a25a00cc-19cd-11e9-8813-cb9dec761e73_story.html.

286. "Interrogation of ISIS kingpin Jamal Al Mashadani 'to Be Aired on Iraq TV,'" *The
National*, November 30, 2018, https://www.thenational.ae/world/mena/interrogation
-of-isis-kingpin-jamal-al-mashadani-to-be-aired-on-iraq-tv-1.797758.

287. "Manama Dialogue: Saudi FM Denies Riyadh Is Changing Alliances, Says
Relations with US Are 'Ironclad,'" *Arab News*, October 27, 2018, http://www.arabnews
.com/node/1394686/middle-east.

288. Donald Trump (@realDonaldTrump), "....after 18 long years. Syria was loaded
with ISIS until I came along. We will soon have destroyed 100% of the Caliphate, but
will be watching them closely…," Twitter, February 1, 2019, 5:35 a.m., https://twitter
.com/realdonaldtrump/status/1091329137699184640.

289. US Central Command, "January 30: CJTF-OIR Strike Summary Jan. 13–26, 2019,"
January 30, 2019, http://www.centcom.mil/MEDIA/PRESS-RELEASES/Press
-Release-View/Article/1744872/january-30-cjtf-oir-strike-summary-jan-13-26-2019/.

290. Joyce Karam, "Syrian Kurdish Leader: No Timeline for US Withdrawal," February
1, 2019, https://www.thenational.ae/world/mena/syrian-kurdish-leader-no-timeline
-for-us-withdrawal-1.820686.

291. US Department of State, "Meeting of Foreign Ministers of the Global Coalition
to Defeat ISIS," January 29, 2019, https://www.state.gov/meeting-of-foreign-ministers
-of-the-global-coalition-to-defeat-isis/.

292. Middle East Center for Reporting and Analysis, "Tensions Rise in Mosul as
Hashd al-Shaabi (PMU) Warns US Forces against 'Provocative' Patrols," February 2,
2019, https://www.mideastcenter.org/research-blog/tensions-rise-in-mosul-as-hashd
-al-shaabi-pmu-warns-us-forces-against-provocative-patrols.

293. Delil Souleman (@DelilSouleman), "#Leonora, a 19-year-old #German national

who fled fighting between #SDF and Islamic State m(#ISIS) jihadists in the frontline Syrian village of #baghuz…," Twitter, February 1, 2019, 9:57 a.m., https://twitter.com/Delilsouleman/status/1091395226617462785.

294. "Iraq Angered by Trump Idea to Watch Iran from US Base," BBC, February 4, 2019, https://www.bbc.com/news/world-middle-east-47118889.

295. Turkish Defense Ministry statement, February 23, 2019, https://www.msb.gov.tr/SlaytHaber/2322019-56163.

296. Michael R. Pompeo, "Remarks at the Meeting of Ministers of the Global Coalition to Defeat ISIS," US State Department, February 6, 2019, https://www.state.gov/remarks-at-the-meeting-of-ministers-of-the-global-coalition-to-defeat-isis/.

297. Wladimir van Wilgenburg (@vvanwilgenburg), "GEN Dunford: So we had a campaign that was designed to clear ISIS from the ground that they had held, and we always had planned to transition into a stabilization phase where we train local forces…," Twitter, February 22, 2019, 4:11 p.m., https://twitter.com/vvanwilgenburg/status/1099099500105351169.

298. "Joint Statement by Presidents of Iran, Russia and Turkey at End of Sochi Summit," Mehr News Agency, February 15, 2019, https://en.mehrnews.com/news/142523/Joint-statement-by-presidents-of-Iran-Russia-and-Turkey-at-end.

299. "Remarks by Vice President Pence at the 2019 Munich Security Conference, Munich, Germany," February 16, 2019, https://www.whitehouse.gov/briefings-statements/remarks-vice-president-pence-2019-munich-security-conference-munich-germany/.

300. "Iran's Regional Record Very Bright: Spox," Islamic Republic News Agency, January 4, 2019, http://www.irna.ir/en/News/83158623.

301. Lindsey Graham, "Graham Applauds Trump Decision to Leave Troops in Syria," February 21, 2019, US Senate press release, https://www.lgraham.senate.gov/public/index.cfm/2019/2/graham-applauds-trump-decision-to-leave-troops-in-syria.

302. Sirwan Kajjo, "Kurds Laud US Decision to Keep Some Troops in Syria," VOA, February 22, 2019, https://www.voanews.com/a/kurds-welcome-us-decision-to-keep-some-troops-in-syria-/4800912.html?fbclid=IwAR3ozYY8r-S8jU9TocTq9DZoRCCWVPDr7ykfmRSvmTZDaCIZe7u7000MTDk.

303. Pompeo, "Remarks at the Meeting of the Ministers."

304. "The Torment of Christians Living in Syria's Khabur Valley," France 24, September 22, 2017, https://www.france24.com/en/20170922-video-christians-syria-islamic-state-group-khabur-river-valley.

305. Gabriel Chaim Facebook post, February 24, 2019, reposted on AfterISIS.com, https://afterisis.com/2019/02/24/gabriel-chaim-the-day-i-saw-life-passing-before-my-eyes-describing-the-last-battles-against-isis-near-baghuz/.

306. Hisham Arafat, "ISIS Killed My Father, Took My Mother: Traumatized Yezidi Children Share Tragic Abduction Stories," Kurdistan 24, February 25, 2019, http://www.kurdistan24.net/en/news/02fd3d09-5ee0-446d-ad2e-45c25e6055ad.

307. Javad Zarif (@JZarif), "As Iran, Russia & Turkey ready a summit in Sochi to work for peace in Syria & UN Court rejects US excuses & readies to rule on US theft of Iranian people's assets…," Twitter, February 13, 2019, 8:53 a.m., https://twitter.com/JZarif/status/1095727782494171136.

308. "Russia, Iran, Turkey Have No Plans for Joint Military Operations in Syria – Lavrov," TASS, February 24, 2019, http://tass.com/politics/1046172.

309. "Daesh Terrorists again Evacuated by US Copters from Syria's Deir Ez-Zor – Report," Sputnik, July 10, 2018, https://sputniknews.com/middleeast/201810071068679412-syria-deir-ez-zor-daesh-terrorists-evacuation/.

310. "Worse Than Mubarak," Foreign Policy, February 27, 2019, https://foreignpolicy.com/2019/02/27/worse-than-mubarak/.

311. AFP, "Former IAF Commander: Israel Hit over 100 Hezbollah Targets," Israel National News, August 17, 2017, http://www.israelnationalnews.com/News/News.aspx/234069.

312. Anna Ahronheim, "What Comes after ISIS? The Day after Daesh," Jerusalem Post, February 19, 2019, https://www.jpost.com/Middle-East/The-Day-after-Daesh-581005.

313. Hassan Hassan, "A Hollow Victory," CTC Sentinel 12, no. 2 (February 2019), https://ctc.usma.edu/hollow-victory-islamic-state-syria-high-risk-jihadi-revival-deir-ez-zors-euphrates-river-valley.

314. Zachary Cohen, "US Intelligence Chief Contradicts Trump on ISIS Defeat," CNN, January 29, 2019, https://edition.cnn.com/2019/01/29/politics/world-wide-threat-assessment-syria-isis/index.html.

315. Ned Parker, Ahmed Rasheed, and Suadad al-Salhy, "Iraqi Forces, Images Testify to Atrocities in New Fighting," Reuters, March 20, 2014, https://www.reuters.com/article/us-iraq-anbar-specialreport/special-report-iraqi-forces-images-testify-to-atrocities-in-new-fighting-idUSBREA2J11720140320.

316. Steven Aftergood, "Secrecy News: Special Operations Forces Aiming to Expand," Federation of American Scientists, April 16, 2018, https://fas.org/blogs/secrecy/2018/04/sof-2019-crs/.

Acknowledgments

This book would not have been possible without the support of my family, including my parents, Joel Frantzman and Lucy Abbot; my wife, Kasaey Keren Damoza Frantzman; my sister, Julia Frantzman Diaz; and other members of my family, including my late grandparents Leo and Sally Frantzman, and Frank and Lucy "Bideau" Abbot, who inspired me. When I began covering the war on ISIS, my wife and I were recently married, and when I decided to put down the camera and start writing the manuscript that became this book, we had the first of our two children. It was for them that I decided the trips to the front line had to take a hiatus. In the battle for Mosul, a Kurdish Peshmerga reached for my hand to help me into a truck to go into the village of Fazalia, as the battle was raging in October 2016. I stopped him and said I couldn't go. I thought about my home and realized that it wasn't worth it.

Along the way, I met many inspiring people who helped and encouraged this project; what follows is a partial list. Laura Kelly, who traveled with me to Turkey, Jordan and Iraq. Eric Mandel, who helped to arrange my trip to Egypt. Paul Hirschson, who hosted me in Senegal. Mira in Dubai, Mohammed Misto, who traveled with me in Kilis, numerous friends in Kurdistan including Vager Saadullah, Kawyer Ahmed, Zach Huff, Alan Duncan, Kareem Botane, Majd Helobi, Hussein Yazdanpanah, Sarhang Ahmed, Dana Zangana, Bahram Yassin, Naser Basha Khalaf,

371

Qasim Shesho, Faridon Abbas, Sherkoh Abbas, Rodi Hevi, Sirwan Kajjo, Wladimir van Wilgenburg, Dyari Mohamad, Aresh Saleh, Ryan D. O'Leary, Sarhad Qadir, Nadia Murad, Vian Dakhil, Adam Lucente, Ceng Sagnic, Lisa Miara, Chris Scurfield, Emile Ghessen, Meredith Holbrook, Alex Pineschi and so many others who helped me in Kurdistan, Iraq and Turkey. News editors at the *Jerusalem Post* Ilan Evyatar, Noa Brummer, Allyn Fisher Ilan and Maayan Hoffman, as well as Erica Schachne; my editors David Sands at the *Washington Times*, Harry Kazianis at the *National Interest*, and Sandy Tolliver at *The Hill*. In addition, members of the us military who helped facilitate interviews, including Daniel Allen Hill and Dante Brown. Also Jonathan Spyer, my colleague and friend, who helped found the Middle East Center for Reporting and Analysis, and Alberto Fernandez, David Patrikarakos, David Hazony, Yaakov Katz, and David Brinn, who encouraged me to publish a book, were all instrumental in helping me prepare for this endeavor. I want to thank the *Jerusalem Post* for giving me the opportunity to tell the story of these struggles in the Middle East to the world.

My first-draft editor Adam Haskel and the publisher, Gefen Publishing House, including Publisher Ilan Greenfield, Senior Editor Kezia Raffel Pride, and Project Managers Devorah Beasley and Daphne Abrahams, were integral to making this a reality.